C. Day-Lewis made a reputation as one of the 'thirties poets' – the group that included W. H. Auden, Louis MacNeice and Stephen Spender – whilst writing successful detective stories under the pseudonym of Nicholas Blake. He was Poet Laureate from 1968 until his death in 1972.

His personal life was one of great complexity. C. Day-Lewis formed strong human attachments and suffered divided emotional loyalties. This biography recounts frankly, but without sensationalism, Day-Lewis's marriages and infidelities. Wherever possible Sean, his eldest son, lets his father tell his own story through previously unpublished letters and through the autobiographical content of his verse and prose. He tells the story with a mixture of affection and detachment.

The book tells of Day-Lewis's solitary childhood, dominated, after the early death of his mother, by an emotionally demanding father. It traces the emotional and poetic development, recalls the short-lived involvement with Communism and the well-publicised success of the thirties and forties. The biography ends with a moving account of the poet's last years, when literary taste turned against his work, and he suffered ill-health.

By the same author
Bulleid, Last Giant of Steam

Sean Day-Lewis

C. Day-Lewis
An English Literary Life

London
UNWIN PAPERBACKS
Boston   Sydney

First published in Great Britain by George Weidenfeld & Nicolson Ltd,
1980
First published in Unwin Paperbacks 1982

UNWIN® PAPERBACKS
40 Museum Street, London WC1A 1LU, UK

Unwin Paperbacks
Park Lane, Hemel Hempstead, Herts HP2 4TE, UK

George Allen & Unwin Australia Pty Ltd,
8 Napier Street, North Sydney, NSW 2060, Australia

British Library Cataloguing in Publication Data

Day-Lewis, Sean
   C. Day Lewis.
1. Day Lewis, C. – Biography
I. Title
821'.912   PR6007.A95Z /
ISBN 0-04-928046-5

Reproduced, printed and bound in Great Britain by
Hazell Watson & Viney Ltd, Aylesbury, Bucks

For Cecil and Mary

in grateful memory

Contents

Illustrations

Preface

This is a biography by a son about his father, written within the decade of the subject's death. These circumstances naturally create suspicion. It may be thought that either the writer is engaged in public relations or some kind of vengeance. During the course of my researches I was told, 'You want, ambivalently, the heroic father figure, and at the same time, subconsciously, to destroy him.' For all I know of my subconscious this may have an element of truth; doubtless my motives are mixed. The reader will judge whether my conscious self has been successful in his attempts to avoid these extremes. My conscious hope is that I have provided not a picture of a hero or a villain, but of a complicated and much-loved man of many contradictions; and that any new understanding will help towards more appreciation of his poetry, which was the point of his life.

A few words about my relationship with Cecil may be useful as a guide. As a young father in the 1930s and 1940s he was conscious of the need not to repeat his father's mistakes in the way of emotional smothering. In childhood, for reasons probably connected with parental inhibitions about the physical display of love for a son, I was 'disturbed': a sleep-walker, a fire-raiser, a nightmare-dreamer, a bed-wetter. A reference to the last of these afflictions may be found in that prolonged verse in-joke, included in *Letters from Iceland* (1937), 'W.H. Auden and Louis MacNeice: Their last Will and Testament', in which Wystan wrote, 'I leave the wheel at Laxey, Isle of Man,/To Sean Day-Lewis ...'. According to the local guidebook, Laxey 'is the home of the world's largest water wheel'. Aged five I was taken to Birmingham for an inspection by Auden's physician father, the dedicatee of *Letters from Iceland*.

Some visitors detected a certain bleakness about the Day-Lewis household at this time, but intensity in family life is a mixed blessing and in his autobiography, *The Buried Day* (1960), Cecil rightly described our relationships as affectionate and easy. In the same book he wrote: 'With my own children, though I was often as impatient and sometimes as unjust as my father was towards me (and suffered for it the pangs which I am sure he suffered), I always tried to say I had been in the wrong when I knew I had been.' Because his outward face was so calm his occasional explosions of temper were the more impressive. Once, when we were living in Devon and simultaneously caught each other cheating in an elaborate game of hide and seek Cecil had invented, he blew up and chased me through our long garden hurling windfall apples at my retreating form. We both retired shaken to separate corners of the house and soon he came to apologize, sounding unusually sheepish. That this was the worst moment of conflict my memory retains shows that on the surface at least our relationship was harmonious.

In a way I probably gained over my younger brother in being a 'guilt figure', a supposed victim of early mistakes. Cecil sometimes knew my mind quicker than I did. He was a generous but realistic encourager, concealing his disappointment at my comprehensive failure as a schoolboy and making the most of my tiny triumphs. He gave much practical help, concealing the trouble this caused him; and he was a good material provider who never asked for gratitude or gave the smallest hint of the money worries which frequently fussed him. His lyrical singing of Tom Moore ballads and his dramatic readings to us from John Buchan, Conan Doyle and Charles Dickens planted seeds; so did his availability for ball games and his pleasure in winning them. He often contributed to the family newspaper I ran, using energy needed for his own work.

Through my second decade Cecil worked in London, leaving his family in Devon, and was preoccupied with love affairs. My brother and I were deposited at boarding schools. At the time, when I thought a 'mistress' was somebody who taught school juniors, this gave him a scarcity value which increased his popularity in comparison with my mother. In the early 1950s he embarked on a second marriage and from then on my meetings with him were mainly planned events. All these things made for at least some of the distance that a biographer needs. I have tried to maintain the distance by avoiding the phrase 'my father'. The fact remains that within its limitations, and Cecil believed in limitations as much in his personal dealings as in his verse, our relationship remained affectionate and friendly. Like most offspring of famous men I could never quite lose the need to try and impress him, but I have no reason for revenge or destruction, quite the contrary. I find in myself pale reflections of many of his characteristics, and this may just have misled as well as helped the biographer.

The case for researching this book so soon is that Cecil's generation has more or less reached its allotted span. Some of those who shared their memories of him with me have already died, and others died before I reached them. To have waited would have been to lose valuable witness. The case against my timing is that the feelings of the living cannot be ignored and are inhibiting. I believe that discretion is the worst part of biography and that the drawing of veils signals a concealment that may be titillating. Yet the biographer must pay some regard to requests for privacy, particularly if revelation adds nothing substantial to knowledge of the subject. In dealing with Cecil's last twenty years I have named all whom I know to have been important to him and have followed his own precept of laying bare his life (in his verse), without connecting all events and emotions directly with those he loved.

The name, by the way, is Day-Lewis. It was created, with hyphen, in the Dublin of 1863 when the brothers Frank and George Day entered the business of their uncle Fred Lewis. Cecil dropped the hyphen from his writing name in 1927, as a gesture of inverted snobbery. At the end of his life, when he came to believe, wrongly, that Day had native Irish origins, and so disliked being addressed as Mr Lewis, he put the hyphen back where he could. In this book, to save confusion, I have used the hyphen throughout, except in book titles.

To an extent I have let him tell his own story. He spent his life learning to understand himself and this is what his verse is about. His novels and detective novels, even his criticism, contain much autobiography. There is also *The Buried Day* about the first half of his life, and his childhood and youth in particular. This is a reticent book and inaccurate on dates and, as he acknowledges, is in some ways informed by the 'representative truth' of his 'personal mythology'. It is also graceful and evocative to a degree I cannot match and has provided this book with all its uncredited quotations.

Christopher Isherwood wrote in his autobiographical *Christopher and His Kind* (1977) that his circle was bad at putting dates on letters. 'I get the impression that their writers regarded letter-dating as something beneath their dignity as artists – something bank-clerkly, formal and mean spirited', he wrote. Cecil evidently felt the same way, and I have had to arrive at the placing of letters in this book by deduction from their contents. I shall not be surprised to be told about minute mistakes of chronology. I have nevertheless made use of letters where possible for they best display his private voice and underline that against his sometimes melancholy spirit Cecil was a great lover of life.

Sean Day-Lewis
Hammersmith, London W14

Acknowledgments

Before her death my mother Mary patiently answered my questions about her life with Cecil and together we went through her diaries. Despite the still open wounds of bereavement, Jill, his second wife, also gave me much time and attention and let me see such few papers as Cecil left. I am grateful to them both, and to Rosamond Lehmann who generously volunteered to share her memories of her long relationship with Cecil, though the subsequent interviews cannot have been easy for her. My wife Anna encouraged me in writing the book and corrected the completed manuscript. I also owe special debts to David Blount for his memoir on Cecil as a Cheltenham schoolmaster, to John Curtis for being such an understanding publisher, to Nicholas Llewelyn Davies for his Nicholas Blake research, to Sir Rupert Hart-Davis for sage advice and the use of his library, to Victoria Glendinning and Barbara Gough for sensitive editing, to Lord Hartwell and the Rt Hon W.F. Deedes for giving me six months' leave from the *Daily Telegraph*, to Ian Parsons and Norah Smallwood for originally commissioning the book and making painstaking suggestions about its subsequent cutting, to Margaret Stephens for her research on Cecil's sales figures, and to John Whitehead for sharing his unique knowledge of MacSpaunday.

I have acknowledged the books of which I have made use either in the text or in the references at the end. My thanks are due to Chatto and Windus for permission to quote from Cecil's autobiography *The Buried Day*, to Jonathan Cape for permission to quote from his poetry and novels, to the Hogarth Press for permission to quote from his poetry, to Basil Blackwell for permission to quote from his *A Hope for Poetry* and *Poetry for You*, to A.D. Peters for permission to quote from Nicholas Blake's detective novels, to Hamish Hamilton for permission to quote from Stephen Spender's autobiography *World Within World* and to Bodley Head for permission to quote from Samuel Hynes' *The Auden Generation*. My thanks are also due here to the libraries which have provided me with letters and other material: the Humanities Research Center of the University of Texas at Austin, USA; the University of Birmingham Library, England; the Lockwood Memorial Library of the State University of New York at Buffalo, USA; the King's College Library at Cambridge, England; the BBC Written Archives at Caversham, England; the University of Iowa Libraries at Iowa, USA.

Others who have helped, many of them taking much time and trouble on my behalf, include: A.F. Alington, Kingsley and Jane Amis, Sir Colin Anderson, Dame Peggy Ashcroft, Peter Aldersley, Elizabeth Barber, Frank Beecroft, Sir Lennox Berkeley, Kenneth Bredon, Professor R.L. Brett,

Kate O'Brien, Win Bryan, Barbara Cameron, Charles Causley, Leonard Clark, Alison Claybourne, Professor F.W. Clayton, Sylvia Clayton, Peter Cochrane, Billie Currall, W.P.C. Davies, Bertha Dawson, Daniel Day-Lewis, Nicholas Day-Lewis, Richard Day-Lewis, Tamasin Day-Lewis, A.S. Duffy, Georgina Dye, Hermione Eccles-Williams, Marilyn Edwards, Mark Featherstone-Witty, Charles Fenby, the Rev. G. Fitzgerald, Sir Robert Fraser, G.A. Gascoigne, Albert Gelpi, James Gibson, Eric Gillett, Giles Gordon, Lawrence Gowing, Robert Greacen, Geoffrey Grigson, Madge Hales, Frank Halliday, Elaine Hamilton, Stuart Hampshire, John Harris, Brian Harvey, Sir John Hewitt, Teddy and Joyce Hopcraft, John Horder, J.E.C. Innes, Daisy Jeffares, P.J. Kavanagh, Michael Kennedy, Betty Kenny, Charles King, Francis King Snr, Francis King Jnr, Philip Larkin, Laurie Lee, John Lehmann, G.L.E. Lindow, Elizabeth Logan, Alison MacDonald, Mary Malone, Louis Marks, Gordon and Margaret McDonnell, Diana McLoghlen, Ed Mendelson, Jacquie Meredith, Liz Millett, Violet Mitchell, Naomi Mitchison, the Rev Arthur Morris, Ryo Nakanuma, Benedict Nicolson, Charles Osborne, Eileen Osborne, Molly Patterson, Hugo Philipps, William Plomer, Sir Victor Pritchett, Alice Prochaska, Hilda Purvis, Ian Purvis, Bryan Reed, Edgell Rickword, W.N. Roughead, the Rev Samuel Rowe, Joan St George Saunders, Patrick Savage, Professor E.R. Seary, the Rev S.P. Semple, Alfred Shaughnessy, Linda Shires, Rosemary Simmonds, Stephen Spender, Doreen Squires, Norman Swallow, Hallam Tennyson, Anthony Thwaite, M. Timms, Paul Vaughan, K.H. Vignoles, Elizabeth Walter, Geoffrey Warner, Oliver Warner, Rex Warner, Hedley Warr, M.J. Weir, Laurence Whistler, Eric White, J.B. Widdowson, Sir Hugh Willatt, Basil Wright, Norman Wright, P. Xuereb.

C. Day-Lewis Chronology

(a) autobiography; (b) adventure story for boys; (c) criticism; (d) detective novel; (n) novel; (t) translation; (v) verse.

1904 Born at Ballintubbert, Queen's County, Ireland.

1905 Moved to Malvern, Worcestershire.

1908 Moved to Ealing, West London.
Mother, Kathleen Day-Lewis, died at Ealing.

1909 Moved to Central London.

1912 Entered Wilkie's Prep School, London.

1917 Entered Sherborne School, Dorset.
Moved to Edwinstowe, Nottinghamshire.

1923 Entered Wadham College, Oxford.

1925 *Beechen Vigil* (v).

1927 Master at Summer Fields School, Oxford.

1928 *Country Comets* (v).
Master at Larchfield School, Helensburgh, Dunbartonshire.
Married to Mary King at Sherborne Abbey, Dorset.

1929 *Transitional Poem* (v).

1930 Master at Cheltenham Junior School, Gloucestershire.

1931 *From Feathers to Iron* (v).
Son, Sean Francis, born.

1933 *The Magnetic Mountain* (v), *Dick Willoughby* (b).

1934 *A Hope for Poetry* (c).
Son, Nicholas Charles, born.

1935 *A Time to Dance* (v), *A Question of Proof* (d).
Retired as schoolmaster, became full-time writer.

1936 *Noah and the Waters* (v), *The Friendly Tree* (n), *Thou Shell of Death* (d).

1937 *Starting Point* (n), *There's Trouble Brewing* (d).
Father, the Rev Frank Day-Lewis, died at Edwinstowe.

1938 *Overtures to Death* (v), *The Beast Must Die* (d).
Moved to Musbury, Devon.

1939 *Child of Misfortune* (n), *The Smiler with the Knife* (d).

1940 *The Georgics of Virgil* (t), *Malice in Wonderland* (d).

1941 *The Case of the Abominable Snowman* (d).
Editor at Ministry of Information, London.

1943 *Word Over All* (v).

1944 *Poetry for You* (c).

1946 Reader at Chatto and Windus, London.

1947 *The Poetic Image*, Clark Lectures at Cambridge (c),
     Minute for Murder (d).

1948 *Poems 1943–1947* (v), *The Otterbury Incident* (b).

1949 *Head of a Traveller* (d).

1950 Moved to Central London, end of first marriage.
     Commander of the British Empire.

1951 Elected Professor of Poetry, Oxford.
     Married to Jill Balcon at Kensington Register Office.

1952 *The Aeneid of Virgil* (t).

1953 *An Italian Visit* (v), *The Dreadful Hollow* (d).
     Daughter, Lydia Tamasin, born.

1954 *The Whisper in the Gloom* (d).

1956 *A Tangled Web* (d).

1957 *Pegasus* (v), *End of Chapter* (d).
     Son, Daniel Michael Blake, born.
     Moved to Greenwich, London.

1958 *A Penknife in my Heart* (d).

1959 *The Widow's Cruise* (d).

1960 *The Buried Day* (a).

1961 *The Worm of Death* (d).

1962 *The Gate* (v).

1963 *The Eclogues of Virgil* (t), *The Deadly Joker* (d).

1964 *The Sad Variety* (d).

1965 *The Room* (v), *The Lyric Impulse*, Charles Eliot Norton Lectures at
     Harvard (c).
     Companion of Literature.

1966 *The Morning After Death* (d).

1968 *The Private Wound* (d).
     Poet Laureate.
     First Compton Lecturer at Hull.

1970 *The Whispering Roots* (v).

1972 Died at Hadley Common, Hertfordshire.
     Buried at Stinsford, Dorset.

I

⌒~1904–1929⌒
All's Dark or Dazzle There

Our youth time passes down a colonnade
Shafted with alternating light and shade.
All's dark or dazzle there....*

A traveller in the South Midlands of Ireland who takes the road out of Stradbally for Carlow will soon climb to Windy Gap. From this height the land can be seen falling away through Co Laois, across the border of Co Kildare and the Barrow river to the Wicklow mountains blue in the distance. Tiny in this benevolent plain is Ballintubbert, otherwise Baile an Tobair or the town of the well, a Laois hamlet cosily tucked in the crotch of gently rising hills.

Ballintubbert House, elegant and shabby, whitewashed and slate-roofed with a porch and two rows of tall sash windows, is the chief architectural feature of the settlement. It was here, in early 1902, that the Rev Frank Day-Lewis and his wife Kathleen made their first marital home; and it was here, on Wednesday 27 April 1904, that their only child Cecil was born.

King Edward VII, on a Royal Visit to Ireland, spent that day at the Punchestown races on the other side of the Wicklow mountains. It is recorded that the King's weather was 'a trifle fitful, but appreciably warmer . . . grey billows of clouds hanging low over the distant blue mountains looked more threatening than they were'.[1] Nothing is recorded of events that day at Ballintubbert beyond the fact of the birth of the future Poet Laureate.

> No one is left alive to tell me
> In which of those rooms I was born,
> Or what my mother could see, looking out one April
> Morning, her agony done,
> Or if there were pigeons to answer my cooings
> From that tree to the left of the lawn.†

* 'O Dreams, O Destinations' (*Word Over All*, 1943).
† 'The House Where I was Born' (*Pegasus*, 1957).

In later life Cecil would sometimes speak of 'we Irish', more often of his Anglo-Irish background. In the eighteenth century it was clear that the Anglo-Irish were the Irish who belonged to the Episcopal Reformed Church, otherwise the Church of Ireland, enjoying a legal ascendency over both the Roman Catholic majority and the Presbyterian minority. By 1904 the phrase should have become as archaic as the phrase Anglo-Saxon in England. The tradition was maintained through snobbery and the anxiety to retain the vestiges of the power and privilege inherited through the continuing British connection. As a romantic exile most of his life Cecil was able to see his Anglo-Irish people as 'landlords, but never of a land rightfully ours': notable for their wit, elegant writing, military skills, Georgian architecture and picturesquely decaying way of life.

Cecil recalled that in his youth he had wished to 'travel light, unencumbered by the past': he avoided asking questions about his relations. His father was of the same mind, separating himself as far as he could from 'the horde of relations, his own and my mother's, which littered Dublin and overflowed into England'.

Selective knowledge helped Cecil in his romantic inclinations. He remembered that both his grandmothers had impeccable Anglo-Irish credentials, in the sense that they belonged to successful and long-established Church of Ireland families. His father's mother was a Butler, enabling him to claim remote kinship not only with the Dukes of Ormonde but also William Butler Yeats. His mother's mother was a Goldsmith, descended from an uncle of the great Oliver. Cecil also fancied a possible maternal connection with Nicholas the Black, a Welsh pirate who survived to become a respectable Co Galway wine merchant; and with Jane Eyre, who lived at Eyrescourt, Co Galway, when the father of the Brontës was a boy in Co Down.

In his last years Cecil became addicted to the idea, put to him by John Kelleher, Professor of Celtic Studies at Harvard, that the Day family were originally the Ó Deághaidhs of Co Clare. In fact the Days first appeared in Kent, part of the south-east of England. A successful early-nineteenth-century Kentish Day contrived himself a family crest – scroll with shield over, wings each side with wreath, hand clasped and in each wing a star – and a motto, *Dum Spiro Spero* (While I Breathe I Hope), which might have been written with Cecil in mind.

Cecil's paternal grandfather was born Frank Edward Day at Berkhamsted in Hertfordshire in 1846, the son of a draper turned London and North Western Railway clerk. He was fourth in a family of ten children, too many to support comfortably even when his father was promoted to station master. In his unpublished memoirs Frank Edward casually records that when he was four or five 'my uncle [Fred Lewis] married to my mother's sister came to spend Christmas with us. And as he had no child at home, or abroad as far as I know, he asked who would go to Ireland with him, and I answered

"I will". So the matter was settled with my parents and I was taken off to Dublin....'

Fred Lewis was a wholesale soap refiner and perfume and pomade manufacturer. According to Frank Edward he was 'the pioneer of this business in Ireland ... the output was large, and as there was little or no competition the profits were large also'. In their middle teens both Frank Edward and his brother George entered the business and on 27 October 1863, both had their surname changed by deed poll to Day-Lewis.

Frank Edward Day-Lewis married Elizabeth Mary Butler in 1868. Their sixth child, Frank Cecil, was born at Pier View House, Sandycove Avenue West, on the outskirts of Dublin, in 1877. Frank Cecil, like his father before him and his son Cecil after him, was to be deprived of his mother at a very tender age. Elizabeth died in 1880 from some complication associated with yet another pregnancy. Within a year Frank Edward had married again, and Frank Cecil was cared for through the rest of his childhood by a stepmother.

Frank Cecil appears to have been the most gifted and ambitious member of the family and the one regarded with most pride by his father. Though his brothers like him attended high school in Dublin, he was the only one who took a place at Trinity College, where he studied for holy orders in the last years of the century and in 1900 took a divinity testimonium. Shortly before this a rich friend of the family had offered to make him his heir if he would go into his business. That he resisted this temptation may either testify to his strength of vocation or a desire to escape from the merchant to the professional class, or a bit of both.

I have not been able to discover how and when the Day-Lewis and Squires families became close. They both lived in Dublin, they were both active in the Church of Ireland, and their mutual attraction was to lead to two marriages. The name Squires can be traced like that of Day to the south-east of England. George Squires was born in 1820 at Old Windsor in Berkshire and his wife Caroline Sabine a year later at Canterbury in Kent. William Alfred, the first of their twelve children, was also born at Canterbury, in 1843. Soon afterwards the family moved to Ireland, where the Rev George was Vicar Choral at Cashel Cathedral in Co Tipperary for thirty-three years.

Cecil's maternal grandfather, the Kent-born William Alfred Squires, was married to Annie Victoria Goldsmith in 1864. His civil service career led him to the pinnacle occupied by the Superintendent of the General Register Office at Charlemont House in Dublin. His wife gave him ten children. The last of these, Kathleen Blake Squires, was born at 11 Charleston Avenue, Dublin in 1878. The baby of the family was also its favourite – high-spirited, affectionate, gentle and amusing. As a girl, she had a delicate, vivid face, full of character: beautiful one day and plain the next, never uninteresting. Her eyes were dreamy, her long and narrow features determined, and her rich auburn hair tumbled about her shoulders.

Frank Day-Lewis was ordained deacon at the Church of Ireland Cathedral of Tuam in Co Galway in 1900. He stayed there as a curate until he became a qualified priest in 1901. At the end of that year he was appointed by the Rev Robert Armstrong, Rector of Stradbally in Queen's County, to be curate-in-charge at Ballintubbert. The slight rise in salary, and the large house to which he moved before Christmas, encouraged him to embark on an early marriage. Frank and Kathleen were wed at Christ Church, Leeson Park, in Dublin, on 2 January 1902. She was twenty-three and he twenty-four.

Frank and Kathy came to a parish where the land-owning Protestant population was about ten per cent of the whole. The Rector had the assistance of two curates and for his £150 a year Frank was rarely required to do more than conduct the 11.30 am Sunday service in the minute church across the field at the back of his Ballintubbert home. His people went to church without question and when they got there they knew their places. The Butlers had the front two pews, the Webbers had the two pews behind them, then came the Merediths, the Glyns, Copes and Wilkinsons. The men congregated on the steps of the church, waiting a few moments after the last peal on the bell and the first exhortation before condescending to take their seats. The service took its course in a similarly predictable way. Frank was no innovator.

The social life expected of the curate and his wife was more demanding, though equally bound by ritual. Canon Armstrong was not popular. He was considered 'too modern' in his style, he was constantly at odds with his senior parishioners, and what is worse he was 'a snob who consorted with the aristocracy'. Frank learnt from this and did not attempt to cultivate acquaintances above, or below, his station. He was accepted by the gentry because he was a Butler, a kinsman of the Caroline Butler of Ballyadams who played the harmonium at his church and the Rosie Butler who took his Sunday School. He and Kathleen embarked on a perpetual round of afternoon teas and, if nothing else, became connoisseurs of seed cake. There was no shortage of Protestant young and in summer there were picnics involving twenty or thirty people, paper-chases and tennis parties. Each family had its own tennis court, usually mossy and so damp that the balls quickly turned as green as the shrubberies from which they so often had to be retrieved.

The young couple made themselves liked, the more outgoing Kathleen particularly so. They also made it obvious to all that they were city people out of their depth in the country and quite incapable of dealing with the practical problems that kept occurring. 'On the whole they had a pretty good life, it always seemed such a warm, cosy little place down there behind the hill, and we always enjoyed going over there as children', remembered

Mrs Jeffares, a parishioner, seventy years later. 'But when things went wrong the Day-Lewises simply couldn't cope.'

Canon Armstrong resigned and died in October 1902, to be succeeded the following January by the Rev Alan Stuart. When Kathleen started her pregnancy in the summer of 1903, Mr Stuart decided to spoil her by presenting her with some of the first asparagus cut from his garden. The curate thanked him warmly and next time he called he was triumphantly escorted to the Ballintubbert back garden by Frank's sister Lilian. The prize asparagus had been planted.

Frank's mind was impressionable, susceptible, fluid, his opinion easily swayed by circumstance or by the last speaker. He did his best to erect prejudices to control this flux and he belonged to the Trinity College tradition discouraging enthusiasm and looking at dissent with lofty disdain. It is probable that he revered that wily giant of Cecils, the third Marquess of Salisbury, Prime Minister from 1895 to 1902, approved both for his piety and his insistence that Home Rule for Ireland would be a shocking betrayal of Irishmen loyal to the crown.

Salisbury's death in August 1903, at the start of Kathleen's pregnancy would have made a considerable impression on the curate. When his son was born it perhaps seemed appropriate, for more than one reason, that he should be christened Cecil, a name the poet heartily detested from his adolescence to his death.

The business of registering the infant was neglected. Cecil was over six months old when Frank made the necessary 'statutory declaration' on 2 November. The birth was registered for the district of Ballylynan in the Superintendent Registrar's district of Athy. The registrar, Mr L. Lacey, seems not to have been at his best. Day is treated as a Christian name and Lewis as a surname, until column eight, where Frank Cecil Day-Lewis of Ballintubbert is listed as father.

It must have been soon after this that he began making plans for moving to England. His ambition was not satisfied by the simple duties and pleasures of Queen's County (now Co Laois). He and Kathleen had accents which betrayed their genteel Dublin origins and doubtless they admitted to being Irish. Yet, like their fellow Protestants, they behaved as foreigners in their own land. Kathleen may well have been sad to leave behind her loving family. For Frank advancement was all, and he was the kind of Victorian who used the expression 'master in his own house' and expected his wife to serve his wishes. England was the hub of the Empire, and preferment in the Church of England the most desirable of ambitions. The fact that both man and wife had English-born fathers made the move across the Irish Sea the more natural. Frank commended himself to the Rev Canon Raymond Percy Pelly, Vicar of Malvern Priory in Worcestershire, and was appointed curate. When Cecil was about eighteen months old, the Day-Lewises moved to Worcestershire.

Roots are for holding on, and holding dear.
Mine, like a child's milk teeth, came gently away
From Ireland at the close of my second year.*

In 1905 the Malverns had been developed within living memory. The grandiose hotels at Great Malvern had been built since Princess Victoria made hydropathic cures fashionable by staying there in 1830; the second industry of private education was still growing. The Priory dominated the town as it had done since 1085.

When Frank and Kathleen lifted the infant Cecil out of their chocolate and cream Great Western Railway train at Great Malvern in the late autumn of 1905 they must have been comforted by the prospect. The one main street, Church Street, was a steep hill, bordered on one side by the Priory churchyard and on the other by very successful shops. Frank would have noticed with special approval the golf links lying above open country to the south of the town. The Assembly Rooms were in frequent use. One week there might be a Frank Benson company playing Shakespeare, next Bransby Williams presenting characters from Dickens. John Philip Sousa brought his band to play marches during his European tours, and Earl Roberts came to state the case for a 'National Service' army to meet the threat of war with the increasingly powerful Germany.

The family moved into a largish red-brick house called Jesmond. Its front windows looked over a well-cultivated garden and a field to distant houses appearing small against Ruskin's 'little mountains' immense and brooding in the background. Frank established himself as a conscientious and earnest priest, always working hard for further qualifications if not for the parishioners. Looking back seventy years later, Violet Mitchell, ten years younger than Frank, remembered him as 'a pale, delicate-looking young man when he came to Malvern'. She went on: 'I remember him fainting at an early Communion and Canon Pelly lifting him to a chair and putting his head between his knees. The curate carried on all right then. I also remember walking with him the day he was going up for his Bachelor of Divinity exam, how anxious he was.'

Cecil was remembered as a patient baby 'dressed in a little blue frock and sitting in his push chair'. In later life he himself could only recall isolated images from this period, like the evensong picture of swans floating in a pool illuminated by evening light, with church bells chiming in the background. He was riding in his pram and his mother stopped it so that he could watch the scene.

The bells that chimed above the lake,
The swans asleep in evening's eye,

* *The Whispering Roots*, 1970.

> Bright transfers pressed on memory
> From him their gloss and anguish take.*

By early 1908 Frank must have been worried by the deterioration of Kathleen's health. Whether or not her fatal disease was correctly diagnosed at that time, he decided that her chances would be better in London. He took his last baptism at Malvern on 28 June 1908, and soon after this he moved his family to Ealing on the western outskirts of London. Kathleen's cancer had attacked her lymph gland and she was suffering from a kind of leukaemia.

The family were living at Church House in Warwick Road, a building which stood on the site now occupied by Ealing Technical College. Frank took no regular job at this time and so was able to devote himself entirely to his wife. Cecil was either protected from any scene of distress, or drove such scenes from his mind. Afterwards he recalled seeing his mother for the last time.

I am taken into a bedroom. My mother is lying in bed. I notice a smell like fish-paste. I am put into her arms and she kisses me. . . . I can remember no pain, no perturbation, no sense of parting. I was brought away to a neighbour's house, ignorant of what was happening at home, and all I can remember of it is that there was a fire lit in my bedroom and a too heavy eiderdown. . . .

Kathleen, unable to breathe because of a swelling in her pleura, died on 23 December 1908, and was buried at South Ealing Cemetery on Boxing Day. She was thirty.

In his novel *The Friendly Tree* (1936), where the heroine Anna is put into Cecil's youthful circumstances, there is a mention that 'nothing of her mother remained now except the tarnished silver-framed photograph on the study desk and the constrained visit every Christmas-tide to a suburban cemetery'. This is the only hint that Cecil ever gave that he associated his mother's death with the festival. Thinking of the bereaved father and son struggling through that Christmas Day of 1908 one is not surprised that they both tried to erase the memory from their minds. As time went on Cecil instinctively shrank from asking his father questions, for fear of free-ing emotions too strong for him.

He was left with the isolated pictures of his own mind, a photograph of his mother in late childhood, and her album.

An album in which she pasted short stories and sketches she had written for parish magazines, contains also a few poems in her own handwriting, composed after her marriage. They have no poetic merit: but one or two of them hint at a man's failure to understand a woman, and it may well be that, had she lived longer, her sadness at certain insensitivities of my father would have hardened into resentment; for she was, I believe, a woman intensely vulnerable, but at the same

* 'The Innocent' (*Word Over All*, 1943).

time, for all her gentleness, capable of bitter resistance against domestic bullying or emotional exploitation.

From this loss stemmed much that gave Cecil universal value as a poet and frailty as a man: his inability to become rooted; the long, lingering immaturity which caused him to cling to the last vestiges of childhood and then adolescence long after he had physically outgrown them; above all his obsessive search for his personal identity so confused by the continual conflict of contradictions within himself, which would be the one unbroken thread of his verse and his life.

> I am one who peered
> In every stranger's face for my identity,
> In every mirror for a family likeness,
> In lakes and dewdrops for the antiself.*

In a 1971 interview with Mark Featherstone-Witty, for a Durham University magazine, Cecil tried to analyse what first made him express himself as a poet. 'I would think that probably it was being an only child, therefore having a pretty lonely childhood – an agreeable one, but lonely – playing by myself all the time till I went to my private school. What else would there be? My mother dying when I was four ... all deprived children do go a bit queer and my form of going queer, I mean I didn't become a delinquent, I became an incipient poet.'

There is perhaps a thesis waiting to be written in support of the gloomy but popular idea that creative writers are really saying, 'Listen to me, I am lonely and unhappy.' Of the MacSpaunday poets [the animal invented by Roy Campbell, comprising MacNeice, Spender, Auden and Day-Lewis], with whom Cecil was associated in the 1930s, Louis MacNeice had a mother who suddenly disappeared from his life when he was six, afflicted with agitated melancholia brought on by an operation, and who died when he was seven; Stephen Spender lost his semi-invalid mother when he was twelve and his father when he seventeen.

Having tidied his affairs in Ealing, in early 1909 Frank took a curacy at Christ Church, Lancaster Gate. A pompous Victorian Gothic edifice, with a high thin spire, facing Kensington Gardens over the Bayswater Road, this was among the most fashionable churches in central London. At first father and son were living at Maxilla Gardens in North Kensington, a street now submerged by the Westway striding above it. Later they lived more conveniently in a maisonette near Paddington Station, at the corner of Craven Terrace and Craven Hill. Here they were joined by Agnes Olive Squires, always known to Cecil as 'Knos', an elder sister of Kathleen's and the most saintly person in Cecil's life. She sacrificed her own satisfactory

---

* Sketches for a Self-Portrait' (*Poems 1943–1947*, 1948).

existence in Dublin and, aged thirty-four, travelled to London to care for
her nephew with the devotion and tenderness of a second mother.

> ... Hers the patience
> Of one who made no claims, but simply loved
> Because that was her nature, and loving so
> Asked no more than to be repaid in kind.
> If she was not a saint, I do not know
> What saints are....*

Though Knos was a softening factor she did not remove the bond of
abnormal tension between father and son. Cecil received from Frank 'the
full force of a love which had nowhere else now to turn', of a young man
who wanted to be father, mother and, in some emotional sense, husband
to him. 'Throughout childhood, I hero-worshipped him; and later, when
the bond began to strangle me, my struggle to break free was all the more
painful for both of us.' Despite the adult attention lavished on him, and
him alone, he did not try precociously to merge with the adult world, but
rather closed in on himself in an instinctive attempt to preserve his integrity.
He was thought of as a dreamy child with little capacity for attention and
observation. He acquired a talent for forgetting which seemed to him
'bottomless'.

The Rev William Goldsmith Squires, brother of Knos and Kathleen, had
been ordained a Church of Ireland priest in 1892. In 1908 he was instituted
as Rector of Monart, a rural parish near Enniscorthy in Co Wexford. His
ministry there was destined to last for thirty-six years, and in 1909 Knos
took Cecil to the rectory for the first of many summer holidays. More than
anything else in his childhood, the Monart experience penetrated below
the conscious surface and was absorbed by the mythopoetic process. He
could remember the sounds of asses warning of approaching rain, but not
the rain; the rectory garden and its views became as Constable described
the landscapes of Claude: 'All is lovely – all amiable – all is amenity and
repose; the calm sunshine of the heart.'

Most of a chapter in *The Buried Day* (1960) is devoted to Monart: the
straggling one-storey house, the lush garden, the serene views across the
Wexford plain to the Blackstairs Mountains, the rector and his sisters Alice
and Agnes, the gardener Johnny Keyes. In particular the sensual memory
of running in bare feet on the meadow dew was a recurring one in Cecil's
poetry and prose.

To those who regularly attended matins at his modest, hill-top church,
the rector was a respected figure. He looked tall and dignified and his sermons were 'extremely educated'. He was so punctual in his social visits
that 'you could set the clock by him'. As an inspector of schools in the

---

* 'My Mother's Sister' (*The Room*, 1965).

Ferns diocese he was thought of as fierce, liable to ask trick scripture questions as he looked, unsmiling, through the oval-shaped granny glasses perched on his nose. To his loquacious sisters he was largely silent. In Cecil's childhood memory he was the inexhaustibly kind Uncle Willie, always willing to enter the child's world, with eccentric characteristics and mannerisms that made him a constant delight.

When I visited Monart in the middle 1970s the rectory was being rebuilt for private use and the garden was a bulldozed wilderness. Cecil's hero figure, the gardener Johnny Keyes, was still about, an eighty-six-year-old beekeeper and church sexton. He remembered none of the lyrical incidents of Cecil's autobiography. He only regretted that he had once misjudged Cecil and never apologized. He found that the lid had been taken off one of his hives and that all the bees inside had died: he blamed Cecil and did not discover until later that another boy was the culprit.

Back in London, Knos set her nephew reading and writing and taught him the beginnings of arithmetic, history and geography. Cecil's earliest literary memories were of nursery rhymes and the newly published Beatrix Potter stories. He became, by his own account, 'an addict of books' at six, repeatedly reading a collection of Greek legends called *The Golden Porch*, and Rudyard Kipling's *Just So Stories*. Not much later he turned to the adventure stories of Henty, Kingston, Collingwood, Rider Haggard, and above all Sir Arthur Conan Doyle's *The White Company* and *Sir Nigel*.

His sense of rhythm was also developing. Having read the dactylic inscription 'How to Develop a Beautiful Bust' in a magazine advertisement, he repeated it constantly, and not only because Knos contrived to be so deliciously shocked, with her disapproving, 'Don't be so bold Cecil', when the words were called out in the street or on a bus. He told numerous interviewers over the years that it was at this pre-school time that he produced his first poem:

> Avatory, avatory, avatory!
> Baby fell down the lavatory.

Knos was well qualified to awaken Cecil's love of music. She had been trained as a singer at the Royal Irish Academy of Music and accompanied her contralto voice from the piano or harmonium. She sang arias from Handel's *Messiah*, decorating them with a luscious *portamento* scooping which made them sound more Victorian than baroque. She launched Cecil's love affair with the *Irish Melodies* of Thomas Moore, though she added as much syrup to his 'The Last Rose of Summer' or 'She is Far From the Land', as she did to such traditional Edwardian favourites as 'Kathleen Mavourneen'.

Because Knos made herself so available she was under-appreciated. Frank, busy with his clerical duties, remained Cecil's first hero. He was a difficult hero, as inconsistent in his reactions as he was unpredictable in his moods. He was most obviously irritated by impertinence or answering back, which he would normally punish with a box on the ears, though there were other times when he apparently encouraged Cecil's pertness, or spoiled him with unwise kindness. Major crimes, like spending pocket money at the sweet shop next door instead of saving it for the Church of England Missionary Society, were met with a lowering of the paternal eyelids and a hurt expression designed to convey more sorrow than anger. 'This succeeded in piercing me with guilt', Cecil remembered. 'I both suffered and profited from the contradictions in my father's character. His behaviour, so remote from the uniformity of treatment which children are supposed to thrive on emotionally, so capricious and unreliable, made me timid, wary, over-adaptable perhaps and too anxious to please; but it also made me sensitive to the moods of others, and sharpened my sense of justice, my indignation against injustice.'

Frank was generous to his son with presents and endearments. He treated Cecil's illnesses or nightmares with sustained tenderness, and had a boyish streak which enabled him to join in childish games or jokes without strain. He also had a central insecurity which made him overstress his authority as Victorian paterfamilias. This insecurity was in some measure passed on to Cecil and showed early in his need to be the centre of attention when others were about, and his need to win. 'If playing draughts with my father, I lost a game, I sometimes disappeared under the table (to kick it over would have been unwise) and wept tears of bitter chagrin', Cecil wrote.

At home the curate always had at least one living-in servant, a succession of Irish nursemaids, and at one extravagant period a grave, bearded man-servant. In other ways Frank was mean: he bullied Knos over her very modest housekeeping accounts and thus ensured that their meals were frugal.

To the outside world the Rev F.C. Day-Lewis was a correct, professional clergyman. He took much trouble with his dress and was accordingly admired by his younger female parishioners. On a Sunday morning he could be seen walking up Craven Terrace to one of the many Christ Church services, resplendent in shiny top hat and tail coat. Photographed in this costume he would hold a stick in his right hand and adopt the pose of elegance made fashionable by King Edward VII. He had a strong sense of clerical etiquette, conducted services in a fine baritone voice, and was intolerant of fellow priests who showed slovenliness or eccentricity in church, or who smoked in public.

Cecil accepted Sunday morning church-going, family prayers and grace before meals as a feature of life. Sometimes he would dress in a sheet, recruit Knos to be his congregation, stand on a table and deliver his own sermons. On Sundays he enjoyed dreaming through the morning service and then taking part, usually wearing a sailor suit, in the dress parade of Christ Church parishioners from the Bayswater Road to the statue of Achilles, and back. He was not invited to join the church choir, its boys being recruited from the lower classes.

He was alone a lot of the time: playing with his model cars on the parapet of the balcony, or sailing his model cutter on the nearby Round Pond in Kensington Gardens; lying awake in his bedroom listening to the plangent sound of a German band playing popular tunes below his window, or the clunks, whistles and staccato puffing of Great Western train movements between Paddington and Royal Oak. Outsiders sometimes appeared on the edge of his world, usually lady parishioners who liked taking him for drives in the park or on their shopping expeditions. Meetings with other children were much more rare, which meant that he approached all but the smallest children's parties with dread.

At the age of eight, after returning from his Monart summer holiday in September 1912, Cecil became a schoolboy. He went to Wilkie's, a preparatory school that was fifteen minutes away on foot down the Bayswater Road. The owner and headmaster, Herbert Wilkinson M.A., lived in Orme Square and the adjacent school buildings were in St Petersburgh Place. Sir Max Beerbohm, a pupil there in the 1880s, wrote forty years later that it provided 'low and earthy tuition'. Cecil, who for some reason always looked back with a romantic glow on the academic institutions to which he was committed, considered it 'a humane and lively school'. Wilkie's was, in some ways, unorthodox for its time. There were no religious observances beyond the two prayers with which each day started. Intellectual ability was encouraged and respected. Placings were decided by merit in work rather than 'character' or success with ball games. Wilkinson himself was a classical scholar who helped his pupils to win many scholarships, particularly at Eton: his discipline was stern rather than harsh, he had patience and knew when to relax or increase pressure on a pupil. School lunches were generous, especially when compared to the hashed dishes Knos was obliged to provide.

As a previously solitary boy Cecil must have approached school, wearing his first dark blue and pink cap and blazer, with some misgivings. Yet in memory there was neither apprehension nor alarm, thanks to 'the love and security I had enjoyed at home'. He soon discovered qualities within himself which made it possible for him to adapt with comparative ease: 'physical energy, for instance, and a potential capacity for running with the herd, and competitiveness'.

For two years Cecil was a successful schoolboy. He enjoyed the meals, and the nose-blowing explosions with which the headmaster indicated that eating was over. He enjoyed games: in the noon break the boys went to Kensington Gardens, where they would play Grand Chain in winter and rounders in summer; on wet days there was unofficial cricket in the glass-roofed, stone-flagged gallery also used as a cloakroom; twice a week they were taken to Wormwood Scrubs in eight-seater wagonettes to play cricket or football. To begin with he managed mathematics without trouble, quickly learning the multiplication tables and advancing rapidly through fractions and decimals before reaching the stout wall of incomprehension which was to confront him for the rest of his life.

He had his bad moments. In his first week he wet his trousers rather than draw attention to himself by asking to be 'excused'. He was later made miserable by a pair of leggings that he was forced to wear when walking to school in the rain; no other boy wore leggings and he was therefore marked as a non-conformist. He aroused the hatred of one boy and returned home one day with a black eye, insisting, under the schoolboy's code of honour, that he had collided with a door. He suffered a bout of diphtheria and was plunged into dread of an operation for the removal of his tonsils and adenoids which was consequently threatened. For a time he suffered from acute growing pains in his left side.

In June 1914 Cecil and Knos took their usual afternoon boat train from nearby Paddington to Fishguard. After three weeks or so at Monart the family travelled for a holiday at Kingstown, on the coast outside Dublin. Here Cecil went down to the shore one morning and found the high water mark of the beach littered with sacks. The first one he looked into contained a dead dog, the next a dead cat. The troop-ships that had been lying out in the bay were no longer there. The soldiers on board had been ordered to destroy their pets before they sailed. Next day Frank arrived to take Cecil and Knos back to London. They were restored to Craven Terrace on 4 August, when Britain declared war on Germany.

The change in London life brought about by the Great War was very gradual. On the class-room walls 'appeared those maps of France and Flanders, the Western front a snaking line of flags, Allied and German, which from time to time were moved a centimetre westwards, a few millimetres to the east – tiny shifts which marked, we were told, great victories or strategic withdrawals'.

In October, while the British Expeditionary Force was experiencing the first bloody battle around the Belgian city of Ypres, Cecil made his entry in the 'confession book' kept by the pupils of Wilkie's. It is the first example of his handwriting still extant, and gives his answers to seventeen set questions:

1. The best place to hang a bunch of mistletoe? From your nose; 2, Your favourite motto? 'Never Say Die'; 3, Your greatest ambition? Telling fortunes; 4, Your ideal man? Mr Asquith; 5, Your ideal woman? Mrs Churchill; 6, Your opinion of motor cars in general? Horribly smelly; 7, Do you believe in spiritualism? Yes; 8, Your ideal way of spending Christmas Day? Up the chimney; 9, Your idea of absolute misery? Going to Carr to tea; 10, Your favourite picture? 'Death of Von Molthe'; 11, The most suitable place for a flirtation? Sitting on the gas-bracket; 12, Your favourite play? Charlie's Aunt; 13, Your favourite

song? Rule Britannia; 14, Your favourite musician? Mendelssohn; 15, Your
favourite magazine? Primer of Latin Grammar; 16, The most unselfish thing
you could do? Listen to Abrahams; 17, When did you feel at your worst? At
my christening. Autograph, C. Day-Lewis. Date, 29.10.14

The distant war became more disturbing. Frank elected to become a
'temporary chaplain to the forces', his son remembering 'how splendid he
looked when I first saw him in his Army uniform, and the leaden misery
in my stomach at his departure'. The bond of Cecil and Knos was strengthened by the falling away of the constraints and anxieties caused by Frank's
exacting presence, but neither Cecil's work nor his conduct satisfied his
elders and he became lazy and comparatively unruly.

During the following year he settled again. In Easter week of 1916, as
a few other Irishmen in Dublin challenged the British Empire, Cecil was
given his first, sturdy, black bicycle on his twelfth birthday. He soon
became an expert on the street geography of his central London patch,
bounded by Kensington Gardens and Hyde Park to the south, Shepherd's
Bush to the west, the northern purlieus of Bayswater, and the Edgware
Road to the east.

Frank was then attached to the East Lancashire Regiment and in camp
at Witley Park in Surrey. Cecil and Knos took their 1916 summer holiday
there in a cottage beside the camp, and Cecil embarked on long bicycle
rides into the country. Frank sometimes roared in regimental manner at
his unfortunate batman, but generally showed himself better suited to the
open-air life and the unemotional camaraderie of men than to the female-
dominated, tea-cup existence of churchy Lancaster Gate. Cecil hero-
worshipped him more than ever. The war remained distant, though he was
aware of the detonations of military training, the death of an instructor
killed throwing himself on a bomb accidentally knocked from the hand
of a recruit, marching feet and men singing as another detachment departed
for the slaughter in France.

Soon afterwards Frank was transferred to the Royal Field Artillery depot
at Wetherby in Yorkshire. Cecil and Knos had a 1917 holiday in this town,
during which his father gave him his first riding lessons. 'If I was timid
at the start, my desire to show up well in my father's eyes made short work
of such timidity', Cecil remembered. 'I do not, indeed, remember that I
was ever frightened of horses; and besides, my trust in him was so absolute
at this time that I could not imagine any great harm happening to me while
I was with him.' In adult life Cecil was far from being a horsey man, but
as a thirteen-year-old he was exhilarated by riding. With hindsight the
silver trumpets of Wetherby, sounding the last post, signalled 'the end of
my childhood's long day'.

In his last year at Wilkie's, Cecil had friends. There was the brilliant
scholar Daniel Dannreuther who later committed suicide. There was the
future Sir Colin Anderson, who became a director of numerous enterprises

public and private and chairman of the Royal Fine Arts Commission. Cecil passed his door each morning and accompanied him on the walk to school. There was a boy called Dawson, the son of a professional billiards player, who was frequently host to boys who liked to try their skills on his father's practice tables at their house in Cleveland Square. Sir Colin remembered him more than a half century later for his habit of taking dog excreta off pavements, rolling it into balls and throwing these missiles at his unappreciative schoolfellows. Cecil also remembered him: 'Wrestling one day with Dawson in the Square gardens, I received my first innocent hint of sexual feeling, which until then I had only experienced in sleep.'

Above all there was the third hero of Cecil's life, Nicholas Llewelyn Davies, one of the star-crossed family adopted by J.M. Barrie. They had arrived at Wilkie's in the same term, when Nico seemed to Cecil 'an altogether superior kind of being'. He 'possessed the magnetism which very occasionally distinguishes one small boy from the crowd of his fellows, and so often vanishes during adolescence'. A photograph of him at the time shows a small boy in Eton collar and top hat, with a perfectly formed round face and prominent front teeth.

The friends shared sweets called 'My Queen', or bottles of a deep red, fizzy cola, and on one momentous occasion they ventured together into a Marble Arch cinema to see a spectacular version of the Carthaginian War. Once Cecil was taken to Nico's home at 23 Campden Hill Square and caught a glimpse of his guardian Uncle Jim, the small, dark author of *Peter Pan*. Some of the characteristics of Herbert Wilkinson, the boys' headmaster, are written into J.M. Barrie's creation of Captain Hook. Wilkinson was first mentioned by Barrie in *The Boy Castaways*, and headmaster and school were given more prominence in the 1902 story *The Little White Bird*. In early drafts of *Peter Pan* there is a Kensington Gardens scene with Captain Hook disguised as a schoolmaster called Pilkington.

In his last year at Wilkie's Cecil was captain of both football and cricket – 'a distinction less dazzling than it sounds, for we were fairly bad at games'. At this time he also had his first air-raid experience, watching from his bicycle as a squadron of Gotha bombers were used to bomb the City of London, killing 158 people. Soon after the raid he found a piece of shrapnel near the place where he had stopped with one foot on the kerb.

Despite the war Wilkinson's standards for manners, Latin grammar and food were maintained. Parents who did not aspire to Eton, where the annual fees were approaching £200, were directed for some reason to Sherborne, the north Dorset public school. That summer Cecil sat for the Sherborne scholarship examination, with Wilkinson himself invigilating. 'One of the questions in the English paper gave a stanza of poetry and invited the candidate to compose a second stanza – with the same metre and rhyme scheme. Wilkie's quiet approval of the stanza I had written made me, quite irrationally, confident that all would be well. All was well. A week or so later a telegram came from Sherborne to say that I had been placed third in the scholarship list', Cecil wrote.

In Thomas Hardy's *The Woodlanders* the chastened Grace Fitzpiers walked and sat with the good-hearted Giles Winterbourne in the Abbey of Sherton Abbas, before taking her lunch at a cheap, old commercial tavern. Seeing her there, looking so out of place among the 'mixed company of dairymen and butchers', he wished he had taken her to 'the dignified' Earl of Wessex Hotel in that town, where years before he had made cider in the court-yard and seen her on her honeymoon. Sherton Abbas is Sherborne and the Earl of Wessex was the Digby, the hotel from which Cecil was launched on his secondary schooling, in September 1917. Dorset was to become his nonpareil of English counties, and it is there that his mortal remains are buried.

By an odd, almost Hardyesque, coincidence two sons of widowed church of Ireland clergymen were delivered up to Sherborne that term. One was Cecil and the other, starting aged ten at the associated preparatory school, was his fellow MacSpaunday poet, Louis MacNeice.

Waiting at the Digby, Cecil felt only the usual 'general diffused bewilderment' of the new boy. The dark hotel had retained its mid-Victorian dignity, but it no longer inspired confidence, having lost its able-bodied male staff to the trenches, and now being held together by an old waiter who moved in a 'painful, splay-footed shuffle'. Equally tentative was Frank, perambulating with Cecil in the hotel garden and intending to explain the mysteries of sex: a topic that had not arisen, either for schoolboy pleasure or for adult preaching, at Wilkie's. Having made the attempt, and quite failed to say what he was talking about, Frank delivered his son to Kenneth Tindall, housemaster of Harper House.

Sherborne in 1917, as now, was a mellow market town characterized by the warm, golden-brown stone used for all its major buildings. It lies in a valley on the upper reaches of the River Yeo, sheltered by wooded slopes and dampened by the prevailing south-west wind blowing from the Blackmore Vale.

At that time the school was in the middle of the long reign of Nowell Charles Smith, headmaster from 1909 to 1927. Cecil, who was as generous in his judgment of his schoolmasters as he was in his retrospective view of schools, saw Smith as an 'enlightened Chief' pulling the school 'out of the last of several crises which have chequered its history' and moving the institution from barbarism into civilized ways. Cecil noted his 'sweet smile which won so many hearts', saw him as 'this noble-hearted and utterly un-showy man' and 'the most disinterested man I have ever personally known'. It was also true that Smith was out of touch with much that happened in his school, which in many ways was as barbaric as it had ever been.

Cecil's arrival coincided with the furore caused by the publication that

July of Alec Waugh's *The Loom of Youth*. The apprentice novelist had been at Sherborne from 1911 to 1915, when he was expelled for 'homosexual practices'. Waugh had probably considered himself immune from such retribution because he was, when caught in the throes of his love affair, top of the school batting averages. His undisguisedly autobiographical novel was written in a passion of nostalgia and resentment. Cecil, who knew nothing of all this, merely observed the wrath aroused. Members of the staff, some of them portrayed in the book and some not, ensured that it was widely read by threatening that anybody caught reading it would be beaten. For a time all sermons in the school chapel included a ringing commination against the book. Both Alec Waugh and his father were removed from the Old Shirburnian roll, and his younger brother Evelyn was diverted to Lancing.

The Sherborne prospectus held the chapel to be the centre of school life; in reality it took second place to the playing fields. It was not so much the school of the enlightened Nowell Smith, more the school of G.M. Carey – otherwise 'the Bull' and represented in *The Loom of Youth* as Buller the games master. Cecil had the good fortune to avoid the reign of terror which was his teaching method, but noted him on the rugby touchline 'yelling for blood ... with strangled, fierce yelps'.

Cecil went straight into the Lower Fifth Classical, under the charge of the Rev Henry Robinson King, 'a gentle, moody, often distrait man, with white hair and a drooping white moustache, who looked like a minor Victorian celebrity and whose son-in-law I was to become'. 'Crusoe' as he was known at the school, or 'Claremont' as he became when transmuted into the genial, tolerant and good-humoured 'dear old fellow' of *The Loom of Youth*, was one of the school's rare civilizing influences. He had been at Sherborne since 1883. In 1898 he had founded the Duffers literary society and married an Edinburgh woman, seventeen years his junior, who gave him five children. When Cecil first walked into his form room H.R.K. was already sixty-two.

Though H.R.K. was a pessimist, sometimes petulant and easily bored, his passion for English literature, specially Shakespeare, Milton and Wordsworth, proved infectious. He was famous for his recitations, sometimes delivered, in the intervals of his long bicycle rides, to cows who were said to gaze at the reader with an expression not immeasurably more bovine than some of his own *Stolidi*, his Duffers. He had earlier served the literary cause through the Powys family; he had tended the sprawling genius of John Cowper Powys when he was a Sherborne boy from 1885 to 1891. In his *Autobiography* (1934), J.C. Powys wrote that 'of all the masters, it seems to me, Mr King's love for the school was by far the deepest, and his benefactions, both material and spiritual, far the greatest. He was one of those men who by some massive instinct of their whole being gather up as they go about the world the lasting essences of life and savour them with a calm and constant satisfaction.' Cecil, for his part, credited H.R.K. with 'infecting me with his generous enthusiasm for English poetry'.

During Cecil's first term at Sherborne his father resigned his military chaplaincy and became Vicar of Edwinstowe, a country village on the edge of Sherwood Forest about to be transformed by the expansion of the north Nottinghamshire coalfield. Cecil had his first Christmas there in 1917 and then returned to Dorset for the term that saw the turning point in the relationship of father and son. The hero of Cecil's childhood was now gradually discovered to be a man of neurotic insecurity.

The immediate cause of the new tension is obscure. It may have had something to do with a 'sex scandal' that came to light at Harper House that term. The 'good-hearted and attractive' head of Cecil's dormitory was caught in bed 'having a do' with one of his younger charges, and was asked to leave. 'The rest of us, since our extreme youth put us in the category of "more sinned against than sinning", got off with a warning and a touchingly sympathetic talk from our housemaster, who was too nice a man to be able to credit, then or later, how far the dry rot in his house had spread', wrote Cecil. The talk apparently did nothing to inhibit Cecil's own masturbatory experiments with his contemporaries, and these in turn did nothing to diminish the heterosexual responses of his adult life. In general Sherborne masters either believed or pretended to believe in the sexual innocence of their pupils. This meant that when they stumbled over boys in the act of 'immorality' they felt obliged to over-react. Fortunately, either through laziness or lack of conviction, this policy was not zealously policed. Here at least, Cecil had some advantage over his literary contemporaries, who were so repressed at their public schools that they spent their sexual lives defying their boyhood authorities.

> When bullying April bruised mine eyes
> With sleet-bound appetites and crude
> Experiments of green, I still was wise
> And kissed the blossoming rod.*

Two months before his fourteenth birthday in April, Cecil received a letter from his father while lying in the Harper sick-room, suffering from measles. Frank's lines of 'small, beautifully-formed handwriting' were 'laden with reproach and self-pity, as if they had been written in blood from his own wounded pride; and such was the effect it had upon me that seldom afterwards did I open a letter from him without a sense of effort, a faint feeling of suffocation. "You have broken my heart", he wrote. He had said this to me before, said it more than once; but this time, seeing it written down, I was for a while entirely convinced of its truth and stood convicted in my own heart for the crime of having broken his'.

* Transitional Poem, 1929.

Years later Cecil decided that the motivation for this letter was an idoliza-
tion equal to his own for his father. Frank had so identified Cecil as his
better self that he felt his son's alleged disgrace as his own. In that Easter
term of 1918, Cecil first felt battered between guilt and self-pity.

Then a light appeared on the horizon, a saving scepticism moved closer. I had
not been so irredeemably wicked; and even if I had, my father would survive
it, and he should have thought less about his own feelings than about the ordeal
I had been going through. Something tough, buoyant, resentful and realistic in
me – a self I had hardly met before – came to my rescue. From this moment,
the old relationship with my father was doomed, for he had let me down when
most I needed it. The man I had idolized lay in fragments, and I was too young
to understand, too much hurt to accept, the real man behind the idol.

In the early 1960s Cecil wrote in a poem about the emotional strain on
parents as their children grow into independence, of the way 'love is proved
in the letting go'. In his own youth, parents who were of the upper middle
class, or aspired to be so, did not question the need to send their sons away
to boarding schools at twelve or thirteen, if not before. In making his sacrifice Frank found any emotional 'letting go' almost impossible, and this meant
that Cecil felt obliged to fight the more strongly, and callously, to escape
from a relationship he unconsciously knew to be smothering. Frank must
have been sorely confused at this. At one moment Cecil was accepting his
love, the next rejecting him. The smothering father had all unknowingly
created a pattern which would show in Cecil's later relationships of love,
in the way Cecil kept a part of himself reserved and independent against
the day he needed to break free for fresh air.

Cecil's emotional conflict with his father, when he was still a more or
less new boy at Sherborne, ensured that his public school had a lasting effect
on him. School – insulated from the outside world, self-important, artificial and anxiety-ridden – now became as important to him as home. It
has been observed that the generation of writers who emerged between
1925 and 1935 were obsessed by their schools. Cecil did not write directly
of school experience, as did W.H. Auden and Christopher Isherwood, and
he showed no overt sign of obsession with Sherborne. The school influence
can nevertheless be seen in a number of his lasting characteristics: his developed sense of responsibility; his worship of heroes, specially games-play-
ing heroes; his willingness to live or work with others in the position of
leader or follower; his wish to belong as an insider and the concomitant
tendency towards conformity.

At his preparatory school Cecil had learned to avoid the role of outsider,
a state which 'does not strike me as a source of gratification, let alone a
cause for self-congratulation'. As a public man in later life he admitted that
'my disposition has always been to conform'. He had his flirtations with
romantic rebellion, but always beneath was 'the man who longed to come to
terms with society or wanted a society with which he could be reconciled'.

At Sherborne his instinct was to discover which way the herd was running and then keep close. As soon as possible he mastered and observed the taboos, totems, catchwords, gradations and general mystique of the 'half savage tribe we were'.

He won a contest for treble voices that year, narrowly beating his future brother-in-law Alec King into second place; he was shaping well as a scrum half; he had the romantic protection of the unorthodox head boy of Harper, the future radio actor and, later, thriller-writer V.C. Clinton-Baddeley; he became involved in the Saturday evening play-readings conducted by Clinton and their housemaster Kenneth Tindall. On Monday 11 November he was able to enjoy the school celebrations at the news of the armistice finishing the 'war to end wars'.

Christopher Isherwood has said that he and his contemporary writers 'were all suffering, more or less sub-consciously, from a feeling of shame that we hadn't been old enough to take part in the European war'. Cecil never, as far as I know, identified such irrational feelings in himself and consciously he felt little but profound relief at having escaped the ordeal, as well as awed fascination for the enormity of its horror. It was one of his lasting disappointments that he lacked 'the epic breadth of mind' to attempt for this war what Hardy in *The Dynasts* did for the Napoleonic Wars.

These feelings did not reach the surface until the following summer, when he and Frank went to stay with a clergyman friend at Falmouth in Cornwall. Cecil was hypnotized by a bound set of magazines giving an illustrated history of the war. 'I went through from beginning to end with an extraordinary feeling of recognition. . . . It is, perhaps, a dominant trait of such natures as mine that we come to reality – such reality as we ever do compass – at one remove, unconsciously holding it off until our conception of it is fully formed within us, or our own response is ready; and then a phrase, a scene, an illustrated magazine releases from within us what is not so much an experience as a re-creation.'

In the early part of 1919 Cecil was to be found 'scribbling away' at his verse in the Harper day-room with twenty or thirty other boys 'banging around' him. Normally such unorthodoxy as this, and his habit of going off to rehearse the soprano solos of Handel's *Messiah*, might have been punished by his peers. His success in taking second place in the school's junior steeplechase that March ensured that he would be able to pursue his eccentricities unmolested.

In July he took the School Certificate examination and won a distinction or credit in every subject apart from mathematics, which he failed. In September he was promoted to the Lower Sixth Classical where he found the work more difficult and began to lose confidence. This made for a new social diffidence and a tendency 'to pretend comprehension where I did not fully comprehend, and to take refuge either in a kind of intellectual slickness or in a deliberately exaggerated naïveté when I was with people cleverer than myself'.

Altogether easier for him was the empty ritual of becoming a 'confirmed' member of the Church of England. If mutual masturbation was 'having a do', Confirmation was 'getting done'. Boys were 'done' according to their age group, and the procedure included a private interview with the housemaster, popularly supposed to be a kind of sexual confessional. Cecil later claimed that all the boys in his batch managed to avoid the issue by saying they had not quite grasped the doctrine of the Holy Trinity, thus putting the theatrical rowing man Kenneth Tindall somewhat out of his depth. Cecil accepted without question that his turn had come and hoped that the laying-on of hands would in some way provide him with a faith to go with the tradition and habit of Christianity that he had learnt. In the event his Confirmation merely confirmed that he would have to look elsewhere for his religious fervour.

In October, debating in the school's Sophists' Club, he spoke third on a motion that 'the world would have been a better place without the civilization of the twentieth century'. According to the official report 'he denied that happiness was the real aim of life, as the last speaker had said; but he tried to place the question on a more moral basis altogether. Finally, with an ornate peroration, he brought before the audience two pictures, the one of the old-time happiness of the tiller of the soil, the other of the modern inmate of the slum.' The budding socialist romantic, as well as the poet, was beginning to find his voice.

The first term of the new decade was the most difficult Cecil ever had. Led by a 'swarthy, saturnine, Welsh rugby forward' the thicker members of the Harper day-room declared that Cecil had 'got above' himself and should be 'dealt with'. Throughout the term he had 'an ever-present sense of being marked down for a victim'. The Sabbath was the day consecrated for major bullying rituals, and for ten Sunday afternoons Cecil waited for the knock on the door of his study. The knock came on the last Sunday of term.

I was first made to swallow a concoction of ink and bad cheese, which certainly lowered my physical resistance. I was then pushed under a row of desks, the lids of the locker-seats were thrown back against the desks to make a sort of pent-house roof, and brown paper was lit at either end of the tunnel created thus. Next I was dragged out, choking but not burnt, and put through a series of running-the-gauntlet courses, in which toasting-forks, wet towels and D's knotted rope figured. Finally I was taken upstairs and thrown, still in my Sunday clothes, into a cold bath. This ordeal could not have lasted more than a quarter of an hour; I had managed not to be sick, or to weep, or to utter a sound throughout.

Cecil's response demonstrated his acceptance of conformity. He remembered D shaking his hand and saying, 'You took it very well', and

himself, half disbelievingly, replying 'I deserved it'. He admitted the power
of the social group, the need to respect social codes and public opinion,
and he felt that his ability to take his ordeal without breaking down gave
him 'a pass into manhood'. More woundingly, he was left with a fear of
people standing together and whispering among themselves, and an inclination as a young man to see hostility where it did not exist.

On the surface his school life now became easier. He walked about with
a gait of pride, tipping his head slightly to one side as fashion dictated. In
September he acquired a sympathetic new housemaster called Armine Fox
and was invited to join H.R. King's exclusive Duffers, where there were
tea and ladies as well as the reading of literary papers.

The pages of the school magazine indicate that in March 1921 he was
taking part in a Sophists' debate, opposing the motion 'that Europe is played
out'. In May he wrote his first printed poem, the opening work in an exercise book headed 'Clivus ad Parnassum' and 'Early Poems – First Series';
and with a quotation from W.B. Yeats, 'Dream then, for this is also sooth'.
The two stanzas were originally called 'A Fragment', but in the *Shirburnian*
that term they became 'Reverie'. They were signed with the initials K.B.,
the initials of his mother Kathleen Blake.

> A gentle breeze, stirring the tree tops;
> A faint whisper, a rippling stream:
> The sun-splashed shadows in the green copse –
> A cuckoo calls – the woodlands dream.
>
> Nature a'drowse, scent-laden visions
> Before my eyes, and mem'ries dear,
> Born of stillness; gentle-eyed slumber
> Soothing my heart – songs sweetly clear.

For more than three years now Cecil had been spending his school holidays
with Frank and Knos in the large, raw, red-brick Edwardian vicarage of
Edwinstowe, a few hundred yards from the edge of Sherwood Forest. He
was more solitary than he would have been in London, not only because
he was growing away from Knos's simplicity as well as Frank's possessive-
ness. He lived, in more ways than one, between two worlds. On one side
were the big houses of the Dukeries – Welbeck, Clumber, Thoresby, Ruf-
ford – which he entered rarely, and never as an equal. On the other side
was the equally inaccessible terrain of the miners, farm-workers, rail-
waymen and shop-keepers. The vicarage had a rose garden, but it was over-
cast with the smells and deposits of the nearby Mansfield and Clipstone
collieries. He walked alone and doleful in the forest and was dutiful in his
attendance at his father's church. He engaged his father in fiercely competitive ball games and enjoyed learning to drive on his second-hand Calcott.
He watched abstractedly from the vicarage windows as long Great Central

coal trains clanked along the embankment above the fields on the far side of the village.

All this time Frank was wondering whether or not to re-marry. He was still short of money, though his stipend was now £600 a year; this was partly because he insisted on a staff of first one and then two maids, as well as a gardener 'mercilessly harried' into producing copious quantities of vegetables. Knos had to be as careful as ever with her housekeeping accounts. The vicar had good reason to believe that one Mamie Wilkinson, whose family had been parishioners of his at Lancaster Gate, would consent to be his second wife. She had the attraction of 'good family' and her own money. But Frank felt an obligation to Knos and loyalty to Kathleen's memory, and he involved both his Bishop and Cecil in his prolonged agonizings.

Eventually Cecil tipped the scales, encouraging the marriage, partly because of a temperament which would always be attracted by the prospect of a radical change in his life, and partly because he expected that 'a step-mother would at least do something to relieve the grinding boredom of the holidays in Edwinstowe – an expectation which was to prove extremely ill founded'. It was later that he came to regret with bitter sadness the sup-planting of Knos, who had spent over twelve years at the prime of her life as his second mother, loving and cherishing him and yet being treated by the Day-Lewises as something of a doormat. Knowing the Church laws as well as Frank she would have had no expectations of becoming his wife, but she must have wept more than a tear or two as she returned in 1921 to Ireland. This was at the time of the final excesses of the Anglo-Irish War, which ended a few months later with the founding of the Irish Free State.

Frank and Margaret Kathleen Maud Wilkinson were married at Christ Church, Lancaster Gate, on 1 June 1921. Cecil was given leave from Sher-borne and officiated as best man, dressed splendidly in hired morning dress. The bridegroom, who had lived through thirteen years of celibacy, was forty-four. The bride was forty-nine and too old, it transpired, to provide him with more children. She was installed at Edwinstowe together with a gross quantity of hideous Victorian furniture and knick-knacks, plus her skittish old father, Major Wilkinson, late of the Durham Light Infantry, who survived the Crimean War, but not for long his transplantation to dank Nottinghamshire.

Mamie was a plump woman, with a tiny mouth and a small beak of a nose set between fleshy cheeks. Cecil saw her as 'well-meaning, affec-tionate, capable of a pleasing gaiety', and the possessor of a mind rigidly locked in the past and protected from the present with stubborn compla-cency. She had been educated in Germany, which may or may not have set her mental rigidity, but which certainly made her fervently anti-German. She loved her new husband dearly but lacked the imaginative equipment to discover and relieve his insecurity. When Frank was in a hectoring, bullying mood she sat there assuming a meek expression, as inert as a bolster. Rightly or wrongly Cecil believed Frank needed somebody to 'stand up to him, laugh him out of his self deceptions and sting him out of his egotism', but she was not made that way.

The relationship between the seventeen-year-old Cecil and Mamie deteriorated swiftly during their first summer holidays together in 1921. He was, in his own phrase, 'prickly as a porcupine – an awkward handful for any stepmother'. Keenly and unkindly aware of his intellectual superiority he made her a butt. She encouraged this by either not realizing, or pretending not to realize, that she had a problem child on her hands. She insisted on being called 'Mother', an untruth Cecil avoided as much as possible. Behind her back she became known to him as 'the step-d', otherwise the step-dragon. Only sometimes, discouraged by beating his head against her prejudices, would he turn from her to the more rewarding business of provoking his father. That she survived intact in such a household indicates a woman built on dreadnought proportions.

By stages Mamie took the life-style of the vicarage back into well-to-do Victorian provincialism. Long, starchy meals were served by starched maidservants who were obliged to work within the bounds of her protectiveness towards her possessions. Every drawer and cupboard was locked, and all the keys were in turn made secure in her bureau. The key to the bureau was constantly mislaid. The heavy furniture she brought to the house made the rooms smaller. Vast oil paintings now glowered from the walls and there was a horde of atrocious ornaments and bibelots kept under glass domes or behind the glass doors of cabinets.

The change in their circumstances did little to mellow the deteriorating relationship of father and son. When specially bored Cecil would pick a quarrel with Frank, using his more agile mind to drive the vicar from position to position until he reached his last line of defence: 'When you have had my experience of life, you will see that I am right.' Cecil did not always have the sense or grace to accept this as a victory, but would pursue his opponent with: 'What use is "experience of life" if you so hopelessly misinterpret it?' His pertness would bring the encounter to an end in an explosion of bad temper.

One incident in particular seemed to typify all that was wrong in this relationship. Cecil had been visiting a young girl, with whom he had been enjoying a chaste friendship, and was later than usual in returning home, partly because a fog made bicycle-riding impossible. He knew his father would be upset and heard him bellowing in the distance. 'He shouted at me all the way up the drive, followed me into the house and up to my room, shouting down my attempts to explain why I was late', Cecil remembered. The episode rankled for years and made Cecil the more sceptical about 'parental love – a love which could thus betray its essential egotism at the very moment when self-forgetfulness and sympathy might justly have been expected of it'.

> Love I desired, but the father I loved and hated
> Lived too much in me, and his images of me
> Fretted a frame always outgrowing them:
> I went into the wilderness bearing all
> My faults and his ambitions on my head.*

Returned to Sherborne in September Cecil was newly grand: head of Harper House, a school prefect and a member of the Upper Sixth Classical, being pointed towards an Oxbridge scholarship. 'I enjoyed my power, took its responsibilities seriously, and was in the way to becoming quite a prig', he wrote.

A new boy at Harper that September was Basil Wright, later to be a pioneer of British documentary films in the school of John Grierson. 'Being sent to Sherborne in 1921 was very like being sent to a German concentration camp and I am not joking', remembered Wright more than half a century later. 'The mental and physical cruelty which one underwent, from prefects and from older boys not worthy of being made prefects, was something really appalling. I was miserable, bruised, bullied, rather despised even by people of my age, because I was a bookworm.''

Wright saw Cecil as a saving grace, doing his best, with the backing of the vague but effective Armine Fox, to remove such brutality.

In the dining room we had a system by which all the boys moved one place up every day and a prefect sat at the head of each table, so that once every ten days or so you sat twice next to a prefect, once on his left and once on his right. The first time I sat next to Cecil, who I regarded as God, or at least a man of about 60, he engaged me in conversation. Somehow we got on to books and he impelled me to start talking about the books I liked. He then, as it were, descended to earth and became extremely personal, charming and exciting. He told me about other books I should read and suddenly I realised that there was some humanity left in the world, that there was something worth living for. I could not be grateful enough for what he did then.

Cecil used the cane infrequently and was not specially demanding of his fags, but he worked the system. Another fag of the time became the Rev Murray Gawne, a Hampshire rector. When he wrote to Cecil on his appointment as Poet Laureate a letter came back saying 'he remembered me and feared that, on one occasion when he had beaten me for burning his tea toast, he lammed into me rather brutally and hoped I had now forgiven him. This was perfectly true. I was young at the time and remember I was near to tears.'

Wright's general view of Harper House in 1921 is supported by another new boy of that term, later to become the Rev Gerald Fitzgerald. In his

* 'Sketches for a Self-Portrait' (*Poems 1943–1947*, 1948).

first year a senior boy, 'and the only one who was brilliant at games', was 'sacked' after being caught in bed with a younger boy. The other boys were treated to 'a long, passionate sermon' from the headmaster and 'an embarrassed and pointless lecture' from the housemaster, making the point that such sexual exercise was 'not playing with a straight bat'. Cecil, on the other hand, provided 'ten minutes in the day-room of simple, down-to-earth common sense, worth vastly more notice than either lecture or sermon – and getting it'. He said he realized that talk of 'blessed innocence' was nonsense, but homosexual practices created scandal and were therefore to be discouraged. His own interest in small boys had by this time become more paternal than physical.

Cecil would have liked to be a more successful games player than he was. He was never good enough for the cricket 1st XI and was only once picked for the rugby 1st XV, but he did lead the Sherborne PT squad which won the Public Schools Physical Training Shield two years running. He also had his cerebral successes. In June of 1922 he won both the Barnes Elocution Prize, named after the nineteenth-century Dorset poet William Barnes, and the School English Verse Prize. The winner of the latter award was required to read his original work at speech day, or 'Commem' as it is known at Sherborne, to the school, the staff and the parents. Thus it was that Cecil made his first public appearance as a verse reader, declaiming his own 150-line 'St Ambrose':

> 'Ambrose for bishop'! ... a voice clear and sweet
> Rings out above the din of shifting feet. ...

He had now fallen under the spell of early W.B. Yeats. 'I read *The Wind Among the Reeds* at my public school, and it had a considerable effect, this very Celtic twilight kind of verse, which I was just right for then', he told Hallam Tennyson in a BBC radio interview at the end of his life. He must have been even more familiar with the book before this, *The Rose*, to judge by what he was writing at the beginning of 1922. His 'Lament of Maureen' is dedicated 'to W.B.Y. in all humbleness', and another poem that year actually begins

> I will arise, and fly on the wings
> Of the whistling wind at dawn,
> Back to the land where the colleen sings
> In the asphodel flush of morn.

Cecil also showed the first signs that year of being an embryo Poet Laureate. On 28 February there was a royal wedding between Princess Mary, daughter of George V, and Viscount Lascelles, described by Cecil as 'a soldier of Britain'. The poet saw this as a magnificent occasion involving 'crowded roofs' and 'a thousand trampling hoofs'. The spectators, including 'the noble from his mansion, the burgher from his trade' and 'the barefoot beggar in his rags' shout repeatedly as 'the steady-marching infantry comes swinging down the street'.

> Honour and beauty and loyalty acclaim
> The jewel of virginity and the warrior of fame.
> High hearts beating with the joy of morning skies,
> Proud eyes sparkling to a nation's thund'rous cries:
> Beneath the golden wings of love two spirits are made one,
> And Christ, the mighty conqueror, is smiling on his throne.

In September 1922, Cecil returned for his final Sherborne year, somewhat bored with power. 'During his last year he withdrew himself noticeably, reading a great deal in his study and appearing only at meal-times or to address the house on matters of moment', remembered Geoffrey Warner, then a new boy. Cecil saw himself as 'a tinpot Alexander with no more worlds to conquer' brooding 'arrogantly in my tent'. He would emerge from his tent wearing a soft collar and a large knot to his tie and a lock of hair falling beside his temple, in his efforts to look less like Alexander and more like W.B. Yeats. He afterwards accused himself of displaying 'the bolshie mentality', a kind of 'superficial perverseness – the simple arrogant desire to be different'.

In fact his revolution did not extend much beyond mildly provocative contributions to the *Shirburnian*, of which he was now a co-editor. The headmaster was pleased to use him as an occasional chauffeur; other masters gave him games of golf; the school doctor began his wine education. He took military training seriously and was proud to be a Company Sergeant Major in the Officers' Training Corps. He played Florizel in a production of *The Winter's Tale* and conceived 'a brief and hopeless passion' for his dark-haired, daffodil-carrying Perdita, one Norah Kirkpatrick. In June of 1923 he won the school English verse prize for the second year, his 'The Power of Music' being composed under the familiar Yeats superscription 'Tread softly, because you tread on my dreams'.

In July he looked on as the Prince of Wales, the future King Edward VIII, visited the school, the day before his much publicized lunch with Thomas Hardy at Max Gate. Hardy was to become Cecil's greatest literary hero: now he was 'only a bicycle-ride away' and yet 'might have been an undistinguished native of Northumberland for all that many of us knew about him'. That month Cecil was more concerned about winning a university scholarship: he had failed the previous year, which was why he was a schoolboy beyond his nineteenth birthday; this time he won a classical exhibition at Wadham College, Oxford, 'on the strength of my English essay and of an entirely spurious reputation as a rugby footballer'.

It was an important month for him in another way. He lost his heart to the flapper-figured Constance Mary King, daughter of that civilized Henry Robinson King who had greeted him as his form-master on his first day at Sherborne. Nearly two years older than Cecil, she had spent the last two terms in London, training in mime and the 'Greek dance' at the then fashionable Ginner-Mawer School. She returned to Dorset in the middle of the month and his previously quiescent interest in her blossomed over the next fortnight.

'Her beautifully cool voice and the grace of her movements distinguished her among the bevy of masters' daughters who, like Marcel Proust's "band apart" at Balbec, moved mysteriously on the fringe of our monastic life: she had, too, an air of independence for which, in my role of the cat-that-walked-by-itself, I felt a strong affinity', wrote Cecil. 'An only daughter with four brothers, Mary, though in no way a tom-boy, had certain acquired traits of boyishness that made it easy for me to approach her – a frankness of address, a mind both idealistic and satirical, a lack of feminine subtlety and disingenuousness which at this time I should have found an insuperable barrier.'

Mary had noticed Cecil long before this, as a boy of striking appearance who walked alone about the Sherborne streets with books under his arm and his head at a tilt. On 30 July she wrote in her diary: 'Met Day-Lewis, he gave me his paper on W.B. Yeats to read. Irish eyes which see dreams. Prize giving. Evening concert, spoke to Day-Lewis in the rain outside.' He said he would keep in touch and next day he went home to Edwinstowe, at last an Old Shirburnian.

Cecil later saw his school career as setting the pattern of his adult failures. 'My knowledge, my achievements, had been a too quick crop, facile and superficial, which would never mature. I was fated to be a good starter but a poor finisher. My enthusiasms would always burn out as fast as they flared up: my first impressions, often so vivid and accurate, would never deepen into true poetic profundity.' There is an element of truth about this autobiographical passage, but at least one Sherborne memory was given a measure of poetic profundity after lying dormant for nearly thirty years. Here was Cecil again mooching among the stalls of the Abbey Way rooms used for chrysanthemum shows:

> Something touched him. Always the scene
>   Was to haunt his memory –
> Not haunt – come alive there, as if what had been
> But a flowery idea took flesh in the womb
> Of his solitude, rayed out a rare, real bloom.
>   I know, for I was he.*

He told in his autobiography how he grew to reject the public school tradition 'with its false heroics, its facile religiosity and distorted values'. This did not prevent his supporting the tradition first as a schoolmaster, then as a parent and finally as a public man. As a Sherborne parent of the

* 'The Chrysanthemum Show' (*Poems 1943–1947*, 1948).

late 1940s and early 1950s he could very quickly become bored with the place and its people. Ruminating in his study he declared that he was 'never able to revisit the place without falling under its spell...'

At Edwinstowe Frank had acquired a curate, the newly ordained Rev Arthur Morris. This young man found Frank 'a little portly and beautifully turned out, lazy, conservative in outlook and with a streak of jealousy in his make-up'. Mamie he saw as 'a kind, motherly, hospitable woman, and Cecil as 'slim and volatile and good-looking, with a really beautiful light tenor voice'. Frank 'tried to make Cecil toe the line about church-going. Cecil was not a mutineer but now and then he rebelled and would not sing in the choir. They were both very Irish, up and down, riotous one day and black the next. They were not really on such bad terms, but they were too much alike and yet different'. Morris also observed that Cecil 'was a bit of an intellectual snob, he was not very kind about his step-mother. She was a target for his sallies and was defenceless, he could not help making her a butt'.

Cecil, in the holiday between school and university, played tennis with athletic local clergymen and sat in the sun reading Yeats and Swinburne. He was conscious of the grime and smell from the local pits smirching the vicarage garden and heard from his father of accidents in which miners were killed or maimed. He proclaimed himself to be on the political left partly to be provocative at the vicarage, and his social conscience was unconsciously born.

This was the setting for Mary King's first visit in September. She stayed for six days and only on the last of these did she detect the 'disgruntlement' which sooner or later descended on the vicarage. According to Cecil they now 'became close friends'. His father took to Mary, 'though he professed himself unable to understand what we had to talk about that kept us up so late. My stepmother felt she should chaperone us if we walked in the forest after dusk; but she need have had no apprehension – we were babes in the wood.' Mary was a nature-worshipper and at this time her essentially practical mind was somewhat clouded with ethereal fancies about fairies, dryads, naiads, pixies and the like, not to mention various theosophical notions. Under her influence Cecil tried sublimating his previous erotic interest in 'slightly undraped actresses in shining magazines' with 'a chaste passion for trees'. He gazed for hours up the trunks of birches and beeches, willing himself into communion with them.

When Cecil arrived at Oxford in early October the last of those who had fought in the war, and survived to continue their academic studies, had just left. The undergraduates had almost all gone straight to the university from their public schools. Cecil found that life at Wadham had 'a certain Edwardian opulence and leisure': he was impressed at being addressed as 'Mister' and at the large size of his room. He looked out with disdain on the 'outbreaks of wild nonsense and high spirits' by the sporty-hearties, and the tittupping affectations of the aesthetes. He saw himself as 'lonely and inexperienced with mildly gregarious tendencies and a keen desire to be liked'. He was 'a predestined victim' for what he called 'Learner-Bores', friendly, good-hearted plodders who for the rest of their lives would start every sentence, 'When I was at Oxford...'

Two of the forty-eight freshmen at Wadham that Michaelmas term became the closest friends of his life. The first was Rex Warner, soon to be identified in verse by Cecil as 'the hawk faced man', a kindly, gregarious, laughing man, a fastidious scholar with a generous spread of character. He was later to become a poet, novelist, essayist, travel writer, translator from the Greek, teacher and academic. The second was Charles Fenby, bespectacled and laconic, a drawling and worldly-wise man, later to become a journalist and editor, an accomplished technician with an introverted administrative style, who ended his career as editorial director of the Westminster Press group.

Fenby remembered his first view of Cecil as a boy 'haughty and aloof'. In his obituary tribute to Cecil for the *Wadham College Gazette* Warner agreed with this. 'My earliest impression of him is of a tall and good-looking undergraduate, extremely well-dressed in the clothes affected in those days and known as "plus-fours". He seemed to me reserved in manner, even rather icy, and I regarded his general bearing and the expression of his mouth as supercilious and perhaps "stuck-up".' He added, writing for Fenby as well as himself, that 'this judgment was very wide of the mark. He had the most affectionate and generous disposition and the apparent iciness of his demeanour served only to mask the fact that he was just as shy as I was myself.'

Both friends considered that the Oxford chapter of *The Buried Day* was inaccurate about them. Cecil 'frequently attributes to his friends virtues which they would never claim to have possessed or adorns them with amiable vices to which they were not subject', wrote Warner. There can be no doubt that Warner had the most brilliant mind of the three and could, as Cecil once versified, 'praise an apple/In terms of a peach and win the argument'. Fenby, on the other hand, was the most sure of himself. He was 'socially confident and sensible, he was gay in manner and active in the Oxford University Dramatic Society, he was very modern, he had read the latest books, knew about the new plays and had a sense of news', remembered Warner.

Cecil produced a romantic picture of the trio striding 'rapidly about the still academic city, three tall young men conducting one of the three-cornered arguments, half serious half frivolous, in which we exercised our brains like sophists by inconstantly changing sides...' Warner acknowledged that there was 'a truth of feeling' about this. He added that Cecil had an 'often melancholy temperament', sometimes disappearing into fits of gloom which were boring for everybody else. He would regularly 'get in a great state after a letter from his Dad'.

It was not a vintage time for Oxford dons, but there was the young Maurice Bowra. He had just become Dean of Wadham and was also tutor for Honour Mods, so both Cecil and Rex Warner moved at once into his formidable orbit. 'The brisk, short figure; the inflections, staccato or slurring, of his voice; the curl of the mouth as he delivered one of his outrageous witticisms; the urbane effrontery of his manner – all the characteristics of this inimitable man were freely imitated by his pupils, and he was already well on the way to being a legend before he was 30 years old', remembered Cecil. Upon those who had 'pretensions to brain' Bowra loosed 'the full force of his personality – its flash and paradox, its challenging, testing, sometimes merciless edge'. Cecil found him 'at once endearing and alarming' and, though he became a friend and admirer of the man who did so much to place Wadham with the élite of Oxford colleges, he would always regard him as 'best taken in smallish doses'. As well as being a 'galvanizing' teacher of the dead languages he had an infectious enthusiasm for English poetry. 'He conveyed to me his own passion for the middle Yeats; and he urged me to read *The Waste Land* at a time when, according to Dr Leavis, Dr Leavis was the only teacher in any English university to have acknowledged the genius of T.S. Eliot.'

At the end of his first Oxford term Cecil went back to Sherborne. He stayed at Harper House and thrilled at least two of his former fags by producing a copy of *Lansbury's Weekly*, including the words of 'The Red Flag' printed on the back page. 'Cecil taught me to sing "The Red Flag" and we agreed that it sounded even better with the first half in the minor key', remembered the Rev Gerald Fitzgerald.

Cecil also renewed his friendship with Mary. She took him to the favourite King haunt on the slopes above Sherborne, the cosy tree-protected 'prairie'. There he was introduced to her personal, bracken-touched oak, the one she called her 'Friendly Tree'. She had taken to calling Cecil 'the piper' and she brought her piper home to supper. Afterwards she confided to her diary: 'I miss the human element in CDL – the piper talks as sprite to sprite, as artist to artist, but not as friend to friend.'

In fact Cecil was now falling 'deep in love' with Mary, but was still preoccupied with his own problems and looking at mirrors. He was not the right person to give necessary extra confidence to a girl who had been brought up amongst boys, felt herself under-valued and yet inferior because she was not one, and was shy about displaying her femininity. He remembered her at that time as 'a very virginal young woman who had little or no experience of men outside her own family', who 'sorely needed at this stage a lover who should take the initiative, a man older than herself'. Cecil suffered from 'a vein of passivity . . . my cowardice and the inhibitions

which had been stealthily building up for years', all of which ensured that
he would 'follow a lead rather than take it'.

The pattern of their long courtship was set. In term they would write
to each other, Cecil from Oxford and Mary from London. When term
was over they would both make for Sherborne, and less frequently Edwinstowe. In the midst of this Cecil 'wished to live like a Poet, walk and eat
and drink and think like a Poet, above all to be recognized as a Poet'. He
was sufficiently successful in this to alarm his future mother-in-law, the amiable Connie, who began warning Mary that she must never marry a poet.
There was no danger of immediate marriage. On the prairie the young
couple were engaged in what Cecil called 'a sort of *Idylls-of-the-King* fantasy' in which Mary 'held court and I doubled the roles of court jester and
her favourite (though neither pure nor parfait) knight'. He added, 'Both
my upbringing and the public school tradition had given me the chivalric
attitude towards woman as a creature who, whatever indignities one might
subject her to in one's erotic fantasies, in the flesh was a virgin, a saint, an
ideal, and must remain unattainable until, after long and faithful service
on her lover's part, she of her own accord stepped down from the pedestal
into his arms.'

In his autobiography Cecil wrote that during his Oxford time his father
'mentioned from time to time the sacrifices he had made to send me to
the university'. On such occasions Cecil doubtless replied that his leaving
exhibition from Sherborne, his first exhibition at Wadham, and a second
one awarded after his third term, made up over half the annual £210 which
kept him at Oxford and during vacations. 'I myself scraped along without
getting into debt; but I could not afford subscriptions to university societies,
or the giving of parties, or travel, or pub crawling', remembered Cecil.

Rex Warner pointed out that despite their mutual poverty Cecil always
managed to 'dress elegantly'. It was a matter of priorities. Warner managed
to spend two months of the long vacation in France for about £15 a month
and had 'jolly good meals' within the budget. 'It was very difficult to get
Cecil abroad', he added. 'I didn't go abroad because I was afraid of making
a fool of myself speaking a foreign language and people laughing at me',
Cecil confessed in a 1968 *Observer* interview. At twenty, he was even mildly
resentful about those who did go abroad. Here he is writing to Warner
from Edwinstowe in late July 1924:

I have been intending to write for the last month or so, but when a man goes
off hob-knobbing with a lot of damned Dagoes in some god-forsaken part of
the globe, what can you expect? Damme, sir! Aren't there a hundred places in
God's own country – I refer to England – as good as this Brittany, wherever
it is. 'How should they know England who do not England know: O to be in
England where the turnips grow.' I don't profess to understand these poetical
fellows, but – bless my soul! – they have a knack of bringing a catch in a man's
throat, curse it all.... I like your 'essential verse' – essential to whom, by the

way? – with its fine disregard for vain fripperies such as metre and sense.... A youth at the Sherborne Preparatory School, being asked in a recent exam, 'Who was John the Baptist?', wrote, 'He was a man who sat in the wilderness wearing camel fur and a girdle of loins about his neck.' S'n'absolute fact! I had an idyllic time at Sherborne, of which more possibly when I see you... Please write again in the intervals between reading pornographic classics and holding pornometric liaisons with innocent French rustics.

Earlier that month both friends had been participants in a Maurice Bowra reading party at Hartland Quay on the North Devon coast. The group perched as nakedly as they dared on a variety of rocks and considered the comedy of Aristophanes. At the end of July Cecil sailed on his first journey to the new Irish Free State and discovered that life at Monart Rectory had changed little through the decade of 'troubles'. There had been a night during the Civil War when armed raiders burst into the house and began searching for a suspected arms cache. 'Stand back!' barked a man with a gun. From his chair the Rev William Goldsmith Squires replied gently, 'I must stand up before I stand back at all events.' Such calm took the hostility out of the meeting and presently the raiders withdrew, but the rector's sister Alice had had a bad fright. This may have been a contributory factor in her death at the end of 1923. Now her younger sister Knos, aged just fifty, had with renewed sacrifice taken her place as housekeeper, harmonium player and parish wife. Cecil read Lucretius and gladly renewed his old relationship with Knos, his second mother.

In September he was back at Edwinstowe for a visit from Mary. Writing in her faery fanciful way she recorded that there were 'days of tearing depression – my knight is sad because I cannot give him more and I know not the way of mine own heart'. After she had gone Cecil wrote to her that 'the sun was shining down all the woodland ways and the beeches of our vigil took me into their spirit; so that I could not be sad because their Dream-Maker was not there to see'.

Returned to Wadham for his second year Cecil had different rooms overlooking the main quadrangle in front, and the Warden's garden behind. He and Rex Warner started a literary society called the Jawbone, which held meetings presided over by the actual jawbone of an ass, procured through the London store of Selfridge's and supposed to represent the instrument by which Samson slew the Philistines. The members read papers, and their latest verses: they also 'told one another how wonderful they were', and from time to time, according to Cecil, 'persuaded a real writer to address us'.

Cecil had written to Warner from Co Wexford complaining that 'one [Harold] Acton of Oxford notoriety, that unsexed model for pornographists, had the astounding audacity to refuse certain poems of mine for his anaemic collection of drawing room ballads, Oxford Poetry.... The monumental temerity of that hairless eunuch in depriving Oxford Poetry of the only verse that would have raised it out of the slough of mediocrity leaves me gasping.' Cecil had nevertheless acquired some prestige in the eyes of his fellow Jawbone members as four pages of his verse, including the rejected poems, were included in the *Ten Singers* anthology of Georgian poetry published by Fortune and Merriman in October.

These poems appeared in *Beechen Vigil*, Cecil's first slim volume of verse which he later disowned but which was the apple of his eye when it appeared in June 1925. He had paid for publication with a legacy of £25 and steeled himself to be his own commercial traveller, touring the bookshops of Oxford and Nottingham. 'There is nothing quite like one's first book or one's first love, and in the case of the former this is often providential', he wrote in his autobiography. 'Mine . . . contained among other juvenilia a poem entitled 'Rose-Pruner', which my stepmother thought one of the gems of English poetry, and which Rex used to declaim ruthlessly aloud whenever I got above myself.'

> Meanders around the rose-beds, gnarled, clay-brown,
> Old Tom the pruner, snic-snac up and down.

All the reviews of this volume seem to have been written by his future brother-in-law Alec King. In *Oxford Outlook*, King commended Cecil's 'aloof imagination and somewhat noble diction'. He thought the poet had 'something to say, and says it memorably, in a style of verse which seems already to be individual and distinctive'. In the *Shirburnian* he added that the slight book, 'beautifully printed in the best modern fashion and with an appropriate cover of beech-leaf green', shows a style 'distinctive and felicitous'.

Other reviewers turned over the two-and-sixpenny book and wrote of other things. Cecil was nevertheless much heartened by this publication and the acceptance of two of his poems, 'Sonnet' and 'Autumn for the Mood', for *Oxford Poetry 1925*, Patrick Monkhouse and Charles Plumb having replaced Harold Acton and Peter Quennell as editors; in sanguine moments he considered he was now a poet of 'accepted achievement'.

Encouraged by Maurice Bowra's 'excellent tutoring', both Cecil and Rex Warner were aspiring to a First in Honour Mods. In his *Memories* of 1966, Bowra remembered Warner's 'remarkable gifts and promise . . . the ideal pupil, since he had been badly grounded at school and found in Greek and Latin all the charms of novelty'. Cecil 'was already a poet and applied his literary gifts to the translation of classical texts with an adventurous originality'. In his fifteen Mods papers Warner received thirteen alphas and two alpha-betas. Cecil could only manage a sound Second and decided he must be a bad examinee.

Mary was still much perplexed by her feeling and her lack of feeling for her piper. She probably said more than she knew when she confided

to her diary that March, 'I believe I am half a boy in thought and feeling.'
When she was a young girl some aunt or nursemaid had told her that compared with her brothers, she looked plain. This thoughtless remark had
always rankled. In a male-ruled household with a submissive mother she
felt at a disadvantage and consciously and unconsciously had made herself
as boy-like as possible. She sometimes displayed a forthright, demanding,
even aggressive domestic style which was an understandable manifestation
of her need to survive as an individual but which her gentle brothers found
surprising. In another social milieu, such distortion might have sent her
striding towards lesbianism. But if boy homosexuality was treated at Sherborne as something to be hidden behind a veil of guilty secrecy, lesbianism
was as unthinkable as it was supposed to have been to Queen Victoria.
Mary was not expected to fight that side of her nature because that side
was not acknowledged; yet she did feel compelled to fight it, and from
a position of complete ignorance.

Cecil also was ignorant of this, and of the effect on his loved one and
her sense of intellectual inferiority when he and his peers tried to impress
her and each other with their conversational dazzle. At Oxford she was
admired, and not only by Cecil, but she felt an outsider in the midst of
so much word-play. 'It does not seem possible in Oxford to make a simple
remark, everything is twisted into an epigram', she wrote after a May visit.
Then, 'I am finding myself more terribly alone than before', and 'Why do
men of experience want to kiss me, poets and the unusual few love me,
and most men utterly ignore me?'

For Cecil this becalmed relationship remained both frustrating and
attractive. Afterwards he pictured her engaged on 'the long and difficult
task of weaning me from my adolescence'. He wrote that 'her loyalty, her
deep capacity for affection, and her honesty – a kind of gritty sub-stratum,
inherited perhaps from her Scottish and North Country parentage, beneath
the youthful softness of her mind – were qualities I soon recognized. They
would gently purge me of my self-defensive cynicism, so that I should discover in myself a tenderness, a spring of altruism, a power to sympathize
with someone other than myself, which had been latent hitherto.'

What is more, the King family itself gave him something new and therapeutic. 'Never before had I lived in a household that was civilized, relaxed,
various, yet a close network of relationships. Here consanguinity seemed
a bond, not a fetter; love was given, not exacted; there was no talk – or
at least I never heard it – about the sin of ingratitude.' That August Cecil
joined the King summer holiday beside Loch Linnhe, Argyllshire, in the
West of Scotland. H.R.K., now seventy, had just retired from the staff at
Sherborne after forty-two years of service, but was still a vigorous walker.
One Sunday he held the company enthralled with a recitation from Shakespeare, Milton and the Dorset dialect verse of William Barnes. In Victorian
manner he remained decidedly the head of the family, but Cecil noted that

his wife, the 'charming, shy' Connie, was 'easily entertained or fluttered by her husband's temperamental changes of weather' yet 'had adapted herself to him without losing her flavour'. Moreover their children, 'so diverse in personality and interests, formed a remarkably close community which had its own customs, catchwords and private jokes. Talk leapt madly about like a fire-cracker, from nonsense to high seriousness.'

The particular problem of Cecil and Mary did not disappear. 'All day I had been with him and at night we talked by the river. Always we hammer away at the same question in the same old way', wrote Mary. 'I cannot love and he cannot leave me.' The King boys took Cecil in their stride, though finding his earnestness somewhat eccentric. Charles, the youngest, fourteen that summer, said that he was 'spellbound by Cecil's enthusiasm for poker patience or whatever family game was being played. His concentrated effort was unprecedented and he was always determined to win, it seemed extraordinary to us. Even on bicycle rides he was absolutely indefatigable, determined to battle on up hills, however heavy our hired bicycles. He also had an explosive laugh, ending in a high shriek.'

Graham Greene has pictured Oxford as 'a man pegged out on a table for examination' with his legs lying up the Banbury and the Woodstock roads.[2] The triumvirate of Warner, Fenby and Day-Lewis, now embarking on their third Oxford year, moved out from their Wadham rooms to 22 St Giles, a small old house overlooking what Greene presumably considered to be the very crotch of the city, covered with the fig leaf of a church and churchyard. The trio went into the churchyard sometimes 'when we felt the need for a gesture of especial significance' and discussed God, immortality and sex. Resting above this Church of England temple of the body was the draughty, uncomfortable, old repertory theatre where Cecil began to acquire his 'life-long insensibility to Ibsen' and his 'passionate, inextinguishable devotion to Chekhov, a writer who in his plays and short stories has indeed said, but with all the saving grace of his felicitous compassion, that we are not put on earth to be happy'.

Rex Warner was only partially successful in broadening Cecil's literary tastes and philosophical understanding. He suggested that Cecil should put away Michael Arlen's *The Green Hat* and turn to Henry James or Proust. Cecil resisted such commands, knowing, as he said in his 1972 BBC radio interview with Hallam Tennyson, that he had to 'come to authors in his own time', a time which was 'rather slow and provincial'. Warner proved more immediately persuasive about rugby football. In his own phrase he 'played rugger with some fervour', performing as a wing three-quarter for Gloucestershire and once being picked to play for the West of England against the formidable New Zealand All Blacks. More than any literary achievement he confessed pride in a comment of the *Stroud News* that he was 'perhaps the most dangerous man in the West of England'. When captain of Wadham he played as a centre three-quarter, and Cecil endeavoured to feed him from fly half. The two of them practised several elaborate tactical movements – scissors running, overhead passes and the like – 'which cost us dear when we tried them out in Cuppers'.

The only other ball game which Cecil played regularly was golf. 'My opponent on several occasions was a tall, unsmiling, taciturn don who irritated me by driving from the tees with an iron.' He was the Professor of Experimental Philosophy – Professor Lindemann, who became the friend, collaborator and scientific adviser to Winston Churchill and was raised to the peerage as Lord Cherwell. Why he should have chosen Cecil as golf partner history does not relate, for it appears they could not find anything to say to each other.

Having found his two friends Cecil was diffident about strangers. When the trio chanced to meet an outside acquaintance Cecil would stand back a pace or two, 'not jealous or disgruntled, but like a confidential secretary who knows he is indispensable and is therefore quite happy to efface himself'. Although secretary and then president of the Jawbone he usually let others break the ice when established writers came to lecture or read their verse. He had 'neither the wish nor the intellectual resource to exploit them', and it did not occur to him to use them as a means towards establishing himself in the literary world – 'I looked upon writing as a vocation, not a career.'

He did nevertheless receive encouragement, notably from Robert Graves, who was 'percipient or charitable enough to detect some promise in my terrible first book of poems'. Presumably Graves continued to prefer *Beechen Vigil* to Cecil's political verse of the 1930s which he then described as the sentiments of 'a simple-minded Red', who had mistakenly approached too close to the 'synthetic' Auden.[3] Graves, who had poignant memories of Wadham as a war-time recuperation centre where officers tried to regain peace of mind before being tossed back to the Western Front, was then living on Boar's Hill. Seeing him first at a bus-stop Cecil decided that this was the way a poet should look: 'blunt-featured, shock-headed, with a butcher-blue shirt, a knapsack and a manner withdrawn yet agreeably arrogant'.

Another who spoke to the Jawbone was the poet and novelist L. A. G. Strong, a former Wadham man now teaching at the North Oxford preparatory school Summer Fields, who was to become a guardian angel to Cecil. Apart from him, the society attracted several of those, later vilified, 'facile versifiers' who passed during the 1930s into Geoffrey Grigson's *New Verse* vocabulary of abuse: Laurence Binyon, for instance, and Humbert Wolfe.

Cecil was then much impressed by Wolfe, a busy Jewish civil servant employed at the Ministry of Labour to charm strikers' deputations, 'one of the wittiest men I have ever met, a figure of flamboyance and panache'.

For a short time Wolfe became his major influence. One consequent poem was 'Naked Woman with Kotyle', written on a dance theme for the Ginner-Mawer magazine the *Link*, and reflecting on a particular Greek vase-painting. Sadly the seriousness of this austere and sexless effort was rather punctured when Cecil began its recitation to the Jawbone by announcing the title. Tom Hopkinson, later editor of *Picture Post* and other journals, commented quietly, 'Lucky chap, old Kotyle.'

Cecil's lack of a naked woman was this term making him, as Mary commented, 'all untidy in his mind'. At one stage he stopped writing to her for over a month while she agonized alone in London. 'It will not do and it cannot be, this reiterates itself in my mind whenever I think of Cecil and today I have been out with his father', she wrote to herself. And 'I am accused of unkindness to Cecil because he gives me more than I can return, have I not tried to break away rather than make unhappiness?'

Fortunately for Cecil he had a friend to whom he could turn, a woman who was not only sympathetic but, as luck had it, a trained psychiatrist. The remarkable Margaret Marshall, a soldier's daughter four years older than Cecil, had been married to a doctor with a practice in Frank's Edwinstowe parish. She was small and neatly-shaped and sallow-complexioned with a long nose and a sensual mouth. She had, as Cecil observed, an 'air of practicality, of clinically earnest attention, lightened from time to time by a lewd giggle'. She caught her first glimpse of Cecil when he drove his step-mother over to call on her but declined to get out of the car. They met at a tennis party where she noted his violent approach. 'He would throw his racket at the net when things went wrong, he really loved to win, he would even play Monopoly with a wicked gleam in his eye', she remembered in old age. They took to each other in a platonic way and read each other their verses.

Soon afterwards she ran away with Douglas Marshall, the talented lieder singer who became her second husband. Divorce was 'a subject, like cancer, which one mentioned at the Vicarage only in shocked, shifty mutters', but, to his credit, Frank 'made no more than token resistance' when it was first suggested that Cecil should go to stay with the Marshalls at their Greenlanes chicken farm near Guildford in Surrey. Tragedy was already in the air as Marshall had contracted tuberculosis, but he was well enough to teach Cecil 'more about singing... than I have ever learnt from anyone else'. Moreover the marriage was an obviously happy one.

Margaret was something new for Cecil: 'agnostic, unconventional, a bit raffish, deliciously disrespectful about so many of the social values and observances I myself had begun to detest'. She had a 'somewhat intense and dominating personality' which she relieved with a coarse tongue and a touch of the clown. Cecil came to think of her as 'an enchanting substitute for the elder sister I never had'. She encouraged him to talk. She 'showed me the only kind of power that I have ever valued, the power of self-knowledge'; she 'gave me, in effect, when I was lost, a compass and a map of the country I was lost in – a map of myself'. It mattered less whether the map was accurate than whether it was helpful in making sense of available facts and showing a way forward. Quite without censure she made it clear that he must grow up, start looking outward, stop intoxicating himself with his fantasies and self-pity. Her interest 'flattered and reassured' him.

Mary had completed her training and in January 1926 she moved to Ipswich to begin work in East Anglia as a peripatetic dancing teacher. On her way there she had a day in Oxford. Afterwards: 'Today came a letter from my piper, full of strange bitterness of longing, we had not one moment alone on Saturday.' Yet, writing to Rex Warner that same New Year, he wished it to be known that all was well. 'As long as one realizes one is being romantic and has a good firm landing place in reality, I see no harm in "thinking among the clouds": it is surely the difference between personal and consciously objective poetry.... You see, I am innately a romantic, though I think that now I have got this part of me well under control.'

At Oxford Cecil sat 'sluggishly mooning on the window seat of our panelled, first-floor sitting room', surviving mainly on a diet of milk choco-late and digestive biscuits. The three friends had drawn closer. Charles Fenby had conceived an affection for him close to love, but was sceptical about Cecil's motives for continually inviting him to Edwinstowe during vacations. 'I think it was just that he was at loggerheads with his father and needed other company', he told me. Rex Warner believed more con-fidently in his friendship with Cecil, which did survive every test of time and absence. Yet when the General Strike started on Monday 3 May the attitudes of the trio could not have been more contrasted. Warner went to Hull to conduct trams, Fenby stayed working for his approaching Finals, and Cecil (according to Mary's diary) 'is thrilled with the romance of Labour's stand and will fight for them if need be'.

The Fabian Socialist G.D.H. Cole, then a Reader in Economics, had just begun his 'Cole Group', a discussion group for leftish undergraduates, meeting weekly at his Holywell house. It now formed a University Strike Committee which recruited Cecil. He became one of the drivers maintain-ing liaison between the Oxford strikers and the TUC headquarters in Lon-don. Such militancy did not last. After being declared redundant as a driver he moved on to London and the Hyde Park Hotel unit producing the *British Independent* on behalf of the Archbishop of Canterbury's mediation move-ment. They had hardly produced their first number when, on 12 May, the strike collapsed and the miners were left to fight on alone. Cecil wrote, 'my own sacrifice to the cause of mediation being my one decent suit, which was ruined with violet ink'.

In June the triumvirate broke up. Charles Fenby took a Second in Modern History and began work as a reporter on the *Westminster Gazette*.

Rex Warner had a sudden nervous breakdown which happened, according to his own account, 'because I was working too hard'. Cecil would have to find new companions for his last Oxford year before taking his Greats Finals.

He began his summer vacation with a long visit to Margaret and Douglas Marshall at Greenlanes. They gave him another helping of self-knowledge, and when he crossed the Irish Sea to Monart in August his mind was clearer. On 2 September Mary joined him there, Cecil meeting her at Enniscorthy with pony and trap. After dinner the next day they went out to look at the stars. 'We were beneath the laburnum by the gate with the stars shining on us steadily...', Mary recorded. 'Monart was magic in her ways. There was no passionate entreaty in our kiss, only starlight and lightness, warmth and happiness.'

'At Monart, that summer, the knot that had held me powerless was cut', wrote Cecil in his autobiography. 'We went out one night, and by the gate into the meadow we kissed for the first time. When at last I went to bed, in the shabby little room I had shared with Knos as a child – it smelt now of the apples which had been stored there through the winter, and was swimming with moonlight – I was in a daze of glory, flooded with incredulous joy like a prisoner miraculously released after years of solitary confinement....'

> In a windless garden
> At the time of plum-gathering
> When the hedge is plumy
> With Traveller's Joy,
> Beautiful gay candid
> My love came to me.*

On 15 September they moved on to give Knos a few days of seaside holiday at Ballinacallig, Brittas Bay, in Co Wicklow. A week later Mary was back in Sherborne and Cecil in Edwinstowe. She wrote in her diary, 'In two years, if all is well, I shall marry', and told her parents she was engaged.

Cecil was not happy to be undertaking a fourth year at Oxford, particularly as 'I knew virtually nothing, and lacked more and more the will to concentrate on the required subjects.' His interest in philosophy was slight and he found that each proposition of Plato or Aristotle, Hume, Berkeley, Spinoza or Kant 'seemed to be irrefutable – until I read the opposing viewpoint'. His studies simply made it 'more difficult than ever to make up my mind about anything at all'. As far as possible he therefore avoided study, taking in only 'a token amount of reading and lecture-going' and spending his time 'in desultory reading – text-books of psychology, poetry, romantic fiction – or pottering about Oxford, or writing verse or day dreaming'.

Thinking of the future he only wanted two things: to write poetry and to marry. He would also have to earn a living, and the most obvious way

* 'My Love Came to Me' (*Country Comets*, 1928).

of doing that was schoolmastering, 'a fate worse than death', which he refused to contemplate. His unrest was not helped by the fact of his being a year older than almost all his fellow undergraduates. He suffered increasingly from those moods of black depression which had started in his late teens, and which 'for many years were to sweep over me out of the blue, drenching me with misery and rendering me so morally impotent that I could not descry any gleam of reassurance through their mirk, nor make the least move to free myself'.

He was helped to an extent by Wilfrid Cowley, destined to become a housemaster at the mildly progressive public school of Bryanston in Dorset, who now moved into 22 St Giles. He had an imperturbable demeanour and was so courtly in his manner that Rex Warner nick-named him 'the Baron'. He dressed like Byron, enjoyed arguing and was full of literary and political gossip. He loved to take a theme and develop it along wild, comic lines. He was very much Mary's favourite among Cecil's Oxford friends, for he was prepared to operate on the level of whoever he encountered.

Maurice Bowra persevered with Cecil's social education, taking the diffident poet to that Jacobean manor house five miles from Oxford where nearly everybody who figures in literary biography and autobiography of that period seems to have gone sooner or later. He already had a tenuous connection with Lady Ottoline Morrell of Garsington, as she was a half-sister of the Duke of Portland, whose private golf course Cecil used during his Edwinstowe holidays. Lady Ottoline was kind to him, later inviting him to tea from time to time, but he was never close enough to indulge in the gossip which was the main reward she received from the grander figures on whom she bestowed her favours. On that first visit Cecil went about 'slinking gloomily amongst the peacocks' while the eminent men stood on the terraced lawns 'rapt in discussion and display'. Nobody thought to talk to him apart from an affable Magdalen undergraduate, Henry Yorke, whose first 'Henry Green' novel came out that year.

Having long ago given up hope of a First, Cecil was determined to achieve the next most distinguished class of degree, a Fourth. In later life, verbally and in print, he claimed to have contrived a place in this class: '. . . it is a mystery to me why the examiners did not fail me altogether'. The Wadham records show that he actually took a prosaic Third.

W.H. Auden, an exhibitioner in Natural Science from Gresham's School, Holt, had arrived at Christ Church in October 1925. There is no agreement about when Cecil first met him. Whatever the date Cecil remembered an initial call on Auden at his Christ Church rooms, 'the windows of which seemed to be permanently covered with sack-cloth curtains, Wystan claiming that he could only work by artificial light'. Auden, whose memory was marginally the more reliable of the two, wrote in 1972 that he encountered

Cecil 'very soon after I came up to Oxford in 1925' when 'he was sharing digs with Rex Warner'.[4] Certainly it was during the first half of 1926 that he brought Cecil together with the young Merton composer Lennox Berkeley, who was persuaded that Cecil should give the first performance of three of his songs at a Musical Union concert in the Holywell Rooms. This was not an unblemished triumph. Cecil had 'no trouble' with a setting of Du Bellay's 'The Thresher', which he regarded as 'one of the most musical pieces of song writing produced during our period'. This was followed by two 'rather unmelodious' settings of Auden poems, one appropriately called 'Trippers' and telling of some passengers in a motor coach. Cecil did much tripping during rehearsals with Lennox Berkeley, and on the day stalled completely: 'I just managed to limp through the first, but in the second I broke down and had to start again, the song being received by the audience with a sustained outburst of silence.'

Cecil had the advantage of being nearly three years older than Auden, and a published poet. Yet, as Auden wrote in 1932, 'Before a man wants to understand, he wants to command or obey instinctively, to live with others in a relation of power...'[5] Cecil also accepted this sentiment and instinctively became an Auden follower, or perhaps Deputy Leader (Poetry) of the Auden Gang. Using Christ Church as a convenient hotel for writing and entertaining his friends, Auden was, as Spender has observed, a 'confident and conscious master of his situation'. Cecil saw it the same way and almost at once became 'a willing disciple', trying to adapt his classical romanticism to Auden's austere intellectual ambiguity. He was at once impressed that such an 'exceptional intelligence' as that of Auden was being devoted to poetry. He was still more impressed by Auden's vitality: 'a vitality so abundant that, overflowing into certain poses and follies and wildly unrealistic notions, it gave these an air of authority, an illusion of rightness, which enticed some of Auden's contemporaries into taking them over-seriously.' Before long Cecil conceived 'certain half-conscious reservations about him', but conceded that Auden's exuberance 'redeemed the dogmatism, the intellectual bossiness, and the tendency to try and run his friends' lives for them'.

In *Oxford Poetry 1926*, jointly edited by Auden and Charles Plumb, Cecil and Rex Warner had four poems each. Auden, with the approval of Basil Blackwell, selected Cecil as his co-editor for *Oxford Poetry 1927*, and in that year the two poets drew close to each other. In an introductory letter for Cecil's 1968 bibliography Auden wrote, 'To you I owe my first introduction to the later poems of Yeats and to the songs of John Dowland. Vice versa, I *think* I am right in saying that I introduced you to the poems of Thomas Hardy and Robert Frost, for both of which I had developed a passion while still at school.'[6]

Cecil remembered that 'often during the summer term of 1927, we shared a punt or walked around Oxford, Wystan's favourite walk being past the gas-works and the municipal rubbish dump'. The Auden walk has been nicely described by Stephen Spender.[7] He 'walked very fast on flat feet, with striding angular movements of his arms and legs and jerkings up of his head'. As he walked, Cecil noted, he talked 'incessantly, his words tumbling over one another in the hurry to get out, a lock of tow-coloured hair falling over the brow of his rather puffy but wonderfully white face'. He had not yet come to the view that poets should look like stockbrokers, for on these walks he would affect a black frock coat, of the kind then favoured by lay readers, and would carry a starting pistol.

Cecil proclaimed himself 'jealous of Auden's superior powers and higher reputation' and took for a time to writing 'pastiche Auden', but he also felt himself to be 'in competition' with Wystan. Maybe Auden was sometimes patronizing in his tributes to Cecil's powers, but he was always ready to admit Cecil as a serious colleague. In his 1972 tribute he was concerned to show that Cecil wrote verse which only he of the so-called 'Poets of the Thirties' could have written: '... what poets of the same generation have in common is the least interesting thing about them. What really matters is the way in which they differ, for every genuine poet, major or minor, is unique, a member of a class of one.'[8]

As soon as Cecil's Greats Finals were over in the summer of 1927 the two poets adjourned to a public house at Appletreewick in Yorkshire's Wharfedale. The initial object of the visit was to write what Auden called 'the somewhat pompous' introduction to *Oxford Poetry 1927*. The editors wrote alternate paragraphs, Cecil going in first, as though taking part in a game of intellectual consequences. 'We were in deadly earnest,' remembered Cecil, 'but we took out an insurance policy, in the form of deliberately portentous prose styles carrying pastiche to the edge of burlesque, against any risk of solemnity or self-importance.'

The rivalry of the colleagues was also allowed occasional expression as when, during a moorland walk, they both had the same thought about a dry-stone wall ahead of them:

A hundred yards from the wall, as if on a common impulse, we both began to walk faster: at 50 or 60 yards, we broke into a trot, and we were sprinting all out over the last 30 yards or so. Arriving simultaneously at the wall, we gave each other an amused but also sheepish look. I see now, beneath this absurdly trivial occurrence, the glint of mutual rivalry. But if it did exist, it was natural enough at our age that it should; and we had a complementary respect for each other. It was at Appletreewick, I think, that we wrote down the names of all the living English poets we could remember: we then sorted them out into three columns: in the left-hand column we put those whom we already excelled, in the middle column those we would excel one day, and in the right-hand column (an extremely short one) the poets whom we had little hope of ever equalling.

There were almost certainly no sexual longings on this holiday. Cecil had long emerged from his homosexual phase. Auden, repressed by the pernicious 'honour system' through which Gresham's sought to prevent physical relationships between boys, had trained himself not to have sexual expectations among members of his own class. On the other hand the holiday did give an impetus for Cecil's *Transitional Poem* (1929) sequence, the first for which he retained any regard at the end of his life. In this Auden is one of the four people Cecil said he had 'loved and chosen'.

> Last the tow-haired poet, never done
> With cutting and planing some new gnomic prop
> To jack his all too stable universe up: –
> Conduct's Old Dobbin, thought's chameleon.
> Single mind copes with split intelligence,
> Breeding a piebald strain of truth and nonsense.

When in the throes of philosophy at Oxford, Rex Warner would frequently repeat to Cecil the saying of Lao-Tze: 'Of everything that is true, the converse is also true.' Few people can have been more consistent in their contradictions than Cecil. That is the central axis of this story and explains why his search for himself, the continuing thread of his life and poetry, was so difficult. Cecil's autobiographical views of his young self as he entered and left Oxford thus have to be read, like many of the statements about himself in *The Buried Day*, as the truth, nothing but the truth, but not the whole truth. He wrote that the Cecil of 1923 'must have been an awkward customer in many ways, with his moodiness and fitful enthusiasms and the rudeness to which his cult of intellectual honesty could tempt him.' In four years Oxford had tried to give him a lighter touch and an acceptance of compromise, but, 'although I was more at ease now in society, and although my affection flowed freely towards those I felt at home with, my mind was still introverted, dreaming, idealistic, ruled too much by abstractions and humiliated by its own lack of experience'.

At the same time, he was certainly taking a business-like attitude to publication. In November 1926 he had joined the Society of Authors, and in January 1927 had written to the Society from 22 St Giles asking whether he could detach himself from the publisher of *Beechen Vigil* for his second book of verse, *Country Comets* (1928):

Dear Sir, I should like your advice upon the following point. In the summer of 1925 I published a book of verse with Fortune Press, paying about half the cost of publication myself. No contract was made with them, but I wrote a letter to them saying I was prepared to give them the first refusal of my next book. I now have material sufficient for another book; but as the Fortune Press never advertises, and I was not very satisfied with their last production, I want to change my publishers. Many of these poems have appeared in reputable weeklies, so I am confident that I could get a better publisher. I should like to know what is the best course of action to take, and how far I am bound by the letter I wrote. In sending me some royalties recently the Fortune Press wrote, 'when you have enough material for another small book you may care to communicate with us', which suggests that they do not consider me to be legally bound to them. If possible, I do not wish to let my MS into their hands, as their methods are most dilatory and rather careless.

A few days later he was advised that he was not legally bound to Fortune; the Society suggested that if he was morally bound he could offer the manuscript and then refuse the terms..

No conceivable terms would have been sufficient to buy his bread for more than a week or two, but his manner of trying to find himself a job was rather akin to the 'desultory and doomed-to-failure spirit' with which he had approached his Oxford Greats. That summer all his energies were spent on his holidays, and the occasional job interview was reluctantly fitted into his full social and artistic time-table.

After the Yorkshire interlude with Auden he travelled, on 7 July, southwards to Sherborne where Knos joined him and he took part in a song and dance recital produced by Mary, now wearing the jade and silver engagement ring with which he had presented her the previous December. The elaborate recital, given three Drill Hall performances in aid of the Abbey's Lady Chapel Restoration Fund, included a mime play in voluminous Victorian dress, *While Aunt Matilda Sleeps*. Mary was one of the Aunt's two straying nieces and, according to the *Western Gazette*, 'Their beaux (Mr Cecil Day-Lewis and Mr Alec King) were striking examples of the sartorial art of those days.' Cecil also rendered groups of Hebridean and Dowland songs, the *Shirburnian* commenting that 'he was more at home in the second, which he sang with great feeling'.

Following this he had three weeks at Edwinstowe and then joined the King family in the Lake District. In later life he claimed that he had always disliked the Lake District, because the mountains do not keep their distance and therefore become oppressive, but he made no complaints that August. It was here on 19 August, after a day at Keswick and an evening of singing, that Cecil and Mary surrendered their long-preserved virginity to each other.

A week later the lovers travelled together to Edwinstowe where Cecil was due for an interview. The unlikely idea was that he should work in miners' welfare: one of the local collieries was starting an adult education scheme and the manager was a friend of Cecil's father. He attended his interviewers in Nottingham on 26 August, wearing a dark-blue sombrero and floppy orange bow-tie, an ensemble selected to impress the colliery management with his poetic status.

Moving on from Edwinstowe, Cecil and Mary were the guests of the Rev Arthur Morris, now a curate at Mansfield, and his wife Alison. Her main memory of his visitation was a charade in which Morris impersonated George v offering the Poet Laureate's crown to Cecil, an honour refused 'with terrible grimaces and oaths'. Then they all four drove to Blakeney in Norfolk for another three weeks of holiday. Morris remembered that the holiday was notable for the discovery, or invention, of one of those strange, unreal birds that made their appearance in Cecil's life from time to time. This one snored outside his hotel window at night and he called it 'the Breathing Bird'. There were sailing and picnics, golf and billiards, marsh walks and a pilgrimage to Norwich Cathedral, and some picture-posing intended to reflect the kind of melodrama then popular in the silent cinema. At one stage Frank, regarded by Alison Morris as 'a real humbug, pretending the whole time', came with Mamie to stay at nearby Cromer. Alison felt mildly aggrieved that Mary stayed on and did not leave Cecil for a third week on his own; but her friendship with him was to blossom later.

Beneath his unrestrained pleasure in holiday activities Cecil was now becoming more worried about his job prospects. Having failed in his care-less attempt to break into miners' education he 'nearly accepted a job at some school in Turkey – or was it Japan? – but I had never been abroad in my life and the prospect of foreign ways and foreign tongues and foreigners daunted me'. Instead he decided that he must try to establish himself in literary journalism. In mid-September he moved into Charles Fenby's Bayswater flat, armed with the £5 which was all he had left from the sale of his classical texts to Blackwell's of Oxford. He was interviewed at the *Spectator*, which had published three of his poems and which needed an assistant for its literary editor, but was turned down. Fenby brought him home a new novel by Edward Thompson to be reviewed for the *West-minster Gazette*. 'I had written a few reviews for university magazines, but not of fiction', Cecil remembered. 'I read the book; then, for hour after hour, I sat trying to think of something to say about it. I could not. Not one single word. My brain had seized up. In the end Charles had to write the review himself ... my £5 was exhausted now and my nerve broken.'

Not for the last time in this story L.A.G. Strong now intervened in his guardian angel role. Since going down from Wadham in 1920 he had been teaching at the Oxford preparatory school, Summer Fields. 'He told me there was a last-minute vacancy on the staff and urged me to try my hand at teaching, if only as a temporary measure', wrote Cecil.

'I remember very well being sent up to London to interview him', recalled A.F. 'Bobs' Alington, then a tweed-suited assistant master, famous for leftish sympathies and the son of the recently retired headmaster. 'I found him in a small room with a gas fire, having recently come down from Wadham, and as far as I remember he interviewed me. At any rate we agreed that he should come to Summer Fields. ... I claim to have elicited the facts that he had been a prefect at Sherborne and in the 2nd xv.'

For Cecil the move back to Oxford, during the last week of September, involved some swallowing of pride. 'I took the post, with the feelings of a spinster, no longer as young as she was, accepting an unattractive and socially inferior suitor in order to get away from home', he wrote. He had resisted the teaching profession 'partly because, half aware how unformed I was compared with many of my coevals, I specially feared a profession which threatens its practitioners with chronic adolescence and tends to shut them off from the "real world" of men that I so wistfully desired to enter'. He also resisted partly, he thought, because he was 'doomed to this profession through incompetence to hold any other kind of job'.

The school, boasting the wholesome motto 'Healthy mind in a healthy body', was founded in 1864. Its large grounds stretched from the Banbury Road to the River Cherwell. School statistics show that of the 2,800 boys who attended during its first 100 years, 951 went to Eton, compared with 189 to Winchester, 171 to Harrow and 147 to Radley. The roll of honour then included two Prime Ministers, two Lord Chancellors, thirteen judges, seven ambassadors, one Archbishop and any number of high-ranking service officers.

In 1927 the institution was ruled by the Rev Cyril Williams, a pompous and conservative headmaster with a vinous countenance and a sarcastic turn of mind, who never looked at the person he was addressing. 'Please, sir, can I go to the Vinery?', boys would ask when needing to excrete. 'I don't know whether you can my boy, but you may', was the unvarying reply. Julian Amery, the future Conservative Cabinet Minister, who arrived as a boy at Summer Fields when Cecil was teaching there wrote in his memoirs, *Approach March*, of the conditions he found. The day started with cold baths – a queue of naked boys in a draughty bathroom, supervised by an officious under-matron – then the pupils were marched to breakfast for grey, lumpy porridge and bad rissoles. Work was conducted in crowded schoolrooms with hard benches. The Vinery consisted of non-flushing earth closets which had 'a terrible stench'. Included in the meals was a form of stewed mutton which they called 'cats' meat', and a bread-and-butter pudding so economical with currants that it was known as 'Brother where art thou?'.

Much of this apparently escaped Cecil's notice, though he did confirm in his autobiography that the milking of the school to provide dividends for at least two families produced a strain felt by all. Numbers of boys had increased faster than buildings and sometimes two classes had to be taught in one room. The heating was not generous: 'The icy damp of the North Oxford winter gripped us for weeks on end, and from the draughts which swept the corridors I contracted a nagging neuralgia difficult to throw off.'

Cecil was nevertheless impressed by the honours board and insisted that the school was 'exceptionally good of its kind', adding that if the boy was 'treated as a clever little animal rather than as a miniature intellectual, I shed few tears over it; for I had no theories about education, no vocation for teaching, and no quarrel with a system that made teaching relatively easy'. It was a system built on drill and fear, with the cane used freely to punish bad work.

Cecil once told Benedict Nicolson, another pupil of this period, that he hated teaching at Summer Fields and, whenever he could, escaped to a public house in the Banbury Road with 'the only congenial companion he could find among his colleagues'. In *The Buried Day*, on the other hand, Cecil remembered that the boys 'were, many of them, quick-witted and attractive, tending perhaps to be rather spoilt, but with an ease of manner and a charming touch of independence which reflected the homes they came from. As for the staff, in a few weeks they had radically changed my attitude towards teachers and the teaching profession.' They put him at his ease and encouraged his 'first faltering steps'. 'Gay, unstuffy, diverse in gifts but alike in their concern for their charges my colleagues at Summer Fields did really seem a band of brothers.'

Whatever the truth of this, the presence on the staff of a sympathetic fellow writer was for Cecil a decided bonus, though at this time, aged thirty-one, Leonard Alfred George Strong had published short stories and verse but none of the novels with which he made his name. He was a Devon man with an Irish background, recently married to Sylvia Brinton, the daughter of an Eton housemaster. He had a big head and a small body, a throaty voice with a trace of Irish brogue, and a sadistic streak which he did not always conceal from his duller pupils. He was also a well-informed but unmalicious gossip, continuously amusing, endlessly kind to his friends, a tireless encourager of the young he liked, and in the end, maybe, too interested in people to work hard enough at his writing. At this time he was much under the spell of J.M. Synge and W.B. Yeats, having got to know the latter in Oxford between 1919 and 1922, and his earthiness was touched with Celtic twilight. He was the sort of man who could report that over lunch with Evelyn Waugh he had seen 'elemental evil spirits' dancing behind Waugh's chair.

Cecil described himself as an 'amateurish' schoolmaster, whose 'poetry-making and the lessons impressed on me by my relationship with my father, stopped me from ever getting too closely involved with the boys'. In class he had to learn as he went along, frequently having to teach subjects of which he knew little, even arithmetic. Julian Amery wrote that Cecil's heart 'was clearly not in teaching'. By contrast Alfred Shaughnessy, who was to have a long career in the theatre, cinema and television, considered himself 'lucky enough to be taught Latin by C.D-L' in a style that included much striding about the classroom and dramatic declaiming of Cicero. Benedict Nicolson, elder son of Sir Harold Nicolson and Vita Sackville-West, was conscious that he knew more French than his teacher Cecil.

He took part in a number of other activities. There was a memorable production of Shakespeare's *The Merchant of Venice*; Shaughnessy was an eleven-year-old Old Gobbo, Ben Nicolson was Antonio, his younger brother Nigel was Nerissa and the future Bishop Batty was Shylock. L. A. G. Strong was assistant producer and designer. Cecil's 'beautiful voice was heard during the play in an original setting of "Tell me where is fancy bred"', and Mrs Strong 'again carried out her unobtrusive but effective duties at the piano'.

Outside school Cecil spent his afternoons in Oxford, at the cinema, watching rugby, talking and singing with Wystan Auden and Rex Warner. The latter was back at Wadham reading English and recalled in 1974, 'We used to go for long and talkative walks in the neighbourhood of the gasworks, a locale already sanctified by a phrase in *The Waste Land*, and I can remember expeditions in canoes with Wystan and Cecil up evil smelling tunnels.'⁹ As well as ordering a reorganization of Cecil's life and poetry, Auden was trying to broaden his musical taste. 'In the teeth of his loud, confident but wonderfully inaccurate piano accompaniment I finally mastered *Ernste Gesänge* of Brahms', he remembered. His singing was more relaxed on evenings spent with the Strongs at Summertown, being accompanied here by the competent Sylvia in Irish songs.

Most evenings were spent in his 'pleasant room' in the gate lodge, working on his *Transitional Poem* sequence, opening and re-opening 'the scars of my unequal struggle with the philosophers'. Middle-period Yeats, 'I think, had the greatest influence on me rather than the early or later style, because it was the style from which I derived some of the *Transitional Poem*, the first adult book of poetry which I was to write'; he explained to Hallam Tennyson in their 1972 BBC radio interview. In his *A Hope for Poetry* (1934), Cecil claimed Hopkins, Owen and Eliot as the 'immediate ancestors' of the post-war poetic movement. Yet in his 1972 interview Cecil spoke for the MacSpaunday group of poets:

We didn't use the revolutionary techniques which Eliot had used ... he and Ezra Pound made the poetic revolution and we didn't carry it on at all.... I see now we were almost reactionary ... having played around with kinds of Eliotesque phrases we went back to the kind of poetry we best understood. I, for example, went back to what everyone counted a sort of neo-Georgian poetry. Of course, it wasn't, anyone who thinks my poetry is neo-Georgian needs their head examining. They have never seen Georgian poetry. Mine was simpler and more straightforward, more almost classical, than any Georgian poetry.

In November a minor fruit of the Appletreewick week appeared in the shape of *Oxford Poetry 1927*. The same month Cecil signed an agreement with Martin Hopkinson of Covent Garden to produce his second volume of juvenilia, *Country Comets*. This volume had already been rejected by several publishers. The agreement with Hopkinson was that Cecil would pay any deficit there might be if the sale after six months failed to cover the cost of production. The book appeared on 8 February 1928, its twenty-four poems representing 'rather more than half' Cecil's work since the twenty-four included in *Beechen Vigil* (1925). He acknowledged permissions from ten journals in Oxford, Cambridge, London and New York. A foreword tells that 'the poems here, being all direct products of a single conflict whose recurrence I could neither expect nor desire, may compensate as a human document for what they lack in maturity and restraint. They are printed therefore, with one exception, in the chronological order of their writing.' Cecil came to regard the book as an 'embarrassment', but *The Times Literary Supplement* certainly gave it a warmer welcome than it did his last volume forty-two years later.

If nothing else *Country Comets* provides a clear signpost to the future. The way in which the poems form a sequence, rather than a miscellaneous assemblage, proved to be a hallmark of the MacSpaunday group of poets. The conflict of the sequence, between positive and negative aspects of Cecil, more than between a single-minded chaser and his chaste girl-friend, showed the way to a large proportion of Cecil's future self-absorbed verse. There are several warning signs of trouble to come in his marriage. In 'The Perverse', for instance, he faces one of the recurring truths of his life, that the journey is better than the arrival.

> His pretty came among the primroses
> With open breast for him. No more denied
> Seemed no more ideal....

During the various school holidays of 1928 Mary and Cecil made a pre-marital progress round their friends and relations spread about England, mainly in Mary's new, open-top Austin 7, soon nick-named 'the pumpkin'. Their marriage date was fixed for the end of the year and, because Summer Fields could not afford a second married master, he knew he must move on.

In retrospect his last summer term at the school seemed idyllic, with 'the elms freshly green and the Cherwell sparkling beyond the playing fields and the salvia-red blazers brilliant under the sunshine'. In white shorts and Sherborne School sweater he greatly enjoyed the annual Hay Feast on 25 June: a lavish strawberry picnic held inside circular castles made of hay just cut from the water meadows, followed by a free fight, involving masters and boys, held with the object of capturing the other castles. Cecil used this event in his first Nicholas Blake detective novel, *A Question of Proof* (1935), where a body is found in one of the hay castles.

In the middle of July he was offered a new job at Larchfield School, Helensburgh, twenty miles from Glasgow, at £300 a year. In early September he and Mary inspected what was to be their first marital home, 128 West King Street, Helensburgh. It was a sound and small and entirely undistinguished slate-roofed, pebble-dashed council house, in a new estate which looked across the Clyde estuary to Greenock. Mary at once demonstrated her practicality and her willingness to do ninety-eight per cent of the required domestic chores. Three days were spent staining floors, supervising workmen and organizing the kitchen. By the morning of his first day at Larchfield, Wednesday 12 September, Cecil had got a severe but workable home, though he chose to live most of that bachelor Christmas term in school.

Helensburgh, Dunbartonshire, the 'Wimbledon of the North' as Cecil called it, has a front on the Firth of Clyde. By the late 1920s the peak of river traffic had passed, but the yowlings and mooings of steam whistles, as much as the hills overlooking Loch Lomond and the mountain ranges, blue with distance and snow-capped until late spring, gave the place romance. Granite-faced, grey-plastered Larchfield was established as an Academy in 1845 to cater for the still expanding middle-class development. In its day it had produced Bonar Law, Sir James Frazer, Jack Buchanan, and John Logie Baird, who had given the first demonstration of television in January 1926; but, according to Cecil, the school 'appeared to have rather exhausted itself in doing so'. The headmaster was T.T.N. Perkins, an untidy man with a moustache, very conscious of his authority, and conscious also of having come down in the world after a double blue at Oxford. As he grew older the school gradually ran down.

The institution had officially become a preparatory school in 1919, but in 1928 it did not insist on boys leaving before their fourteenth birthdays as did Summer Fields. To his dismay Cecil found that some of the seventy or so boys – twenty-five of them boarders – were 'large, hairy men'. As master in charge of rugby he found that he had a 1st xv of giants and a 2nd xv of pygmies, so that he spent much of his time 'chasing all over the field, plastered with Scottish mud, trying to tackle the whole 1st xv one after another'.

The school aimed to give boys 'a Christian and a liberal education'. Cecil spent much of his first term trying to educate himself in 'that weird, consonantless variety' of the Scottish tongue spoken around Glasgow. He found the boys 'serious, good-humoured, rather uncouth and unsophisticated', as yet untainted by the prevailing social atmosphere of 'prosperous bourgeois gentility'. He was not greatly attracted to the adult company either in the masters' common room or beyond, so much so that the prolonged but vigorous sermons which he was forced to sit through with the boys on Sundays were actually a high spot of his life. Where possible he escaped to Glasgow for a pub-crawl with 'the admirable Mr Snodgrass', a veteran of the 1914–18 war and the father of a fellow master. 'When in drink he saw me not double but as a whole platoon, or even a company of men, drilled me on the station platform, entrained me, and when we returned to Helensburgh, marched me with ear-splitting words of command along the sleeping avenues homeward', wrote Cecil.

H.J. Weir, a pupil of this period, remembered Cecil as 'a young and enthusiastic master who took an interest in all sides of school life, including games. Being slim and wiry, he was always pretty fit. He coached and refereed rugby and took an interest in cricket. As a teacher he maintained good discipline and also tried to instil some real interest in his subject. He was quite a popular master, though I seem to remember that he had a fairly quick temper and we didn't take too many liberties in his class'.

Out of school he was still working on the *Transitional Poem* sequence. He sent the opening poem of Part Four to W.H. Auden, who would provide its superscription, 'The hatches are let down/And the night meets the day/The spirit comes to its own/The beast to its play': these being the last four lines of an epithalamium written for Cecil's wedding at the end of the year. The twenty-one-year-old Auden had finished at Oxford that summer and now wrote back from Berlin enclosing his chorus 'The spring unsettles sleeping partnerships . . .' from the verse charade *Paid on Both Sides* on which he was working. The play has a wedding scene with a dedication to Cecil. The Auden letter was critical of the poem Cecil had written him. 'What I feel about this poem and also about what I can remember of several others of *Transitional P.*, is that you are not taking enough trouble about your medium, your technique of expression', wrote the severe Wystan. At that time Auden was still living in a middle-class household, and he ended with the news that he had 'just returned from a midnight feast with the maids, having eaten too much duck. . . . I and my boy together would make D.H. Lawrence look rather blue: he is the most elemental thing I have yet met: I think my fiancée will have this quality which I feel in need of at present.'

Cecil, with his father and stepmother, arrived in Sherborne on Christmas Eve and joined forces with the Kings for the festivities. Boxing Day was also the wedding eve and there was a party at Greenhill, attended by the bridegroom, the best man (Rex Warner) and their friend Wilfrid Cowley, 'the Baron'. There was music in plenty with Cecil offering the four items of Brahms's Opus 121, *Vier Ernste Gesänge*, taught him by Wystan Auden: 'I found these sombre songs so deeply sympathetic that I was to create consternation among Mary's assembled friends and relatives by singing them on our wedding eve, and in particular by the conviction I imparted to my rendering of the passage that begins "O Death, how welcome art thou to him that is in want".'

There was apparently no reading of the verse epithalamium (Appendix I) which Auden sent from Berlin for the occasion, despite its reference to 'the accurate matching of a man and woman'. Perhaps this was not the occasion to consider the image of 'a pretty boy' who came to Sherborne, causing 'splendid seniors' to buy his photograph, or the prep school time when 'lust howled in a boot-hole underground'. Auden's mind was preoccupied with Christopher Isherwood's comparison of the Icelandic sagas with their prep school days at St Edmund's, Hindhead. Thus there are obscurely menacing, saga-like hints about sudden death, failure and cowardice, not to mention an unwelcome forecast that Mary would conceive a son on the first day of the honeymoon.

Next afternoon, on Thursday 27 December 1928, Cecil and Mary were married at Sherborne Abbey, well over five years since they had talked to each other during that Duffers' reading of Shakespeare's *A Midsummer Night's Dream*. She was now twenty-six and he twenty-four. The officiating clergy were their fathers, the Rev H.R. King and the Rev F.C. Day-Lewis. After a reception for about 250 guests in the Big School room Cecil changed from the obligatory black and white costume to a bright green shirt and daffodil tie, and he and his bride drove west in 'the pumpkin' for a first honeymoon night at the Royal Clarence Hotel, Exeter. Next morning they drove on to North Devon, pausing only at Barnstaple to send a letter to Mary's brother Charles asking if he would kindly locate and destroy a used condom inadvertently left in a bedroom at Greenhill, 'as H.R.K. might not understand'. They reached the Hartland Quay Hotel by early afternoon.

'We were young for our age, idealistic, proud; a loving couple, but in public so undemonstrative to each other that few could have guessed it', remembered Cecil. 'I fancy that even more than most young couples, we had a sense of being united *against* the world, though in fact nobody had disapproved of our marriage.' They rejoiced in the winter sun and the lonely Atlantic beating against the jagged coast-line. She called him 'Monkey' and he called her 'Winkle' as they clambered about the rocks where four years ago Cecil had perched as a member of the Maurice Bowra reading party from Oxford. They walked along the cliffs in the teeth of a tearing wind to inspect Hartland Lighthouse, and they drove to nearby Clovelly. Cecil read aloud from his *Transitional Poem*. They listened to the protesting sea and Mary said, 'It's wilder here than at Padstow.'

This comment about Padstow, which amused Cecil, may be taken to indicate the insularity of the couple. Mary had spent two months of 1922 in Italy as a companion to an aunt, living frugally but getting to know the natural, artistic and architectural warmth of Florence, Siena, Assisi and Perugia. She was not to leave Britain again until 1970. Cecil had never been beyond the British Isles and, apart from a Paris weekend in 1938, would not do so until 1947. They did not have time to take a honeymoon abroad and, with an income of £400 a year including allowances from their two families, they were not specially wealthy. But it probably never occurred to them to seek a warmer climate. Sensual lingerings were not in their Sherborne-trained natures, and enthusiastic reports from Wystan Auden in Berlin reinforced their view that there was something undesirably decadent about abroad.

'Though I had lost my faith, I had not discarded the Christian view of marriage in so far as it stresses the absolute responsibility of the partners for each other. It was a responsibility I eagerly accepted, and by which I hoped I should be matured', wrote Cecil. He added, with a touch of contradiction, 'There was the delighted sense of being in haven at last, and with it the exhilaration of setting out from harbour, on a voyage I dared hope might be prosperous and could not imagine as less than life-long.'

As it happened, Mary had met somebody the previous autumn, Diana Jordan, a young, neat and talented teacher of dance just arrived at Sherborne School for Girls, with whom she could probably have lived in contentment all her life. But Mary, to her ultimate cost, had now learned to love Cecil and was committed to him for life. She had cultivated the supposed masculine virtue of stoicism and was an intensely private person who, though far from frigid behind closed doors, generally shrank from emotional confrontation as from physical contact; in this respect her inhibitions matched those developed by Cecil in his battle to escape from the smothering love of his father. Hartland was maybe a fitting place for such a partnership to begin, a place of austere grandeur, subdued in its colours and clear in its outlines, more enlivening than comforting, a meeting place of a restless force and a constant object, the transitory and the permanent.

By 10 January they had moved into their new Scottish home, with its well-polished austerity, plain and simple furniture, whitewashed walls and fresh-air-filled separate bedrooms. Mary made the care of the house and garden her department and either fell, or was pushed, into the role of mother figure. As Cecil put it in his autobiography, the part of him which was 'the little boy who didn't want to grow up ... started an underground campaign', and he frequently had to be nursed out of minor ailments like influenza, tonsillitis, abscesses in the gums or bronchitis. In fact he retired to bed with flu less than a week after his return to Helensburgh.

W.H. Auden, arrived on 27 February from Berlin and stayed for a week-end of walking, music and eating. 'Wystan rapidly ate his way through our stock of provisions, his tremendous energy needing constant refuelling', recorded Cecil. There was much literary talk. Middleton, Donne and Housman were praised; Owen, D.H. Lawrence, Yeats and Eliot were considered. As to Cecil's unfortunate Oxford encourager Humbert Wolfe, he was, according to Auden, a 'typists' poet' who 'made us sick' with his 'dapper' thoughts and 'slick' lines. Back in Berlin Auden remembered such talk and wrote what he called 'a technical exercise instead of a bread and butter letter', an eighty-one line verse letter (Appendix II). At the end of this he sent his love and said he hoped he went down with Mary 'alright'.

Cecil was again at a low ebb with flu on 26 March when he received a letter from Leonard Woolf accepting his *Transitional Poem* for autumn publication by the Hogarth Press. He at once despatched a card to Auden telling him the news, chasing the previously despatched verse 'Letter to

W.H. Auden' which was to be published as an epilogue in Cecil's 1931
sequence *From Feathers to Iron*:

> Daffodils now, the pretty débutantes,
> Are curtsying at the first court of the year:
> Their schoolgirl smell unmans young lechers. You
> Preferred, I remember, the plump boy, the crocus.
> Enough of that. They only lie at your feet.
> But I, who saw the sapling, prophesied
> A growth superlative and branches writing
> On heaven a new signature.

Auden replied from Berlin enclosing the poem to survive in his *Collected
Shorter Poems* (1966) as 'A Free One'. 'It is splendid news about the Hogarth
Press. I liked the poem immensely and was duly flattered', Auden wrote.
' "On a northern fell within the sound of hammers" is exactly my phantasy
of myself. It's a little hard that my little weaknesses should be exposed in
dedicatory verses. . . . It's not the bad poets who are successful that one is
jealous of, but the good ones like yourself whose medium happens to be
a simpler one, because then one can't be superior about it. I am incredibly
happy, spending my substance on strumpets and taking part in the white
slave traffic.'

That May was a beautiful one. While others took part in the General
Election campaign – which introduced the female, or 'flapper', vote, and
resulted in the first Labour Government – Cecil and Mary spent more and
more time in the country, and particularly the bluebell woods around Loch
Lomond. On 4 June Frank and Mamie came to stay and Cecil retired to
bed with tonsillitis; three days later his father and the 'step-d' departed for
Edinburgh and he felt better. He was up and about during Knos's stay later
in the same month, and for her part she went about 'endearing herself at
once to our friends'. A letter to L.A.G. Strong during that June suggested
that Cecil neither had nor wanted any friends in this part of Scotland.

We are vastly looking forward to seeing you again – I'll bring a stock of songs.
How do you suppose my stock stands at Summer Fields? I don't think we can
stand more than another year in this hole, and both Cyril and Bobs said fervently
'When are you coming back to us?' I'm afraid this was only a rhetorical question,
but I should leap at any chance of getting back. Anyway, I can talk to them
when I'm with you. The parents and the directors at this place make life a positive
misery: as an amiable drunkard of my acquaintance here said to me – 'D Lewish
mark m'words, th'directorsh'r a shower of bastards. . . .' I can do nothing in this
shower of bastardy; I sit about and contemplate rasping satires but nothing comes
of it. I have though, emended a hymn verse:

> Can a mother's tender care
> Cease toward the child she bare?
> Yes it can; but still, the Lord
> Will not hit her with a sword.

– Try it: it sings very pretty.

If you have any money, get the Brahms Quintet in B Minor (Columbia): the clarinet is ravishing and the whole recording absolutely the snake's hips. The people in this place are snub-nosed, commercial, bowler-hatted, puffed-up, dysenteric, sweating; they are excrement without bowels, arrogant without grace; they are like a man who goes up with a dispatch-case into a fenced city and returns at eventide full of loose conversation. Faugh, the nasty helots, the burberried barbarians!

At the end of July, after nostalgic times with the Strongs at Oxford, Cecil and Mary went on to Amberley for the marriage, on Wednesday the thirty-first, of Rex and Frances Warner. Cecil was best man and provider of a marriage poem, in which the last of the three sections praises Rex's intellectual honesty and Frances's beauty and hopes the couple will be 'glad of their conjunction' and 'outstay/The accidents of noon'.

The opening sixteen-line stanza of this poem, hardly changed and quoted by Cecil in *A Hope for Poetry*, was later used in Poem 5 of *The Magnetic Mountain*. This 1933 sequence represents a more obvious surrender to the Auden influence than the earlier *From Feathers to Iron* (1931), at first sight a surprising reversal. In fact the latter sequence was a reflection on the particular nine months before my birth in 1931. Work on *The Magnetic Mountain* started before this, when the Auden influence was closest.

Meanwhile Cecil's *Transitional Poem* was published in October, a sequence of thirty-four lyrics in various stanzas, divided into four parts. In so far as the MacSpaunday poets were to create a poetic revolution this was its first public manifestation, and it was certainly greeted by reviewers as something new, largely on account of the images of modern civilization which mingled with Cecil's personal conflicts. The work points the way to various 1930s preoccupations, arguing the relationship of loyalty and belief; stating the dilemma of the poet hesitating between allegiance to his relations and friends and familiar middle-class way of life, and his attachment to a philosophy of more or less revolutionary thought and action. The sequence looks forward in hope to the attainment of single-mindedness, a state in which there are no claims apart from the one exclusive faith, an absoluteness which Cecil never remotely achieved.

In 1960 Cecil could still look at the sequence with 'feelings of affection, tinged with awe – how on earth did I produce such a relentlessly and unexpectedly *highbrow* poem at that time?'

Samuel Hynes has observed that 'the most striking thing about *Transitional Poem* is how conventional it is, how well it attaches itself to the English tradition: the verse forms are regular, the allusions are classical, the natural details are Romantic. Romantic, too, is the constantly present "I", the poetic sensibility focussed always upon its own condition.'[10]

Certainly the only debt to T.S. Eliot is the gathering of explanations and footnotes at the end, a device dropped when the sequence was 'collected', and which imitates *The Waste Land*. In the verse itself some have been able to find the voices of Donne and Marvell as well as Yeats. As with the Auden *Poems* of 1928 the sequence was given numbers rather than titles, an austere gesture which became fashionable in the 1930s, discouraging to anthologizers. He had already dropped his hyphen with *Country Comets* – 'a piece of inverted snobbery', as Cecil later confessed – and he now dropped his disliked Christian name as well, writing for the rest of his life as 'C. Day Lewis'.

More importantly the sequence starts the work of making a mythology of his generation, another echo of Yeats. The book is dedicated to Rex Warner. In Poem 8 Cecil also declared his allegiance to Mary, with whom 'I ran the gauntlet for my prime'; W.H. Auden, 'the tow-haired poet'; and his pre-marital counsellor, Margaret Marshall:

> She next, sorrow's familiar, who turned
> Her darkness to our light; that 'brazen leech'
> Alleviating the vain cosmic itch
> With fact coated in formulae lest it burned
> Our tongue. She shall have portion in my praise,
> And live in me, not memory, for always.

Here is yet another Auden cross-reference. The second of his 1928 *Poems* reflects on his Appletreewick holiday with Cecil, mentions 'a crooked valley', crumbling stone sheds, an 'awkward waterwheel', a 'deserted mine', where he spoke with a poet of 'Margaret the brazen leech' and 'that severe Christopher'. I have not discovered what experience, or joke, caused Auden to think of Margaret in this way, but the phrase was to acquire a sadly ironic connotation. After the death of Douglas Marshall from tuberculosis she made an unhappy and short-lived marriage with the poet's elder brother, Dr John Auden. When the marriage led to conflict Cecil and Wystan found themselves on opposite sides, the first cloud on a friendship that gradually became more distant, first through ideology and then geography, after the early 1930s.

Whatever Cecil and Mary may have thought of the Scottish middle class they dissembled effectively enough. They were befriended by Jim Allen, a retired ship owner, and his wife Janet, who according to Cecil 'gave us the special warmth of kindness – a steady glow like a peat fire's, unspectacular and dependable – that is Scotland at its best'. Hilda Purvis, the widow of a Larchfield director and medical officer, remembered that 'both Cecil and his wife made a great impact here socially – it was in the days of musical afternoons and evenings and they were very much in demand'. Mary persuaded people to take part in music and dance entertainments, introducing the Larchfield boys and other natives to 'Greek dancing'. 'We all leapt about in scanty tunics and shields, it was something that had not been done in Helensburgh before and when we had to do it for an audience I was so embarrassed that I absolutely ricocheted around the stage', remembered one victim.

As if to double the embarrassment Cecil had that Christmas term of 1929 joined forces with the music master, E. W. Hardy, to produce a Larchfield school song. Sending me a copy in 1973 the then headmaster, J.B. Widdowson, wrote with some understatement: 'In all candour I cannot think that it is a great piece, though it doubtless suited the mood of the day well enough.' It was dedicated to T.T.N. Perkins, but not used again after he was persuaded to retire.

> School of the mountain and the lochside
> School of the white and blue,
> Make our hearts as bright and brave
> As the mountain and the wave
> So Scotland may be proud of you.

Having composed this Cecil was understandably eager to leave the country and on 30 October wrote to Cheltenham Junior School applying for a post teaching scholarship classics. Maurice Bowra was a Cheltenham College governor and had 'promised to blast the place for ever if they do not fall for me', Cecil wrote to L.A.G. Strong. He added that the job 'rises from £300 to £700'. This November letter also revealed that 'the licensed critics have been inclined to cock the leg at *Transitional Poem*, but here and there one observes the ranks of Tuscany scarcely forbearing to cheer'.

In this month Cecil was also in touch with Naomi Mitchison, the novelist, poet and childrens' writer married to a Labour politician, daughter of the physiologist J.S. Haldane and sister of the geneticist J.B.S. Haldane. She was encouraging contributions to the *Realist*, a journal which was intended to relate art and science but which folded after one verse-less number. He wrote to her from Helensburgh.

I was very pleased to get your letter and to know that you liked *Transitional Poem*. I am engaged on a satire [*The Magnetic Mountain*] at present, and have not written many short poems lately suitable for publication: perhaps the *Realist* might like the one I enclose ['Letter to W.H. Auden']: it is not much 'tinctured with science', to use Ella Wheeler Wilcox's expression, but it might be of interest as showing the attitude of a modern poet to his work. As you say, my poems have a philosophic basis – though it is a series of intuitions, rather than a pre-reasoned plan. I am afraid I haven't enough knowledge of the sciences to claim a scientific basis: but I do think they have recently brought to light an enormous amount of material which ought to be used – as the 17th century metaphysicals used the renaissance materials – for conceits and illustrations of every sort. Perhaps the poet does not need a very detailed scientific knowledge, since he is more or less bound to use data which has already become familiar. Do you think the *Realist* would like an article on this subject?

Again, a week later:

I am very grateful to you for helping me with the *Realist* people: they are going to take the poem, I think, and are encouraging about the article (which is not yet written). The first two parts of that poem are my 'reactions' to the work of a friend of mine [W.H. Auden]; his writing is very obscure, which perhaps accounts for the difficulties of my poem.

He and Mary had Christmas at Edwinstowe and spent the morning of their first wedding anniversary on 27 December driving to Cheltenham for his interview with the Cheltenham Junior headmaster. After a two-hour conversation Cecil drove 'the pumpkin' on to Sherborne. On the thirtieth he left alone for London and missed the letter offering him the Cheltenham appointment. Mary sent him a telegram to which he replied next day, New Year's Eve.

'Divine Winkle, The annunciation has just taken place; Cheltenham Boys' School has averted the perpetual reproach of rejecting Teacher Lewis, I see; or have I interpreted your telegram wrong? I think not', he wrote. 'Are you still beautiful? I am', he concluded.

2

~1930-1939~
On a Tilting Deck

I sang as one
Who on a tilting deck sings
To keep men's courage up, though the wave hangs
That shall cut off their sun. *

As I write, Alice Prochaska's *The Young Writers of the Thirties* exhibition at the National Portrait Gallery in London is still fresh in the memory. For over four months of 1976 the fresh young faces of W.H. Auden and Christopher Isherwood, Stephen Spender, Louis MacNeice and C. Day-Lewis looked out from posters on underground stations and elsewhere. Some 35,000 people went to look at the exhibits. Much space was used in literary journals and newspapers, some of it occupied by the two survivors of the Auden Gang, Spender and Isherwood.

Everybody was at pains to point out that there were other writers at work in Britain during the decade, some of them significant and some influential; that the real heroes were the writers and intellectuals who actually went and fought against Franco in Spain; that the Gang were not a gang, but a pigeonhole used by critics; that its so-called members never met; that they could not seriously be considered as literary equals; that the differences between the members were more interesting than their similarities. Yet even writing which set out with the intention of diminishing or dismantling the Gang apparently had the opposite effect; the very juxtaposition of the names re-established them as a characteristic and unified voice of the decade and put another layer of concrete on the belt enclosing them. Any publicity is binding publicity.

Cecil himself agreed that 'the movement of the 1930s certainly helped the poets whose names were connected with it to a more than fair share of attention'. He further acknowledged, in his 1972 BBC radio interview with Hallam Tennyson, that there was 'very little poetic reason' for the mythological invention of MacSpaunday. They were all subject to the influence of Auden, but Cecil was the only follower so spellbound that, by his own account, 'I had to free myself.'

* 'The Conflict' (*A Time to Dance*, 1935).

The writers of the Gang were all subject to 'the weather of the times' and were agreed that the weather was too bad to be ignored. Even in comparatively comfortable Britain it was a rotten decade, starting in slump and ending in war. Surveying the home scene the young writer with a social conscience was confronted by stagnation and poverty; an impotent Labour Government followed by a musclebound National Coalition, both getting every conceivable decision wrong; a rising tide of pacifism just twenty years too late; the potential evil of the Fascist solution. Writers who moved about the European continent, if only in search of sexually desirable and co-operative boys, saw Fascism begin to realize its potential.

In a 1935 letter Stephen Spender reflected that Cecil was lacking in depravity. Certainly, until the very end of the decade when he also became a sexual adventurer, Cecil's settled and orthodox middle-class family life was at an opposite pole from the pleasure and pain enjoyed by the homosexual members of the Gang prominent in Christopher Isherwood's volume of autobiography *Christopher And His Kind*. And precisely because school and domestic life at Cheltenham were so sheltered, Cecil was enabled to keep alive, longer than others, his dreams of 'that promising land ... somewhere beyond the rail tracks'. He travelled just far enough to see Alexander Dovzhenko's Soviet epic about the relation of man to the soil, *Earth* (1930), and left the cinema feeling that the film 'was the most beautiful and moving – the most *real* thing I had ever seen. It gave an emotionally convincing picture of a society in which the power of every man and woman could have full exercise.' This experience helped him towards a collection of 'heterogeneous ideas which served to plug the hollow in the heart where a god should be', and the illusion that man could, under Communism, put the world to rights.

In retrospect he believed 'there was generosity as well as absurdity in this', for he and his friends 'did at least make some attempt to imagine the conditions we did not share ... and we were prepared to help destroy a system that perpetuated itself by such hideous human wastage, even though our own pleasant way of life would be destroyed in the process'.

He never pretended that he could change class. One of the disconnected images I retain from my earliest childhood in Cheltenham is of Cecil talking to some working-class comrade, cloth cap held respectfully at his side, in our front garden. I tried for some time to pull Cecil away from this 'rough beast', this vaguely threatening figure from another planet. When the man had gone Cecil turned on me crossly for my rudeness, but it was also significant that although the conference was a long one the visitor was never asked into the house. As well as a religious quality, Cecil's Communism had an element of romance; he took a romanticized view of the British worker which could not survive too much contact; and a romanticized view of the enemy, the forces of reaction, as 'a sort of composite caricature' taking in the Government, the Church, the Press, the Law and other branches of what is now identified as the Establishment.

He also had some intellectual conviction that only the Communists and their allies were capable of confronting the Fascists. This was not surprising in view of his guilt about prevailing middle-class comfort and awareness of the way in which the British press and radio were controlled.

All the same the extent to which Cecil was involved has been exaggerated. Though he was marginally the most and longest committed Communist of the Auden Gang he did not join the Party until well into 1936, several months after he retired from schoolmastering, and before that he was scrupulous about not airing his politics in the classroom. In the summer of 1938 he withdrew from politics in favour of poetry. During the two years plus that he was a political activist his greater concern was to earn enough, through writing, to support a wife and two small sons. Moreover, it was at the very start of this period that he was stopped short by the unfavourable critical response to his Communist morality play *Noah and the Waters* (1936), and began finding his way back to his personal poetic preoccupations. Even in his political verse he was what he remained, a divided man.

He was, in other words, very much a part-time Noah, prepared to give up his spare evenings to ark-building but otherwise doing well in and by the existing system – to the extent of writing an unexceptionable weekly novel review column for the *Daily Telegraph*, and detective story reviews for the *Spectator*. Newspaper proprietors could perhaps feel that his threat to evict them at gunpoint would not actually be carried out until the coming of the Communist flood.

> Scavenger barons and your jackal vassals,
> Your pimping press-gang, your unclean vessels,
> We'll make you swallow your words at a gulp
> And turn you back to your element, pulp.
> Don't bluster, Bimbo, it won't do you any good;
> We can be much ruder and we're learning to shoot.
> Closet Napoleon, you'd better abdicate,
> You'd better quit the country before it's too late.*

In retrospect Cecil was the only member of the Gang to recall with any pleasure or pride the bright-eyed innocence of his 1930s political stance and to claim 'honourable wounds'. The more popular view is that in so far as the poets were committed politicians they were also gullible dreamers, as ineffective in their work as on the platform, because, as Auden himself decided by 1939, 'The honest truth, gentlemen, is that, if not a poem had

* Poem 20 (*The Magnetic Mountain*, 1933).

been written, not a picture painted, not a bar of music composed, the history of man would be materially unchanged.'[1]

There may also be some support still for the view of the poet Roy Campbell that the attitude taken up by MacSpaunday was so well publicized that its main effect was to advance the sales of MacSpaunday books. Quite apart from the inability of the MacSpaunday beast to co-ordinate its movements in life as it did in Campbell's imagination, the facts about sales do not support his argument. In the early years of the decade the sales of the young poets were small enough to support the Maurice Bowra assertion that Cecil's income from verse was 'sufficient to keep him in contraceptives'. Even the first Michael Roberts anthology, *New Signatures* (1932), supposed to be such an important landmark, only sold 1,000 copies in its first year. Cecil's first three Hogarth Press volumes only did half as well as this in their first years. By contrast, he wrote, *A Time to Dance* (1935) 'sold very well from the start'. Comparatively well maybe, but his last and best-selling collection of the decade, *Overtures to Death* (1938), sold only 1,773 copies at 5s each.

Against this it may be added that the influence of MacSpaunday was out of all proportion to its sales and by the end of the decade there was a potential audience of perhaps 50,000, which read little magazines and kept in touch with this part of the literary scene. As Samuel Hynes has observed, there is a sense in which 'new poets become a renascence when a public wants and needs a renascence'.[2] These poets 'were celebrated almost before they were published because they seemed to offer new responses to new problems'. For a significant section of the intelligentsia belonging to the following generation or two the Gang were heroes: Cecil particularly so because his success was matched with good looks, an elegant outward style of dress and mannerism, sexual orthodoxy, an unambiguous political commitment and a clear-cut way of expressing himself.

In a sense Cecil's gratitude for this response was misplaced because the inflation of his reputation, and the critical reaction against this, came too soon. Cecil was both the oldest of the MacSpaunday poets and the slowest to mature into independence. In some ways, emotional and intellectual as well as poetical, the decade formed the end of his adolescence. It was a searching, learning decade for him and he only found his true voice as it ended.

As Cecil and Mary made their usual round of relations and friends in the first days of 1930 their main concern was their impending move back to England in April. He returned to school for his last Larchfield term on 9 January and three days later wrote in gratitude to L.A.G. Strong: 'I've got the job at Cheltenham: also a monstrously good review of *Trans. P.* in the *Irish Times* by F.R. Higgins – are you responsible for that too?', he began. 'Your hand is detectable behind most of the fortunate things that have happened to me in the last few years.... Did you see Auden's play [*Paid on Both Sides*] in the *Criterion* – balmy, but full of good stuff; his style is amazingly homogeneous considering the number of its influences....'

Having completed his Berlin year Auden was in London tutoring the young Peter Benenson, later to be the founder of Amnesty International. He wanted a job that would give him more financial independence; Cecil recommended him as his successor at Larchfield and the idea was accepted. 'Whereas Day-Lewis had natural ability to teach in a rather earnest and serious manner, Auden had too much of a sense of fun and the ridiculous ever to make a teacher', remembered the pupil of both, H.J. Weir. One parent suggested to the following headmaster 'that he should not have any more poets on his staff'.

Cecil and Mary left Helensburgh on 3 April, 'the pumpkin' loaded to its canvas roof with luggage. At Carlisle 'the Austin began to lollop lethargically and eccentrically like something in a fun fair, and looking down I saw that half the wire spokes had given way under the weight of our belongings, and the back wheels were perceptibly not circular any more but turning oval-shaped'. Altogether the journey to Edwinstowe took two days. On the tenth they had a day in Birmingham with Auden and his family, mostly to talk about Helensburgh. On Friday 25 April, in a sunny hour of sweet scents two days before Cecil's twenty-sixth birthday, they moved into a rather cramped flat at Belmore House, Bath Place, near the centre of Cheltenham.

Cheltenham College was opened in 1844, on the Rugby public school model, its gothic buildings rising beside the Bath Road. It had become military in its bearing, so that the parade ground, the chapel and the playing fields (where Gloucestershire play three matches at the annual cricket festival) were regarded as three indivisible parts of the Holy Trinity. It was not all that different in style from Sherborne, but lacked anything of the melancholy beauty and softening quality given by Dorset surroundings. In the 1930s the Junior School, where Cecil taught, catered for about a hundred boys. Though its red-brick Edwardian premises were divided from the College by the Thirlestain Road the school was run very much as a satellite of the College and Cecil thus had to answer, more than once, to two headmasters.

Belmore House, where Cecil and Mary had the ground-floor flat, was a depressed, grey-plastered place of no distinction inside or out. They had an enormous kitchen, a tiny dining-room and sitting-room, and, as at Helensburgh, separate bedrooms. It was from there that Cecil cycled to the Junior for the first time in the last week of April, there to teach Classics and English to the scholarship form and French and History lower down.

At school Cecil found a certain amount of suspicion about him. He was known to have 'committed poetry' and had not been altogether successful in masking his 'potential subversiveness behind short hair and a keen interest in games'. The long and leathery College headmaster, H.H. Hardy, was not satisfied that the new master had a proper detestation for D.H. Lawrence, and had shared his doubts with the Junior headmaster, a small, chubby, red-faced man called Bowers, who reminded Cecil of 'a very superior coachman'. In the Bowers study and in the masters' common room there was 'a certain air of suspended judgement'.

Away at the beginning of term, playing a batman in Anthony Asquith's film *Tell England*, was the Junior master to whom Cecil would grow closest. Lionel Hedges was a useful amateur actor and also a games master better known as a batsman than a batman. Now a Gloucestershire irregular he had played for Kent while still a boy at Tonbridge School, and during his four years as an Oxford undergraduate had made himself known as a master of the funny anecdote as well as the square cut. Cecil saw him as a 'brisk, broad, compact figure' with 'a face that must have been handsome in youth but was at 30 running to fat'. He was also a heavy drinker, reckless with what money he had, and he and Cecil spent more evenings at the Beehive public house than were approved by either Mary or her friend Eileen, Lionel's good-humoured and handsome wife.

The main butt of Cecil and Lionel was a solemn fellow master called J.D. Parker, who was given to making remarks of such banality that he originated a new form called the Parkerism. He would look at a building and say, 'A house is nothing without windows', or at a wet day and say, 'It is awfully depressing when it rains.' Hedges and Day-Lewis jointly kept a book where all Parkerisms were recorded.

At the end of the first term at Cheltenham Cecil and Mary decided to start their own family. This decision made they travelled north for a voyage from Mallaig in a new Bermuda-rigged cutter just bought by their Helensburgh friends Jim and Janet Allen. On 31 July the four of them set sail on the boat's maiden journey, to the Outer Hebrides. At Barra Mary had to go to bed ashore with tonsillitis and the party was held up for four days. The rest of the voyage, sailing about South Uist, Skye, Dunvegan and Portree, was sun-blessed and beautiful, and they got back to Mallaig on 8 August in a mood of serenity.

They then joined the King family holiday at Easedale Lodge in the Lake District, and Cecil was able to spend five days with W.H. Auden and his family at their nearby Wescoe cottage near Threlkeld. In the Christmas term that followed Mary conceived her first child.

> Come on, the wind is whirling our summer away,
> And air grows dizzy with leaves.
> It is time to lay up for a winter day,
> Conserve earth's infant energy, water's play,
> Bind the sun down in sheaves.*

* Poem 4 (*From Feathers to Iron*, 1931).

Christmas that year was celebrated at Sherborne, his father-in-law commenting that 'when the charades began Cecil was really great – I again felt that the boy might make his living off this astonishing exhibition, if he was willing'.

There were moments during the first half of 1931 when Cecil thought he might have to make his living in a different way. Bowers of the Junior had stumbled, in the 'Imperial Library' of Banks the Promenade bookseller, upon the *Transitional Poem*. In a highly embarrassed interview he eventually reached his objection to the sequence, that it was 'extremely, excessively, er, SEXUAL'. The interrogation fizzled out, leaving Cecil with the feeling that he had been given a warning. Soon afterwards, on 10 March, he received a letter from the College headmaster, accusing him of 'Bohemian' tendencies. An assistant master at the College had seen him wearing a green shirt, while whitewashing the walls of his flat, and another observer had reported the poet attending a concert with a stock about his neck under his dinner jacket: this was intolerable conduct, the staff must be properly dressed at all times.

Before replying he took the advice of a College master who, unlike the colleagues who reported all departures from convention, was a friend. Frank Halliday was a sensitive Yorkshireman who loved literature and eventually became a professional writer himself. His autobiography tells how he first heard of Cecil as 'a young married man who liked Beethoven and César Franck' and was 'said to write poetry'.[3] He met the newcomers during their second term and registered Mary 'with a ballet-dancer's hair and figure and a dairy-maid's complexion', and Cecil 'reserved and almost severe, until his mouth curled into a smile and he began to speak with the trace of an Irish brogue'. Halliday was also a shy man and his mask was an offhand manner, at first discouraging. The discouragement had been overcome and by this March, Cecil and Mary had become friends with Frank and his wife Nancie, and they all spent a long time discussing the best response to the headmaster's outburst.

None of which prevented the perversity in Cecil's make-up from coming to the fore: he came to believe that he had it in him to destroy himself, and on 14 March he went some slight way towards this by answering H.H. Hardy with 'a sarcastic and saucy letter'. Cecil's St Patrick's Day post consequently contained 'a tremendous rocket' which put his future in some doubt. This was followed at tea-time by the kindly Mrs Hardy, a warm-hearted peacemaker. With a pregnant wife Cecil felt he could not afford war and it was agreed that he would go to the headmaster and apologize. At the interview on 19 March Hardy accused him of 'intellectual superiority' and Cecil was abject in his promise not to repeat his various offences: 'I saved my job and the immediate future, and was humiliated for years to have crawled thus.'

As soon as term was ended Cecil caught the Great Western Railway's

'Cheltenham Flyer' to London, where he entered a nursing home to have his tonsils removed. Convalescing, he turned back to his verse sequence recording his personal experience of Mary's pregnancy, and looked forward in hope.

> Twenty weeks near past
> Since the seed took to earth.
> Winter has done his worst.
> Let upland snow ignore;
> Earth wears a smile betrays
> What summer she has in store.*

In June Cecil and Mary visited Charles Fenby, lately established as editor of the *Oxford Mail*, and attended an Oxford showing of John Grierson's pioneering documentary of 1929, *Drifters*, and Alexander Dovzhenko's *Earth* – the Russian epic which so swayed Cecil's movement to Communism. He saw this film against a threatening background: there were already $2\frac{3}{4}$ million unemployed and the Labour Chancellor of the Exchequer, Philip Snowden, was about to announce the bankruptcy of the Government, requiring public expenditure cuts of £96 million, including £66 million off unemployment pay. All this served to intensify Cecil's vision of a new world, a fantasy that his temperament could fit with the verse he was writing and which therefore helped the poetic 'interplay and consonance between the inner and outward life, between public meaning and private meaning'. The 'struggle and joy' implied in the revolutionary idea 'shed an atmosphere of exhilaration over the contemporary scene, giving familiar objects new value, or at least showing them up with the clarity, the apocalyptic, disturbing, attentive look of things seen in a brooding light before a thunderstorm'.

Also that month Nancie Halliday had tried to get a copy of Cecil's *Beechen Vigil* from Banks the Cheltenham bookseller. The shop replied: 'We very much regret the publishers are out of stock of *Beecham's Virgil* by Cecil Day-Lewis, but we have noted to send you a copy as soon as possible.' Halliday sent the note on to Cecil with the comment: 'I take it that this is another translation of the *Pilliad*?'

The humour of friends helped ease the waiting for my arrival. 'Pog', as I was called, was due on 28 July. Mary busied herself; Cecil played earnestly competitive games of shove-halfpenny in the dining room with Rex Warner and Lionel Hedges; Pog stayed where he was. There was a drive to A.E. Housman's Bredon, and a visit to the cinema. The unemployed Warner grew tired of waiting and went home, and shove-halfpenny turned to poker patience. On 31 July Knos arrived and Mary went into a local nursing home to have Pog induced. Cecil was asleep at Belmore House

* Poem 10 (*From Feathers to Iron*, 1931).

when his first-born was finally delivered by forceps at 5.20 am on a fine and windy Monday 3 August.

> Come out in the sun, for a man is born today!
> Early this morning whistle in the cutting told
> Train was arriving, hours overdue, delayed
> By snow-drifts, engine-trouble, Act of God, who cares now? —
> For here alights the distinguished passenger.
> Take a whole holiday in honour of this!*

On 13 August 'the pumpkin' was sold to Diana Jordan to pay for their new baby. A week later the family of three left by train for the christening at East Quantoxhead, on the Somerset coast near Watchet. By 24 August, the day on which Ramsay MacDonald told his Labour Cabinet that they were out and he was in as leader of a new National Government, the Day-Lewises were installed for a month's stay in the rectory of the generous Rev Arthur Morris. Mary soon noted a mutual passion in the eyes of Morris's wife Alison and Cecil; it was not the last time Cecil would be in love elsewhere while his wife recovered from pregnancy.

Poem 5 of *From Feathers to Iron* tells Mary that 'We must a little part,/ And sprouting seed crack our cemented heart'. Those who 'would get an heir' must bear an 'initial loss' for 'A part of each will be elsewhere'. The following poem celebrates the view that 'Now she is like the white tree-rose', and the description was inspired less by the new mother than by Alison. Their fun at East Quantoxhead, where they played through the anxious weeks which ended with the Japanese attack on Manchuria and Britain going off the Gold Standard, was ephemeral and child-like. Alison was dissatisfied in a marriage which would soon end; Cecil was engaged in exploration. The honourable rector and the stoic Mary watched quietly.

The encounter and its consummation was to be remembered in Cecil's first straight novel, *The Friendly Tree* (1936). Here Alison is characterized as Evelyn Crane: a woman of classical features and patrician air and gawky gait, a 'fatal' woman born lucky, with an aristocratic disregard of consequences, one who lost interest in conversations before they were over and was at home in expensive shops. Evelyn's affair with the Cecil character, Stephen Hallam, ends with copulation amidst bracken, interrupted by a symbolic passing hunt and encouraged by the still more symbolic 'muted savagery' of its horn. This climax proves to be an anti-climax, and Steve abruptly decides that he must not see Evelyn again and must return to his wife: 'Evelyn is nice, exciting, a new country, but Anna is where I am at home,' he declares. 'You were right, Anna, when you said I was not cut out for a Don Juan. My senses do not run on a separate circuit from my conscience: they would always be found to create obligations which morally and emotionally I should have to accept.'

* Poem 29 (*From Feathers to Iron*, 1931).

Mysteriously, in a 1936 letter to the novelist Hugh Walpole, Cecil wrote that 'there are people who are much more like types out of a book than real people, aren't there? – and I rather think that Evelyn is one of those'. He added: 'I must say that I was properly sickened by Stephen's behaviour over Evelyn! But the affair had to take place to round off the pattern of the book.'

Certainly Cecil maintained a platonic friendship with Alison for some years after the month at East Quantoxhead and as a starter he sent her this unpublished sonnet, including the kestrel of his *The Magnetic Mountain* (1933).

> Dear, when at last you bow your wayward head
> And like a rose to iron frosts consent,
> When all your golden gallantry is spent
> And little left for you but to be dead:
> Remember how your cool and woodland eyes
> Caught fire once from the sun and burned for me,
> How at high summer stretched before the sea
> Your naked breasts tore heaven by surprise.
> Over the world of heather where we lay
> Joy like a kestrel hovered in the wind,
> He swooped, he soared, he left the wind behind
> Carrying our sweet bodies worlds away.
> You gathered all that grows at beauty's prime
> Will have enough to warm a winter time.

In the midst of all this I was baptized Sean Francis by the Rev F.C. Day-Lewis at East Quantoxhead parish church on Thursday 17 September. Mary recorded that I was 'naughty for the rest of the day', and that when the family left for Cheltenham four days later 'Pog was screaming'. Back home on 22 September, Cecil wrote to L.A.G. Strong:

I send my new book [*From Feathers to Iron*]: I wish you could review it for the *Spectator*, but imagine it is too late for that. I hear Sylvia is going to have a child: is this so? It sounds delightful. Ours was born in August, a boy, Sean Francis: this sequence of poems was written during the nine months. I am still on approbation, but have gained ground recently by presenting the head-master's wife with a stuffed white seal.

The new book, *From Feathers to Iron*, was published as No 22 of the Hogarth Living Poets series while Cecil was still in Somerset. It consisted of twenty-nine lyrics and the epilogue 'Letter to W.H. Auden'. It was greeted with some enthusiasm by reviewers already wondering whether MacSpaunday could be seen as a movement. Michael Roberts, who would become the animal's leading anthologist, used the *Poetry Review* to hail the new work as 'a landmark, in the sense in which *Leaves of Grass*, *A Shropshire Lad*, *Des Imagistes* and *The Waste Land* were landmarks'. Poets had been trying for thirty years to be participants in the social order, rather than fugitives and rebels, and to use images and metaphors drawn from applied science. 'Mr Auden's *Poems* . . . showed the first marked advance, and now, in *Feathers to Iron*, we have the full solution: these images are used, not for their own sake, not because the poet's theory makes him choose images from contemporary life, but because they are structural: the thought requires precisely that expression.' Roberts also used the newly fashionable word 'propaganda', suggesting that Cecil had provided 'propaganda for a theory of life that may release the poet's energies for the writing of pure poetry as well as provide him with definite standards which will make satire possible again'.

Other critics have pointed to the clash between the railway symbolism of Auden Country and the Day-Lewis images of nature, actually better tuned to a story of pregnancy and parturition. Soon afterwards, in *A Hope for Poetry* (1934), Cecil wrote that for him the sequence 'expressed simply my thoughts and feelings during the nine months before the birth of my first child: the critics, almost to a man, took it for a political allegory; the simple, personal meaning evaded them'. He includes the 'perpetual interplay of private and public meaning' in the work of MacSpaunday but considered that in this case the sequence contained 'a political significance of which I was quite unconscious while writing it'.

February 1932 was the month of *New Signatures*, the slim volume produced by Michael Roberts and John Lehmann at the Hogarth Press, which later became part of the 1930s mythology. In tone it can now be seen as more of a feeler than a 'generation's manifesto' as suggested by Leonard Woolf.[4] It did contain some of the disillusion brought about by the failure of the Labour Party, and some of the desire for something stronger and more Left, but not all the contributing poets were involved in this way and they shared only a note of apprehension. The book enabled Cecil to trail *The Magnetic Mountain* with three poems from the sequence. The other poets included were W.H. Auden, Julian Bell, Richard Eberhart, William Empson, John Lehmann, William Plomer, Stephen Spender and A.S.J. Tessimond.

The Belmore House flat had appeared to diminish after my arrival, and my cot had to be placed in Mary's small bedroom. She and Cecil looked for a house on the edge of town. They went to look at Box Cottage in Charlton Kings, with its view across farm and fields to the bold Cotswold escarpment of Leckhampton Hill, and knew it was the place for them. After a fortnight of anxiety and disappointments they managed to borrow £600 to buy the freehold. It was a delectable small house with a Cotswold-tile roof and walls which, once the enveloping ivy was torn away, were seen to be made of mellowed brick. There was an L-shaped vegetable garden at the back and on the front lawn a syringa tree 'whose frail and brilliant blossoms almost suffocated us with their perfume for a week or two each summer, until a wind sent them streaming like white tears on to the grass'. All was concealed from the lane by a huge old box hedge, so making a paradoxically 'sequestered, escapist kind of place for one of the new come-down-out-of-that-ivory-tower poets'. One small room at the front of the house was to serve both as Cecil's study and bedroom, another at the back was earmarked for Mary and a third was to be my nursery and sleeping-place.

Work on improvements was set in motion and the Day-Lewis trio left for their summer holidays with the Kings and Knos at Kincraig, beside the Scottish Cairngorms, where I had my first birthday looking fat-faced, smiley and contented.

W.H. Auden had completed two years and an extra summer term at Larchfield. He had enjoyed himself there, regarding it as 'quite dotty, like the school in Evelyn Waugh's *Decline and Fall*. The headmaster was a cari-cature of a man, throwing his authority around while his dying wife lay listlessly all day on a chaise-longue in the summer house on the lawn, in full view of the boys. For all his sympathetic nature, Wystan relished this ghoulish situation: the whole set-up was so gloriously surrealist.'[5] That Christmas term he moved closer to Cheltenham, taking up a post at the Downs School, Colwall, near Malvern, and starting on the three happiest years of his life. On 13 October he called on Cecil at Belmore House, the first of many visitations between the two poets during term-time.

Just before this Cecil had made an initial contact with Geoffrey Grigson, the Auden-admiring critic who was to develop a sustained hostility to Cecil's work over the remaining forty years of his life. Born a Cornishman and the seventh son of a clergyman, Grigson was an Oxford contemporary of Cecil's. He had gone from there to journalism, starting his career on the *Yorkshire Post*, where he was proud to have written probably the only newspaper leader on the death of D.H. Lawrence in 1930. Since then he had arrived in London, carving out a name as a critic with a sharp pen on the *Morning Post*, where he had become literary editor. At the end of 1932 he was planning his *New Verse*, the most influential and entertaining little magazine of the generation, a journal where he could counteract the Sunday paper reviewers – 'all Georgian attitudes; no sharpness of vision anywhere'[6] – and display his strict literary values and his qualities of inde-pendent mind, vigorous intelligence and jaundiced ferocity. At this time Cecil accepted Grigson happily, and without reservation, as a champion of MacSpaunday. He wrote first at the end of September:

I meant to write some time ago thanking you for your encouraging remarks about my poetry and to suggest Auden as a yet worthier subject for attention. I see from the *Bookman* that you have now arranged us in the correct order – 1, Auden; 2, Day-Lewis – but I shall chase him home, you can rely on that, and I think we'll make the pace pretty hot between us. I hope you will like *The Magnetic*

Mountain book when it comes out; I am stealing some of Auden's thunder for it, but I don't believe either of us will be the worse for that. Please understand that I'm not paying idle compliments when I say how encouraging it is to find some one reviewing poetry seriously, and as the most important kind of writing, and not as something that novelists do in their spare time. By the way, Auden's (and my) frequent use of school imagery is due more to our profession than to lingering adolescence. And I don't think Empson is a stayer – I doubt if he'll do much more, though what he has done is good. Graves, I feel, does himself down by perpetually writing about how difficult it is to write poetry just now. My final order – another professional weakness! – is 1, Auden; 2, Day-Lewis; 3, Spender.

Then again on 6 October:

I think your idea for a magazine of poetry a good one, and I shall be very willing to contribute. I'm not sure about *Voice* – wasn't there a magazine of verse running not long ago called *Voices*? a bad one, I mean? I feel rather drawn to *Counter-Attack* as a title for a paper with the Auden-Spender-Self bias – a bit melodramatic and Mosleyish, perhaps. I do feel that the most important thing for a production of this sort is that it should have some sort of spiritual coherence, otherwise one gets just another of these Georgian flower shows – masses of unrelated colour. It seems to me that there is no point in any collection of verse unless something arises out of the juxtaposition of the several contributors which is more than the sum total of their individual achievements: and for this to happen one must have a certain identity of aim, outlook or what you will amongst the contributors – even though it means that one must forfeit a good deal of alien poetic merit. What do you think? Also, I am for anything that will help to throw open the park to the public: it makes one despair to think that one is preserved for an aesthetic aristocracy. What can one do about this? Something must be done, I'm sure. I don't mean that we should go about distributing our work in tube trains: but that contact should be made between us and the sort of people who are at present being spoon-fed out of novels and wireless talks. We can give them something with more kick in it, if they could only be induced to taste. I'm sure they would find plenty in Spender's work and mine and some of Auden's which had meaning for them: someone is wanted who will arrange a meeting, prepare the contact. Why don't you take it on? As you know, our writing is half propaganda: we can't help it: nobody else seems to be doing anything about 'this England of ours where nobody is well'. And its so silly to be spilling propaganda only into the mouths of a few incurable neurasthenics. I feel somehow that it is really quite a practical matter, the purveying of our brand of salvation – a matter of distribution and advertisement and business methods; though it does sound lunatic enough, put like that. We may be quacks, but I don't think so. I feel you would be doing the state some service by getting us across. I'm afraid this letter has been grossly egoistic and uncalled-for. Do come and see me if you are ever hereabouts: I hope to be in London next holidays.

He wrote two more short notes that month, the first accepting that Grigson was 'probably right about the title' and instructing him not to be 'too commonplace and reserved', the second enclosing some sample verses of *The Magnetic Mountain* for inclusion in the first issue of *New Verse* to be published in January. In the event Grigson used two poems from the sequence. Another poem trailing the volume was printed that autumn by the *New Statesman*, where it caught the eye of Naomi Mitchison. Cecil wrote to her with thanks.

I was so glad to hear that you like the *New Statesman* poem: it *is* a good one: it's one of a long sequence, *The Magnetic Mountain*, which will be out early next year I hope. It is comforting having one's views fairly definite at last; though in another way distinctly uncomfortable – the views being of a type likely to lose me my job here, where one can't expect the authorities to read between the lines and realise how salutary and pro-British it all is really! I am quite certain that Wystan and you and myself and the rest of us have in our various ways got hold of the right end of the stick; and that does give me an amazingly peaceful feeling in my centre, though with the rest of me I am frightened to death with the sense of personal and public insecurity. I've seen Wystan several times this term: the most remarkable thing to me about him is that, though he is in ways quite a different person, his poetical mind hasn't changed in the least since I first met him at Oxford: which seems to me a sure sign of his worth – if one needed one.

Before the end of the year Cecil was able to send the completed book to the Hogarth Press, where it was greeted by Leonard Woolf as 'the best thing you've done' and 'the best long poem that I have read for many a long day'.

On the evening of Thursday 12 January 1933, the day before the Adelaide Test Match that started the 'bodyline' controversy, Cecil was with Charles Fenby at the *Oxford Mail* office. 'Isn't that cricketer L.P. Hedges a friend of yours? He has just died,' said Fenby. 'I had not even known that Lionel was ill, I felt as if all the blood was running out of me,' remembered Cecil. It was the first time since the departure of his mother that anybody close to him had died, and this particular death seemed to be against nature: Cecil was much cast down.

It was a bad month, but few forebodings were raised in Cheltenham when, on the thirtieth, Germany acquired a new Chancellor, Adolf Hitler. There was more head-shaking in the military town ten days later when the Oxford University Union voted 275 to 153 'that this House will in no circumstances fight for its King and Country'. Between these events, on 4 February, Cecil wrote to Geoffrey Grigson.

I'm glad to hear that *New Verse* is going well. The Hogarth Press are doing a limited edition of *The Magnetic Mountain* as well as the ordinary one and I'm supposed to be touting round for possible buyers; if you would care for one of these then the thing to do apparently is to write direct to the Hogarth Press. I hope you will like the book: its cumulative effect is pretty considerable I feel.

On 12 February he wrote to L.A.G. Strong suggesting that he might also like to order himself a copy of the limited edition. He added that he had 'done 20,000 words of my blood-curdling story'. This referred to *Dick Willoughby*, the second in a series of 'tales of action by men of letters' which Strong was editing in Oxford for Basil Blackwell. Strong himself wrote the third of these boys' adventure books, *Fortnight South of Skye*, and Rex Warner wrote the eighth, *The Kite*. Cecil finished his contribution, his first published prose book, on 17 March.

Four days later he and Mary were at last able to move into Box Cottage at Charlton Kings. It felt large after the flat and room was found for a nurse-maid, Rosemary Whitlock, as well as me. One who helped with the move was Eileen Hedges, nick-named 'Jinnie' by Mary, whom the Day-Lewises were trying to help through her mourning. Jinnie remembered Cecil at this time as 'a wonderful teacher and adored by all the little boys, especially the not so bright or homesick ones, for whom he had great tenderness and compassion'. She found that, contrary to his own account, 'he cared very deeply about people and couldn't bear cruelty or ridicule. I remember once a party of us were dining at a rather plush restaurant when in came a very old, very dirty, very drunk woman who sat herself down at a table and began shouting and swearing. Most of the party started to laugh, all except Cecil, who really lost his temper with us and made us feel ashamed of our-selves.'

March 1933 saw the publication by the Hogarth Press of both Cecil's *The Magnetic Mountain*, described by the New York *Partisan Review* as 'perhaps the most important revolutionary poem as yet written by an Englishman', and the second Michael Roberts anthology, *New Country*. The latter included four poems from the former, as well as Cecil's prose 'Letter to a Young Revolutionary'. This was addressed to one Jonathan Smith, a twenty-five-year-old university student thinking of joining the Communist Party.

The letter illustrates the way in which politics had become religion for Cecil: '. . . the prime essential for the revolutionary is faith: an absolute belief in revolution as the way to, and the form of, new life . . . the certainty of new life must be your starting-point', he wrote, incidentally giving himself a text and a title for his second novel, *Starting Point* (1937). 'Not jealousy, not pity, not a knowledge of economics, not hate even, or love, but certainty of new life . . . revolutionary works without faith are vain.' He went on to knock 'protestant democratic liberalism', 'the burden of the individual conscience' and the souring and stultifying Oxford idea that, 'Of everything that is true, the converse is also true', before giving Smith his final instructions: 'You must go first – you must do the exploring – and explorers, though they may die unhonoured, have lived honourably.'

The letter, one of whose fantasies sees Jonathan shooting some 'bloated capitalist, cad, liar, bully, beast and public nuisance', is complementary to the thirty-six fervent lyrics of *The Magnetic Mountain*. The sequence contains a mixture of the authoritarianism of T.E. Lawrence and the escape

of D.H. Lawrence. The iron mountain represents the goal, marvellously
sturdy beside the feather values of the old life, and the sequence can be
taken as a parable about leaving a sick country to go and find a healthy
one. The book is dedicated to Auden; it has two poems in which Auden
is addressed and it is more influenced by Auden's style than any other work
of Cecil's. Compared with Auden's *The Orators* (1932) it is very clear and
hard in identifying the enemy, but it leaves some doubt about how the
new country beyond the railhead would work. It also shows a revealing
nostalgia for what might be left behind, with its suggestion of taking a
light engine 'back along the line/For a last excursion, a tour of inspection',
which should be superfluous. The patriotism is not entirely between the
lines.

> You that love England, who have an ear for her music,
> The slow movement of clouds in benediction,
> Clear arias of light thrilling over her uplands,
> Over the chords of summer sustained peacefully;
> Ceaseless the leaves' counterpoint in a west wind lively,
> Blossom and river rippling loveliest allegro,
> And the storms of wood strings brass at year's finale:
> Listen. Can you not hear the entrance of a new theme?*

In *New Verse*, Geoffrey Grigson reviewed the two books together and
condemned the Roberts compulsion to pretend that the Auden Gang was
a unity. 'How, as an artist, is Auden united with Day-Lewis, Day-Lewis
with Spender, Spender with Upward?', he asked. In contradiction to his
later view he allowed that 'Day-Lewis cannot make himself entirely a bad
artist'. Yet his new poems did not differ as they should from his letter. He
was allowing verse, in Spender's words, 'to spill over into our world of
confused emotions'. Other critics admired the way that the impetus of the
verse carried the sympathetic reader over the passages of Communist-
induced self-righteousness.

As with the Day-Lewises' first married home at Helensburgh, an early guest
to stay at Box Cottage was W.H. Auden. He was with Cecil and Mary
for the weekend of 29 April, before going on to his summer term at the
Downs School. No sooner had he arrived than he asked Mary, 'Can I have
something to eat?' He consumed the banana he was given, and then
another, and then another, until he had eaten his way through all five in
the bunch. At night he slept on a camp bed in the sitting-room, under sheet
and blankets plus all the coats and macs he could find from the passage
outside, and any movable carpets he could find on the floor. It was that
summer on a school lawn that he had his transcendental experience, 'one

* Poem 32 (*The Magnetic Mountain*, 1933).

fine summer night in June', discovering 'what it means to love one's
neighbour as oneself', recorded in *Forewords and Afterwords* (1973).

The Auden and King families again met during their Lake District summer holidays in August, and Cecil saw something of John Auden as well
as Wystan. Cecil and Mary returned to Cheltenham in time for the publication of *Dick Willoughby* in mid-September. This first of Cecil's two Dorset-
set, full-length adventure novels for boys is a strenuous and hearty story
about a Tudor teenager, suggesting that the heart of the author was in the
same place as the hearts of those who wrote *Kidnapped* and *Westward Ho!*.
It celebrates the virtues of courage, magnanimity and endurance, as well
as deploying an exotic line in horror with a phosphorescently leprous phantom, and a villainous servant with a cork nose and eerily sibilant breathing.

Such horror was remote enough to be acceptable and the book sold some
copies during that October. But letters to L.A.G. Strong that autumn
expressed disappointment at the unwillingness of any American publisher
to take up the tale. They also contained news that he had 'practically finished
a detective novel'.

In the event the novel, the precursor of a canon of twenty, proved difficult
to finish and the publication of *A Question of Proof* was still eighteen months
in the future. It was being written like so many others out of necessity.
The picturesque roof of Box Cottage was letting in the rain and £100 was
needed to repair it properly. Cecil had read a vast number of detective novels
and it occurred to him that he might be able to write one himself.

He was not single-minded in this. At the same time he told Leonard
Strong, 'I've just finished a ballad ['Johnny Head-In-Air'], 150 lines or so,
rather good – I think, which will probably be printed in the *Twentieth Century*: it's far too long for anyone to pay for it.'

With Mary seven months pregnant it was decided to have Christmas
at home for the first time, entertaining Stephen Spender. He approached
Mary's elaborate preparations in mock shock: 'If I had known you kept
Christmas I would not have come.' Mary, who had a residual belief that
left-wing poets meant what they said, took this remark literally and was
mildly shocked herself. Cecil, who was expanding *A Hope for Poetry* from
a paper for the Cheltenham College Masters' Essay Society into the first
book about MacSpaunday written by one of its limbs, was grateful to be
able to talk it over with Spender.

He also wrote to Geoffrey Grigson: 'I'll let you have a poem or two
to look at by the New Year. I shall be in London from the 9th to the 12th
[January 1934] and should like to see you then: perhaps you will suggest
a time to meet. I've been commissioned to write a short book on post-
war poetry and am finding rather a shortage of material: it would be nice
to talk about it with you.'

After starting 1934 with a visit to the Rev Arthur and Alison Morris
at East Quantoxhead, Cecil was in London from 9 to 12 January, staying

with Leonard Strong and having lunch with Stephen Spender and another *New Signatures* poet who was to remain a friend for life, William Plomer. If he had been able to accept an invitation to lunch with Grigson during those days their relationship might have been cemented, and Cecil might have received less savage treatment in the future. As it was, Cecil still considered Grigson a friend when he wrote on 17 January, but not for long after that.

I'd be grateful if you could let me know how to come by some of MacNeice's poems. I'd like to say something about him in my book, if he fits in, but I don't want to base criticism on that first book of his [*Blind Fireworks*, 1929]. Perhaps you could sell me any old issues of *New Verse* in which poems of his have appeared – and you may know other papers. I don't want to write to him personally, because you say he is apt to take a long time about sending things, and because it would not be very satisfactory for him if he sent me some of his work and then I wasn't able to say anything about him in the book.

In February his continued doubts about *A Hope for Poetry* were expressed in a letter to Lady Ottoline Morrell:

Thank you very much for the book of Stephens [*Strict Joy* (1931) by James Stephens]. I have not had time to read much of it yet, but some of the poems are very attractive. I feel his prose is the best work he produces: the *Crock of Gold* must be an immortal. My book is nearly finished now; it has given me a shocking inferiority feeling, when I compare it with criticism by Eliot or Edmund Wilson, but there may be some value in it that I can't detect. I look forward very much to seeing you when I am next in London.

The birth of Cecil's second child was accomplished with less fuss than the first. Medical opinion agreed that it would be acceptable for Mary to stay at Box Cottage. Her diary recorded that on 7 February, 'Sean was packed off to the Hallidays and Nurse Elizabeth Peel arrived from North Finchley.' Nicholas Charles was born during the afternoon of Saturday 17 February and Mary considered that he was 'not bad looking'. Cecil bought a pineapple to celebrate and the baby-care gospel according to Truby King, which had been imposed on me, was mostly left on its shelf above the kitchen dresser, though consulted for reassurance from time to time. Rosemary Whitlock continued to look after me, Nurse Peel managed Nicholas, and the only upset occurred one evening when Cecil and Mary came home unexpectedly early and, according to Rosemary, 'caught the Nanny entertaining her young man in the kitchen', something that was not done without permission.

In May, Cecil made his first broadcast, a BBC Midland Region talk from Birmingham on 'Spring in the Cotswolds'. It seemed innocuous enough, but next morning the handsome Don Johnson, now in his third term as headmaster of the Junior, said: 'You're in trouble again, Cecil, some parents have telephoned me, complaining that you insulted the King in your broadcast last night.' Much investigation followed and it was eventually discovered that after Cecil had disapproved of Henry VIII in a history lesson a boy had reported at home that 'Mr Day-Lewis said the King was a bad man.' It was decided that this 'rudimentary historical judgement somehow got confused, in the addled wits of some colonel or mem-sahib, with the present monarch and my radio talk'.

A new friend at this time was John Moore, a still unknown writer born at nearby Tewkesbury, who used his knowledge of country pursuits for his writing and played an increasingly conspicuous part in the public life of the district. He would make his name in the late 1940s with his 'Brensham Trilogy': *Portrait of Elmbury*, *Brensham Village* and *The Blue Field*, a chronicle of Gloucestershire life. That month Moore took Cecil sailing in his dinghy on the Severn. Later Cecil bought the boat and Moore turned to flying, taking the poet into the sky as his first passenger.

During the summer term Lloyd Kay, manager of Banks bookshop, involved Cecil and John Moore in his plans for a Cheltenham Literary Society. At a dinner on 11 July Cecil was elected chairman, with the popular novelist Francis Brett Young as president. Soon afterwards Cecil wrote of this to L.A.G. Strong:

They have started a literary society here, of which by some quaint whimsy I have been elected chairman. We are starting off with a cracking great banquet on October 4, to which a number of well-known authors are being invited. I am writing to ask if you will be one of the number and make one of the speeches. You get expenses and I hope a good dinner and some publicity – we have 100 members so far: and if you are not in Scotland then I do hope you will manage to come down: it is time you and Sylvia explored the hinterland of Charlton Kings, and we should both love to have you here. Congratulations on *Corporal Tune*: it is the stuff. I've a long poem in next month's *Life and Letters* I think you will like.

Among the boys who left the Junior at the end of that summer term was David Blount, the son of a bank manager. He had been a rewarding pupil and Cecil was to remember him and his father as Detective Inspector Blount of his detective novels, a man who started his Scotland Yard career with 'the impersonal eyes of a bank manager'; over the years the character became more like Cecil's Scottish rugby international friend and literary agent, W.N. Roughead.

Some forty years later Blount remembered Cecil's correctness in keeping politics out of the classroom, his ability to spend complete English classes reading dramatically from *Nicholas Nickleby* and other such books, his disinterested willingness to give free private tuition to the best minds, his painstaking efforts to avoid the usual clichés of school reports, his generously given talents as singer and actor. According to Blount, Cecil started with the advantage of a striking physical appearance 'both boyish and aged' and 'a certain hauteur of manner', best observed as he rode his tall black bicycle with a kind of 'statuesque panache ... his head at a characteristic tilt and his chin aloft', from Box Cottage to school.

He won his pupils by being 'simply himself'. He 'conveyed the impression that he didn't care whether we liked him or not, or indeed what we or anyone else thought of him, and this was a novel experience'. It was also a novel experience when he set the reading of his *Dick Willoughby* as a 'holiday task', thus ensuring that each boy in the class would have a copy bought for him.

That summer Geoffrey Grigson had sent questionnaires to the poets in whom he was interested, asking them for their opinions on the state of their craft. Twelve replied, of whom four declared themselves to be apolitical, two said they were Communists, two (Dylan Thomas and David Gascoyne) claimed to believe in revolution, Wyndham Lewis found himself 'exactly midway between the Bolshevist and the Fascist', and nobody admitted to being Conservative or Fascist. Among those who did not reply were Auden, Spender and Day-Lewis. Cecil gave his reasons, or some of his reasons, in an August letter to Grigson.

Yes, I received the copy of the questionnaire: I meant to write and tell you that I would rather not answer it, but I forgot. One or two of the questions I felt quite incapable of answering, and some of the others seemed to me unanswerable in any brief space. Actually several of them are dealt with indirectly in my book, which will be out on September 1st [*A Hope for Poetry*]. I'm asking Blackwell to send you a copy. There are (at least) four printer's errors in it, which will provide the enemy with a good basis for criticism. I'm afraid I haven't got anything by me that I can send you for *New Verse*.

This apparently marked the parting of the two men. Cecil had contributed the political poem quoted from at the head of this chapter to the July issue of *New Verse*, but in October he was to move his allegiance to the new *Left Review*, the official organ of the British section of the Communist-run Writers' International.

It was at this monent, also, that Cecil received the kind of boost which does not go down well with those who would guard the strictest standards of literary criticism. On 15 August the Londoner's Diary of the London *Evening Standard* carried a ten-paragraph item under the heading 'England's Great Man':

Recently Mr Winston Churchill and Colonel T.E. (Aircraftman Shaw) Lawrence met at the country house of a British Minister.

The two men had a discussion in which present company was excepted, on the dearth of great men in the post-war period.

Mr Churchill scouted the idea that there were any great men in England at the present moment.

Aircraftman (Colonel T.E. Lawrence) Shaw was more optimistic. He claimed that he had discovered one great man in these islands.

His name is Cecil Day-Lewis. He was, of course, unknown to the other guests.

Mr Lewis was born at Ballintubrer [sic], in Ireland, in 1904. He is a scholar of Wadham, which in the late Lord Birkenhead, Sir John Simon and C.B. Fry has already three modern celebrities on its roll.

Lord David Cecil, another literary idol of the younger generation, was a don there for some years after the war.

Mr Lewis's claim to greatness is based on his poetry. He has four volumes of verse to his credit.

Here is a sample:

> *Farewell again to this adolescent moon;*
> *I say it is a bottle*
> *For hapless poets to feed their fancy on.*
> *Once mine sucked there, and I dreamed*
> *The heart a record for the gramophone.*

When he is not writing poetry, Mr Lewis is a schoolmaster.

The quotation is from Poem 24 of *Transitional Poem*, and the poets should have been not 'hapless' but 'papless'.

Preparations continued for the October banquet of the Cheltenham Literary Society. On 20 August, Cecil had taken his family to Edwinstowe and six days later he wrote from there to L.A.G. Strong.

We've definitely fixed October 11 for the banquet, and look forward to seeing you then. I managed to finish my detective novel and sent it to Peters [literary agent]: he thinks it a good one and says there should be no difficulty about finding a publisher. My book of criticism, *A Hope for Poetry*, is coming out on September 1. I should like to know some time what you think about it: there are about three ideas in it of some value and a few amusing pieces of pure frigidity, but for the rest – *je m'en fiche*. I hope you're having a fine time in Scotland and being fecund.

The Curtis Brown literary agency had made overtures to Cecil at the end of the previous year. He asked Strong's advice about this and was directed instead to A.D. Peters. So began a partnership of great trust and friendship which lasted without a ripple of conflict until Cecil's death.

'Pete' was born August Detlof, the fourth son of a Schleswig-Holstein farmer, and was adopted at the age of three by an aunt who ran a girls' school in Brighton. After toying with journalism he started his agency in 1924, serving such as J.B. Priestley, J.C. Squire, Gerald Bullett, Martin Armstrong, Edmund Blunden, Rebecca West and Sheila Kaye-Smith. With Cecil were added such writers as Margery Sharp, C.S. Forester, A.E. Coppard, Evelyn Waugh, Margaret Irwin, Frank O'Connor, and Cecil's Gloucestershire friend John Moore. Cecil found Peters a sane encourager who rarely raised false hopes and whose knowledge and love of good writing could be respected without reservation.

There were other advantages at this firm. One was Peter's ultra-efficient yet warm-hearted assistant Margaret Stephens, and the other was W.N.

Roughead. 'Roughie', who became one of Cecil's dearest friends, was a hero to Cecil before they met. Cecil had watched him play as hooker in the Oxford University rugby x v of 1925, against the giant New Zealand All Blacks, 'the bravest and most skilful display of open rugby I have ever seen'. The balding but appropriately named Roughead, son of a distinguished Edinburgh criminologist, was at the same time a member of the Scottish x v. He had joined Peters straight from Oxford in 1927, and though he did not share his boss's devotion to work he had the same infectious feeling for still pleasure, 'satisfaction without exhaustion' as V.S. Pritchett has put it, which soothed Cecil's more moody temperament.

The agency did not handle *A Hope for Poetry*, which appeared on 1 September. Geoffrey Grigson complained that it was 'a bad book' which 'Mr Day-Lewis, instead of writing for his equals or betters, has written to persuade others to read himself, Mr Spender and Mr Auden. An inferior purpose has bred an inferior book, evasive on the poet and politics, ridiculous often in judgement... and in prose style as cheaply poetical as Mr Humbert Wolfe or Mr Basil de Selincourt or any other Sunday journal buffoon. There is a nasty resemblance between *A Hope for Poetry* and a romance for boys written not long ago by the same writer.'

Whatever may be thought of that – and the last sentence does suggest a man more fascinated by his own sword-play, or bill-hooking, than interested in his opponent – more indulgent reviewers welcomed such a clear account of what MacSpaunday was doing. Over forty years later it is still regarded with affection by those it helped to an understanding of the new poetry. It had six editions in its first ten years, and in the late 1970s was again being reprinted in the United States. The book is dedicated to Maurice Bowra, a guest at Box Cottage that July.

The first edition had eleven chapters, the opener claiming Hopkins, Owen and Eliot as 'our immediate ancestors', and the next three looking at each of these. The sixth chapter, considering how poetry is used by modern society and attacking literary critics, was particularly admired by William Plomer when he wrote to commend the book. 'Altogether I think you have written one of the best books about poetry I have ever read, and certainly the only one by anybody of our generation', Plomer added.

Replying, Cecil wrote: 'Stephen [Spender] saw the book in MS and liked it; and there is no one whose approval could make me feel happier than yours and his.' This was sadly at variance with the put-down in his *The Thirties and After* (1978) where Spender wrote that although *A Hope for Poetry* might be taken as a manifesto for the 'thirties poets' it was 'a book I have never read'.

The opening banquet of the Cheltenham Literary Society, at which Naomi Mitchison discussed the justification of fairy tales, detective stories and other escapism, and Wystan Auden talked on 'Literature and Enlightenment', was held on 11 October. Afterwards Cecil retired to bed with

nervous strain and a cold, but was able to write from his sick-room to
Leonard Strong with advice on how to review Dilys Powell's *Dissent from
Parnassus*: 'I feel that too much time is spent making final term's orders
with Wystan, Stephen and myself, and so long before the term is over',
Cecil wrote. 'It's true, I think he's [Auden] certain to be top at the end:
but I only *say* so out of a kind of self-defence.... This perpetual playing
off of one of us against the other must give a number of readers the impression that we are either cutting each other's throats in earnest, or staging
a mimic battle for publicity's sake.'

In November, Cecil was engaged with his part as Feste in a production
by John Moore of Shakespeare's *Twelfth Night*. It was given by the Cheltenham branch of the British Empire Shakespeare Society and Cecil's performance, singing as well as acting, was probably the most polished of his stage
efforts. The Sir Andrew Aguecheek in the production was Frank Beecroft,
a schoolmaster and musician who became a friend and collaborator with
Cecil. For a time they were the two tenors in the Cheltenham Madrigal
Singers meeting at the Ladies' College. Beecroft also remembered, in 1978,
being taken by Cecil 'to a meeting of what I think was called the Cheltenham branch of the Society for Cultural Relations with the USSR, a surprising title at that date, where we saw the Eisenstein film *The General Line*
(1928). This was in a rather sinister back street and a suitably dimly lit hall
where Cecil was helping with ushering and handing out leaflets.'

That November the revolutionary Feste heard from his war hero. Having proclaimed Cecil a Great Man, T.E. Lawrence now wrote from the
Ozone Hotel at Bridlington complaining that *A Hope for Poetry* was 'only
half an argument'. 'So long as you wrote poems I was content with reading
them. Over *Dick Willoughby* I laughed. This, as I say, is different. Probably
you are hardened against letters from unknowns.' He did not say what the
other half of the argument was, but after asking why Cecil's generation
put so much stress on 'those few thought ridden poets' like Donne, Vaughan
and Crashaw, Lawrence proclaimed himself 'glad you concentrated on
Auden, Spender and yourself'. The hero went on to show himself a
confident forecaster. 'Auden makes me fear that he will not write much
more. Spender might, on the other hand, write too much. You have given
numbers of us the greatest pleasure – though for me *The Magnetic Mountain*
was a qualified pleasure.... Poets hope too much, and their politics, like
their sciences, usually stink after 20 years.'

Now a celebrity, Cecil was invited by the BBC's newly formed General
Talks Department to speak in a new *Youth Looks Ahead* series. He despatched his notes in early December to Mary Adams, then an assistant in
the department as well as the wife of a Conservative MP, who wrote on
them that they were 'interesting' and added that 'it's communism, or
rather neo-marxism, but we must be prepared to stand for it'. G.N. Pocock,

the department head, was less sure. He wrote to Cecil that the talk 'looks to me a good deal too difficult for the wireless'. If he insisted on talking about politics instead of literature there would have to be a balancing speaker.

Cecil replied at length pointing out that to his way of thinking literature was 'inseparable from politics in the broad sense'. 'I am well aware that the word "Communist" (and to a lesser extent the word "Fascist") is apt to excite the most violent feelings, not only amongst the general public but in Broadcasting House', but, 'I had no intention of making my talk a piece of propaganda.' The letter ended in a conciliatory manner with the suggestion of a meeting to discuss differences, making it clear that 'the only point on which I am bound to stand firm is that some adequate reference to the relation between politics – the science of living together – and literature should be made.'

As 1935 dawned the BBC's General Talks Department was still agonizing about Cecil's contribution. The family had gone to Sherborne for Christmas and he wrote from there on 3 January saying that as he had had no word perhaps his compromise synopsis could be returned to him. Pocock wanted to go ahead with the talk and asked for the aid of the Director of Talks, Charles Siepmann. A memo at last came back, signed C.A.S: 'The summary seems to me an admirable one, in some ways a great deal better than [Richard] Crossman's. It is a pity there is no room for him in the series of six.' After further discussion it was decided to include Cecil in a series of seven, his talk to be given in London on 21 March for a fee of twelve guineas.

In March, Cecil published three books. His *A Time to Dance* came out from Hogarth Press at 5s, and his three previous books of verse were reissued by the same publisher as *Collected Poems, 1929–33* at 7s 6d. In addition the Crime Club imprint of Collins offered *A Question of Proof* by Nicholas Blake for 7s 6d. It is a measure of the standing which he had suddenly achieved, not to mention the cheapness of newsprint, that Desmond MacCarthy could devote an entire two-column article, forty-two column inches, to the new book of verse in the *Sunday Times* of 10 March. A week later Basil de Selincourt was allowed thirty column inches in the *Observer* to review both poetry volumes.

The title work of *A Time to Dance* was described as 'a symphonic poem in memory of L.P. Hedges'. The spirited first movement announces that Cecil will not sing a dirge or a funeral anthem for his dead friend Lionel, 'But words to match his mirth, a theme with a happy end'. It goes on to describe the heroic-epic flight of Lieutenants Parer and M'Intosh, home to Australia from the war in Europe, in 'a craft of obsolete design, a condemned D.H. nine'. The second movement is an elegy reflecting on Hedge's death; and the third is a theme and variations, using parody and echoes of familiar poetic styles to curse capitalism and look in rapture towards the Red dawn.

Oh hush thee, my baby,
Thy cradle's in pawn:
No blankets to cover thee
Cold and forlorn.
The stars in the bright sky
Look down and are dumb
At the heir of the ages
Asleep in a slum.

The book contains ten other poems, mostly personal but dwelling on the conflict between the past and the future in the poet's present mind. There is a reflection on his younger son Nicholas 'Learning to Talk', a warning to himself that 'Moving In' to Box Cottage must not be an escape, and 'A Poem for an Anniversary' in which Mary is advised to 'Admit then and be glad/Our volcanic age is over'. There are also 'The Conflict' and 'In Me Two Worlds', which he came to regard as 'the only political poems of any value which I wrote'. 'It is significant', he added, that 'though they both end with a confident statement of the choice made, they are both poems of the divided mind, while the shrill, schoolboyish derisiveness which served for satire in other political verse of mine demonstrates the unnatural effort I had to make in order to avoid seeing both sides.'

MacCarthy said he pounced on *A Time to Dance* because he had been impressed and instructed by *A Hope for Poetry*. He found the flight poem admirable in diction and true in feeling, but so intermittent in its use of rhyme that it amounted to 'writing verse on too easy terms'. He nevertheless found that Cecil was 'a poet of exceptional impetus and directness', and specially admired the long ballad 'Johnny Head-In-Air' dealing movingly with 'humanity's weary and difficult march'. De Selincourt considered that 'Mr Lewis's grimness is overdone' but found his vision acceptable: 'He hovers with the kestrel, he even soars with the lark, and, wind-borne in those ecstatic heights, sees a new world coming – this is our chief need'. He thought the first movement of the symphony 'almost pure Hopkins', though more buoyant and less back-breaking than 'The Wreck of the Deutschland'. Elsewhere he was dubious about the 'general application of Owen's consonantal rhyme'. He concluded, 'Mr Lewis is a great performer; but I do hope, if I should meet him on "The Day", I shall get my bayonet into him before he gets his into me!'

Neither of the Sunday reviewers found it odd that a poet about to join the Communist Party should tell a story that celebrated the middle-class stiff upper lip. Communists also needed heroes of the T.E. Lawrence kind and indeed C. St John Sprigg, otherwise Christopher Caudwell, the English Communist soon to be killed in the Spanish Civil War, told the story of Parer and M'Intosh in his *Great Flights* (1936).

As to Lawrence himself, he had written to Cecil the previous 20

December, saying that after all *A Hope for Poetry* 'isn't a bad book at all'. On *A Time to Dance* he added, 'I shall enjoy buying your book, so please don't send it – after all, you don't write so many as all that!' History does not relate whether he was able to keep his promise. Two months after its publication he had the motor cycle accident which resulted, after five unconscious days, in his death.

Among those who certainly did buy the book was Lord David Cecil, who had written an enthusiastic commendation of *A Hope for Poetry* in December, before arriving to stay a night at Box Cottage and address the Cheltenham Literary Society. He thought the new poems 'magnificent'. They 'seem a large advance on anything you have done as yet, and place you at a bound far ahead of all other poets of your particular generation', though the last movement of the symphony was 'jarring and irritable'.

Stephen Spender, writing on 14 March, also considered that the new book 'contains much the most beautiful poetry you have written'. The poetry was showing a new lack of inhibition. 'In all your early work I find that there is a slight stiffness ... too much emphasis on the stiff upper lip ... which puts me off a good deal, and even annoys me occasionally.' He went on,

Edwin Muir said something to me which I think very true, and which I pass on, because I myself would find it very valuable, that often in your work you simply *replace* what you are really writing about with something else, by a very simple process not of symbolism, but of comparison. For instance in 'In Me Two Worlds' one almost sees a *Punch* cartoon with two worlds drawn, one on each side of the sheet, and with Communism written on one and Capitalism on the other, and with you (labelled Cecil) standing in the middle. (Rex Warner often writes like this too. Perhaps you will see what I mean in his work.)'

He was worried that the 'very traditional style' of *A Time to Dance*, 'haunted with a rather beautiful habit of cliché', sometimes ran away with itself.

My only other criticism is a wish that you wouldn't go in for that 'Bogyman, bogyman' stuff. In the first place, I can't see the point of satire that just is the thing it satirises. Secondly, you aren't depraved enough to write like this, you haven't even got a developed and sophisticated enough sense of humour, at least I don't think you have. There are great advantages in being depraved, you know what, one can soak oneself in and emerge from 'the destructive element', but you have different standards, that is all. Or that's how I see you.

If the flight of Parer and M'Intosh was a curious choice of subject for a would-be Communist, Cecil's involvement with the ''tec' could be seen as still more contradictory. As he wrote in 1942, 'the detective novel proper is read almost exclusively by the upper and professional classes. The so-called "lower-middle" and "working" classes tend to read "bloods", thrillers.'[7] He added that 'the detective story's clientèle are relatively prosperous persons, who have a stake in the social system and must therefore, even in fantasy, see the ultimate triumph of their particular social values ensured'.

The first reason why Cecil wrote such novels was to make money. The second was that he was an addict who wanted to introduce others to the habit. He had a third more personal motive, which he called 'the guilt-motive'. He dubiously connected this with the decline in religious obser-vance, with the waning belief in a God who would take the burden of guilt off the individual's shoulders. He saw the story of detection as a kind of substitute religious ritual with the detective and the murderer represent-ing the light and dark side of man's nature, two sides which could both be identified with by both reader and writer. In the end the detective triumphs because he has more or less supernatural powers; if he is not a god he is at least a fairy godmother.

Cecil believed that the guilt-motive accounted for the class-based follow-ing of the form. In detective stories the hero was on the side of law and order. 'The lower ranks of democratic society ... having little or no stake in the system ... prefer such anarchistic heroes as, from Robin Hood down to the tommy-gun gangster, have held to ransom the prosperous and law abiding.' The workers had 'less time and incentive than the relatively leisured to worry about their consciences. In so far as their lives are less rich, the taking of life will seem to them less significant and horrifying ... the general sense of guilt, the specific moral problems which tease the more prosperous classes, affect them less nearly.'

Cecil himself, like so many of the generation that led the movement away from institutionalized Christianity, felt much guilt. He also discovered in his nature a destructive, maybe mostly self-destructive, streak; and he found his activities as Nicholas Blake almost as therapeutic as they were remunerative.

His pseudonym was derived from his second son Nicholas just born, and the Blake family name used by his mother. His detective was Nigel Strange-ways, who starts in *A Question of Proof* every inch W.H. Auden. In succeed-ing novels, as Cecil grew away from that powerful poetic influence, Nigel became increasingly like himself.

He is introduced on page 108 of the first novel, a nephew of the Assistant Commissioner of Scotland Yard, a 'private inquiry agent' who has already made 'pots of money' thanks to 'the Duchess of Esk's diamonds affair and several high-hat blackmail cases which have figured less prominently in the press'. He had been dismissed from Oxford University after two years for answering his Mods papers in limericks: 'Very good answers ... he's a first-rate brain, but it alienated the dons, they have no taste for modern poetry.' He is said to look like 'one of the less successful busts of T.E. Shaw', a 'nordic type' and 'faddy'. His hostess is instructed that 'you must have water perpetually on the boil; he drinks tea at all hours of the day. And he can't sleep unless he has an enormous weight on his bed. If you don't give him enough blankets for three, you'll find that he has torn the carpets up or the curtain down.'

When Strangeways arrives, emerging from a first-class railway compartment, he is recognizably Auden. He walks towards his hostess 'with rather ostrich-like strides'. He blinks at her short-sightedly and bows over her hand 'with a courtliness a little spoilt by the angularity of his movement'. He makes some 'flat remarks, which his loud and exuberant voice somehow redeemed from banality'. He is at once involved in a car chase, to which he responds by singing in 'a raucous baritone, "O death, how bitter art thou to him that liveth in peace, to him that hath joy in his possessions and liveth free from trouble"'. Later he launches into Handel's *Israel in Egypt*, curses his poor sight and decides he is not a 'proper, inhuman, cold-blooded sleuth' as he would 'always believe my friends sooner than the facts'.

The Crime Club was started by William Collins in 1930. By 1935 its authors included Agatha Christie, Freeman Wills Crofts, Philip Macdonald and Ngaio Marsh. A.D. Peters advised that the real identity of Nicholas Blake should be kept secret, and when *A Question of Proof* was published even Collins employees were told no more than that Blake was 'the pseudonym of a well-known writer'. Informed readers inclined to exercise their own powers of detection might have arrived at his identity. It is clearly the book of a young man, exuberant and naïve, yet showing ease and distinction in its prose style. The setting is Sudeley Hall, a preparatory school. Though some of the geography is derived from Cheltenham Junior, the discovery of a body in a hay castle and the character of the headmaster clearly indicate Summer Fields.

There is a nominal link between Michael Evans, the hero of the book enjoying a love affair with the headmaster's young wife Hero, and John Evans of Summer Fields. But this Evans, 'like most games masters, a very nice man indeed', is really a mixture of Cecil and Lionel Hedges. The platitudinous Gadsby – 'you never know what a fellah's capable of when there's a woman in the case' – is a close copy of their Cheltenham butt Parker.

The book is dedicated to Margaret McDonell, the 'brazen leech' of *Transitional Poem*. In terms of British sales it has proved the most successful of Cecil's twenty detective novels; at the last count 193,422 copies have been bought in various hard- and paperback editions, though it has been far outstripped by ten other Blake books in the United States.

Among those who quickly discovered the identity of Blake was Rupert Hart-Davis, then working for the publisher Jonathan Cape. He wrote wondering if Cecil might be prepared to try his hand at a serious novel. Cecil replied on 10 March saying, 'I'm very glad you liked the detective story and it is nice of you to suggest that Cape's would be interested in any serious novel I might do. Actually, my seriousness at present runs into verse and I don't feel it is likely I should be writing a serious novel in the near future.'

At the beginning of May Cecil was back in London for a half-hour Easter Monday BBC discussion with the American poet and academic Paul Engle on 'Modern Poetry – English and American'. Cecil had met Engle after speaking to the Oxford University English Club in February and, though 'I was given so much drink that I couldn't see beyond the first row of the audience', had thought to invite him to stay at Box Cottage in March. They had got on well enough but the broadcast was hard going. Their script submitted in advance was considered by the BBC to be 'too literary and academic' and the rehearsals proved to be unexpectedly long and abrasive. There was some quibbling over the next few weeks about whether his twelve guineas was supposed to cover his travel expenses. In the end he managed to secure an extra 10s 6d for taxi fares.

There were no fees for taking part in Mary's entertainments. Cecil was willingly pressed into service for her recital of dance and song given in aid of the Tewkesbury Abbey appeal, organized by John Moore, that month at Cheltenham and Tewkesbury. The local *Echo* reviewed the second performance and commended the 'superb lightness of action, delicacy of expression and cleverness of movement' of Mary and her dancers. It added: 'Mr Day-Lewis, the young poet, sang a number of traditional and other songs with much beauty of intonation and enunciation, while the seven members of the Cheltenham Madrigal Society rendered their many unaccompanied madrigals with profound ease and finish.'

Less parochial entertainment was afoot when on 18 May W.H. Auden brought his small but imperious friend Rupert Doone to stay at Box Cottage. Doone was the creator of the Group Theatre which had given Auden's *The Dance of Death* in 1933, and the following January would produce the Auden–Isherwood collaboration *The Dog Beneath the Skin*; he had been trained in classical ballet and had worked with Diaghilev. After this visit and another in July Cecil was encouraged to start upon his next verse venture, *Noah and the Waters* (1936). It was not Doone's fault that in its writing the work turned from 'a choral ballet' into what Cecil called 'something in the tradition of the mediaeval morality plays', which was never performed.

Another visitor Auden brought to Charlton Kings in June was Erika Mann, eldest daughter of the German novelist Thomas Mann who was now living in Switzerland after escaping from the Nazis in 1933. Having declined to perform the service himself Christopher Isherwood had asked Auden if he would marry Erika so that she could get a British passport. She had been running an anti-Nazi cabaret company touring the German border and was not well favoured in Berlin. Auden brought his slim and handsome fiancée to Box Cottage on 14 June and next day, as Josef Goebbels, the Nazi head of propaganda, all unknowingly announced that she was no longer German, she and Wystan were married at the registry office of Ledbury, Herefordshire. The marriage was purely one of convenience and later Wystan suggested that Erika's only redeeming feature was that she had managed to rescue the tetralogy *Joseph and his Brothers* from the Mann household. 'I can't say we're friends, but she did us that service,' he would say.[8]

Also at Box Cottage that weekend was Basil Wright, Cecil's grateful fag at Sherborne, now working with John Grierson in the GPO Film Unit pioneering the craft of documentary; Cecil had introduced him to Auden in undergraduate days. Auden was to leave schoolmastering and Malvern at the end of this summer term to join the GPO Film Unit as writer and assistant director. In the following year the Unit would release perhaps its most renowned film, *Night Mail*, jointly directed by Wright and Harry Watt with a verse commentary by Auden and music by Benjamin Britten.

Various factors were now making Cecil wonder if he might also retire from schoolmastering and try to survive as a full-time writer. One was the example of Auden, another was Rupert Hart-Davis's offer to publish any serious novel he might write, and a third was his wish to commit himself to Communism and join the Party. A still more pressing reason was that he was likely to be sacked by the Cheltenham College authorities anyway. In early July he was to face a 'court martial' held by the College governors, and would need all the support that Maurice Bowra could give him. It was bad enough that he wrote Red verse; that was a relatively harmless eccentricity and it would remain unread. It was monstrous that he had written a detective novel implying that he was either having an affair with the charming Canadian wife of the new College headmaster, Dick Roseveare, or wished to have one. At the end of July Cecil wrote of his troubles to L.A.G. Strong:

We are being treated to a lovely firework display here just now: the Governors are holding a court-martial on me tomorrow – charges (a) Smut: no one who could write a wodge of pornography like *A Question of Proof* ought to be allowed to teach in their seminary – rub your eyes, pinch yourself, and look again: yes, it is really true; and (b) Bolshevism. I've got the two headmasters and two members of the Council solid for the Cause, so Lord Lee of Fareham, who is bent on sacking me, may be baulked. But even if he is, I'm getting a bit tired of these intermittent dust-ups, and thinking seriously of cutting adrift from school work. I have written to Peters, who is very kind and encouraging, and thinks that with ordinary luck I should have no difficulty in floating in the writing-market; and I'm quite prepared, if I make the break, to take any work I am offered. Peters suggests that, besides having a shot at serious novel writing, I should try and get some work reading for a publisher: if you hear of anyone who wants a reader, will you croak the good news in his ear? There is no hurry, as I should have to give the school, or the school give me, a term's notice. The only part of the prospect I do not altogether care for is that – so Peters says – I should have to live in or near London at first so as to be in the middle of the market: do you feel it would be really necessary? I should do it, if it was, of course.

The Governors voted to take no action, but Cecil was called to a private interview with the chairman, Lord Lee of Fareham, a Privy Councillor and art connoisseur, former First Lord of the Admiralty and Minister of Agriculture, a man well remembered for his exposure of the munitions shortage in the early days of the Great War. He was seen by Cecil as a small, dark and insignificant-looking man who brusquely motioned the poet to sit down and then launched without more ado into a homily. Cecil remembered only the finale of this. Lee mentioned a talk on collective farming which Cecil had contrived to give to the local branch of the Society for Cultural Relations with the USSR that spring, and went on to ask: 'D'you realize what would have happened to you if you'd done that sort of thing in the Regiment?' Cecil, now too aware of the crudity of his interrogator to be nervous, silently shook his head. 'The Colonel would have handed you over to the subalterns' mess; and when they'd finished with you, you'd have been asked to join some other Regiment.'

Cecil emerged shaking with indignation, believing he had seen something of what was going on in Germany and Italy, not to mention the class war and the 'coming struggle for power' at home. The incident was placed entire in his novel *Starting Point* (1937), where the Lord Lee character is a Fascist-minded industrial tyrant and the Cecil figure a hostile agent within the capitalist system. Meanwhile the ever helpful Strong let Cecil know of a possible vacancy at the more liberal Dorset public school of Bryanston, where his Oxford friend Wilfrid 'Baron' Cowley was on the staff.

No offer came from Bryanston, and by 3 September Cecil was writing again to Leonard Strong, from the Auden cottage in the Lake District, saying that he now had a choice between £250 per annum for three years for three novels, offered by Rupert Hart-Davis and Cape's; and £300 a year from Longmans for the same period as an advance on three novels, and two other books to be given them within five years. He added that 'the shindy at Cheltenham died down, but I think I'll clear out of it next spring at the latest. . . . Verschoyle has given me the detective novel reviewing for the *Spectator*, and I've nearly finished my new one [*Thou Shell of Death* 1936], which is a pretty glamorous piece of work.'

Hart-Davis came to stay at Box Cottage on 14 September and instantly made himself popular with the family: somewhat military in appearance and bearing, yet funny and generously appreciative and compassionate. Cecil suffered from 'corrosive anxiety' about being able to support us all and Hart-Davis reassured him, notably by matching the Longman offer of £300 a year. By the time Hart-Davis returned to London Cecil was feeling strong enough to hand in his resignation at school.

That September ended with the beginning of his last school term and the death at eighty of his first form master at Sherborne, his father-in-law H.R. King. The month also saw publication of Cecil's *Revolution in Writing*, an appropriately red paperback which was No 29 in the 'Day to Day

Pamphlets' of the Hogarth Press. The first of its three essays is the rather neutral script of his *Youth Looks Ahead* talk which had so troubled the BBC before its broadcast in March. The second essay, 'Writers and Morals', is a kind of personal explanation of his position as a would-be revolutionary who had to support his family by bourgeois means though 'the very air I breathe is the air of a society I believe to be rotten'. The third essay, 'Revolutionaries and Poetry', had appeared as an article in *Left Review*.

Cecil's contradictions made him vulnerable. From the Marxist side Montagu Slater, an editor of *Left Review*, slated 'Revolutionaries and Poetry' for suggesting that poets should bring with them some sacred relics of the old bourgeois culture, when they joined the revolutionary class. From the Bloomsbury liberal side Julian Bell, the elder son of Clive and Vanessa Bell, soon to be killed fighting for the Spanish Republic, was equally scathing about Cecil's attempt to deny that his writing was a creation of the bourgeois culture whose subscribers actually constituted his audience. He criticized Cecil and his friends for disguising a personal, neurotic malaise under Marxist ideology and for sentimentalizing the proletariat.

Cecil also found himself under fire at this time from his social democrat friends. In the last movement of his *A Time to Dance* symphony he had notoriously asked, 'Yes, why do we all, seeing a Red, feel small?' The question had provoked Naomi Mitchison, and he replied to her on 27 October.

1. I did not say I *only* felt small seeing a communist: several other people have made me feel small, as individuals; the communist makes me feel small through what he represents – I thought the poem made that quite clear. 2. Quite apart from that, when a poet says I and We, he is seldom referring only – and quite often not at all – to himself: failure to realise this led Wintringham [Tom Wintringham MP, editor of *Left Review* who fought in Spain] to write his 'asinine' reply. And by the way, you should say 'rats' to Wintringham, not me: it was he who said we are inseparable! I don't think I am romantic about communism: at all events, everything I write or say in its favour in a place like this endangers my job, and I've no private income to live on if I lose it: please don't think I'm trying to appear in the least heroic: but it does put me in a different category from most of the Bloomsbury reds – not that you did put me there, but a number of people do. I don't, as a matter of fact, call myself a communist at all; nor ever should unless I was a working member of the party. And, if I didn't care what at least one 'social democrat' says, I shouldn't be making this rather laboured attempt to justify myself. I haven't 'tried' the communist party any more than the labour: it's just that I believe dialectical materialism is much nearer the truth than any other philosophy I have come up against: and that communism appeals to my prophetic (or self-hallucinatory) faculty as being the inevitable next mode of life. Going all out to the left, at the very sober pace I have gone, does not give me a particularly nice feeling: I was quite happy before in my innocence, and am now full of self-reproachings for my own inactivity. How am I to give the Midlands a chance? I should be just as tied at a school there as I am here:

more so, because I've dug myself in here pretty well. And, practically, teaching
and writing leave one little time or energy for other activities.

From the middle of December he could say what he liked. He had been
attached to one academic institution or another for the twenty-three years
since he became an eight-year-old schoolboy at Wilkie's in pre-war London. Now at last he was free. He left the Junior 'in a mellow kind of valedic-
tory haze'. His fellow masters gave him a cheque; the boys presented him
with two cut-glass decanters and bridge-playing equipment; the *Cheltonian*
wished him 'all success in what is bound to be an interesting and significant
career'.

Cecil was also free to make contact with the Communist Party. He did
not do so, he went off to Sherborne with Mary and us boys to enjoy a
bourgeois family Christmas. In January 1936 he was able to publish his
second Nicholas Blake novel *Thou Shell of Death*, 'dedicated to my late
colleagues with gratitude and affection', beginning with a gentle attack on
bourgeois materialism as represented by the habit of giving unwanted
Christmas presents.

Talking to Mark Featherstone-Witty in 1971, Cecil explained that he
mainly started his detective novels with 'a physical place' or 'a closed circle',
locations like a prep school, a government ministry or a cruise liner where
the number of suspects can be limited. This novel was an exception in that
he started with a title, taken from Tourneur's *The Revenger's Tragedy* and
proceeded from that to the idea of death by poisoned walnut. The 'physical
place', the Somerset estate of Nigel's aunt Lady Marlinworth, followed
next. Among the guests there are Georgia Cavendish, a monkey-faced
explorer who arrives in a two-seater car with a green parrot on her shoulder
and a huge bloodhound beside her, and who is 'everything a woman should
be'. She seems to have been to some extent a caricature of Cecil's friend
Margaret Marshall, and she was to become first wife to Cecil's detective,
Nigel Strangeways.

In his 'February 1936', included in *Overtures to Death* (1938), Cecil was
depressed, seeing the month as 'infirm and grey' and 'leaden hearted'. Outside his work room the month began with a visit from William Plomer,
who introduced his friends Lilian Bowes-Lyon, another Gloucestershire
poet who was a first cousin of the Duchess of York, the future Queen Elizabeth, and Laurens van der Post; both of them became literary colleagues
of Cecil.

Speaking to me shortly before his death in 1973, Plomer said he was
shocked on this first visit by schoolmasterly Cecil's insular outlook and his
lack of curiosity about his immediate surroundings. Plomer had been born
and mainly brought up in South Africa, had taught at Tokyo University
and had travelled in the Soviet Union, but quite failed to interest Cecil
in any of these places. He had also been surprised over the years by Cecil's

capacity for hope and his continuing ability to see the 1930s 'not as a dull, dishonest decade but as a time of great hope.'

Cecil wrote in his 1960 autobiography that 'no-one who did not go through this political experience during the 1930s can quite realise how much hope there was in the air then, how radiant for some of us was the illusion that man could, under Communism, put the world to rights'. Plomer wondered if this radiance was itself an illusion, something imagined by a reserved man, secluded by living with the enemy in Cheltenham, something unimaginable to a man who had experienced more of the human nature that was supposed to bring about what Plomer called 'Utopian reckonings'. Plomer considered Cecil one of those men it is easy to like and difficult to know: a man with whom he felt 'compatible in a brotherly way', a man with whom it was pleasant to pass the time but who always held a substantial part of himself in reserve, and indicated that this section of the house was locked against all male comers. It should be added that Cecil had a real talent for making and keeping male friends, who presumably did not want to go through the door which Plomer minded being locked.

In that same February Hogarth Press published Cecil's seventh volume of verse, dedicated to the theatre-loving Charles Fenby, the morality play *Noah and the Waters*. Its point of departure is an extract from the Communist Manifesto which Cecil also quoted in his *Revolution in Writing* of the previous year. 'Finally, when the class war is about to be fought to a finish, disintegration of the ruling class and the old order of society becomes so active, so acute, that a small part of the ruling class breaks away to make common cause with the revolutionary class, the class which holds the future in its hands. . . .' In a foreword the author agrees that the parable 'is probably not suitable as it stands for the modern stage . . . its drama derives largely from the weight and imminence of the issue it represents and little from any conscious dramatic construction'. The issue is 'the choice that must be made by Noah between clinging to his old life and trusting himself to the Flood'. The ruling class is represented by three burgesses who argue realistically for the status quo and, incidentally, forecast the splitting of the atom in defence of capitalism. The revolutionary class is the choral Flood. Noah is a divided bourgeois intellectual of two voices, the first fearful of change and the second favouring commitment to the Flood; he is recognizably a self-analysis of the author.

> I was always the man who saw both sides,
> The cork dancing where wave and backwash meet,
> From the inveterate clash of contraries gaining
> A spurious animation.

On its publication *Noah and the Waters* was received with a universal chorus of critical disapproval, in which even the *Daily Worker* joined; it was Cecil's first experience of such clamour. Geoffrey Grigson in *New Verse* provided the most strident attack with his 'Two Whiffs of Lewisite'. Noah was a 'very dull' morality play with the revolution represented as 'an undifferentiated mass of H_2O, a substance which evaporates quickly, takes any shape and has only the force of gravity'. Cecil was 'a politician, a bewildered moralist, and also a man of letters with unconfessed and vulgar ambitions... Hiding his threepenny self in Nicholas Blake/A thriller writer on the literary make'. He wrote 'fake poetry and fake Auden', he made a 'worthless but worthy noise', he was 'not even truth's pimple squeezer now' and 'needs to be yoicked off his literary perch'.

Cecil considered the best defence against this kind of knockabout was at least to pretend indifference. 'I have seldom received a criticism of my work which helped me in the least either to improve it or to change its tenor', he wrote. He was all the more impressed on this occasion that a critic of some goodwill, Edwin Muir, should have pointed out that his verse was 'deteriorating, becoming facile and careless'. Writing in the *Spectator*, Muir suggested that the Noah allegory made the situation 'more vague' instead of clearer, it clothed 'a poetic fiction in a Marxian idea'. He concluded: 'Mr Day-Lewis has been overpraised as a poet; but he has written some verse from which one can deduce at least that he is a man of talent. This last poem shows nothing but a devastating facility'.

This review was published on 13 March and played a considerable part in directing Cecil back to personal poetry and away from political verse. It is perhaps the supreme irony of Cecil's 1930s political agonizings that he should have been visited four days later by Brian Harvey, a Communist undergraduate who was secretary of the Oxford University English Club. The Party wanted Cecil as a member, for his publicity value as a celebrity if nothing else, and Harvey had been sent as part of the official campaign to recruit him. Harvey recognized that Cecil was not going to join the party lightly, and that his visit would merely be the opening shot of a campaign. 'He was not going to give in easily to pressure, he was earnest and deliberate in his thinking, and everything was going to take a long time', Harvey remembered. A week later W.G. Shepherd of the *Daily Worker* visited Box Cottage for a night and added his voice.

That month Hitler's forces reoccupied the Rhineland for Germany and the Nazi threat grew. This maybe helped as much as the Party emissaries to persuade Cecil that he must emulate his Noah. His delay, he wrote, was partly caused by a 'refinement of bourgeois subjectivism by which I was unwilling to join the party till I was making enough money to be able to assure myself that I was joining from disinterested motives, not as one of the lean and hungry who would personally profit by revolution'. He was also searching for the single-mindedness of a convert joining the Catholic Church. As he put it in concluding his poem 'The Conflict': '... only ghosts can live/Between two fires'. After he joined he did have 'a real sense of tranquillity, a conviction that I had obeyed my conscience and done right'.

Yet, even as this self signed on the dotted line, his poetic muse was unconsciously beginning to move in precisely the opposite direction, thanks to its newly found recognition that he was not Noah. The honest consistency of his inconsistency, of his continuing dilemma as a divided man, could hardly be more sharply revealed than it was here in the first half of 1936. There was a double perception about the line 'Stay away, Spring!', with which he started his 'February, 1936' poem.

Mary welcomed the prospect of Cecil working at home, but it was during his first three years as a full-time writer that they grew apart to a fatal extent. Schoolmastering gave them plenty of gossip, but writing is a solitary occupation and Mary was encouraged to maintain a supply of coffee and biscuits, not to look over his shoulder. She remembered that she did once try to talk to him about poetry at this stage of their lives. 'You know nothing about it', he cut her off, sensing all too quickly that she was pretending an interest that was not really close to her heart. She never needed discouraging twice and a rift was opened between them. They avoided emotional confrontation and maintained a perfectly friendly manner with each other most of the time, still quite frequently going to the cinema and town events together. She provided efficient housekeeping and social ease when he entertained his friends.

'For seven days in the week I was shut away, hour after hour, in my tiny room which, moved by a disastrous impulse, I had painted an unforgiving shade of orange, kept warm during the winter by an oil-stove which gave me headaches, trying to write novels without any of the novelist's equipment', he wrote. When he had time to relax he mostly cycled off alone to bird-watch on the Cotswolds, 'a hobby Rex Warner had infected me with his own enthusiasm for.' Frequently he stayed away lecturing and many of his evenings were devoted to political activity. He recorded that though Mary 'was not hostile to my political views, she did not share them'. In fact his views included a sort of amalgam of D.H. Lawrence and Karl Marx that blamed capitalism for inhibiting the relationship between the sexes, 'poisoning it with a false idealism that encouraged only the self-conscious and cerebral sides of our nature'. To this extent he was repudiating his years of courtship, years which the backward-looking Mary regarded with much fondness.

Mary was still a Liberal, but she inherited her father's conservative temperament. She had a countrywoman's suspicion of change and thought the present rather better than the future and rather worse than the past. She had formed her tastes, persuasions and prejudices and relished the familiar and the traditional. She was loyal and reliable and her modest, private exterior concealed great love. She did not share Cecil's intellectual curiosity and was not attracted as he was by his expanding horizon and public fame.

It was ironic that Cecil should have been spending the first six months of his new life working at a novel to be called *The Friendly Tree*, pausing only to write an introduction for *Poems of Strife*, a Lawrence and Wishart revolutionary anthology edited by Julius Lipton and published in May. The novel is an autobiographical story telling, with no disguise of detail, about his courtship and marriage and concluding that whatever his other adventures Mary would always be home, the familiar country where he was rooted. The book was finished on 9 June and that evening he and Mary and their friends the Hallidays went to the Plough at Tewkesbury for a celebration dinner.

Cecil was now attempting to gather support for his move to persuade the Society of Authors to affiliate with the Trades Union Congress. Among those he tried to recruit was his hero among living novelists, E.M. Forster. The Cambridge man replied that as 'an old-fashioned liberal, if anything, I'm in my usual dilemma, and I don't like the idea of imposing an anti-Fascist test on a non-political organization. And this it seems to me, is what would happen if the Society of Authors was affiliated to the TUC.'

At the annual meeting of the Society at 21 Gower Street on 24 June, Charles King, a Greek translator, proposed 'that a committee shall revise the rules of the Society in such a way as to qualify it for affiliation to the TUC and that this having been done the Society shall apply for such affilia-tion'. Cecil, seconding the motion, said that it would 'put authors in a stronger position for agitating for the amelioration of the highly unsatisfac-tory libel laws'. He suggested also that 'a popular front of writers should be formed to combat the increasing danger of Fascism. The fate of authors in Italy and Germany should be sufficient indication of the necessity for organization and unity.'

Lord Gorell, opposing, said there was no case for him to answer as no reasons for affiliation had been put forward. If there were political implica-tions officers would resign. He was supported by Dorothy L. Sayers and St John Ervine, and the pro-affiliation speakers included Amabel Williams-Ellis (an editor of *Left Review*) and Raymond Postgate. At the end the chair-man, Major Ian Hay Beith, called for a show of hands and declared the resolution defeated without a count being necessary. Only in the 1970s did the Society become affiliated.

Next day Cecil wrote to Rupert Hart-Davis declaring himself 'more pleased than I can say' that *The Friendly Tree* was liked: 'I was really quite frightened about it.' He added that 'the meeting yesterday was indescrib-able: Lord Gorell must be the biggest snake outside the Zoological Gardens – a real twister; however we got about 15 votes against 35 or so, which wasn't bad'.

He was now writing a weekly novel review column for the *Daily Tele-*

graph, whose readers were not burdened with the news that L.A.G. Strong was his greatest benefactor and that Strong's new novel *The Last Enemy* was set at Summer Fields preparatory school where they had been teaching colleagues. On 3 July Cecil reviewed his friend's book below A.E.W. Mason's *Fire Over England* and Seán O'Faoláin's *Bird Alone*. He described Strong as 'a novelist for whom I have real respect. He possesses to a remarkable degree the power of disinterested observation; he handles scenes of violence with just the right mixture of tact and brutality; there is generally more to his novels than meets the eye.' After a plot summary Cecil judged that 'Mr Strong's studies of boys and masters in a happy school are excellent', and after minor complaints about faulty construction in one place and lack of detail in another he told his readers, 'I enjoyed this book as much as you will.'

The following Friday, 10 July, Cecil reviewed Rosamond Lehmann's fourth novel, *The Weather in the Streets*. He had lately met her for the first time at his novelist friend Elizabeth Bowen's London house and had invited her to be a guest at the Cheltenham Literary Society annual banquet the following October: in five years' time they were to become very close. Cecil described her now as 'a very talented writer indeed'. But he went on to say, 'I doubt myself whether she will ever be in the same class as Virginia Woolf, Constance Holme, Rebecca West, Elizabeth Bowen and Margiad Evans – the five women writers of today whose originality is beyond question.' He commended her 'remarkable flair for dialogue', her 'vivid and decorative, neo-romantic manner' and her exceeding cleverness. She could be criticized on points of style, though in fact Cecil found only one over-ambitious phrase to criticize, but her book was 'a notable achievement'.

At the beginning of that fateful July, on the strength of the acceptance of *The Friendly Tree*, Cecil had bought a car, an open-top Morris 8. It was used to transport the family to a holiday at Lyme Regis. Cecil was there, mucking about in boats and mackerel fishing, when the Spanish Civil War broke out.

Stephen Spender wrote on 1 September, announcing that he had finished his book *Forward from Liberalism* and suggesting that Cecil might like to write political notes as a regularly monthly feature for *Left Review*. 'Of course, I realize that the financial sacrifice for you is far greater than for me, if you do free work. But I think if we give *Left Review* backing, it should certainly be possible to double its circulation, and in that case it will be able to pay contributors. Also, I don't think that such notes should be very difficult for you, as you do have plenty to say about contemporary events, I imagine.'

Cecil readily agreed to this; because of the war in Spain his political self was more committed than ever. Yet it was also in this month that the third edition of *A Hope for Poetry* was published with a new postscript commending the 1935 *Poems* of the sceptical Louis MacNeice as 'in some ways the

most interesting' book of verse in the previous two years. His peroration
ended revealingly:

The function of those who uphold the ideal of pure poetry is, by their insistence
on form and integrity, to correct the tendency of the rest of us to mistake gush
for vigour and substitute rhetoric for imagination. Between the two ideals of
poets today, social justice and artistic integrity, a foundation should be laid for
a poetic future not unworthy of the traditions we have inherited and the society
some of us hope for and are fighting for.

October began for Cecil with the publication of his first straight novel,
The Friendly Tree. There is little Communism about this. The hero Stephen
Hallam is a Red from a Nottinghamshire coal-mining district, with a
courtly brother called 'the Baron', but his efforts to talk politics are constantly cut short by his more important task of courting the heroine Anna
Charteris, and his urban homeland is much less lovingly described than the
wind and sunlight on the hills, the pacing clouds, woods, and the flight
and song of birds on her Cotswolds. Anna is Mary in her looks and manner-
sims, her chaste reservations and her Georgian taste. The very title, preferred by Rupert Hart-Davis to Cecil's original *The Sunny Tree*, refers to
that small oak on the slopes above Sherborne where the youthful Mary
communed with nature. Yet the initial circumstances of Anna are those
which blighted Cecil's youth: she suffers from a widowed father, Edward
Charteris MA, a headmaster, who lives too much in her and asks more reassurance of her in the way of gratitude and attention, obedience and respect,
than she can give.

Cecil later held that his three autobiographical novels of the late 1930s
were bad because it was not until the next decade that he began to be interested in people. They are nevertheless valuable as signposts in his own progress towards self-knowledge, as well as being a repository for his current
social conversation pieces. One of the few favourable reviews came from
L.A.G. Strong. 'The novel has had a rather disheartening reception on the
whole, so yours was the more timely and cheering', Cecil wrote in thanking
him. Strong had lately been in Dublin, and Cecil asked him: 'Do you know
whether I have been turned down for the Irish Academy? – Lennox Robinson wrote to me a month or two ago and said that Yeats was proposing
me, but I've heard nothing since.' In the event Cecil was black-balled for
his Red views.

With W.H. Auden, Paul Engle and Edwin Muir, Cecil wrote an introductory essay for an edition of *Selected Poems by Robert Frost* published
that November by Cape. Inevitably, Geoffrey Grigson in *New Verse* considered Auden's essay 'of interest, the others patronising or commonplace;
Day-Lewis as usual, pompous, artificial, obvious, writing like a respectable
don who has written poems and contributes to the *London Mercury* and
the *Oxford Magazine*'. As to Frost, he was 'as precisely genuine as Day-
Lewis is sincerely Wardour Street'.

Despite Grigson's hostility Cecil was increasingly in demand. So much so that his *We're Not Going to do Nothing*, a pamphlet also published in November as a reply to Aldous Huxley's pacifist declaration *What Are You Going to Do About It?*, was mainly written for him by Rex Warner. That Warner was successful in achieving Cecil's style was confirmed by *New Verse*. Seeing the by-line as a bull sees a red rag, Grigson's magazine found the pamphlet 'badly written, badly argued, badly informed, a silliness answering a silliness in dead terms of literature'.

In *International Literature* the Marxist critic D. Mirsky had unwisely criticized *New Verse* for 'systematically hounding Day-Lewis for what it regards as an excess of Communist loyalty'. This gave Grigson the sort of opening which he relished, to wield his bill-hook in this Christmas number. 'We have not been attacking Day-Lewis for an excess of Communist loyalty', he slashed.

We have been attacking him as a bad poet, a muddled writer distinctly respectable, bourgeois and ordinary in his way of writing which differs altogether from his no doubt sincere political ideology.... Perhaps if Mirsky understood English rather better he would realise the unrevolutionary nature and the downright badness of Day-Lewis's verse in manner and meaning. We recommend him also to have a dip into Mr Day-Lewis's most ordinary, mob-sucking novel *The Friendly Tree* just published.

December 1936, the month of Edward VIII's abdication, was a gloomy one for Cecil. He was feeling low from an attack of bronchitis; and he was feeling guilty because he believed he ought to volunteer to fight in Spain with the International Brigade and he 'lacked the courage to do so', a guilt not damped when Auden told him he was going to Spain in the New Year.

On the twenty-third the family were conveyed northwards for Christmas at Edwinstowe, with both Nick and myself suffering loudly from whooping cough. I have a few isolated memories of this uncomfortable time, in particular of Cecil being given by his father a handsome blackthorn walking-stick, both men hovering awkwardly about each other as the gift was made. As a loyal reader of Cecil's books Frank may well have recognized himself in *The Friendly Tree*, an unflattering portrait including his need for profuse and articulate thanks whenever he gave presents, his 'irritability and tenderness, fun and pomposity, injustice and generosity, censoriousness and indulgence'. I did not pick up anything reproachful in the atmosphere, or any foreboding that this would be the vicar's last Christmas, just an atmosphere of thin ice and people being careful that it should not be broken.

Before the end of January 1937, both Auden and Spender were in Spain, though some way behind the lines. Safe in Cheltenham, Cecil sadly registered the deaths of other literary volunteers, John Cornford and Ralph Fox. Cecil had found Fox, with Mrs Harry Pollitt, one of 'the two most likeable Party high-ups I met – gentle, unbigoted, yet firm-minded personalities, whose devotion to the Cause had not diminished them as human beings'. Later in the year a memorial volume for Fox, 'a writer in arms', was published with a Pollitt introduction, jointly edited by Cecil with John Lehmann and T.A. Jackson.

Marjorie Pollitt was one of the several Party speakers put up at Box Cottage when they came to speak to the tiny Cheltenham cell, or at public meetings, on behalf of the Popular Front. Cecil's cell 'never numbered more than ten or 12' and included 'one or two school-teachers, a waiter and several men who worked at the Gloucester aircraft factory'. Cecil was considered an 'interllectual' and was therefore put in charge of political education. He read *Das Kapital* and the thoughts of Lenin, as well as the Communist Manifesto; he began to half understand the dialectical materialism and economic theories which he was teaching and to learn the 'abstract, inflexible and hideous' Party jargon; but 'never can there have been a more signal instance of the blind leading the short-sighted'. He felt he was fulfilling his need to be part of a close community, and that although he was not sharing the life of the workers, 'I was at least in contact with it now, in a position to learn a little about its manners and exigencies.'

Efforts to involve the local Labour Party in Popular Front activities were 'received with the embarrassment a bishop might show if publicly asked by a tart to contribute money to a good cause'. Cecil mostly left to others the tasks of distributing leaflets and selling the *Daily Worker*, and when there was a cancellation of a planned open-air meeting by the fountains in the Promenade, at which he was to introduce the chief speaker, 'my shame at the feeling of relief was almost as great as the relief I felt'. He had 'steeled' himself to speaking in halls all over the country, but to judge by the observation of Louis MacNeice was not quite a firebrand:

One evening there was a gathering of some 50 people – mainly writers – to oppose Fascism. Day-Lewis and Goronwy [Rees] were the speakers. Day-Lewis spoke first, in his tired Oxford accent, qualifying everything, nonplussed, questioning. Then G, who was just as Oxonian as D-L, took over and spoke like a revivalist, flashed his eyes, quivered with emotion, led with his Left and followed with his Left, punch on punch, dogma on dogma, over and over-statement, washed in the blood of – well, nobody asked of whom, but it certainly made you stop thinking.[9]

At Cheltenham Cecil was appreciated. A fellow member, Mrs M. Timms, said she thought of him as chairman of the branch: 'He was a very valuable and conscientious comrade, extremely modest and very well liked', she wrote. 'I can vividly remember him singing and reciting at our monthly socials, when there were about forty active members. He also helped produce very successful plays such as Clifford Odets' *Waiting for Lefty* and *Where's That Bomb?*'

For a time he wrote, as Stephen Spender had suggested the previous September, a monthly political 'Topic of the Month' for the *Left Review*, mostly calling on sympathetic writers to join with Communists in opposing Fascism. In the November issue he had suggested that the 'Fascist bluff' should be called. The 'anti-Fascist countries' had more arms and indeed 'the preponderance is so enormous that even a maniac like Mussolini would not dare challenge it – let alone a comparatively cautious man like Hitler'. In the same number he had 'dared assert that, if a play like *Waiting for Lefty* had been performed for the benefit of the TUC at Plymouth its emotional effect would have swept away the sophistries of the Citrines and the Bevins'.

In June of 1937 he brought his readers nearer home with an article headlined 'Goings-on in Gloucestershire'. He revealed that Lord Bathurst, 'the biggest (and most reactionary) landowner' in the county was trying to set up local militia units for defence against the Germans. 'The biggest laugh of all is that some local Blimp has offered £100 for the equipment of the units with red coats, which would make them more attractive to the girls of the village.' There had been 'slanderous statements' at the Cheltenham and District Peace Council that the militia was being set up with 'Moscow gold'. In fact the backers were the English Mystery, 'a ludicrous association of high-hats drawn from the landed gentry' and believing in 'aristocratic dictatorship'. It is hard to know whether the article constitutes investigative journalism or a fictional germ for the Nicholas Blake thriller *The Smiler with the Knife* (1939), dealing with the threat to national security of 'the English Banner'.

In the first months of 1937 Cecil was also working on a Socialist symposium *The Mind in Chains* to be published that year by Frederick Muller. One of the contributors, Edgell Rickword, had recruited others. They included Anthony Blunt, exposed in 1979 as a former spy for the Soviet Union, and who here wrote on 'Socialist Realism in Painting'. 'I think it's going to be quite a decent little book: some of the essays are excellent', Cecil wrote to his editorial assistant Brian Harvey from Sherborne in April. Among the other writers were Rex Warner, Edward Upward, Arthur Calder-Marshall, Alan Bush, Charles Madge and J.D. Bernal. Cecil's introduction evokes the preface to *Prometheus Unbound* and contrasts Shelley's 'exalted and just vision of the human mind' with the capitalism that 'has converted the physician, the lawyer, the priest, the poet, the man of science, into its paid wage labourers'. He says that the symposium 'could never have been written were it not for the widespread belief of intellectual workers that the mind is really in chains to-day, that these chains have been forged by a dying social system, that they can and must be broken – and in the Soviet Union have been broken; and that we can only realize our strength by joining forces with the millions of workers who have nothing to lose but their chains and have a world to win'.

Cecil's political views were regarded as eccentric rather than dangerous by the townsfolk and neighbours who knew him. Living next door to Box

Cottage were the Hopcrafts, an old brewing family from Northampton-shire. The ebullient, bullish Teddy owned and managed the Cheltenham Original Brewery which later disappeared into the Whitbread group, and he and Cecil shared the services of a gardener called Bloxam, Communist and capitalist alike paying 7s 6d a day for his help. Cecil preferred not to have a wireless set or any newspaper but the *Daily Worker* at Box Cottage, so Mary was often with her friend Joyce Hopcraft listening, or reading Cecil's novel reviews in the *Daily Telegraph*.

Nicholas Blake's 1937 detective novel, *There's Trouble Brewing*, was dedicated to Joyce and Teddy and researched with several visits to the Cheltenham Original Brewery. It includes a fisherman called Bloxam. The germ of the story came from Teddy, whose father had known of an incident where a worker died through falling into an open, boiling, copper vat. Blake places his action at Maiden Astbury in Dorset, a Hardy country town where Nigel Strangeways is invited to lecture the local literary society on the strength of his 'little book on the Caroline poets'. The novel has a breathless finale in which there is a threat that the brewery will blow up with all the main characters inside. There is not much in the book to indicate troubled times, much less a Marxist author, but, as Nigel puts it, the case 'does add force to a certain cliché – there's trouble brewing'.

Some time in 1936, Cecil had publicly thanked Hugh Walpole for his encouragement of young writers, and in subsequent correspondence had added that this was 'a nice change after the denunciations of St John Ervine, Priestley, etc.!' In February 1937 Walpole invited Cecil to join the selection committee of the Book Society, started with Walpole as chairman in 1928.

Cecil knew this invitation placed him in difficulty. The fee would be useful, he regarded it as an honour to have been asked, and he would have an opportunity of influencing public reading habits. Against this the Book Society was considered in radical literary quarters to be safe, bourgeois and respectable, part of 'the System' he was supposed to be fighting. Also the extra work would give him less time for writing verse. He sent Walpole an equivocal reply and asked the Communist Party for advice.

The Party said that Cecil should accept, should join anything which took him nearer the corridors of power; and he wrote to Walpole again saying, 'Very well: I'll sign on, and gladly.' Cecil remained troubled. 'I've just said I would join the selection committee of the Book Society; Walpole was pressing about it: I feel I may have been a b.f. to do so, what do you think? Still, I can always resign', he wrote to Leonard Strong.

It was in May, the month of George VI's Coronation and the arrival of Neville Chamberlain as Prime Minister, that Geoffrey Grigson treated his *New Verse* readers to the news that Cecil had sold out. 'C. Day-Lewis, the poet (a member of the International Association of Writers for the Defence of Culture), has joined the selection committee of the Book Society', he announced.

On this committee Mr Day-Lewis no doubt will be Change, Revolution, Youth, the Rising Generation. But this ends his stance as the Poet writing thrillers (result: respectful knowing reviews of each thriller) and establishes him as the Thriller Writer, the Underworld Man, the yesterday's newspaper, the grease in the sink-pipe of letters who has posed for ten years as a spring water. Think of Hardy, Yeats, Housman, Flecker, Pound, Lawrence, Eliot, Graves, Auden, Spender, Madge – could one have gone so treasonably against what is real? Mr Day-Lewis and his Legend are now liquidated: the liquid has flowed to its only shape and low level in the old sardine tin of Respectability. Mr Lewis has drained himself off, a Noyes, a Binyon, a Squire, a dullard. We can get along without him.

Visitors to Box Cottage in the first months of the year included Amabel Williams-Ellis, the *Left Review* editor working for Spanish Medical Aid; Rebecca West, who spoke to the Literary Society about travel writing; and W.H. Auden who had returned to England at the beginning of March. Wystan had not served, as he had expected, as an ambulance driver in Spain. He had been in Barcelona and Valencia doing some propaganda broadcasting for the Republicans, but he did not feel that he had been useful. When he signed the Box Cottage visitor's book after his one night stay on 1 April his handwriting was shaky and had lost the tiny but sure formation of previous entries. He continued to believe with Cecil that Franco must be fought, but the anti-religious bias he had encountered on the Republican side had disturbed him. He did his best to conceal his doubts from Cecil and worked on at his 'Spain' poem, published in May in aid of Spanish Medical Aid. The more zealous supporters of the Popular Front were nevertheless disappointed that the poem proved to be so detached.

While others fought and died Auden went back to Colwall for a therapeutic summer term of teaching at the Downs School, and Cecil took Mary to stay at Lyme Regis, and to order a new sailing dinghy at nearby Weymouth. They were in Lyme on 26 April, the day before his thirty-third birthday, the day Franco's German bombers reduced Guernica, the Holy City of the Basques, to rubble.

In June there was a by-election at Cheltenham, and the local Labour Party became less embarrassed by Communist support for its candidate. Cecil took the chair at a Charlton Kings pre-polling meeting on 21 June, and introduced the Labour leader Clement Attlee with an idealistic speech. Next day he drove his Morris 8 about the town, so enveloped by red rosettes that at one point it boiled over. The result was an easy win for the Conservative-supported candidate.

On 24 June Knos arrived from Ireland, and six days later she and the family departed for a month at Lyme Regis. We lived in a house in Coram Avenue with a view across the sea to Golden Cap and the lesser peaks of the Dorset cliffs, which would be featured in Nicholas Blake's *The Beast*

Must Die (1938). On 7 July he was able to write to L.A.G. Strong about his second straight novel, *Starting Point*, dedicated to Leonard and Sylvia.

I'm sending off today or tomorrow a proof of my novel: the general feeling about it (shared by myself) is that there are some good things in it but it doesn't hang together: you and Sylvia will have to take the good parts as your own, and grin and bear the rest. I'd be very interested to hear any technical (or any) criticisms you have of it. . . . We're having a bumper time here: I've bought a sailing-dinghy, so prayers for those in peril on the sea would not come amiss.

We returned to Cheltenham on 28 July and early next morning Cecil was woken by the telephone. Mamie was on the line from Edwinstowe to say that Frank had died in the night from a quite unexpected coronary thrombosis.

I drove straight up to Edwinstowe, feeling numb – no need to harden my heart any more against the associations of home-coming. I turned right, from the Edwinstowe-Mansfield road, into the drive. On my left was the vegetable garden where my father had harried a succession of gardeners; then the herbaceous border, tactlessly blazing now with summer flowers; then the tennis lawn, with its pergolas of rambler roses on one side and on the other a steep grass bank rising up to the rose garden and the house.

Frank had come to stay at Box Cottage for the last time on 12 April. He was stooped then and grey and a little pot-bellied as he approached his sixtieth birthday; disappointed by many things, maybe a touch jealous that even his uncouth brother-in-law Willie Squires had lately been preferred, as Chancellor of the Irish diocese of Ferns; enjoying the reflected glory of Cecil's success and yet wishing that his son wrote 'proper books', regretting that they had for so long been on different wavelengths. 'It was typical of my warped attitude towards him that when he told me that his health had deteriorated, and that doctors had told him to take things easier, my immediate reaction was to dismiss this as just another appeal for sympathy,' Cecil confessed.

He now found Mamie 'grieving bitterly' and, though she had plenty, worrying about money. He found Frank lying on the bed 'from which last night he had half fallen in his sudden death-agony, decently composed now, with lilies beside him and a crucifix stuck in his folded hands'. Cecil cast a cool eye on death, his feelings too confused and contradictory to surface. 'I had never seen a dead person before, and had not known how small the dead look: my father's head seemed to have shrunk, and his face was the face, almost, of a stranger – a waxwork face which looked so remote from the living, the human, that it made death all the more impenetrable a mystery. I held the back of my hand against his cheek for a few moments, then I left him.'

Cecil registered the death at Ollerton and comforted his stepmother as best he could, with pity rather than love. 'A day or two later – on a burning, brilliant morning', they followed Frank's coffin through the wicket gate, across the meadow where father and son used to punt a rugby ball together at Christmas-time, and so into the churchyard. Mamie 'leant on my arm, and I felt as dry and emotionless as if I had been her solicitor or my father's undertaker'. After the service the body was put in a motor hearse and 'conveyed half-way across England' to be laid in Mamie's family tomb at Bath. 'I drove her there behind the hearse – an interminable journey through the blazing heat of that day – in the last of my father's long sequence of second-hand cars.'

For years after this Cecil continued to dream of his father and their love-hate relationship. Even in 1960 he could write that he was still finding traces of Frank in himself: 'inherited characteristics, and the marks of my first and longest ordeal by love. I can pray now that, when alive, he did not know how much both he and I had to forgive each other for.'

> Oh, black frost of my youth, recalcitrant time
> When love's seed was benighted and gave no ear
> To others' need, you were seasonable, you were
> In nature: but were you as well my nature's blight?*

He returned to Cheltenham on 6 August and was somewhat cheered by L. A. G. Strong's response to his *Starting Point*. He wrote thanking him:

Many thanks for your letter: it delighted and encouraged me no end – I'd begun to take a very depressed view about the book, what with one thing and another. I think you're right about the wine-stain, it's a manufactured sort of repetition – the kind of thing that looks all right in a detective novel but nowhere else. I still like Theo's shooting of his mother best in the book: it was a sort of deliberate accident, like those slips of the tongue that psychologists revel in. I was afraid that the middle section, starting with Anthony's leaving Windover, dragged rather badly: but if it kept you interested I'd ask no further reassurance about it.

I've had rather a lousy time lately, with my father's funeral, and all his affairs in a bit of a mess, and fobbing off deputations of sobbing parishioners. Mary is off to Scotland next week, and I shall settle down to some stern dinghy-sailing on the Severn. Rex Warner's *Wild Goose Chase* is coming out next month – I shall be glad to hear what you think of it.

Cecil began to spend more time at Oxford. His *The Mind in Chains* symposium had been published in June. He was now preparing a three-volume verse anthology for children, *The Echoing Green*, commissioned by the Oxford publisher Basil Blackwell. In selecting and introducing this he exercised what he called 'the measure of intuition and experience which any teacher of English will be able to draw upon after eight years' work with children of 11 to 14'. He acknowledged that 'taste' was only learned after tasting everything, and so he included narrative, dramatic, satiric, religious,

* 'Son and Father' (*Pegasus*, 1957).

lyric and comic verse; the sonnet, the epigram, the epitaph, the ballad, the folk song, the madrigal and the nonsense rhyme.

At the same time he was working with Charles Fenby on their *Anatomy of Oxford*. Maybe 'working' is too strong a word: Fenby's perhaps partial memory was that he gathered together almost all the material for this compilation of town and gown oddities, while Cecil chiefly supplied his selling name. 'One day I said, look here you must be able to say you have contributed something to this book, go and look something up in the Union Library. He got into a terrible state about this, said he was not a member of the Union and might be challenged by one of the stewards there. He had a strong sense of propriety and of property', remembered Fenby. Against this the preface makes much of 'the pleasure this work gave its compilers ... the joys of research are simply the joys of Eden before the Fall, pure self indulgence. As you browse away one rich pasture leads to another yet more delectable – and the Oxford meadows are evergreen as the Elysian.'

Whatever the truth about the proportion of work, Cecil appreciated the chance of observing the Oxford community through 'the good sense, the informedness and seriousness' of its newspaper editor. He found Fenby both calming and stimulating and 'admired his sober questioning of many of my own flightier opinions, both political and literary', so different from the 'logical yet violent unorthodoxy' of Rex Warner.

During this time the *Sunday Times* reported a 'proctorial faux pas in the Royal Oak public house, when youthful-looking Mr Day-Lewis and a friend were mistaken for undergraduates'. Cecil had been 'engaged in a shove ha'penny contest when the proctorial cortège entered and attempted to "prog" the poet'. The writer added that the incident had 'afforded young Oxford an opportunity of airing an old grievance against the system which prohibits the undergraduate to frequent the bar of any hotel, restaurant or tavern under risk of a heavy fine'.

At evenings and weekends Fenby gave Cecil what he described as 'my first grown-up contact with the English countryman', a contact which was sufficiently detached to enable him to see this 'solid and sly' breed as a romantic generalization, a kind of human being whose voice and movements communicated 'the regular rhythm of a life under the seasons' and was 'robustly all-of-a-piece'. His rootedness and single-mindedness, real or imagined, were enviable qualities to Cecil. 'Imperceptibly, a longing for the countryside, for some more rooted life, began to grow within me', Cecil remembered.

He was able to see the Oxfordshire landscape overhung with 'an elegiac air, a melancholy I found haunting and enervating, which flowed perhaps from the contrast between these long settled places and the deepening insecurity of the world that lay about them, and which reflected itself in the weedy fields, the roof-rent barns, the exhaustion and dilapidation caused by ten years of agricultural decay'. In other words his natural response to the run-down of British agriculture was passive and poetical rather than active and political, and that after hardly a year in the Communist Party.

He spent more time sailing his new dinghy on the Severn; and in the middle of August began looking for a new house in the country, thinking that Oxfordshire or Berkshire would provide 'a life under the seasons' conveniently close to London.

The second Cape novel, *Starting Point*, was published in September. Its dislocated plot was designed to explain British decadence in both Freudian and Marxist terms. The story ends with Cecil's favourite character Anthony Neale, the aspect of himself the author approved at the time, having reached the starting point: bound to working-class comrades 'by the steel cables of action, the filaments of belief', bound to the hands 'which would guide a new world struggling out of the womb'. The novel is helped along with intimations of incestuous love, homosexuality, and ostentatious self-indulgence in art for art's sake.

The character John Henderson has experiences precisely similar to those of Cecil as an Oxford undergraduate during the General Strike and as an employee called to account for his socialist principles. Another character, the 'aesthetic' novelist Theodore Follett, suffers the bullying that Cecil endured at Sherborne. But it is the noble Anthony who conquers his terror of street soap-box speaking, which used to mean that 'for days beforehand fear had gnawed like an ulcer at his stomach', before going off to fight for the International Brigade in Spain.

Cecil did not believe the novel to be very satisfactory, despite Leonard Strong's encouragement, and was surprised to receive an enthusiastic letter from Edward Sackville-West in Vienna: 'I read a great many novels, one way and another (it is a novelist's duty), but I don't think I ever read one which, in its particular way, was more thoroughly successful.'

Geoffrey Grigson had ended his May onslaught against Cecil, 'the grease in the sink-pipe of letters', with the declaration that 'we can get along without him'. In view of this Cecil was astonished to receive a letter from Grigson that autumn asking for a contribution to the proposed November double number of *New Verse* devoted to W.H. Auden. Cecil replied with a dignity not altogether concealing the wounds which Grigson had inflicted on him.

I have been away, and only got your letter this afternoon. I imagine it is too late now, in any case, to send you a contribution: apart from that, I still don't see how you feel that any honour could be done to Auden by a contribution from someone you believe to have lost his own, to have taken the handful of silver, and in general out-squired Squire. I realise that it is not sending a message to you, and I will try and do something if Thursday of next week would not be too late for you to receive it: I'm full up with work till Wednesday; if that is too late, you might care to ask the Hogarth Press would they mind your reprinting my 'Epistle to W.H.A.' from *Feathers to Iron* – or a few lines out of it. I should not like personalities to get in the way of any tribute we can pay to Auden, though you must admit the personalities have been all on your side.

About the Book Society. The postscript to your letter suggests that I should make you some return in the way of explanation. It is quite arguable that the idea of Book Societies is wrong, though I'm not convinced of it myself. I joined the committee in order to be able to get the work of younger and less popular writers across to the B.S. public: I felt it was legitimate to do this, just as you might use the *Morning Post* or *New Verse* for that purpose. I admit that the financial organisation of the B.S. makes it difficult for them to choose a book likely to be unpopular, but the Recommended list has some effect too. Since I joined, they have chosen or recommended three books which I believe to be good in their kinds, and which they would not have been very likely to notice if I had not pressed for them – *Letters from Iceland, Wild Goose Chase,* and Isherwood's new story. I have found the committee scrupulous in the attention they give to the books that come before them; but then, even before I joined, I never believed that Blunden – for instance – was an opportunist crook. As to the political aspect of it, I consulted my own Party authorities before joining the B.S. and they agreed that it was a reasonable way of trying to bring Left books to the attention of people who would not normally look at them. Nor was Auden in the least shocked by my joining this committee – or, for that matter, by my writing detective novels, another thing which you resent, I believe.

No doubt the Book Society is, looked at from one angle, a racket: but so are the 'literary' pages of daily papers: one has either to stand right outside the racket, or else to use it (as you used your position on the *Morning Post*) to get the better stuff over to ordinary readers. I may have been wrong in taking this course: but you had no justification for assuming so flippantly that my motives were careerist. I knew perfectly well that there would be an outcry from those who automatically give a raspberry whenever the B.S. is mentioned: I can assure you, though, that the committee members are not all people who say 'A grunt would serve as well' – and, even if they were, there would be no harm adding to their number one person who does not think like that. And, as I say, I prefer Auden as a critic of my actions to someone like yourself, who seems to have allowed some personal rancour to replace objective criticism of my own work during the last few years.

I hope you will allow yourself to consider the possibility that, though I may have been misguided, I have not been dishonest: and, if so, let us drop this squabbling and criticise each other – when we must – on rational, not prejudiced, grounds. You will understand that the substance of this letter is absolutely confidential.

Cecil's tribute duly appeared, recalling that 'I met Auden first at Oxford 11 years ago: I knew very soon that he was and would be the best poet of my generation and I have never had any reason to change my mind.' He also continued on the Book Society selection committee. 'I've just received marching orders from the *Telegraph* – owing to the amalgamation, they say: so it looks as if I shall have to prop myself up on the Book Society a bit longer', he wrote to Leonard Strong. The *Daily Telegraph* swallowed the *Morning Post* on 1 October.

Cecil was nevertheless feeling sufficiently comfortable to trade in his exhausted Morris 8 and use what money he inherited from his father on a handsome new Hillman Minx coupé. In this he made several journeys to Bournemouth where his widowed stepmother was settling into the hideous turreted and spired Branksome Chine house which she called 'Edwinstowe'.

Nicholas Blake's 1938 detective story, sparked by seeing me nearly run over by a car, was *The Beast Must Die*, critically acclaimed as among the two or three most successful he wrote. It has sold nearly 300,000 copies in five hard- and paperback editions in the United States, more than any other Blake work; and in Britain it has sold nearly 135,000 copies in three editions, achieving commercial success only exceeded by *A Question of Proof* (1935) and *The Case of the Abominable Snowman* (1941). It is the only Blake novel adapted for the cinema, having been used by the distinguished French director Claude Chabrol for his 1969 movie, *Que La Bête Meure*, a Franco-Italian co-production.

Although the film is shot on location in Brittany and is very French, with a plot transformed by Paul Gegauff's screenplay, it does use the voice of the English contralto Kathleen Ferrier singing Brahms's Opus 121 songs, *Vier Ernste Gesänge*. This was the work Cecil learnt at Oxford with W.H. Auden as his 'loud, confident but wonderfully inaccurate' piano accompanist, and it was from this work that he extracted his title, the composer paraphrasing Ecclesiastes 3.19, as 'The beast must die, the man dieth also, yea both must die.'

Dedicated to L.P. Hedges' widow Jinnie, and her new husband Tony Osborne, the story starts and ends at Lyme Regis though it is otherwise set in Gloucestershire. A detective novel writer called Frank Cairnes is discovered by Nigel Strangeways to have murdered the rat-like hit-and-run driver who killed Cairnes's son, and is finally allowed by the humane detective to escape trial and die in his dinghy out on Lyme Bay 'fighting a clean enemy for a change – the wind and the waves'.

As the New Year dawned Cecil was still an active politician, going hither and thither with Rex Warner, both of them still looking, to such a sceptical observer as V.S. Pritchett, 'starry-eyed and very exalted' and rather proud in their public school exclusivity. Underneath this façade Charles Fenby's realism was beginning to take effect.

'Faced with the choice of being an amateurish political worker or trying to make myself a better poet – a dilemma in which my poetic habit seemed hopelessly at odds with genuine public spiritedness – I as usual prevaricated and procrastinated', remembered Cecil. When it came upon him his revulsion from his political self, though not from Communism, 'was almost apocalyptic'.

It happened during an anti-Fascist meeting at the Queen's Hall in London, soon to be destroyed by German bombs, at which Cecil was down to speak on the warping of children's minds in Germany and Italy and was only one of several well-known writers on the platform. On his feet he found himself 'possessed of a spirit and a fluency greater than I had ever had before, on such occasions, experienced'. At the end the applause and the comments of his friends told him that he had spoken with 'considerable power'. He was not gratified, for half-way through his speech, by his own account, 'I seemed to detach myself from the man who was so eloquently holding forth, to hover above my own shoulder and with X-ray eyes to look penetratingly down. I heard myself speaking – with sincerity and fervour: I saw myself enjoying the exercise of power over an audience: it was a good cause, and I could approve of every word I was saying, yet to my detached self up there it was as though reality had evaporated out of the performance. When I sat down, all in one piece again, I distinctly heard above the applause a small voice saying three or four times inside my head, "It won't do, it just won't do."'

He continued with his political work for some months after this, but he had decided that although 'it was the right thing to do, I am the wrong person to be doing it'. In February he began looking, without success, for a Thames Valley house: not so much because he wanted to live in the country, more because, as he said, he hoped to be able to cut himself off from meetings, committees and the day-to-day work of the Party

On 12 April he and Mary began an Easter holiday in Dorset, planned mainly to give her mother a breath of sea air at Lyme Regis, but with a vague idea that they might find a home in the area. Two days later they crossed the border into Devon and found a house which seemed to have been planted on a hillside specially for them. They had decided to buy 'Woodlands', above the Axe Valley village of Musbury, even before they took Connie King for a second look on Easter Tuesday. They returned to Cheltenham and negotiated a loan of the necessary £1,600 on the strength of Mary's securities. By 9 May, the day on which Cecil reached the half-way mark of his life, he knew that in the summer he would be able to take his muse, and his family, where he was sure they could belong.

For the next three months he continued with his somewhat public and political way of life. He took the chair at a meeting to draw attention to Japanese aggression in China; he lectured in Wolverhampton on Byron, and worked on his Byronic narrative about an episode of the Spanish Civil War, 'The Nabara'; he spoke at Left Book Club branches and continued to write committed articles for the *Left Review*. In July, most surprisingly, he was persuaded to leave the British Isles for the first time in his life, to attend a Paris weekend rally organized for the Popular Front by the International Association of Writers for the Defence of Culture, 'For Peace and Against the Bombardment of Open Cities'. Cecil had played a leading part in establishing the Association's British section and was now chairman of an executive committee that included Harold Laski, Rose Macaulay, Kingsley Martin, Goronwy Rees, Hugh Walpole and Rebecca West.

He crossed the English Channel with Rex Warner and a strong prejudice against both the French and all intellectuals: the former prejudice was part of the reaction of his generation against the uncritically reverent view of French culture taken by the preceding generation; the latter set up by Warner himself as he went through his earlier anti-Establishment phase. As Cecil put it, 'A certain perversity in his mind, together with his broader interests and his predilection for the more raffish bar-room types, rendered him intolerant of intellectuals, in whom he found a clique-mentality both shallow and pretentious.' By the time he got back to Cheltenham on 26 July, after only four days away, Cecil's prejudices were more deeply ingrained than ever.

Warner remembered that Cecil made him 'come to the conference and sat there refusing to say a word of French to anybody'. His insistence that all French intellectuals were both tedious and insufferably pretentious was well fed by the Communist poet Louis Aragon, who advised at length that the English comrades should make an alliance against the forces of reaction with the Royal Family. Cecil nodded towards English writers he knew, including Rosamond Lehmann, who was there with Goronwy Rees and the Soviet-seduced spy Guy Burgess, but he and Warner largely kept to their own company. John Lehmann was one of those who noted Cecil 'stonily watching' while such as Aragon, André Malraux and Ilya Ehrenburg held forth: a marked contrast with Stephen Spender, an ardent attender of writers' conferences, glowing 'like an illuminated Shelley'.[10]

If Spender was glowing, it was because he enjoyed the give and take of free speech, not because he was committed to Marxism. Soon he would be instrumental in detaching Cecil from any dogmatic belief about a beautiful future based on the model of Stalin's Soviet Union. Clearly the bright-eyed days were over: Auden had spent the first seven months of the year travelling with Isherwood in China and the United States, deciding to abandon the struggles of his native land; MacNeice maintained his morose political silence; Spender had evidently moved so little forward from Liberalism that he could return there with almost imperceptible movement. Cecil was at least sufficiently obstinate not to see Stalin and Hitler as much of a muchness: the struggle to achieve belief had been a difficult one and he was now loth to let go. To some extent he remained a believer when, on 2 August, he 'noiselessly slipped the painter'. Next day I was given my seventh birthday party in the very long grass which was the lawn of our hideaway home in Devon.

The village of Musbury nestles comfortably in the lower eastern slope of the Axe Valley, half way between the small carpet-making market town of Axminster and the English Channel at Axmouth and Seaton. Above

the village rises the 577 foot hill known as Musbury Castle, taking its name
from the Iron Age camp fort whose mud walls are still to be found at
its crown.

Brimclose, as Mary and Cecil renamed their house, was originally two
cottages, built perhaps 300 years before to house the gamekeepers and
foresters of the local Drake estate. It is a long low building with massive
stone and cob walls and a thatched roof, not so much perched on the hillside
as strongly-rooted, a natural growth and a refuge which the president of
the immortals had designed to be there. The grounds of three and a half
acres included a cider-apple orchard, from the top of which it was possible
to look down the valley to the sea and the great chalk cliff-face of Beer
Head; and a neglected tennis court on which the previous owners kept
goats.

Inside there was a long living-room with low oak beams and king posts,
stone-floored and rush-matted with a large, copper-hooded fireplace, providing cool in summer and draughts in winter. The water supply was reliable, from a spring rising above the house. There was no electricity or piped
gas or telephone, and the cottage had a damp and inadequate lean-to kitchen
at one end, and a similar bathroom at the other.

> To another bathroom, shires and years away –
> A makeshift one tacked on to
> The end of a cottage, it smelt of rusting pipes,
> Damp plaster. . . . *

Electricity and telephone were ordered, and had to be wired half a mile
up from the village; an architect and builders were instructed to build a
new kitchen with guest room above; and Cecil and Mary together went
to work on the wilderness of the garden. 'The clearing of our neglected
land at Musbury during the first year there – rooting up great patches of
nettles, attacking overgrown hedges with a bill-hook, cutting down a few
old trees, sawing them up, splitting the logs with beetle and wedge – all
this gave me intense satisfaction . . . as though I were clearing my own life
of tangles, excrescences, dead wood, rank growths', Cecil remembered. He
did not have a moment of regret for the old life left behind: 'All that
mattered to me was the present, into which I had escaped after so much
living in the future.' Temporarily he felt, as he always would when moving
to a new home, 'born again'.

For a few months, as warm summer turned to damp autumn, as south-
westerly gales began battering at the front of the house, and rain turned
the steep, deep lane behind into a water-course, it looked as though Cecil
might have reached his real home, the place where he could at last put down
roots. Brimclose gave him and Mary a new bond, something to be com-
panionable about besides their two sons. They even shared a bedroom,

* 'Stephanotis' (*The Room*, 1965).

though their beds were in opposite corners of it, a room transfused with morning light as the sun rose over Musbury Castle. Here, the literary-minded could say, was a writer beginning to acknowledge that his true poetic place was in the English tradition of natural, pastoral poetry; a poet now shedding his chrysalis composed of Auden and Owen and Hopkins influence, elliptical syntax and syncopated rhythms and Eliot waste product; showing his true colours in the clear, earthy, knowing, brooding influence of Thomas Hardy, well placed to review new territory on the western margin of South Wessex. If there was an ideal home for such a poet he must have found it on this harmonious hillside. Yet before his first year at Brimclose was completed he knew that even this place could not heal his divided mind.

Switch love, move house – you will soon be back where you started,
On the same ground,
With a replica of the old romantic phantom
That will confound
Your need for roots with a craving to be unrooted.*

Cecil's first letters from Brimclose give a good idea of his state of mind. One, on 24 September, was to Frank Halliday, his comrade schoolmaster at Cheltenham, '... this war has been coming so long we shan't be sorry to get the bloody thing over and done with: it is, I must say, both gratifying and disconcerting to find Marxist theory working out like a chemical experiment before our eyes, though no doubt it would be more fun if we didn't have to supply the material for the experiment ourselves', he wrote.

We are living a wonderfully escapist life here, which I must say suits me just for a change. The local pub is excellent, full of Shropshire Lads and foul-mouthed veteran rose-pruners: my form at darts has been quite electrifying, and every now and then I put in a dirty crack at Chamberlain, which is received very well for this sort of pocket of Liberalism – they all read the *News Chronicle*, for instance. I have not seen much of the local gentry yet, but there is a house not far from us called 'Ruma Kita', which must contain something pretty fierce, and further across the hill lives with his French wife an artist who has, I am told, been hung at the Royal Academy. So what? I hear some queerish tales in the pub about the local upper crust, which appeal both to my love of scandal and my sense of the class-war. Our bath-water, by the way, has taken to rising up out of the earth in the middle of the lawn: it can't be long before my statues sweat blood and an eight-legged lamb is born in the paddock.

Writing in the same spirit to L. A. G. Strong, he said, 'we are enjoying this place no end: the view from the house I can only describe as panoramic, the garden is full of the strangest creatures, and if only they'd get to work on building our spare-room, you'd both be able to come down and see for yourselves. As it is I don't think it will be ready till Christmas now. The local pub is terrific: the first snatch of conversation I heard the first

* 'Ideal Home (*The Gate*, 1962).

time I entered it was "...so I sharpened a stake and stuck it up her arse", and this was a pale foretaste of what was to come.'

His latest book of verse was sent to reviewers as Londoners were taking their first air raid precautions, trenches were being dug in the parks and massive evacuation planned: the *Overtures to Death* title seemed just right. This fifth and last of Cecil's 1930s volumes of verse is indeed dark with the silhouettes of bombers and fighters, and the acrid smoke of guns curls from its pages.

> .... but no such blaze
> Briefly can cheer man's ashen, harsh decline;
> His fall is short of pride, he bleeds within
> And paler creeps to the dead end of his days.
> O light's abandon and the fire-crest sky
> Speak in me now for all who are to die!*

The first ten poems maintain the oppressive, despondent atmosphere of this opening, the Munich mood. The political militant has retired, it is now too late for action, there is nothing to do but wait passively for disaster. Cheltenham's 'Regency Houses' are sadly 'unstuckoed' and they symbolize the property of a condemned society; they will crumble, but they will not be replaced by something better. Then follows the title sequence, seven poems in which Death is directly addressed, both with ceremony and in witty vein, as an enemy, a counsellor and a friend. Nonchalance partly dispels the depressed mood and the following poems contemplate in clearer light Cecil's own responses, his theoretical belief in action and his 'aspen hesitation/Dithering on the brink'. This leads to 'The Volunteer', a tribute to those who did fight in Spain for the International Brigades; and to 'The Nabara', a heroic narrative based on the story of G.L. Steer's *The Tree of Gernika*, about four Republican trawlers manned by Basque fishermen which engage in an audacious and hopelessly unequal battle with a Nationalist cruiser. The appearance of this a mere six months before the complete surrender of the Republicans to Franco's Fascism gave it great poignancy for its time. The book ends with a group of eight personal poems which point the way to Cecil the 1940s poet.

The volume was dedicated to the 'old-fashioned liberal', E.M. Forster, who wrote at the end of October saying he was ashamed of his tardiness which was not due to "'age's dim recalcitrance" for I like the book and was proud to be connected with it'. He had been, like many, in 'a queer state these past weeks, alternating between gloom and resolute cheerfulness, and in neither state is one an intelligent correspondent'. Britain was in a dilemma. 'Either we yield to the Nazis and they subdue us, or we stand up to them, come to resemble them in the process, and are subdued to them that way. Your poems, particularly the long one, offer the possibility of

* 'Maple and Sumach' (*Overtures to Death*, 1938)

heroic action, and many will be satisfied by that, but not you or I', he suggested. Forster went on to write of his disillusionment since he spoke up for Communism in Paris three years before and his view that Russia 'seems to be going in the wrong direction'. Maybe Communism 'will restart after the next European catastrophe and do better. . . . I know you won't mind dedicating your work to someone who has less faith than yourself, though it seems the wrong way round.'

In the autumn issue of *New Verse* 'Commitments'; Stephen Spender wrote on 'The Left Wing Orthodoxy', which he characterized as 'respectability coupled with a certain amount of log rolling'. He went on to face the sins of Cecil in joining the Book Society selection committee; and W. H. Auden in accepting the King's Gold Medal for poetry, having been selected for the honour by a committee chaired by the Poet Laureate, John Masefield. 'Undoubtedly, from the point of view of the older generation, these successes, which Day-Lewis and Auden probably regard as tactics, are part of the process by which the English writer, who has a good heart at the age of 20 and is therefore a socialist, develops a good brain at 40 and becomes a conservative.'

Cecil was sufficiently stung by this to write angrily to Spender, receiving in return a somewhat bewildered response. Trying again, in a calmer frame of mind on 12 November, Cecil said: 'I was offended by your article, not because it attacked me as a "public figure", but because it seemed to imply that I could only be on the Book Society through dishonesty of my own, through "writing in a style and developing an attitude adapted to the quotations printed on publishers' advertisements". I think you would be "furious" if someone said that about you.'

As to Spender's decision to write for *New Verse*, Cecil reminded him that in Paris he had suggested that Geoffrey Grigson should be exposed as 'the complete intellectual snob'. He added that 'if Grigson had said the scurrilous things about you that he has said about me, I should certainly refuse to write for his paper – is this just the seamy side of public school education coming out?' There was no point in protesting to him about his attacks on people: 'He thrives on that kind of thing: the one thing he cannot abide is being taken no notice of. . . .'

Turning to Spender's suggestion that Cecil's political and Book Society work might be having an adverse effect on his poetry, he agreed that this was a proper area for discussion. 'But your article nowhere gave any evidence for or even stated a deterioration in my work as the result of these activities. . . . If you could show me a worsening of my poetry and establish a cause-and-effect between that and my present activities I would drop them', Cecil wrote. The article had gone the other way about: 'Day-Lewis has become respectable, therefore one fears the worst for his work: ditto Auden and Spender, though they are not quite so respectable yet.'

Beginning a lengthy defence of his efforts on the Book Society selection committee, Cecil declared, 'I joined it, with very considerable misgivings, as you know, more because the Party said it was the tactical move than for any other reason.' The committee might be a 'racket', but it was sensible to use it 'in order to win the influence which writers always have had in the community'. For the same reason he was now making other personal contacts by going about Devon 'talking to WEA groups and that sort of thing', although he admitted, 'I came to live here because I felt that too much political activity was drawing off energy that ought to go into my verse.'

Cecil evidently still considered himself a loyal member of the Communist Party. 'I still believe that working for the C.P. may be able to provide me with the synthesis which, as you say, and I agree, I need; and might it not do the same for you?' he wrote. 'I wish I could influence you to stay in the Writers' Association.' The long letter concluded with the suggestion that they should meet and discuss the matters more in London.

Spender's reply from his Brook Green flat in Hammersmith was almost as long, and included an invitation to Cecil to spend the night of 5 December with him. 'We'll get some Irish whiskey, if that's what you really like, and have a talk.' The letter is about the artistic conscience: 'Whoever cares enough about poetry to write it, cares about it more than for anything else.' He considered that the Communist Party 'hasn't the slightest interest in poets as poets; they are just interested in anyone who can transfer his reputation to them'.

In June 1976, Spender spoke on the BBC Radio 4 programme *Kaleidoscope* about the 'Young Writers of the Thirties' exhibition showing at the National Portrait Gallery.

I'm rather surprised from this exhibition to see how close I really was to Day-Lewis, I'd rather forgotten about that. . . . I think my letters to Day-Lewis are rather mean, as a matter of fact. I'm always writing to him to say how good his poems are and then going on to say, but I think they're rather terrible, or something. . . . Well, by 1938 of course, it seemed to me that for Day-Lewis, Communism meant the village pub. In fact I'm sure it did really. His group of chaps. And I was rather anxious to point out to him that Communism meant Stalin and I think in fact that really is why Day-Lewis broke with Communism. Because I think I did have one conversation with him in which I did manage to persuade him that he ought not to look at those nice chaps in the village pub, but he ought really to look at what the leaders were talking about and doing.

That conversation took place during the night of 5 December when Cecil stayed with Spender at Brook Green. Cecil still made no complete renunciation, but he did no more political preaching after this and he began to enjoy his chaps at the Red Lion public house in Musbury more for their own sakes, and for the sakes of darts and dominoes, than for political reassurance. Brimclose itself was so remote from political, or any other, man-made noises that 'when we heard footsteps or the sound of cartwheels in the lane, we often rushed to the window to see who was passing, as men crowd to the rails when a ship is sighted in mid-Atlantic'.

Among those whom Cecil encountered at the Red Lion were John Currall and his wife Edna Elizabeth, known to the world as 'Billie'. They were a Warwickshire couple, also new to the village, and they were divided from the Day-Lewises, in the geographical sense, only by the fields and woods of Musbury Castle. The narrow, steeply-graded, high-banked Mounthill Lane leads from the village, past Brimclose and over the brow of the hill, then descends gently to Bulmoor Cross. Here, in a combe of land enclosed by woods, was the small and economically impractical farm on which John Currall had been set up by his parents. Billie found herself standing next to Cecil at the bar of the Red Lion on the day she and John arrived in Musbury in October 1938. She was a hazel-eyed lovely, a youthful child of nature who could never have been contained within the bounds of marriage. Cecil, a year older than she, was at his most handsome, and ready to suspend earnest endeavour, to walk away a little from his mother-figure wife and sow his first wild oats.

> That winter love spoke and we raised no objection, at
> Easter 'twas daisies all light and affectionate,
> June sent us crazy for natural selection – not
> Four traction-engines could tear us apart.
> Autumn then coloured the map of our land,
> Oaks shuddered and apples came ripe to the hand,
> In the gap of the hills we played happily, happily,
> Even the moon couldn't tell us apart.*

In 1960 Cecil recalled 'a wild, preposterous and devouring love-affair which I had embarked on, or rather been shanghaied aboard – a product partly, perhaps, of the hallucinatory and irresponsible Munich period'; and elsewhere in his autobiography he refers to 'a shameless, half-savage, inordinate affair which taught me a great deal about women, and about myself, that I had never known'.

He was more forthcoming in 1968 when he published *The Private Wound*, his last completed Nicholas Blake novel, 'a sort of confessional' by an English novelist he called Dominic Eyre. He convincingly transferred the story to the West of Ireland, where he took his summer holidays during the last years of his life, but, as he told Billie in a 1971 letter to her, it was her book. In fact there is an epilogue where another writer finds the Eyre manuscript and speculates about the story of romantic melodrama so out of character for a novelist of the impersonal Christopher Isherwood camera-eye school. He wonders if the book does not represent 'some conflict, some authentic experience, which Dominic underwent in his thirties.

* 'Jig' (*Word Over All*, 1943).

The central relationship, between him and the woman he calls Harriet Leeson, may have developed in another part of Ireland, in England, or somewhere abroad for that matter.'

Harriet Leeson, known as 'Harry', is a raffish beauty with thin lips, a long mouth and greenish hazel eyes set closely together. She is clearly identified as 'the daughter of a shopkeeper in a town on the Gloucestershire–Warwickshire border, which accounted for her countrified English accent'.

Cecil identified himself in Dominic just as clearly: he has just been offered £300 a year for three years to write three novels; his father was a Church of Ireland cleric who began his ministry at Tuam; he had been brought up in England but was now in Ireland because 'sooner or later a man feels the need to return to his first roots'; he felt an 'odd pull' towards Co Clare – the land of the Ó Deághaidhs; he had 'had one year of bad bullying at school and was still perhaps over-quick to feel, or imagine, hostility'; he has 'a beautiful voice' and was brought up on the *Irish Melodies* of Tom Moore.

The very first page of *The Private Wound* takes us straight into the 'devouring love-affair' of Mounthill Lane, Musbury:

When I remember that marvellous summer of 1939 ... one picture always slips to the front of my mind. I am lying on a bed drenched with our sweat. She is standing by the open window to cool herself in the moonlight. I see again the hour-glass figure, the sloping shoulders, the rather short legs, that disturbing groove of the spine halfway hidden by her dark-red hair which the moonlight has turned black.... She is naked. She turns her head to me and says, 'Come on! You're always best the third time.'

I suppose it's because she still nags at my mind, because in a way she demanded so little ... because she ought to have some little shrine of her own (and without me who will remember her?) – yes, out of mere gratitude I should tell the story....

Harry appears 'with a curious, rolling gait, swinging her arms across her body', a creamy voice and 'a vaguely West-of-England manner'. She discovers that Dominic writes books and elects to call him 'Boo'; Billie, with similarly endearing irreverence discovered that Cecil was a poet and called him 'Po'. Harry, like Billie, 'never pretended to an interest she did not feel.... She asked me how I was getting on in the cottage; she did not ask then, or any time later, how the book was getting on.' Tearfully she tells Dominic about the sexual and economic performance of her likeable husband Flurry. 'He's no good any more.... And we're so poor. If only he wouldn't drink so much.'

Dominic more than once postpones the moment when he demonstrates that he is good. They are among dunes by the sea. 'Harry put her arms round my neck, sunk to the ground with a fluent movement, as if she was a wave-nymph drawing me down. How well I would get to know that liquid, yielding, compelling movement of hers! It was so different from her rather gauche, graceless walk. I had no sensation of falling to the ground: it was like being lowered on a cloud. Her saffron-coloured skirt had ridden up high. She was wearing nothing beneath it. . . . I had a momentary revulsion knowing now she had come out here to seduce me.'

Days pass before he surrenders. Then, 'presently, I enter her again. She seems passive, yet she fits her movements fluently to mine. It is like swimming in nectar, her breasts and belly the little waves. And now her arms clutch me tighter, tenacious as garlands of white flowers strung on wire. I hear that familiar straining noise in her throat – she never cried out loud any time I made love to her – and feel her body melting, collapsing.' Dominic is in love with her and himself. Harry is 'insatiable' and her 'recklessness endeared her to me – and communicated itself to me. She never used contraceptives, for instance, and refused to let me do so. She believed in the "safe period". . . .'

Billie remembered that Cecil 'would get so moody if he was writing' and when he was in a black depression she retreated. In the novel Dominic says that Harry 'would sometimes let a week or ten days pass before she sought me again' and, if they met by chance in this period, 'treated me with indifference . . . she enjoyed stratagems, the more outrageous the better. But then she would lose interest completely, become bored and peevish; and again I would wonder if she had it all worked out so as to keep me her slave, in a state of uncertainty. One day I would think her a paragon of women; the next day, a whore.' Billie remembered how Cecil would be 'angry and agitated' if she had been in the company of other men and 'almost taunted' her with not being able to leave her husband. Sometimes he would put notes into her hand saying, 'Read this when you are alone, my sweet.' Usually there were lines of poetry on them.

A walker standing on the summit ridge of Musbury Castle in afternoon sunlight will see to the west a panoramic, well-ordered landscape, Brimclose neat and contained in the middle-ground, everything beyond mellow and in its proper place, all nature tamed and bonded with man. To the east the country looks darker and wilder and more generous in its vegetation, inviting and mysterious and heart-tuggingly beautiful, and hidden in those woods is Bulmoor Farm, the home of the Curralls.

During 'that marvellous summer of 1939' the *News Chronicle* serialized the Blake novel of that year, partly set in this landscape, *The Smiler with the Knife*. The Chaucerian title of this novel suggests a kind of schizophrenic division, and so did the headline of the biographical newspaper article trailing the serialization, 'The Poet with the Gun'. Cecil was photographed standing on the Castle, looking romantically pensive and windblown and carrying the .22 rifle he used for shooting rabbits and other creatures he could consider pestilential. The photographs unknowingly illustrated another divison in Cecil's mind, finding him on the very borderline between his respectable family life to the west and his 'half savage' love affair to the east.

Cecil and Billie contrived nights away together, sometimes as far afield as rooms in London or Oxford, but more often at local inns. They became increasingly reckless about advertising their love in and around Musbury. On one triumphant occasion they achieved sexual congress while balanced in a tree between the hill top and the farm, and this became their 'personal tree', in which they played games and imagined their castle.

Mary did not frequent the pub, but she could not help discovering what was going on, particularly when Cecil and the Curralls emerged from the Red Lion together and arrived at Brimclose in a 'tired and emotional' condition. There was a scene in early April when Mary felt so plagued and isolated by her inebriated visitors that she retired to bed, and was reprimanded by Cecil for her inhospitality. Before that month was over Mary was increasingly turning for reassurance to her village friend Barbara Cameron, the occupant of Ruma Kita, a woman of rare sturdiness of character, unquenchable humour and very occasional ferocity. Cecil spent most of the evening of his thirty-fifth birthday at the Red Lion, while Mary was out at Ruma Kita with Barbara and her family.

'Mary learned to accept Billie Currall. . . . She knew Cecil would never be happy with the same woman for long and she was afraid of smothering him. If Cecil went for a walk she was afraid he was with Mrs Currall, if he was later than usual at the pub she would begin to worry. Poor Mary, she covered up so much', Barbara Cameron remembered.

Looking the other way was always hard, even if Mary did believe the affair would burn itself out. Billie Currall remembered one evening when she was walking up the lane towards Brimclose and met Mary walking down. 'It's quite safe, he's there alone,' said Mary as she hurried on towards the village. That time Billie tiptoed past the house without a glance through its windows. At other times, she admitted, 'I was a bit brazen'; and once Cecil persuaded her into his Brimclose bedroom. She came to think of him as 'really the only man I have loved', which meant that in the second half of the year there were tears mixed with the ecstasy and, despite herself, she began to want him as a husband.

In some ways the first month of 1939 was a melancholy one. W.H. Auden and Christopher Isherwood left for the United States, Barcelona fell to Franco and, the day after I had been rushed to Axminster Cottage Hospital to have my appendix removed, W.B. Yeats died. Cecil spent his working time putting the final touches to the third of his Cape novels, this one bearing a title taken from a Tom Moore *Irish Melody*, 'Has sorrow thy young days shaded?'. Before the end of January he despatched the manuscript of *Child of Misfortune* to Rupert Hart-Davis, to whom he wrote again on 9 February:

I am really delighted you like the book so well. I should like you to write in the dedication 'For Rupert and Comfort' [his wife], if you would like the dedication: I had intended it to be a sort of Christmas present, but then I thought you ought at least to see the thing before you had it thrust upon you. Sean came back from hospital on Monday and is in excellent form. What about the length? I'm told you are not allowed to sell a novel at 8s 6d unless it is over 110,000 words and I have an awful feeling that *Child of Misfortune* will add up to about 109,500, thereby ruining poor old Cape's with costs of production. If it's a matter of 1,000 words or so more I could probably think up some episode to fill it out.

One of the first visitors to Brimclose the previous autumn had been Basil Wright. He had been considering a documentary film idea, suggested by the distinguished Irish director Robert Flaherty, which would show the working of the boats that collected coal in the English north-east and delivered it to gasworks beside the Thames in London, After discussion it was decided that Cecil would write a shooting script for Alec Shaw as director and Wright as producer, the project to be sponsored by the British Commercial Gas Association. Shaw insisted that if Cecil was going to work on the script he should take a trip on a coal boat. This was arranged and, according to Wright, 'at that time Rex Warner was in low water, miserable and so on, and Cecil said why not let Rex come along too, it would be a good break for him'.

Cecil and Rex left Brimclose on 13 April. 'I remember we changed trains at Yeovil Junction', Warner recalled in 1973.

Here my cautious temperament prompted me to suggest that we should buy half a bottle of whisky for emergencies on the high seas. Cecil wouldn't hear of the idea as we'd both been told by Basil Wright that Captain Tickner of the ss *Wimbledon* never stopped handing out drinks. Rather nettled I said, 'All right, I'll buy quarter of a bottle for myself' and did so. At the offices of the Wandsworth Gas Company we were greeted by Captain Tickner (a huge and delightful man) with, 'I hope you boys have brought some booze with you, there's none on the ship.' We laughed nervously at this and Cecil explained to me afterwards that this was one of the good Captain's little jokes. In fact, it was the strict truth. It was only on the southward run (undertaken by Wright and Shaw) that liquor flowed. Maybe an empty ship needs more careful handling than one full of coal. Anyway we got nothing to drink but incredibly strong tea and I'm sorry to relate that Cecil, instead of allowing me to drink my quarter bottle alone, insisted on having one half of this miserable dram. Once arrived at the Tyne, things changed. Captain Tickner swept us into a pub called The Tram, where he kissed all the fat maids and never stopped drinking for days.

They returned to Brimclose on 18 April and next day Basil Wright arrived, to be roundly abused for the inadequacy of his information about Captain Tickner's drinking arrangements. 'We evolved the script in two or three days, sitting in Cecil's room at Musbury', remembered Wright. 'I wrote the pictures and handed them to him and he wrote the dialogue.

He had got a very good visual as well as verbal sense and he regarded the whole thing as a bit of fun. The film was to be called *The Colliers.*'

The most heart-felt line was written for the Captain: 'Three mild and bitters, Alice, and a glass of poison for Mr McCulloch. And don't spill any on the way, lovely.'

The novel *Child of Misfortune* was published in June and the resulting mail suggested that some readers, if not many critics, agreed with the blurb writer that Cecil had now 'attained complete maturity as a novelist'. In fact the book has the strengths and weaknesses of his other straight novels, with an invented plot drawing together innumerable ideas and episodes found again in Cecil's verse, as well as *The Buried Day*. The story is of two brothers, Arthur and Oliver Green, conflicting sides of the author, one destined to be a painter turned cartoonist and the other a Church of England clergyman turned politician. The two are shown progressing through life from childhood to middle age, responding to their complex heredity, which includes a charming, irresponsible and lately deceased Irish father, and a conventional yet careless English mother.

Part One has the boys enjoying Wilkie's school and summer holidays in Wexford and Norfolk. The Green household in Wexford has a kindly Aunt Joyce based on Knos, a Home Rule enthusiast of a gardener based on Johnny Keyes, and, inevitably, a meadow for barefoot running at the top of the morning. The section ends with those dead pets Cecil had found on Kingstown beach at the outbreak of war in 1914. In Part Two Arthur, the more individual of the two boys, goes back to Ireland in the middle of the Anglo-Irish War to try and find his silly Uncle George, and is unconvincingly led to him just before he is executed by the Irish Republican Army for being a Black and Tan informer. The final section is set in the 1930s, when both brothers are stars in the campaign against Fascism. There is a thoroughly detestable Fascist, unreasonably tolerated by the other characters, called Alec Cameron. His organization is called the League of Britons, politically a more sensible title than the eccentric English Banner of *The Smiler with the Knife*.

During the last months of peace Cecil was not exclusively preoccupied with his love affair. He sailed his dinghy alone from Lyme Regis in 'a trance of pleasure'; he killed a cock pheasant at seventy yards with the first shot from his .22 rifle, 'a performance which deeply impressed Rex Warner, though he was less pleased when I sent him to retrieve the game shot out of season on someone else's land'; he even climbed the hill to help the amiable John Currall 'clean out his cow-sheds or make his hay'. What political involvement he had was decidedly anti-Fascist rather than pro-Communist. Here he writes to the now knighted Sir Hugh Walpole:

I've been asked to obtain messages from English writers to be transmitted into Germany through the illegal radio station. This station is listened in to by a great number of Germans, at considerable personal risk as you know, and I feel sure that such messages would buck them up and make them feel they were not altogether isolated. If war breaks out, the Nazis will no doubt make extra efforts to jam this station, but they have not succeeded yet. I should be most grateful if you felt able to help over this. The message should be from half to a page of typescript.

Brimclose visitors, on the turn of June and July, included Mary's brother Francis King, now teaching at Winchester College, and his first wife Barbara. Francis produced a short passage from the fourth of Virgil's *Georgics*, which had been set in an examination, and asked if Cecil could provide a verse translation. 'The passage excited me – particularly the line about bees holding little stones to ballast them when they flew in a gusty wind. I felt I would like to translate the whole of the *Georgics* and soon I began work, my imagination quickened and enriched by all that I had come to love here [in Devon] – the places and the people – and by a sense that this work might be a valediction to them', Cecil wrote.

Visitors in the middle of July included Rupert Hart-Davis and his wife Comfort. They offered to entertain Nicholas and me at their farm near Henley for ten days in August, so that Cecil could play cricket and Mary could have a holiday living with Barbara Cameron and gardening at Brimclose. On 9 August Cecil reported to the Old Broughtians, the literary team assembled by the dramatist Clifford Bax, to play a series of matches in the Bath area. He took part in the two opening games and in the second, at Lacock, he was allowed to bowl, an event which he had been anticipating with pleasure.

'In preparation for this I had been practising on our tennis lawn, against Sean and Nick, a leg-break which fell almost vertically in front of the batsman.... During the one match in which I was allowed to bowl, these high-trajectory deliveries created dismay among our opponents; and Archie Macdonell and Alec Waugh were kind enough to say they had never seen bowling quite like it. In the next match I was fortunate enough to tear a leg-muscle, so that my bowling average remained a respectable one, and for the rest of the tour I supported the team no less effectively as an umpire', Cecil wrote in 1960.

A letter he wrote to Hart-Davis on 17 August, from the Brockham End Hotel at Bath where the team were staying, suggests that in 1939 he was more earnest about his cricketing performance. 'The tour has been a bad one for me – I tore a muscle in the third match, and have umpired ever since: however I may yet head the bowling averages, as I took 5 for 44 in the second match', he wrote.

Legend has it that when Cecil arrived to take us home from the Hart-Davis farm I rushed to him and flung my arms around him, something quite unheard of in our undemonstrative family. When he returned us to Brimclose on 20 August war was only a fortnight away. Knos arrived from

Ireland on 22 August, three days before the Day-Lewis consignment of gas masks. She had time for a single mackerel-fishing trip from Lyme Regis, but departed for home a week after she arrived because of the threat of imminent hostilities.

Cecil thought about his war, wondering how best to help, and survive. He wrote to Sir Hugh Walpole on 26 August.

I am exercised about this war-service business. When I was last in London, Alan Ross suggested that I should ask you about the kind of jobs that writers could do best and would be asked to do. Do you know of anything particular I côuld apply for in this line? I am no good at languages, which I imagine puts me out of the running for a good many jobs, and for this reason I am inclined to join up in one of the ordinary war-services, but I want to go where I should be most useful.

Three days later, without waiting for any response from Walpole, he wrote to Denys Kilham Roberts of the Society of Authors asking for a job at the proposed Ministry of Information. 'I don't think I should be par-ticular about what kind of job I did, but I cannot be quite certain of this as I have very little idea of what kinds of work there would have to be done under the M.O.I.'

Roberts replied on 31 August, the day Britain announced mobilization, that 'until the Ministry becomes a thing of substance instead of a shadow, which it is unlikely to do until War actually breaks out, anything definite in the way of officially reserving services of authors is apparently impossible. All I can do is to say, quite unofficially, that it is likely the Ministry will in fact have use for your services and I suggest that you should not at present attach yourself to any other branch of National Service.'

On 1 September, the day Germany attacked Poland, Cecil took a train to London for a selection committee meeting of the Book Society. He returned to Devon on the breakfast train next day, noticing Big Ben and the Houses of Parliament to his right as the express picked its way out of Waterloo station, and wondering if all this might soon be a smouldering ruin. Mary's diary for Sunday 3 September recorded the essentials of that day: 'War 11 am. Fine and sunny. Listened to the Prime Minister. Picnic in garden. Evacuees arrive.'

No evacuee climbed the hill to Brimclose, no storm materialized, noth-ing changed. 'We picked our apples; the rough touch of branches as we climbed the fruit trees was reassuring in this ghostly time when war dis-tantly oppressed us like a premonitory haunting of the mind', Cecil wrote. He cared for his wife and his mistress and his sons and he relaxed with the labouring denizens of the Red Lion, a combination that combined 'to relax and to coarsen me, bringing out against my old fastidious, over-cautious self a care-free and roughshod one that often shouldered the other aside'.

Visitors came as usual. I remember approaching the high bank above our tennis court – cricket ground and being struck with awe by the sight of Cecil and Rex Warner at play, bowling at each other furiously, every nerve and sinew apparently stretched by the competition. They looked to me like two bulls disputing for mastery of a herd, and I became rooted where I stood, until I was noticed and told to retire to safety. Others who stayed that autumn included Frank Halliday, quietly absorbed in his painting of Brimclose; and the amiable celebrity-hunting John Garrett of Raynes Park Grammar School, Rex's latest headmaster. John Garrett became famous for his gallant action on Seaton beach: during a pub-crawl frolic Billie Currall plunged fully clothed into the sea and Garrett took off his shirt to dry her so that she was ready for the next pub.

Between frolics Cecil worked slowly at his *Georgics* translation. When, in December, the *Times Literary Supplement* called for 'the poets to sound the trumpet call' and meet the Nazi threat to 'belief and freedom' with 'fresh songs of deliverance', the writer of *Overtures to Death* was scornful.

> Where are the war poets? the fools inquire.
> We were the prophets of a changeable morning
> Who hoped for much but saw the clouds forewarning:
> We were at war, while they still played with fire
> And rigged the market for the ruin of man:
> Spain was a death to us, Munich a mourning.
> No wonder then if, like the pelican,
> We have turned inward for our iron ration,
> Tapping the vein and sole reserve of passion,
> Drawing from poetry's capital what we can.*

In December he was able to send fifty lines of the *Georgics* to Paul Engle at the University of Iowa. 'It looks as if this war is going on for ever: our Mr Chamberlain has got his blood up properly, after being led by the nose, duped and bullied by everyone, and he'll probably declare war on Russia, Japan, Iceland and Terra del Fuego if and when we have won this one', Cecil wrote in an accompanying letter. 'What I am really aiming at is being appointed Official Poet to the Royal Navy, with the rank of Rear Admiral (at least), but I doubt if the authorities will see their way to it.'

Cecil's last book of the decade, *The Smiler with the Knife* by Nicholas Blake, was rather overtaken by events through not being published until October. A peace-time atmosphere was necessary to this story of a conspiracy, within a patriotic organization called the English Banner, to stage an armed rebellion and provide Britain with a Fascist dictatorship under a Mosley-like caricature called Chilton Canteloe. The book is dedicated 'for Roughie' (W. N. Roughead) and has a title drawn from *The Knight's Tale* of Chaucer.

At the outset of the novel Nigel and Georgia Strangeways have moved

* 'Dedicatory Stanzas to Stephen Spender' (*The Georgics* of Virgil, trans., 1940).

like Cecil and Mary to Brimclose, Musbury, and it is Georgia who says, 'I don't want to leave here at all, ever, and I believe I never shall.' The descriptions of Cecil's new house and grounds and the wet weather we faced during our first autumn there are precise. Musbury village becomes Folyton and Cecil's favourite pub is thinly disguised as the Green Lion. The English Banner is represented in the village by a Major Keston of Yarnold Farm, a holding which he has turned into an arms dump, and Yarnold is really Bulmoor, the home of the Curralls. The story of the ghost of Bulmoor Cross is a version of the favourite story of Jack Frost, the Musbury village bore of the time.

After travelling about England and resourcefully destroying the Banner conspiracy Nigel and Georgia return to Devon to find a summons awaiting them at their cottage alleging that their hedges have not been properly clipped. It was appropriate that Cecil's 1930s should end on this note of ironic anti-climax. In *Transitional Poem* (1929), his signpost to the decade, Cecil had thought on what happens 'when nature plays hedge-schoolmaster'. Since then there had been many lessons and some hedging. Now he had come full circle, physically and poetically, and for a time was allowing nature, his and that around him, to be the teacher.

3

〜 *1940–1949* 〜
Desire Going Forth

No doubt for the Israelites that early morning
It was hard to be sure
If home were prison or prison home: the desire
*Going forth meets the desire returning.**

The decade of the 1940s put Cecil 'under a stress such as I have never known' and gave him 'sweet influences that for long enabled me to bear it': for the poet of the divided mind and the divided heart this paradox of hurt and delight proved as encouraging to his muse as it was wounding to his nervous system. In so far as there ever was a MacSpaunday animal it had now divided into its constituent parts and Cecil was free to be himself, and to serve the English lyric tradition as strengthened by Thomas Hardy. 'My life seemed to grow again, flowering in wider sympathies and a sensibility less crude, while my work was enhanced by the joy and the pain which seemed to purify vision and enlarge it, to show me poetry everywhere – in the most commonplace things outside me as in the precious strata of my own past experience, unworkable till now, but now opened to me by a seismic disturbance of the whole being', he wrote.

The combination of the *Georgics* of Virgil and the geophilic verities of Devon country life, and the rumblings of a war approaching closer, meant that Cecil could begin the decade with an illusion of rootedness, a posture of classless romantic patriotism. This was muddled with a strong instinct for self-preservation, schooled in the horrific front-line images of the First World War, which led him to prefer the risks of the London blitz and the grinding overwork of a Ministry of Information editor, to the more obvious dangers of the military life; and he felt uneasy at finding himself on the same side as the foolish or greedy forces of capitalism and the privileged classes that he had campaigned against over the previous ten years.

It is the logic of our times,
No subject for immortal verse –

* 'Departure in the Dark' (*Word Over All*, 1943).

> That we who lived by honest dreams
> Defend the bad against the worse.*

After the defeat of Germany in 1945 the British people returned Labour
to power with a massive majority. Cecil looked on with a generally sympathetic but cool eye: the imperfect realities of evolutionary politics could
only disappoint one who had lived by revolutionary dreams. Mostly he
meditated on his mirrors, looking into himself and, through himself, to
his view of the universe. Sometimes women joined him on his vigil and
for a time, as he saw it, they would sit together contemplating their ideal
selves: happy beginnings leading to harrowing endings.

> It is not of their transience I'm afraid,
> But thinking how most human loves protract
> Themselves to unreality – the fact
> Drained of its virtue by the image it made.†

The first January of the new decade brought cold weather and food
rationing and Cyril Connolly's literary journal, *Horizon*. The first issue contained a *Georgics* extract which Connolly professed to enjoy 'enormously
– particularly your very delicate touch and your use of a colloquial style
that is neither artifical nor journalistic. The texture of your translation is
perfect I think.'

In his autobiography Cecil recorded that at the start of 1940 his 'wild,
preposterous and devouring love-affair' was 'now calming down'. It was
an emotional kind of calm. Billie Currall announced that she was expecting
their child in September. Cecil's immediate shame and panic was short-
lived, for Billie soon made it clear that she would take care of things and
would not descend to moral blackmail. On the surface they continued their
lives as though nothing had happened, but this was a private wound inflicted on others besides themselves and which could never be entirely
healed.

> Now the peak of summer's past, the sky is overcast
> And the love we swore would last for an age seems deceit:
> Paler is the guelder since the day we first beheld her
> In blush beside the elder drifting sweet, drifting sweet.‡

In February there was an invitation from John Cheatle, a witty and
talented BBC producer, to write a Nicholas Blake radio play. Cecil wrote
back saying that Blake 'shows every eagerness to write a radio-drama-mys-
tery-sensation-bombshell for you' when he has time. Cheatle replied that
he would wait until May. His instructions to Blake included 'strict Detection Club rules: characters credible, plot logical, red herrings encouraged

---

* 'Where are the War Poets?' (*Word Over All*, 1943).
† 'The Double Vision' (*Poems 1943–1947*, 1948).
‡ 'Hornpipe' (*Word Over All*, 1943).

if legitimate, writing of high standard (i.e. Nicholas must forget his elder brother Sexton)'. He added: 'On second thoughts don't repeat these instructions to Mr Blake Jnr – I think they are unnecessary and might hurt his feelings.'

Cecil wrote again on 24 February pointing out, 'I have no idea for a plot in my head yet, and next to no idea of how to write for radio.' He nevertheless promised to deliver a script by 18 May and went on:

It has just occurred to me that I might set the drama on board a coastal steamer: this, apart from its almost stunning originality, would (a) enable me to use a great deal of the dialogue I composed for Basil's collier film and which will never now be used, and (b) would give your boys unlimited opportunities for burbling into bedroom ewers – an accomplishment for which they are so justly renowned. It remains to see, of course, whether Basil will at all resent my pinching a few lengths of the Gas Company's property: I'll write to him at once about this. In the matter of characterisation, plot and writing your instructions are – as you say – unnecessary: they will be practically indistinguishable from Shakespeare. As to your point seven, you cannot tell me enough about construction of plot, radio technique, etc, so send me your hints, your brochures, your all – they'll be needed, my God they will. And above all let me implore you, dear J. Cheatle – less of the Mancunian hustle: you've got all the vast and idle resources of the Detection Club to draw on, so give me as much time as you can for this job.

The play was not the only fruit of Cecil's collaboration with Basil Wright. Another was the poetic commentary for *The Green Girdle*, a film sponsored by the British Council about the newly created 'green belt' around London. As well as his own words he used those of other poets including a description of trees by Thomas Traherne. The film was considered good of its short, documentary kind, an early example of the use of colour with Ralph Keene as director, the distinguished Jack Cardiff as cameraman and Richard Addinsell as composer. The voices of the actor Robert Eddison and the radio news-reader Bruce Belfrage were used for Cecil's commentary.

Cecil's most regular and popular visitor at Brimclose, relishing cricket on our very rough 'tennis court' as much as marathon piquet tournaments, was W.N. Roughhead, otherwise Roughie, soon to be called up from his duties at the A.D. Peters literary agency to serve at sea with the Royal Navy. 'I am tempted to adopt your brilliant emendation – sea-cook for sea-coot in my *Georgics* but fear it would ruin my chance of receiving a D Litt (Loughborough) for the translation', Cecil wrote to him after a February visit.

Later in the month Leonard Strong came to stay with his family and he and Cecil made the ground plans for their *A New Anthology of Modern Verse, 1920–1940*, to be published by Methuen in July 1941. A March visitor was William Plomer, then working on the last volume of the diaries of country life in mid-Victorian times written by the Rev Francis Kilvert.

'Plomer has been staying with us this weekend, at his most entertaining, and we visited the scenes of Kilvert's junketing at Lyme Regis and Seaton', Cecil wrote to Sir Hugh Walpole.

In April and May, as Billie Currall bloomed with her unwanted pregnancy, the war news got worse. The Germans invaded Denmark and Norway and their submarines took a heavy toll of British merchant shipping. Winston Churchill became Prime Minister and there was a swift Nazi advance through the Netherlands, Belgium and France.

Cecil divided his time between the *Georgics* and his Nicholas Blake radio play *Calling James Braithwaite*, cannibalized from his script for *The Colliers*. He sent his script to Roughie on 21 May for delivery to the BBC. In a note to John Cheatle he apologized that it was 'rather badly typed as I had to do it myself in a hurry. I think it should play to 45 to 50 minutes, but I found it difficult to calculate the times of the noises off parts.' Cheatle replied that it was 'an excellent script . . . all delightfully Shakespearian'. He nevertheless resented the stage directions: "sound of seagulls, winches, commands, voices, Tyneside accent". This seems to me to be carrying glibness almost to the point of casuistry. I know I am a brilliant producer, but am damned if I will do your hack work for you.' As with other works in this Detection Club series the play was broadcast in two parts: the first on 20 July gave the crime, and the second on 22 July gave the solution.

Cecil and Mary together went to London on 22 May, attending a Detection Club dinner and enjoying a Leslie Henson revue. From there they travelled on to revisit Cheltenham, and Cecil gave a poetry reading in Gloucester. He did not return from his travels to Devon until 31 May. This was one reason why he failed to secure the leadership of the Musbury Local Defence Volunteers, and felt obliged to intrigue for this glamorous position over the first three months of invasion fever.

Winston Churchill wrote: 'The swift fate of Holland was in all our minds. Mr Eden had already proposed to the War Cabinet (on 13 May) the formation of Local Defence Volunteers, and this plan was energetically pressed. All over the country, in every town and village, bands of determined men came together armed with shot guns, sporting rifles, clubs, and spears. From this a vast organisation was soon to spring.'[1] The Musbury platoon was stronger on shot guns and sporting rifles than on clubs or spears, and its determination was chiefly centred on not missing any drinking time at the Red Lion. When Cecil asked one Musbury man if he would enlist, he asked: 'Us don't reckon to fight for they buggers in Axmouth, do us?'

There was a National Day of Prayer on 26 May and the miraculous deliverance of around 337,000 men from the beaches of Dunkirk was completed on 4 June. The LDV in Britain quickly grew to one and a half million men, and before the end of the month Churchill found time to despatch memoranda drawing attention to the 'uninspiring' title of this force and ordering the change to 'Home Guard', whatever the cost in replacing 'arm-lets etc'.

'My own military career was meteoric', wrote Cecil in 1960. 'Starting as a private, I quickly intrigued out of his command an elderly local fusspot [Sir George Pickering] who had, on the strength of a knighthood, been given the job of raising the Musbury contingent. In no time, I was com-manding the platoon myself, and after a few months I became a company commander.... [A contemporary letter from Cecil indicates that on 19 September he was appointed Assistant Platoon Commander, with Sir George promoted to the theoretically superior position of Section Leader.] I had a specious talent, which impressed our charming battalion-com-mander, Col Lethbridge, for planning operations on paper' and he believed 'that – being a writer – I obviously couldn't have anything to do all day and might as well make myself useful. Useful indeed I was to the Musbury platoon, for whenever I heard that a consignment of weapons had turned up at HQ, I dropped the *Georgics* and tore into Seaton to get first pick of them.' As to John Currall, a First Lieutenant of the Warwickshire Regiment in the last year of the First World War, he went off to serve in the Uplyme Platoon.

Occasional pangs of guilt about his failure to volunteer for the full-time armed services maybe added fervour to Cecil's war effort. He had let it be known at the Ministry of Information that he was keen on writing what it called 'vigorous patriotic verse'. This was drawn to the attention of S. J. de Lotbinière, the Director of Empire Programmes at the BBC who in-dicated in an internal memorandum that not all were impressed by the repu-tation of the 1930s poets. 'Beyond some faint recollection that he wrote *Child of Misfortune* and a certain amount of poetry, I don't know much about him. Would he be useful anywhere?'

Hitler and Stalin had signed a pact in 1939 and, except in the Security Services, where the public school old-boy network kept doors open, Com-munists were considered almost as dangerous as Fascists. On 5 July a further BBC memorandum from S.J. de Lotbini ère announced, 'I have investigated the C. Day-Lewis position and find that MI5 said we may use his material but he must not make a personal appearance at the microphone.'

There was no objection to his frequent personal appearances at the Home Guard watching post on Musbury Castle.

> A hill flank overlooking the Axe valley.
> Among the stubble a farmer and I keep watch
> For whatever may come to injure our countryside –
> Light-signals, parachutes, bombs, or sea-invaders.
> The moon looks over the hill's shoulder, and hope
> Mans the old ramparts of an English night.★

★ 'Watching Post' (*Word Over All*, 1943).

The platoon was composed of farm-labourers, cowmen, road-men and carters: some young and some veterans of the First World War. Cecil knew them as pub companions, and as occasional colleagues in hay-making and poaching. They treated him with 'a sort of sardonic tolerance' and 'were willing to be led (though not too far from the village), but would not be driven (except in my car, which we used for night patrols)'. They were prepared to occupy the cleverly camouflaged pill-boxes built along the Axe Valley, but only when they were not dampened by rain or flood-water.

Night operations were a speciality. Cecil prepared an elaborate one to impress the Brigadier, in which the climax was to be an attack on the village window-cleaner's tricycle (disguised as a German tank) with flour-filled paper bags. This was accomplished, but it proved not to be the climax of the evening. 'The operation had been timed to end a quarter of an hour before the pub closed. The combatants arrived punctually at the rendezvous outside the Lion. I drew them up in ranks; and after the Brigadier had expressed his gratification at the keenness and resource shown by all concerned, I gave an appreciation of the night's events, ending my discourse with "On the command, Dismiss, the Company will turn smartly to the right and move into the Lion" – whereupon, before I could issue the word of command, a genial voice rose quiet but clear from the ranks, "First bloody sensible thing you've said tonight, Mr Lewis." '

For a time in September there looked to be a serious possibility of actual fighting. On 6 and 7 September the Musbury defenders were kept 'stood-to' for thirty-six hours, expecting at any minute a German landing on Seaton beach and a quick thrust up the valley. 'We were scared that day, and if the Germans had landed, I daresay we should have been scattered like chaff: but we could see all round us what we should be fighting for – we were on our own doorsteps, after all – and we should have done our best.'

Cecil also remembered this moment in a poem where he visualizes 'men and barges massed on the other side' and mythologizes in Yeatsian manner the platoon 'out to guard the star-lit village'.

I write this verse to record the men who have watched with me –
Spot who is good at darts, Squibby at repartee,
Mark and Cyril, the dead shots, Ralph with a ploughman's gait,
Gibson, Harris and Long, old hands for the barricade,

Whiller the lorry-driver, Francis and Rattlesnake,
Fred and Charl and Stan – these nights I have lain awake
And thought of my thirty men and the autumn wind that blows
The apples down too early and shatters the autumn rose.*

On 22 September Cecil was able to write to Rupert Hart-Davis, now a recruit of the Coldstream Guards at Caterham, about his pleasure that

* 'The Stand-To' (*Word Over All*, 1943).

John Piper was to decorate his planned *Poems in Wartime* book of verse,
and to 'suppose *The Georgics* will be coming out according to plan'. He
added that his 'military genius has won almost instant recognition and I
have been promoted to the dizzy height of Ass. Platoon Commander which
enables me to wear a dinky little strip of blue carpet on my shoulder straps.
Unfortunately it has involved promoting Sir George Pickering ("Flicker-
ing George" to the cognoscenti) as section leader, and as a result I spent
nearly all yesterday quelling a mutiny.'

Another publication of the Battle of Britain summer was Nicholas
Blake's *Malice in Wonderland*, dedicated to Paddie Wright. Wonderland
was the 'biggest, brightest, most ambitious of all the holiday camps that
had sprung up over England during the last year or two'. Nigel Strangeways is called in to investigate the sinister practical jokes of one who signs
his messages the Mad Hatter, and runs to murder before being unmasked
as the Cambridge rugby blue who is the camp's games organizer.

Billie Currall's child, William, was born in September, as the Battle of
Britain reached its climax. Mary walked over the hill to Bulmoor Farm for
a crisis tea, accompanied as far as the gate by Barbara Cameron. She found
Cecil's features in the new baby's face. The two families agreed to continue
their present, and separated existences, with John Currall accepting the role
of the boy's father.

After the birth Cecil bought a pram for his third son and that is all he
ever bought for him. 'When William was born and a baby, every afternoon
when I could manage it, four or five times a week, we would walk for
miles through the country lanes, Po pushing the pram', remembered Billie.
'We would think nothing of six or seven miles' walking in an afternoon.'
On one notorious afternoon, as an act of confession and defiance, Cecil
pushed the pram through the middle of the village.

In Cecil's 1948 verse collection, *Poems 1943–1947*, there is a poem called
'The Unwanted' which can be read two ways. It can be taken both as a
reflection on the creative process, glorious results from unpromising beginnings, and as a comment on this particular birth. It considers first a baby
who was conceived 'A willed one, a wanted one –' but was born 'As ailing,
freakish, pale a one/As ever the wry planets knotted their beams to thwart'.
This is contrasted in the last two stanzas with the flurried conception of
a baby by 'Two strangers harshly flung together/As by a flail of wind'.

> Sure, from such warped beginnings
>   Nothing debonair
> Can come? But neither shame nor panic,
>   Drugs nor sharp despair
> Could uproot that untoward thing,
>   That all too fierce and froward thing:
> Willy-nilly born it was, divinely formed and fair.

Though Cecil had no further contact with this 'divinely formed and fair' Willy, his concern was made clear in his detective novel *The Worm of Death* (1961). Dr Piers Loudron, installed in Cecil's then Greenwich home, is discovered to have fathered an illegitimate son amidst the nervy disorientation of 1940. 'It was more than an "affair" ', Dr Loudron writes in his diary. 'I see it now, I knew it then, as the first time in my life I had acted purely on impulse, whole-heartedly, without calculation or self-regard. From the moment Millie came into my surgery, in the late autumn of 1939, I was possessed by her, I did not care what happened to me, my reputation, my family, as long as I had her love.' Millie had Billie's goodness of heart and tried to cope on her own, but after she died the son Graham was sent away to orphanages and suffered much. When Dr Loudron heard of this he adopted the thirteen-year-old boy, but Graham had been damaged beyond repair and eventually commits patricide.

Cecil's translation of the *Georgics* of Virgil was published by Cape on 4 October with a dedication to Stephen Spender. In a foreword the translator suggested that 'no poem yet written has touched these subjects [agriculture, horticulture and a practical love of nature] with more expert knowledge or more tenderness'. It was a work 'at once serious and charming, didactic and passionate; and didactic verse is the only kind which can be translated literally without losing the poetical quality of the original. The present translation is line for line, and literal except where a heightening of intensity in the original seemed to justify a certain freedom of interpretation.' Cecil had tried to 'steer between the twin vulgarities of flashy colloquialism and perfunctory grandiloquence'. He acknowledged help from his former Oxford tutor, Dr Maurice Bowra, in reading the manuscript and making criticisms.

The seven dedicatory stanzas to Spender begin on a note of self-pity about poets being 'not much in demand these days/We're red it seems, or cracked, or bribed, or hearty'. The second stanza, rather contradicting the first, answers the demand for war poets. The fourth, echoing both Shakespeare and Rupert Brooke, explains what Cecil has been doing while awaiting call-up.

> Meanwhile, what touches the heart at all, engrosses.
> Through the flushed springtime and the fading year
> I lived on country matters. Now June was here
> Again, and brought the smell of flowering grasses
> To me and death to many overseas:
> They lie in the flowering sunshine, flesh once dear
> To some, now parchment for the heart's release.
> Soon enough each is called into the quarrel.
> Till then, taking a leaf from Virgil's laurel,
> I sang in time of war the arts of peace.

After delivering a copy of the *Georgics* to Spender, Cecil wrote to John Lehmann on 18 November: 'I have just spent a very pleasant week-end with Stephen: we are contemplating the idea of starting a correspondence with each other on poetry and living in the world today.' Cecil was glad that the Penguin *New Writing* was 'going forward' but was doubtful about the request to provide it with satirical poetry. 'I don't feel it was ever a thing I did at all well, and am even more uncertain whether I could write that kind of verse just now.'

At the end of November the German Luftwaffe began its attack on Bristol, and the sky to the north from the watching-post on Musbury Castle had a fearsome red-glowing light. The brutal destruction was two counties away but the bombers throbbed ominously to and fro over the Axe Valley – the 'throbbing cello-drone of planes' in Cecil's 'Ode to Fear' – and on their way home their crews off-loaded their remaining bombs into our countryside. No damage was done, though if one particular incendiary had landed on the Brimclose thatch instead of in the garden we might have provided a useful path-finding fire.

December saw Cape's publication of Cecil's *Poems in Wartime*; and the Hogarth Press publication of his *Selected Poems*, chosen from *Transitional Poem* and each of his 1930s verse volumes. *Poems in Wartime* is a paperback comprising eleven works later reprinted in Parts Two and Three of *Word Over All* (1943). There were poems of love for Billie Currall, 'Jig' and 'Hornpipe'; Home Guard poems, 'The Watching Post' and 'The Stand-To'; personal memory poems, 'One and One' and 'The Innocent'; melancholy reflections on the state of war, 'The Dead', 'It Would be Strange' and 'The Assertion'; and present views, 'Windy Day in August' and 'The Poet'.

Richard Church, reviewing the volume in the *Listener*, declared that Cecil had emerged from 'his entanglement of ideas and political proccupations. He is now fully himself. It is an impressive self, and likely to make a permanent mark on the history of English poetry.' For his part Cecil wrote to Rupert Hart-Davis saying he liked Piper's designs for the book 'very much, though the frontispiece does look rather like a picture of a poet with his nose eaten away by clap'. He added:

I am all for keeping at a respectful distance from the war, but don't see how I can avoid being called up in the spring: my battalion commander is very keen to keep me with the boys here, but when he applied for my call-up to be postponed indefinitely they said, 'Nothing doing'. I don't know whether to carry it any further, try Harold Nicolson [Parliamentary Secretary to the Minister of Information 1940–41], for instance: it seems slightly indecent, though I do think I can do useful work writing here, and I'm sure I'm more cut out for a leader of bone-idle guerrillas than for the regular army, in so far as I am cut out for either. What do you think I should do? The Home Guard is jogging along very pleasantly: we now have a wonderful variety of American automatic weapons, but only moderate skill at loosing them off.

Cecil and his sergeant assembled one American First World War machine-gun and took it to the Brimclose orchard to see if it would fire. In the excitement the commanding officer accidentally touched the firing button. 'The muzzle of the gun dragged upwards, and the stream of bullets began to clear the bank and spray over Devon. The sergeant, a serious and admirable man, inquired whether the War Office would pay compensation: but as it turned out, none of the bullets had found a billet, either in man or cattle', Cecil recalled. There was a more dangerous incident on the last night of the year when, after a heavy evening at the Red Lion, Cecil came within two feet of leading his patrol off the high cliffs at Seaton golf links.

In the following year his war would become more earnest, less innocent.

The start of 1941 was cold and brought snow to East Devon. Cecil put the finishing touches to Nicholas Blake's *The Case of the Abominable Snowman* and led his own family and that of Rex Warner in tobogganing on the steeply inclined fields around Brimclose. On 10 January he went to London to be interviewed for a job in the Ministry of Information's Film Division and a week later wrote to Rupert Hart-Davis saying, 'I have not heard the result, but fancy I have not got the job, so it will be the Army for me after all. This war is really getting beyond the joke: hardly any meat down here; no Players'; no Milk Tray chocolates.'

The letter went on to say that Cecil was 'writing a lot of poetry – I feel sure the complete *Poems in Wartime*, when I've added 30 or 40 more to it, will be the best thing I have ever done. I only hope I get a bit more time to deal with the present rush of verse to the head.' He was looking forward to a Home Guard Social at Musbury's Drakes Hall when 'the scenes of debauchery will, I have no doubt, be indescribable'. Meanwhile his room was 'now so stuffed with secret papers and confidential documents about the Home Guard that I shall really have to have a lock fitted on a cupboard somewhere: we also have a dozen A.W. bombs lying in a ditch beside the garage, only waiting for the children to take them up and plug them at passers-by'.

On 20 February he went to Exeter for an army medical examination. After it he wrote to Hart-Davis again saying that he was recommended 'for – of all bloody things – the Armoured Corps. Do you know any one with any influence at the War Office, who could get me into something I could be some good at?'

By early March, with Mary being nursed through quinsy by her friend Barbara Cameron, Cecil had again been summoned to London by the Ministry of Information. On the ninth he returned to Musbury assured of a job as an editor in its Publications Division. He began at the MOI offices, then located in the heights of London University's Senate House in Bloomsbury, on Tuesday 11 March, living in Roughie's flat in Buckingham

Gate, St James's. On the fifteenth he wrote from his new office to Frank Halliday:

As the above cryptic initials signify, I'm now working in the Min. of Inf. (Publications Division): started work (?) here last Tuesday, and only yesterday received my calling-up papers for the Army and was ordered to join the Royal Corps of Signals at some god-forsaken place in Yorkshire. The Ministry is fighting to keep me here, but I doubt if they have enough guns to fight off the redoubtable Capt. Margesson [Rt Hon. David (Viscount) Margesson, Secretary of State for War].

The mild squabble between the War Office and the MOI for Cecil's services continued unabated for the next few weeks. A letter written to John Lehmann on 17 March contained a pencil-scrawled PS announcing, 'Alas, I am being combed out of here.' But it was not until the beginning of April that he actually reported to the Royal Corps of Signals depot in that bleak stretch of Yorkshire that is Catterick, and after twenty-four hours' service he was, to his intense and guilty relief, exempted to return to work at the Ministry. His certificate of temporary discharge was later handed round his drinking companions at the Red Lion in Musbury, and was much chuckled over: 'Period of Service with the Colours, One Day; Conduct during Period of Service, Good.' The day at the training depot with the West Country draft, among 'Mechanics, labourers, men of trade/Herded with shouts like boneheaded cattle' sparked 'The Misfit', a touching poem about a particular recruit who 'stood out from the maul'. He was maybe a shepherd, ploughman or cowman, 'So quaintly dressed/In his Sunday best', and 'One with a velvet hand for all manner of beast' now standing 'bemused,/With the meek eye of a driven thing', part of 'the herd to be branded for soldiering'.

The Ministry of Information was not a widely respected addition to wartime government and was unique in that it inspired no official history extolling its contribution to the eventual defeat of Hitler. It was endowed with what Sir Stafford Cripps called 'unlimited funds' and the public was given little idea of its various functions. In so far as it had a censorship role it was considered an officious irritant, and some outsiders who saw its workings considered it a soft refuge for people who had unfairly avoided battle service. The middle-class creative products of the Ministry, which ideally reflected belief in the force of example rather than exhortation and were comparatively subtle when set beside other examples of 1940s propaganda, were accepted as milk was accepted, with no thought for the cow. In memory the chief result of the MOI was comedy.

In March 1941, Duff Cooper was still the Minister with Harold Nicolson as his Parliamentary Secretary. Four months later Churchill sacked this team and replaced Cooper with his loyal Irish acolyte Brendan Bracken. He was able enough, but had no point of contact with the gifted and mildly anarchic gathering of creative talent under his roof. His craft divisions included one each for films, publications, advertising and exhibitions. The Publications Division had been made into a harmonious and streamlined unit by its Director, Bob Fraser (later Sir Robert Fraser, Director-General of the Central Office of Information and then the Independent Television Authority), with Max Parrish as his deputy.

Fraser was an Australian who had made his name as a Fleet Street journalist, going to the MOI's Empire Division after being a leader writer on the *Daily Herald*. Parrish, the technical expert who trained everybody else in the department, had worked as an editor for Collins the publishers, on the type of guide and encyclopaedia that matches an economic text with generous illustration. The combination of Fraser's flair for attractive popular journalism and Parrish's know-how made for a publishing success which has never really had its due.

The Division was set up when Hilary St George Saunders, then better known as the thriller-writer Francis Beeding, arrived from the Air Ministry with a short text on the Battle of Britain. A straightforward text-only booklet was produced first, looking much like a government White Paper of today. No author was credited, the publication was simply described as, 'An Air Ministry account of the Great Days from 8th August to 31st October 1940'. Then, according to Fraser, 'Max said let's do an illustrated version from this start, and from there our books took off.' The texts, glossing various aspects of the war effort, were mostly provided on commission by the departments concerned, with the MOI operating as publisher for His Majesty's Stationery Office. The writers were often distinguished, but were not normally identified. They had the unfair advantage over other publishers of the time of unrestricted paper; but it was nevertheless due to Fraser and his editors that some of the books sold up to six million copies, and anything which sold only a million was considered to have done badly. An economic price was charged and much profit made for the Treasury.

Writing a tribute to Parrish in *The Times* obituary columns in March 1970, Fraser said that he had been responsible for devising 'a new kind of book, the popular illustrated documentary, to meet the needs of the time.' Looking back in 1976, Fraser recalled Cecil as 'much the best' of the editors who worked for him. 'If he had chosen to stay on when the war ended he could certainly have had the job as Director of the Division.' Others who worked, at one time or another, in Cecil's small editorial section included Nicolas Bentley, Kenneth Bredon, Laurie Lee and J.M. Richards.

Bredon remembered how the energetic Fraser, and Parrish, normally quiet and gentle but capable of violent outbursts, 'respected one another and knew exactly how to exact the best from their senior staff', an exercise that required 'both tact and skill' considering that the staff included 'Cecil, among the most distinguished literary figures of the day' as well as 'the volatile Laurie Lee'. 'They also knew how to use the organization of the

Civil Service to their own ends.... They refused to allow the Division to become bogged down by "normal procedure" and if it was necessary to do so cut across red tape by acting first and explaining later', he said.

Cecil appreciated the help given him by Parrish, 'genial, unassuming, apparently unflappable and a glutton for work'. He added that 'most of us came to the work as amateurs. We didn't stay amateurs for long. Anything I knew about editing I learnt from Max. He insisted, for example, that every caption should be squared off with its photograph – a technical challenge I myself, having written many sonnets, found fascinating.' Cecil would start by preparing manuscripts for the printer. After these had been set up in galley proofs he would assemble a large number of pictures from Barbara Fell's photographs section, laying out up to forty on his office floor so as to decide on one for use. He would then order necessary maps explaining the course and directions of battles. When galleys, photographs and maps were complete they were passed to Charles Lamb's production unit. He had evolved a technique of integrating text and illustration that became ever more sophisticated as the war progressed, and was revolutionary for the 1940s. The mixture was returned to the editor as a photostat. The next stage was caption writing. 'Cecil was, as one would expect, supremely good at writing them', remembered Bredon. The object was to describe a picture in an economical yet vividly informal way, and the captions were written over and over again until every word was as well placed as possible. Later the editor might have to supervise foreign language editions. The style was much influenced by the contemporary pictorial journalism of the British *Picture Post* and the American *Life*; it also constituted still television.

There is no doubt that, as Fraser put it, the Ministry had 'its fair share of passengers', but the editorial work proved 'so absorbing that hours almost ceased to matter'. Cecil was among those who habitually overworked for his £900 a year, and sometimes slept in a bunk bed in the basement. Among the forty or so titles, apart from *The Battle of Britain*, were *Bomber Command*, *Front Line*, *The Air Battle of Malta*, *The Abyssinian Campaigns*, *Ocean Front*, *Combined Operations*, *R.A.F. Middle East*, *The Campaign in Burma*, *The Mediterranean Fleet* and *Ark Royal*.

'Cecil was by no means unfriendly and would often join us in the canteen or at the film shows that the Ministry put on for us in the evenings, but he inspired a certain amount of awe,' said Bredon. 'Some called him "the gloomy poet", but this was an unfair description; a little austere perhaps, but not gloomy. Laurie, the inveterate joker, who had known him longer than most of us [only since they joined the Ministry], liked to tease him a little, which I think Cecil rather enjoyed. I remember Laurie, Olivier Popham [now Mrs Quentin Bell] and I announcing that we were going to start a periodical called *A Hope for Poultry*. I also remember Cecil inventing a Chinese character called "Hoo-Flung-Shit-Hi".'

The MOI was not an institution to inspire verse, though it did provide the setting for Nicholas Blake's first post-war detective novel, *Minute for Murder* (1947). Cecil's facility was sometimes informally called upon, as when he produced his 'Heroic Couplets Written in Honour of Mr H.A. St G. Saunders, on the Occasion of A Banquet Given By Him to Three Moderately Civil Servants':

> We thank you, Saunders, Hilary A. St George
> For a most handsome, nay, gargantuan gorge,
> Washed down (oh, what a pleasing flood, dear Hilary!)
> With noblest juice of vineyard and distillery.
> Had you of such Olympian plenty warned us,
> We should have starved for weeks before, sweet Saunders.
> Our fancy fed upon your fancy feeding,
> We send this flower of verse – called 'Love-Lies-Beeding'.

The work was signed by C. Day-Lewis, Robert Fraser and Max Parrish.

During April and May of 1941 the Luftwaffe made its last attempts to destroy London, before being diverted to the June attack on the Soviet Union. Cecil was there for the worst of this, always fortunate enough to escape with nothing worse than frights, sometimes rather surprised in the morning to find himself still alive. To an extent that now appears unlikely normal life continued. Roughie, then on leave from the Navy, recalled one particular night when he enjoyed 'a jolly good dinner' with Cecil at the Café Royal as 'the bombs came down like hail'. Afterwards they were not allowed back into Buckingham Gate because of an unexploded mine and they 'played piquet the whole night through at the United Universities Club'.

A social engagement in April was the wedding of Stephen Spender and the pianist Natasha Litvin. Besides Cecil the guests included Louis MacNeice, Julian and Juliette Huxley, Rose Macaulay and the *Horizon* editors Cyril Connolly and Peter Watson. William Plomer and Joe Ackerley were other guests, observed by John Lehmann to be 'acting once more the part of satiric chorus in undertones which grew disturbingly merrier as the alcohol began to work.'[2]

Whenever possible Cecil escaped back to Devon. Nothing could be more healing than 'the incense-breathing morn' of Brimclose: 'Whenever during the wartime summers I came back for a week-end from a London dusty and stinking with the rubble of the blitzes, the first thing to greet me as I walked into the garden was an exquisite fragrance of flowering grasses or mown hay drawn out by the night-dew and sweetening the air for miles.'

Writing to Mrs L.A.G. Strong from Musbury on Good Friday, 11 April, Cecil revealed that 'I've been given six months exemption, and when that's finished there should be a good chance of getting another six months. And so on.' Another letter shedding light on his way of life was sent to Frank Halliday from the MOI on 6 May: 'I have to work fairly hard here – nine to 12 hours a day – though it comes rather in spurts and there's a lot of sitting about doing nothing in between. I see a lot of Charles Fenby, who is working on *Picture Post* now.'

As 1941 progressed Cecil had increasing reason to want to be in London, and not only because the air raids were dying down. After a chance reunion during one of the spring blitzes he had fallen in love with Rosamond Lehmann and he had not been rejected. Neither she nor he recorded dates or addresses and it is not possible to be altogether precise about the when and where of this all-consuming nine-year relationship: so important to Cecil for his development both as a poet and as a person; so important to Rosamond that in her vulnerable forties she unwisely and generously committed her whole heart to him. All that can be said for certain is that before the end of the year they were living together in Kensington, the first of several houses in and around London where they found time to be together, and Cecil had embarked on his period of 'double marriage', 'sweet influences' and 'a stress such as I had never known'.

Rosamond Lehmann was born, she writes in her *The Swan in the Evening* (1967), 'during a violent thunderstorm' on 3 February 1901, the day of Queen Victoria's funeral. Her childhood was spent in materially comfortable circumstances at Bourne End, Buckinghamshire, in the Thames Valley, and she went to school in 'the brick and stucco pavilion built by our parents in the garden to house our education'. According to the first volume of autobiography by her brother John she learnt to play the piano, she wrote verse and prose in the high romantic manner and, in family plays, she cast herself for ultra-feminine parts. She also became a Girl Guide. She went on to Girton College, Cambridge, where, amongst other things, she became keen on modern poetry. She was very clever and very sensitive and very beautiful and had developed a personality of such power that no man could regard it with indifference.

> Next you appear
> As if garlands of wild felicity crowned you –
> Courted, caressed, you wear
> Like immortelles the lovers and friends around you.
> 'They will not last you, rain or shine,
> They are but straws and shadows,'
> I cry: 'Give not to those charming desperadoes
> What was made to be mine.'*

She made an early marriage to Leslie Runciman, and became a celebrity at twenty-six with the success of her first published novel, *Dusty Answer* (1927). In 1928 she began a second marriage with Wogan Philipps, then a painter but to become known as the only Communist member of the

* 'The Album' (*Word Over All*, 1943).

House of Lords: they had two children, Hugo and Sally, more or less the same ages as the two sons of Cecil and Mary. Her literary fame, popularity and reputation grew through the 1930s with *A Note in Music* (1930), *Invitation to the Waltz* (1932) and *The Weather in the Streets* (1936). She wrote of the subtleties of the human heart and, as Marghanita Laski commented in 1953, 'No English writer has told of the pains of women in love more truly or more movingly than Rosamond Lehmann.'

One who visited her, when she lived with Wogan Philipps at Ipsden House in the Chiltern Hills of Berkshire, was the undergraduate Stephen Spender. He found her 'one of the most beautiful women of her generation'.

Tall, and holding herself with a sense of presence, her warmth and vitality prevented her from seeming coldly statuesque. She had almond-shaped eyes, a firm mouth which contradicted the impression of uncontrolled spontaneity given by her cheeks, which often blushed. Her manner was warm, impulsive, and yet like her mouth it concealed a cool self-control, and the egoism of the artist. At this age she seemed at the height of her beauty: yet when I look at photographs of her then it seems to me that her features were in fact too rounded, too girlish, and that years confirmed a sculptural quality which one felt then in her presence but which later showed in her features. So that she was one of those women in whom even greying hair was a kind of triumph, a fulfilment of maturity which her youth had promised.[3]

It was not surprising that Cecil should have felt at least half-smitten at those early meetings in 1936, when he and Rosamond were introduced at Elizabeth Bowen's house and she stayed a night at Box Cottage, an honoured guest of the Cheltenham Literary Society. She had isolated memories of subsequent encounters with Cecil: at a meeting of some literary committee she caught his eyes watching her from across the table; at some anti-Fascist rally she sat near him on the platform and after she complimented him on his speech he grasped her hand passionately.

Before the beginning of the war her second marriage had broken up, her children were living with her mother at Bourne End, and she was unhappily occupying a room in the London house of Henry Yorke (the novelist Henry Green) and his wife. Soon after their first unplanned reunion Cecil invited Rosamond to dinner, declared his love and invited her to move to a small flat above his own at Buckingham Gate.

At this time Cecil also explained that he was worried about his impending call-up to the Army, and felt he could be more useful where he was at the Ministry of Information. She knew Harold Nicolson, as indeed she knew most of the leading literary figures of the day, and she offered to approach him on Cecil's behalf. Over lunch she told Nicolson that unless he did something he would be losing one of his 'most useful and brilliant new recruits'. This was probably the crucial factor in keeping Cecil's Army service so short, and he was deeply grateful.

Quite quickly he and Rosamond drew closer and she took him to visit her mother and children at Bourne End. When the lovers went out on the river together she wondered, 'What are we starting?' He reassured her, telling her to put away doubts and to believe with him that his love would last always. Talk of marriage at this stage was largely rhetorical; indeed it seemed best to Cecil that Mary should not even know of his new relationship. So when he and Rosamond moved, after a few months at Buckingham Gate, to a small rented house in Gordon Place, off Kensington Church Street, Mary knew nothing. It was not hard to maintain her in ignorance: all Cecil's letters were written on MOI notepaper and this was the address to which all correspondents were directed; committed to Devon village life, Mary had no contact at all with the gossip of literary London; Cecil was often bored and occasionally exasperated in her company, but he continued to regard her fondly as one who would never knowingly do him harm; he had the ability to keep his life in compartments and had no problem about maintaining his former amiability when at Musbury.

There was also his feeling for Nick and me. 'As you know Cecil and I were agreed on not wanting our own relationship to disrupt our family responsibilities too much,' Rosamond told me. 'You were obviously a "guilt figure" to a strong, perhaps morbid degree, in his mind.' Cecil thought that my disturbed nature in early childhood meant that he had in some way let me down. 'He talked a great deal about you when we were first together. Your sleep-walking was, or had been, a source of great worry to him. He took it as a sign that you were anxious or "disturbed" (because lacking enough love) in early childhood; and he reverted again and again to the incident of your burning your hand very badly on a hot pipe during a sleep-walk. He thought this had been a serious trauma for you and that it affected your development – for a while,' she said.

She helped to give Cecil perspective on this and to coax him out of 'what I called his black ice periods'. She found as had others that 'what was true about him, involved the exact opposite being equally true.... He was a deeply divided personality, hence his periods of withdrawal, of being unable to feel or respond.' It was also true that at this time he did feel great love and tenderness for Rosamond: and because he was flattered by her genuine admiration for his talent, he stilled any doubts he may have had about the extent to which she directed his development.

Throughout the decade when he had been the increasingly fashionable Poet of the Thirties, idealized by younger men of his kind, he had maintained his ascetic, outside, provincial view of the artificial posturing, the sheep-like movements and rapidly changing views, the jealous bitchiness, the stimulating competitiveness of fashionable literary London. Rosamond knew her way about this scene; she was at home with, and courted by, the grandest company, and she was able to coat Cecil's provincial inhibitions with metropolitan sophistication. Under her care, and as his work gradually became less fashionable, he gained in social confidence and began to think of Musbury as a retreat from the world where he belonged.

In June the compulsive celebrity-hunter and headmaster John Garrett had somehow engineered a review in the *New Statesman* by Rosamond of his Raynes Park Grammar School production of *The Taming of the Shrew*. After the performance she and Cecil went to the Wimbledon Common house of one of Garrett's friends. After a glass or two of his customary whisky Garrett strode over to Rosamond and said, 'Come on, you great big beautiful bitch – dance with me,' and together they fox-trotted across the polished parquet with the backing of a gramophone record. Cecil was less upset by the 'beautiful bitch' remark than the action of the normally homosexual Garrett in challenging his sexual prerogative. Rex Warner, still teaching at Raynes Park, was commissioned to try and make peace between Garrett and Cecil. That he did not quickly succeed is indicated in a letter Cecil wrote to Frank Beecroft, his Cheltenham friend also now teaching at Raynes Park, on 1 December. It was hoped that Cecil would go back to the school to perform a Beecroft song setting:

but it will have to remain unsung by me for a bit longer. I asked Rex to tell John I would not be coming on Sunday. It is childish on my part, I fancy, to persevere in this vendetta: but it would be even sillier to come down when I am still feeling badly towards John – and silliest of all to sing to an audience from which the headmaster is conspicuously absent. I'm sure my tenacious Irish vindictiveness will relax after a bit, and then all will be OK. But in the meantime John is doing his consiliatory genuflections and acrobatics to an audience that isn't there.

As a celebrity readily available in London, Cecil now did more broadcasting than ever before. During 1941 he was repeatedly on the air, talking about the Home Guard and Irish childhood memories and Wilfrid Owen and, more improbably, Madame Curie; taking part in discussions; and sometimes being asked to perform unlikely tasks as a verse reader. 'I'd prefer to read Tennyson – a bit out of *In Memoriam* for instance – than Shakespeare: after all, dramatic verse should surely be left to the actors; I'll try a Shakespeare sonnet if you like', he wrote to the BBC producer C.V. Salmon in May.

'I wish we could persuade the BBC to alter their methods a little', he wrote in the duologue introduction compiled with L.A.G. Strong for their *New Anthology of Modern Verse*, which came out from Methuen in July. 'The radio could be a magnificent instrument for the revival and communication of poetry; but at present I do not feel the BBC is going the right way about it.' Poetry was given perhaps fifteen minutes every other week, often just before midnight. 'They announce that somebody is going to read poetry and the impression given is of someone turning on a tap, very ceremoniously but very cautiously, from which a meagre trickle of culture will emerge.'

Altogether ninety-eight British and Irish writers are represented in the anthology as between-the-wars poets. Of the two supreme contributors W.B. Yeats is allowed six poems and Thomas Hardy only five. Others honoured with six are W.H. Auden, Walter de la Mare, T.S. Eliot and A.E. Housman. Cecil included five of his own works – two from *Overtures to Death*, and one each from *Transitional Poem*, *From Feathers to Iron* and *A Time to Dance*.

Nicholas Blake had contrived one detective novel a year since 1935 and, with the help of spotty and yet wholesome-looking war-time paper, the sequence was maintained with the publication in early October 1941 of *The Case of the Abominable Snowman*. The book is set in the Essex mansion of Easterham Manor, modelled on the home of Basil Wright's parents; the danger for Cecil in moving his stories out of his familiar West Country is shown by his referring to Colchester as Chichester. The time was the end of 'the great frost of 1940' and as the children of the house watched their garden snowman melt, 'the crack at the top of his head deepened. A segment of snow slid, smoothly as a camera shutter, off its face. Its face ought to have gone. But it was still there. The squat, shapeless snowman still had a face – a face almost as white as the snow which had covered it, the dead, human face of someone who shouldn't have been there at all.'

For the last time Nigel Strangeways has his wife Georgia in tow; he plays piquet with the now very Roughie-like Detective Inspector Blount of Scotland Yard, and as the case reaches its climax he experiences 'a faint sensation of excitement stirring in the pit of his stomach, a feeling of anticipation, like that of a poet in whom a poem is beginning to move'. Otherwise little is told of the detective's state of mind in his immediately pre-Ministry of Information period.

Cecil himself remained sensitive about his position in the Ministry of Information. This was shown after J.B. Priestley, by now considered a second Churchill in his skill at using the radio microphone to bolster the morale of the civilian population, had scored some easy points at the expense of the Auden Gang. He described Cecil as a 'fire-eating poet' who had behaved like a lamb in joining the MOI, and he was still more scathing about the presence of Auden and Isherwood in the United States. Cecil replied by private letter in indignant defence of himself and his colleagues, calling Priestley's attitude 'malicious and contemptible'. Priestley replied that he had no intention of attacking Cecil: 'The little I have seen of you I liked.' He had himself advised that young artists should 'go on with their own work until they were told they were wanted', and his phrase about the 'fire-eating poet' had been supplied to him.

Cecil had gone on with his work, and in November he accepted an invitation to join the Committee of Management of the Society of Authors. Needless to say his name was put forward at a meeting chaired by L.A.G. Strong. Other names put forward at the same time were E.M. Forster,

Julian Huxley, Harold Nicolson, Osbert Sitwell, Rosamond Lehmann, Phyllis Bentley, Arthur Calder-Marshall and Vita Sackville-West.

In January 1942 Cecil appeared with the Irish tenor John McCormack in an edition of the popular radio light entertainment show *Irish Half-Hour*. Cecil remembered the singer as 'an adorable man, handsome as the top of the morning, racy and bawdy of tongue, a heroic figure with the simplicity of the heroic and a heart of gold'. After he had sung, Cecil recorded, he said 'goodbye to the men in the Forces, speaking with a warmth, a conviction, an utter lack of theatricality that were unbearably moving: "Goodnight", said the old singer into the microphone, "and may God bless you and hold you in the palm of His hand".' He was fifty-seven then, and had little more than three years of life before him.

Increasingly taken up with his metropolitan preoccupations Cecil managed only three short weekend visits to Brimclose in the first six months of 1942. He was not about to see the light in the sky on the nights of 23 and 24 April when the Luftwaffe tore the centre out of Exeter. Jinnie and her family of three Hedges children and two Osbornes, who had lately moved to the Devon county town from Cheltenham, were among those bombed out. They were temporarily installed at Brimclose on 27 April, Cecil's thirty-eighth birthday.

Mary visited Cecil in London for a mid-May weekend and was impressed that he found it necessary to work on Saturday and Sunday. She stayed at Charles Fenby's flat, having presumably been given an explanation of this arrangement that satisfied her; and Cecil found time to give her a dinner at the Hotel Rembrandt and a lunch at the MOI canteen, and to accompany her to a Leslie Henson revue and an Albert Hall concert. She also attended at Broadcasting House when Cecil gave his 15 May talk on British war artists.

In early June he was able to write to Frank Halliday: 'I'm still evading the draft, as you see, but cannot feel I shall get many more deferments. I met [Arthur] Koestler here a few weeks ago – rather a terrifying character, I thought – I expected him to slip and cut me to the bone any moment. ... I'm madly busy, turning out publications by the score and working a minimum of 60 hours a week.'

He had a ten-day holiday at Brimclose at the start of the school summer holidays and, to judge from the short letter he wrote afterwards, on 21 August, to Captain Rupert Hart-Davis of the Coldstream Guards, had to work still harder at the Ministry to make up for this. 'At Musbury the wicket is bumpier than ever and Sean has developed a formidable turn of speed as a bowler. Mary and the children are very well. I'm busier than ever here – anything from nine to 14 hours a day: but have written some poems this year and hope to have enough for a book before very long.'

So continued the grinding year of 1942: Cecil writing a little poetry in the chinks of his life but otherwise preoccupied with the propaganda texts of other men and the sweet consolations of his life with Rosamond. There were Brimclose weekends in September and November; there was a December party asked for by Sir Archibald Clark-Kerr, the new British Ambassador to Moscow, at which Cecil, with Stephen Spender, Louis MacNeice and others, sat at his feet on the floor of John Lehmann's flat; there were more broadcasts, late-night readings in the *And So to Bed* slot from Tennyson, Blake, Herbert and Hopkins. He had a week in Devon at Christmas, suffering from piles.

Even Nicholas Blake was rendered more or less quiescent by the conditions of the day, though he did produce the introduction to *Murder for Pleasure*, 'The Life and Times of the Detective Story' by Howard Haycraft, a Peter Davies publication. Haycraft considered that *The Beast Must Die* was Blake's magnum opus, thanks to its 'sheer mental suspense'; and placed *The Smiler With the Knife*, with Georgia performing as a female superman, in the category of John Buchan's Hannay adventure yarns. The author apparently interviewed Blake, finding 'the poet with a gun' looking like 'a young farmer or aeroplane mechanic', somebody 'strong, almost tough', a 'tall man with a shock of dark hair and a deeply lined face.' Blake told him that detective novels were 'a harmless release of an innate spring of cruelty present in every one'.

When the book was reviewed Raymond Postgate declared that in his introduction Blake had failed to establish his view that the detective novel was for the upper classes because the lower classes read 'bloods' or thrillers. John Strachey commented that Cecil 'writes even better when he is, presumably, pot-boiling as Nicholas Blake than when he is "giving himself to literature" as Day-Lewis'.

Cecil never had qualms about buying an education for his children, whether or not this gave them an unfair advantage over others, and as a Communist it had been made clear to him that his duty was to stay as close to the ruling class as possible even if this did mean patronizing schools devoted to the social status quo.

Thus, as soon as we arrived in Devon in 1938, I was sent to the junior department of Allhallows School, Rousdon, occupying a spectacular, though often mist-shrouded, estate on the high cliffs above the thickly wooded landslip between Lyme Regis and Seaton. Whether this institution really provided its inmates with any advantages during the war years is doubtful. It was trying to be a public school, built about the blessed trinity of the chapel, the parade ground and the rugby field; and it was very proud of its most famous old boy, Marshal of the Royal Air Force Sir Arthur Harris, the man running the British bomber offensive against Germany as the ring was closed on Hitler. It was this school which provided the background for Cecil's late 1950s poem to me about how the love of parents 'is proved in the letting go'.

It is eighteen years ago, almost to the day –
A sunny day with the leaves just turning,
The touch-lines new-ruled – since I watched you play
Your first game of football, then, like a satellite
Wrenched from its orbit, go drifting away

Behind a scatter of boys. I can see
You walking away from me towards the school
With the pathos of a half-fledged thing set free
Into a wilderness, the gait of one
Who finds no path where the path should be.*

By 1942 my younger brother Nick was also briefly at Allhallows, but our progress was not encouraging and before his ninth birthday in early 1943 he was despatched to Sherborne Preparatory School; in mid-February Cecil undertook his first parental visit to the Dorset town where he had also been schooled.

On 1 April Cecil brought Laurie Lee to Brimclose for a five-day week-end, mainly so that his young protégé could research in East Devon for an MOI booklet on the contribution of British agriculture to the war effort. After this earnest start Lee evidently set about his writing task at a properly ruminative pace, for his *Land at War* did not emerge from His Majesty's Stationery Office until 1945, the year after his first published slim volume of verse, *The Sun My Monument* (1944).

Lee was almost exactly ten years younger than Cecil. They were as different as two complicated men can be, yet it is not hard to see why they should have liked and admired each other so much. Though Lee belonged to Gloucestershire, not to Devon, it was to Cecil as if he had discovered that one of his domino opponents at the Red Lion was a first-rate poet: and not just a poet, but a man with the lovely gift of being rooted in his own countryside even when he was somewhere else. For his part Lee was doubtless grateful that a poet of accepted achievement should take him so seriously and treat him so kindly and enjoy his sly, child-like fun. At this stage of the war Laurie was Cecil's closest friend. Before Rosamond Lehmann gathered up her children and took them to live in rural Berkshire she and Cecil and Laurie for a time shared a flat off Walton Street in South Kensington. At this time Lee was a script writer with the MOI's Crown Film Unit, and Cecil was partly responsible for bringing him over to the Publications Division in 1944. His subsequent literary success almost certainly owed something to Cecil's early encouragement.

Laurie visited us at Brimclose several times during the 1940s. Many of Cecil's guests simply stayed, it seemed to his sons, to enjoy Mary's meals and engage in impenetrable adult, literary and political discussion. Some of the braver ones subjected themselves to cricket on our highly dangerous

* 'Walking Away' (*The Gate*, 1962).

pitch, before retiring gracefully into more conversation. Laurie Lee alone was able to become a boy again, initiating games, making bows and arrows, giving out intimations of mischief. I think of him then as effortlessly friendly, smiling and shrewd, but sometimes reduced into silence by depression.

I asked him what he remembered of Cecil. 'I have been much perplexed in my mind since Cecil's death and I have not talked about him to anyone. I don't feel I *can* talk about him, even to you. I only saw him about once in the last ten years, though I don't believe this was his fault. My best memories of him would overlap with some of yours, on visits to Musbury. What remains is either vague or too difficult, although he was the man I liked most among my friends, and was the kindest to me.'

Since 1941 the distinguished actresses Peggy Ashcroft and Edith Evans had been giving poetry readings with music in London canteens and service centres. The idea of expanding this work into the Apollo Society occurred when Peggy Ashcroft found herself in a Cambridge to London train in 1943 with Stephen Spender and his wife, and Cecil. The co-operative organization was launched at the Arts Theatre, Cambridge, on 30 May. The Poet Laureate, John Masefield, was present as the guest of Lord Keynes and the readers were Peggy Ashcroft, Robert Harris and John Laurie, with Natasha Litvin as pianist. Gradually Cecil's life acquired a new dimension as the demand for his reading grew.

The Society, composed of poets, actors and musicians, aimed to 'revive the neglected art of reading poetry and to show that poetry and music can be regarded as complementary'. In the 1953 *Apollo Anthology*, Cecil added that 'its programmes consist of groups of poems preluded, concluded or interspersed with musical pieces, the intention being that the poems and the music should comment upon one another somehow – by a similarity of mood it may be, or association of style or subject, or by a violent provocative contrast. This marriage of two arts, like any other marriage, requires tact, delicacy, intuition, a sense of humour and a capacity for compromise.'

Cecil was listed in the first prospectus as one of the eleven founders and a member of the six-man and two-woman executive committee. Other poets signed up were Walter de la Mare, T.S. Eliot, Louis MacNeice, Edith Sitwell and Stephen Spender.

That summer Denys Kilham Roberts, Secretary-General of the Society of Authors since 1928 and a man with his own unsatisfied literary ambitions, raised some money to start a new literary journal and recruited Cecil and Rosamond, and Edwin Muir, as his co-editors. Rosamond suggested 'Avenue' as its title, but *Orion* was eventually preferred. John Lehmann was somewhat perturbed that the new publication was to have the same purpose as his *New Writing*, an open-minded search for verse, prose stories and essays with no thought for movements or dogmas. Rosamond, in

particular, proved a conscientious editor who wrote a large number of letters
and assembled several distinguished contributions which her brother might
have been glad to publish. In the long run the *Orion* compilers lacked John
Lehmann's single-mindedness, and publication was neither sufficiently
frequent nor consistent to build a following. Cecil was never a very enthusiastic or committed editor, partly due to his other work and partly to
his antipathy to Kilham Roberts.

In early June there was another visit to London by Mary. She stayed four
nights at Charles Fenby's flat, and there were meals at the Café Royal and
the MOI, meetings with Rupert Hart-Davis, Rex and Frances Warner, visits
to the theatre and cinema. Cecil was rather involved with family duties that
month. I broke an arm in a bicycle collision returning from school and
he somehow found the time to visit me at Exeter Orthopaedic Hospital.
The only lasting result of the accident was that I became, like Nick, a school
boarder: an arrangement which made it possible for Cecil and Mary to
maintain their married front for our benefit over the following seven years
or so.

He took a long weekend and a long week at Brimclose during the summer holidays. A fortnight after he left on 10 September, a copy of *Word
Over All* arrived. Inside the cover Cecil had written, 'Mary with my love
Cecil, September, 1943'. Four pages on were the printed words, 'Dedicated
to Rosamond Lehmann'. The poems of Part One told more about Cecil's
new interest. 'The Lighted House' is another example of his repeated equa-
tion of new homes with new loves, and this one does not conclude with
any reflection about all houses being alike and a kind of prison; 'The
Hunter's Game' sees the lover as a bow and arrow compelled by love to
fire at his mistress, 'The huntress, white and smiling, laid – /The victim of
your arrow'; 'The Album' is full of appeals to the loved one, in which
Cecil looks at the old photographs of Rosamond in various stages of her
youth, 'scenes at your heyday taken', considers the hurtful and 'intemperate
gales' of her mature life, and is finally reassured that he has missed nothing
through his forty-year absence.

> I close the book;
> But the past slides out of its leaves to haunt me
> And it seems, wherever I look,
> Phantoms of irreclaimable happiness taunt me.
> Then I see her, petalled in new-blown hours,
> Beside me – 'All you love most there
> Has blossomed again', she murmurs, 'all that you missed there
> Has grown to be yours.'

The fourth poem of the book contains a restatement of Cecil's pattern,
which Mary must by now have found recognizable and only partly reassur-

ing. The 'Departure in the Dark' could be taken to represent anywhere else that Cecil might have been staying as much as Brimclose. If it was really 'hard to be sure/If home were prison or prison home ...', if it was so that 'the desire/Going forth meets the desire returning', why not settle for staying put? Sadly there is a ruling of nature, Cecil's nature anyway, that man should be a 'tenacious settler ... Among wry thorns and ruins, yet nurture/A seed of discontent in his ripest ease'.

Mary was left to wonder for a month. On 27 October she received two letters from Cecil telling of his new love, and offering to divide himself so that he should spend part of his time with Rosamond and part maintaining his marriage, at least until Nick and I were 'launched'.

> HE   It is out at last –
>   The truth that fevered my cheek and frostily glassed
>   My eyes against you: a creeping
>   Incurable disease, it passed
>   Into your heart from mine while we were sleeping.*

Next day, Mary met Cecil off the late Waterloo train at Axminster. What happened after that she expressed with a single surprising word in her diary, 'Peace'. Surprising and yet not surprising: they both considered that angry confrontation might snap the frayed thread holding them together. Something in Cecil still wanted to maintain this thread, and not only because of his fatherly feelings. Mary's love was sufficiently selfless for her to believe that if she was understanding and accommodating about his extra-marital needs he would always come home in the end, in accordance with the closing declaration of *The Friendly Tree* (1936).

Cecil's *Word Over All* is divided into three parts and includes thirty-one poems in all. Six of the works in Part Two and five in Part Three were first published as *Poems in Wartime* (1940). Where the previous book, *Overtures to Death* (1938), had been resigned to doom, this one had the overall spirit of Walt Whitman's 'Reconciliation': 'Word over all, beautiful as the sky,/Beautiful that war and all its deeds of carnage must in time be utterly lost,/That the hands of the sisters Death and Night incessantly softly wash again, and ever again, this soiled world.'

Part One ends with the nine-poem sonnet sequence 'O Dreams, O Destinations', contrasting the experiences and idealism of childhood and youth with the compromise and disappointment of adult life. Asked in an interview at the end of his life which poem he would be most remembered by, he answered that this was not for him to say, but that he thought this sonnet sequence could be described as his most 'concentrated' piece of work.

The concentration will become clear if, with some help from Cecil's *Poetry for You* (1944), we go behind the scenes to see how the second of the sonnets was constructed.

* 'Married Dialogue' (*Poems 1943–1947*, 1948).

Children look down upon the morning-grey
Tissue of mist that veils a valley's lap:
Their fingers itch to tear it and unwrap
The flags, the roundabouts, the gala day.
They watch the spring rise inexhaustibly –
A breathing thread out of the eddied sand,
Sufficient to their day: but half their mind
Is on the sailed and glittering estuary.
Fondly we wish their mist might never break,
Knowing it hides so much that best were hidden:
We'd chain them by the spring, lest it should broaden
For them into a quicksand and a wreck.
But they slip through our fingers like the source,
Like mist, like time that has flagged out their course.

The theme here is one of those that haunted Cecil, the inevitability of children growing up and going out into the world. The sonnet expresses his unease at the prospect of Nick and me going through this process, and mixes images of his own and our childhoods. The first eight lines deal with the children's feelings and expectations, the last six with the protective thoughts of the parents.

His method of working frequently involved a start given him by a key line, which came to him more or less complete and provided a basis for the surrounding structure. In this case the line was, 'The flags, the round-abouts, the gala day'. He thought about this and decided it could have meaning on two levels: these were things which children might get excited about, and could also represent attitudes and circumstances encountered in adult life. The image of the first two lines was remembered from the comparatively recent past when he was living permanently at home and could drive me up from the Axe Valley to school at Rousdon. His route gave a superb view of the valley which, at this stage in the morning, was sometimes veiled by a grey tissue of mist. The image of lines five and six comes from Cecil's pre-1914 Irish summer holidays in Co Wexford, when he watched the Monart Rectory gardener Johnny Keyes clearing the spring that rose in the paddock. 'A scoop of sandy earth beneath a boulder, it was', he remembered in his autobiography. 'When the leaves were cleared out, I could see the sand grains dancing and a spiral shape growing out of them, linking the source with the dimpled surface.'

The later generalized images of a 'sailed and glittering estuary' and 'a quicksand and a wreck' were imagined from the earlier ones, they do not result from observation at Axmouth or Wexford. The final image, 'like time that has flagged out their course', arises from a memory of the two-mile steeple-chase course when Cecil was a fourteen-year-old at Sherborne. He concluded that the origins of the images illustrated the way a poet digs into himself for precious stones, as a miner digs into a hillside. 'However skilful and hard-working a miner is, he will not find any diamonds unless there are some to be found there', Cecil added.

On the whole *Word Over All* has received more critical praise than any subsequent book of Cecil's verse. The main question mark has been applied to some of the war poems: occasional works such as 'Airmen Broadcast', celebrating the triumph of the Spitfire and Hurricane pilots in the Battle of Britain; 'Lidice', remembering the Czech village obliterated by the Germans in 1941; even 'Will it be so again?', regretting that in war it is so often 'That the best are chosen to fall and sleep'. Critics have held that these are duty verses, written because the poet was aware of a situation demanding a poem, rather than being aware of a poem demanding to be written.

Other war-time poems are clearly felt, particularly those like 'Word Over All' itself and 'Ode to Fear', which place Cecil's own fear and 'our time's ghost-guise of impermanence' against his duty to go on recording. The book ends with four Billie Currall poems, all passionate, clear and singable. The tone, as Clifford Dyment has pointed out, conveys 'a wry resignation, a sort of non-gloomy pessimism'. 'The poems in *Word Over All* – I will chance my arm over this – still seem to me far and away the most striking, taken together, that Cecil Day-Lewis ever write, more remarkable technically and more profoundly felt than what went before or what came after', added John Lehmann in 1960.

As with The *Georgics* in 1940, Cape managed to take advantage of the boom in poetry sales with *Word Over All*. Both books sold over 11,000 copies, a considerable advance on any of Cecil's 1930s volumes, none of which reached a 2,000 sale.

On 9 December Cecil was able to broadcast 'The Revenant', a poem reflecting on the Orpheus and Eurydice legend, in the first of a Home Service series produced by Stephen Potter and called *New Poems*. This appears to have been the first work written for his next book of verse, not to be published until 1948. He sent the poem to John Lehmann for possible inclusion in the fiftieth number of *New Writing* and in the letter told that he was now working on translations from Valéry. Rosamond, who could cope with the French language more confidently than Cecil and did not share his prejudice against modern French culture, had suggested that he might do some Valéry translations and offered to put the originals into literal English. He, feeling the need to relieve his slightly obsessive attachment to Hardy, was receptive to the idea of investigating a quite different poet, a rationalist of elegant precision rather than a fatalist of passionate irony. Cecil rendered the twenty-four stanzas of 'Le Cimetière Marin' as 'The Graveyard by the Sea' and for good measure translated the four stanzas of 'The Footsteps'.

In November Cecil took another step towards establishing himself as a metropolitan. On the third he was elected to membership of the Savile

Club, proposed by A.D. Peters and supported by many including Compton Mackenzie, Stephen Potter and Stephen Spender. He accepted the place and paid his first annual subscription of twelve guineas. The Savile was predominantly a literary club – with a distinguished representation of professionals in music, the theatre and the cinema – so he could generally feel he was where he liked to be, among his peers. He never suffered bores patiently though, and, as a guest, I can remember his ill-concealed impatience when put next to a member whose one desire in life was to discuss matters artistic in terms of algebra. Against this it was in the middle 1940s that the members of the Savile, like prep-school boys in the grip of a new group of catch-phrases, were working up the joke about one-upmanship, gamesmanship, lifemanship and the like. Cecil later expressed some mild jealousy that Stephen Potter had had the wit to develop this craze into a literary industry, mythically centred at Station Road, Yeovil, with himself as sole shareholder.

By 1944 the MOI had moved out of the high Senate House to nearby Russell Square House and it was here that Cecil was working as the Germans attacked London with their V1 and V2 missiles. Though the building had had a near miss, during which all its windows were blown out, the editors stayed at their desks even when a prolonged note on the buzzer system indicated that a clutch of missiles was approaching the area. Only when there was a series of short buzzes, announcing that a bomb was heading for the Ministry, did the staff take what cover they could on the north side of the building. Laurie Lee sometimes operated as an independent spotter, crawling out of his window and sitting on the ledge, armed with binoculars and a police whistle.

Rosamond, who that year published her immensely successful novel *The Ballad and the Source* (dedicated to CDL and known as 'The Salad and the Bourse') was now living with her children in Diamond Cottage at Aldworth in the Berkshire hills. Cecil spent his weekends there as often as possible, enjoying the sort of gently wooded countryside which he had wanted for himself when he first thought of leaving Cheltenham. Sometimes he coincided with the children home on their school holidays. Sally, now ten and just started at boarding school, began to adore Cecil as a kind of extra father, and he, who had always wanted a daughter, felt able to respond with the kind of overt affection not customary at Brimclose. Her brother Hugo, then twelve, and, in his own words, 'the prematurely grown-up man about the house', had a more distant relationship with Cecil, whom he remembers as 'a man of great precision, regular hours, nothing ever out of place. His hair was brushed and there were three buttons on his coat, his pencils were sharpened and his notebooks neatly laid out: he was not a spontaneous figure. He didn't at all put himself up as a stepfather; but he paid attention to our juvenile ploys, he was good at playing trains, specially smashes. But he certainly wasn't always there when we were at home.'

Cecil's visits to Brimclose remained infrequent: a weekend in February, one just before his fortieth birthday in April, a third timed for Mary's forty-second birthday in May, and another as June turned to July. My memory is that when Cecil arrived at Brimclose he would link arms with Mary and they would make a slow tour of the garden together talking quietly, and to me everything in the garden appeared well. Yet when they finally parted the one complaint that Cecil was ever heard to make about Mary was that as soon as he arrived on his visits she left for gossip and sympathy with her friend in the village, Barbara Cameron. This is not how it looked to me, though it doubtless had an element of truth and there were certainly bad times throughout the decade when Mary needed immediate reassurance.

'I don't think I am the right person to give impressions of Cecil. We had an antipathy for each other. On my side because his "affairs" made Mary very unhappy. She loved him a lot', Barbara Cameron remembered:

I used to think she was glad of the war years. Cecil was home quite a lot. There were some lovely summers and Brimclose was very peaceful. The war seemed very remote. A lot of the time I think Mary kidded herself that she had the perfect marriage. She liked cooking for him, she liked watching him cut the grass, and she was happy to see him in the porch writing. I think a lot of the time Mary and Cecil were very close. Mary's eyes always shone when she was happy and Cecil knew only too well that a smile from him would make her so. It's all mixed up with growing vegetables, collecting and sorting salvage and making camouflage nets, and amongst and through and around it all was Mary who worked so hard to make her marriage work and Cecil who smiled and invariably got his own way. Their common bond was Brimclose which they both loved.

On 10 February, for the first time since before the war, Cecil contrived a few days in Dublin. Knos visited him there and told of her planned retirement on the coast at Monkstown, when her brother Willie Squires completed his thirty-six-year ministry as Rector of Monart after Easter. Cecil's mind went back to the beginning of this term: pushing Uncle Willie's bicycle up the rough avenue to the rectory, listening to Knos as she scooped her way in luscious, funereal manner over the melodies of Tom Moore.

In Dublin he gave a lecture on poetry at the Abbey Theatre, with the writer Frank O'Connor as his chairman, and read Hardy to the Royal Dublin Society. The pleasure of being greeted in his native land as a celebrity meant even more to him than English plaudits; these came his way in September when he was elected a fellow of the Royal Society of Literature.

In August he was in Devon. He now saw little of Billie Currall, they even frequented different pubs, but he clearly felt nostalgic about his old love that summer. His 'On the Sea Wall' included in his *Poems 1943–1947* tells of a Seaton beach bather who appeared to be the ghost of Billie 'On the very same spot where, five years ago,/You slipped from my arms and played in the breaking/Surges to tease and enchant me'.

The following month, reunited with his present love in Berkshire, Cecil wrote the lines that are now to be found on his tombstone at Stinsford in Dorset:

> *Shall I be gone long?*
> For ever and a day.
> *To whom there belong?*
> Ask the stone to say.
> Ask my song.

Rosamond Lehmann remembered how on that day in 1944 he tossed the poem over the table to her with a flick of the wrist and a mock-modest smile. He called her 'Rose' and the last line begs, 'Quick, Rose, and kiss me'. The poem sprang directly out of a lovers' conversation between them. All the questions were supposedly from 'Rose' and his were the answers. In a way the epitaph chosen at my suggestion for his tombstone was a poignant joint epitaph for Cecil and Rosamond.

In December Basil Blackwell published his *Poetry for You*, a heart-felt 'book for boys and girls on the enjoyment of poetry' dedicated 'to Sean and Nico'. It proved to be one of his successes, selling nearly 120,000 copies at the last count. The foreword is diplomatically well-judged, flattering teachers that 'nowadays poetry is taught much more sensibly in schools' than it had been in his day, when he found himself at Wilkie's as a boy of eight trying to learn by heart, 'It was a summer's evening, Old Kasper's work was done . . .', against the distraction of flies buzzing on the window pane, a smell of scented lime trees and a street musician outside the window playing 'Pop goes the weasel'.

January 1945, the month in which the Allies in the Ardennes defeated the last major German counter-offensive of the war, was a weary one for Cecil. He had returned to London after Christmas, but was suffering from the effects of four years of overwork and a still longer period of emotional upheaval. On 19 January he returned to Brimclose for a fortnight of sick leave. He had no doubt that this was the home he should make for when in need of nursing. Snow fell heavily and at one point Musbury Castle had a six-inch covering. Cecil recovered a little with long walks, sawing, tobogganing, shooting and ping-pong tournaments on the new table he had bought at Christmas. At the end of the month he returned to his desk at the Ministry.

He was still there in Room 608, Russell Square House when Germany signed its unconditional surrender. He did not rejoice: he had too many doubts about the past and the future, and his own war roles; but he nevertheless set to work on an 'Ode to Victory' for broadcasting, and an Albert

Hall pageant. Two days after VE Day Mary arrived at his flat at 14 John Street. They went on from there to a nostalgic long weekend at the Randolph Hotel, Oxford, where Mary was able to enjoy a contented forty-third birthday on 12 May.

On 5 July Cecil was at Brimclose for the General Election, casting his Labour vote in the safely Conservative Honiton constituency. Two days later he recovered his Hillman Minx coupé (attacked as a German tank as part of Home Guard training in 1940) from the Seaton garage where it had been waiting for a new part for four years. He celebrated by shooting two rabbits and a pigeon, useful for the pot with food shortages increasing as the European war ended.

Mary's mother was dying of cancer at Sherborne. When Mary had to take her turn in the sick-room she found the task both squalid and shattering. Constance died late at night on 31 July, the day before her seventy-fourth birthday. Cecil and Mary gathered with the rest of the home-based Kings on 3 August, and next day went to the funeral at Sherborne Abbey followed by interment beside the remains of H.R.K. at Sherborne Cemetery. Cecil left for London after lunch at the Crown. Mary broke down with exhaustion and grief at Brimclose next day.

On 6 August the Americans destroyed the Japanese city of Hiroshima with the first atomic bomb to be used in war and three days later they repeated the dose at Nagasaki. When Cecil came to Brimclose for his summer holiday on 10 August the Second World War was almost over. Five years had gone since Cecil kept watch on Musbury Castle, 'For whatever may come to injure our countryside':

> Image or fact, we both in the countryside
> Have found our natural law, and until invaders
> Come will answer its need: for both of us, hope
> Means a harvest from small beginnings, who this night
> While the moon sorts out into shadow and shape our valley,
> A farmer and a poet, are keeping watch.*

Now the Musbury church-bells were ringing out at last, bells which were to have been tolled as a signal that the Germans had landed and which had stayed silent until this moment when they could declare peace. At the crown of the hill stood wood piled to make a bonfire, just one of the beacons which the following evening would symbolize the thankfulness of the Axe Valley people.

There had been a lot of laughter in the village during the war years; Mary had laughed as much as anybody, but she was now emotionally exhausted. I had never heard her cry before. It was a terrible, wailing sound which drifted down through the floor-boards of their bedroom as I stood

*'Watching Post' (*Word Over All*, 1943).

below in Cecil's study during the morning of 25 August, her cries punctuated with ineffectual mutterings of consolation from him. The ostensible
reason for the outburst was that Nick had been caught smoking and she,
who smoked forty cigarettes a day, did not want him to emulate her. Even
then I realized that more than this must have upset her; and in retrospect
I understood that her crying was for the death of her mother and the
security of childhood and the surrender of youthful idealism and the nagging knowledge that in two days' time Cecil would be returning to the
arms of Rosamond. Next day Cecil had stomach trouble, a sure sign that
his nervous system was being strained. He kept his anxieties to himself, was
weighed down with guilt and saw Mary watching him.

> Take any place – this garden plot will do
> Where he with mower, scythe or hook goes out
> To fight the grass and lay a growing fever,
> Volcanic for another, dead to me;
> Meek is the ghost, a banked furnace the man.*

At the beginning of October she and Barbara Cameron went on holiday
in the Lake District, meeting Cecil in London at the beginning and the
end. On 24 October Cecil came to Brimclose for a long weekend. Mary
met him at Axminster off the late evening train and afterwards wrote 'no
spark' in her diary. Next day, 'Talked to Cecil about self and Rosamond.
There isn't really any way out of this trouble until we are old, nothing
can cure the situation really, but it is good to talk.' On the twenty-seventh
they went to Sherborne to stake their claim in the division of Greenhill
furniture, and to take Nicholas to a picnic lunch beside 'the friendly tree'
on the prairie where they had done so much of their courting.

The Ministry of Information continued in existence. As Nigel Strangeways explains in Nicholas Blake's *Minute for Murder* (1947), 'The public are
sick of stories, photographs, exhibitions, films about the war. We're only
going on with the production because the service departments can't fight
down their lust for publicity – a lust we ourselves, I admit, were first responsible for provoking in them.' Cecil continued to attend at his office though
he no longer believed very much in the work.

Earlier in the year he had accepted a commission from G.M. Trevelyan,
the historian and Master of Trinity College, Cambridge, to give the 1946
Clark Lectures and the preparation of these was now his major activity
both at home and in his office. Among those who doubtless influenced the
choice of Cecil for this task was George Rylands of King's, a fellow founder
of the Apollo Society and a long-time friend of Rosamond.

He had ten days at Brimclose for Christmas that year. He bought Mary
a lamb-wool coat at Exeter and together they despatched their Christmas
card, on the outside an angel-happy design by Paul Cross and on the inside

* 'The Woman Alone' (*Poems 1943–1947*, 1948).

Cecil's new poem, 'The Christmas Tree', later published in *Poems 1943–1947*.

> Put out the lights now!
> Look at the Tree, the rough tree dazzled
> In oriole plumes of flame,
> Tinselled with twinkling frost fire, tasselled
> With stars and moons – the same
> That yesterday hid in the spinney and had no fame
> Till we put out the lights now.

In a broadcast many years later, Cecil explained how he cut the tree from a spinney above Brimclose and bought it into the house for the twelve days of Christmas. Mary snorted on hearing this and pointed out that she had always been responsible for providing the tree. Thanks to her green-fingered skills our trees were used repeatedly, re-rooted in the garden when the festival was over to await the next Christmas. 'Put out the lights now!' was a traditional cry. Mary would never countenance artificial light on her tree, and when the candles were lit on Christmas Day the electric lights in the long, low living room would be switched off.

'January 24, 1946. … I have been painting Cecil and he, in his ingenious and determined way, has taken the opportunity to write a poem', wrote Lawrence Gowing, Cecil's portraitist. 'I have kept my painting room a great deal tidier since I read it. "Who was Gowing?" – "The painter in that poem by Day–Lewis." Collector's fever; I have bought four prints this week. Including the *Death of the Virgin* (by Rembrandt), of which Cecil said, "Some of these angels ought to be in a reform school."' Commissioned by Rosamond, Gowing was working on what was unarguably the most powerful portrait of Cecil ever painted.

'Most of the talk was about Hardy, I remember, and psycho-analysis', wrote Gowing in a letter to me. 'He spoke of a relationship that he had with an older woman [Margaret Marshall] when he was very young – looking back, he saw it as tantamount to analysis, and important in his mental life. … Cecil was continuously inquisitive about my procedure. When a conventional likeness was virtually finished, he was seriously alarmed (I was apprehensive myself) to see a runny wash of cobalt blue slapped all over it. I then repainted the whole thing in one sitting.'

It is a dark picture and some have found it to reflect the ruthless aspect of Cecil's nature. Gowing said that he was not aiming to illustrate 'ruthlessness'.

My intention, so far as it was not necessarily vague, was simply to dwell on the visible shape, which was so noble, and through it perhaps to parallel some of the brooding quality of poetic determination, both constant yet delicate, yet certainly with an element of fierceness, which forbade me to change the shape of his mouth. Of course a painter of my kind is so exclusively concerned with look-ing that he hardly notices what it is that he has seen, let alone considers its moral constitution. It was quite a surprise when Rosamond said 'I wondered what you would do about the chin', and realized that she thought of as a blemish to be tactfully masked, the scar that I had never been conscious of at all.

As the day for the delivery of the first of his Clark Lectures at Cambridge drew near Cecil looked ahead with some trepidation: he was conscious of not being a scholar by temperament, that his Oxford degree was a poor one, that the pedagogic triumphs of a preparatory schoolmaster had come too easily. On 29 December he had read the first lecture to Mary at Brim-close: it was a long time since she had been invited to help in any way with his work, and this reading, as well as being pleasing to her, was a symp-tom of his anxiety to be well rehearsed for the day of the opening lecture, 24 January.

The number of Clark Lectures, established in the late nineteenth century and given annually in the general area of Eng Lit, is elastic, and it was Cecil who decided that his subject *The Poetic Image* merited six lectures, all to be given in the Easter term of 1946. Before making his first entrance in the Trinity dining hall he was in an understandably nervous condition and was grateful for a nip of gin from a flask proffered by the perceptive Ken-neth Clark. Cecil had been aware of Clark's patrician features presiding over the Films Division of the MOI, but they only became friends through the gin incident.

Cecil's experience as a schoolmaster, broadcaster and recitalist, as an ama-teur actor and singer, meant that he knew something about how to work on an audience. A Cambridge University audience, so accustomed to the mainly grim science of academic literary criticism, was likely to be struck by a lecturer who dared to mention the one common factor in the response of all readers for whom a poem has some meaning: 'that common factor – let us be rash, and burn our boats, and call it pleasure'. The influence of Rosamond on these lectures was considerable. Beside *A Hope for Poetry* (1934) they show an author brought out to his potential: 'very excellent they were – original and illuminating; they were also admirably delivered and warmly applauded. I remember how greatly the Master of Trinity, George Trevelyan, enjoyed them', recalled George Rylands. The achieve-ment was the more remarkable in view of the strain of Cecil's life at the time.

Cecil returned to Brimclose next day, 25 January, and Laurie Lee joined him there. The success at Cambridge had done nothing to resolve future courses and Cecil remained in at least two minds about how and where he should live when he retired from the Ministry of Information at the end of the month. Only in minor ways could he clear his desk. On 29 January he wrote to Denys Kilham Roberts saying, 'I have decided not to continue with *Orion* after number three – I've really got too much on

1. Frank Day-Lewis, Cecil's father, at the time of his ordination in 1900

2. Agnes 'Knos' Squires, Cecil's aunt, who became a 'second mother' to him after the death of Kathleen Day-Lewis in 1908

3. The infant Cecil after the Day-Lewis move from Ireland to England in 1905

4. The twelve-year-old Cecil on holiday from 'Wilkies' prep school in 1916

5. With Rex Warner, 'the hawk-faced man', before Cecil's first marriage in 1928

6. With Sean his first child on holiday in Scotland in 1932

7. With Mary his wife at Cheltenham in 1930

8. Cecil on Musbury Castle, 'a hill flank overlooking the Axe Valley', in 1939

9. Billie Currall ('That winter love spoke and we raised no objection . . .') and their child William in 1940

10. With Charles Fenby in the Brimclose garden during the 1940s

11. With sons Sean (right) and Nicholas

12. Living room still life

13. With W. H. Auden (left) and Stephen Spender at the Venice conference of PEN International in 1949

14. Rosamond Lehmann in the same year

15. The 1946 Lawrence Gowing portrait of Cecil which Rosamond encouraged

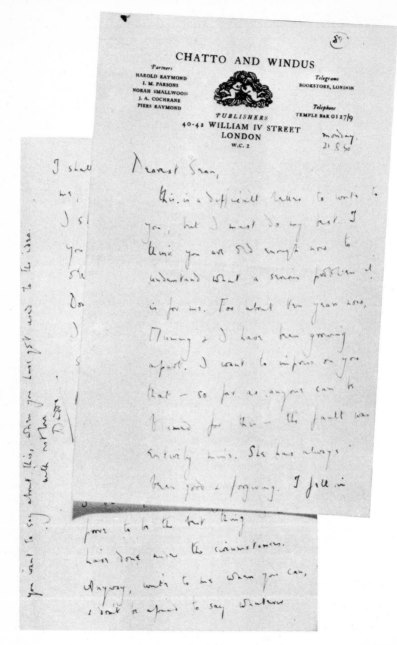

CHATTO AND WINDUS

Partners
HAROLD RAYMOND
I. M. PARSONS
NORAH SMALLWOOD
J. A. COCHRANE
PIERS RAYMOND

Telegrams
BOOKSTORE, LONDON

Telephone
TEMPLE BAR 01 27/9

PUBLISHERS
40-42 WILLIAM IV STREET
LONDON
W.C.2

monday.
21 8 50

Dearest Sean,

This is a difficult letter to write to you, but I must do my best. I think you are old enough now to understand what a serious problem it is for me. For about ten years now, Mummy & I have been growing apart. I want to impress on you that — so far as anyone can be blamed for this — the fault was entirely mine. She has always been good & forgiving. I fell in

I shall
us,
I sl
you
sha
Do
I
s

you want to say about this, when you have just used to the idea.

D——

fairer to be the best thing
I have done under the circumstances.
Anyway, write to me when you can,
I don't be afraid to say whatever

16. Cecil's 1950 letter to Sean announcing the end of his first marriage and the beginning of his second

17. Cecil and his second
wife, Jill Balcon, in the
drawing room of
96 Campden Hill Road
in 1953

18. With Jill and their children, Tamasin and Daniel, reading
congratulations on his appointment as Poet Laureate in the new
year of 1968

19. Cecil as he appeared in 'A Lasting Joy', a BBC television series recorded at his Greenwich home three months before his death

20. Kingsley and Jane Amis at Lemmons, their eighteenth-century Hadley Wood house on the northern edge of London. It was here that Cecil died in 1972

my plate to be able to give it all the attention I ought to.' As it turned
out this third issue, published later that year, was also the last: containing,
amongst much else, Cecil's 'The Sitting', 'Buzzards Over Castle Hill' and
'Statuette: Late Minoan'.

One trouble was that none of the things on his plate offered a continuing
income sufficient to maintain a family and live a complicated double life.
He had been offered a teaching job at a small, progressive private school
close to Musbury, just over the Dorset border, but there were reasons why
he did not wish to try settling at Brimclose again. He had agreed to be
a full-time reader for the new publishing firm of John Lehmann Ltd, which
started in 1945, but while the company was struggling to establish itself
this only offered part-time employment.

On 31 January Cecil left the MOI for the last time and Mary was somewhat
heartened that day to receive a letter saying that he was thinking of spending
the next three months working at Brimclose. In fact he did not reach there
until 9 February, in the meantime having given his second Clark lecture
on 'The Field of Imagery'. He did some work improving the Brimclose
drive, and having finished this he rang Rosamond to make arrangements
for meeting over the third Clark lecture, 'The Pattern of Images', on St
Valentine's Day.

On 19 February Mary recorded, 'Cecil at pub, talk afterwards about
Rosamond'. For the first time Cecil said he could think of 'no good reason'
why he should not go to her permanently. Next day he and Mary left
together for London, a crisis arising because Cecil had forgotten to bring
his reading glasses. 'Whole day a mist of unreality and wondering what
the result will be, it can't end like this', wrote Mary in London while he
was out visiting Rosamond. It did not end like that. Next day Mary accompanied him to Cambridge for the fourth Clark lecture, 'The Living Image'.
'Enjoyed the lecture, sat in Master's chair, very cold, happy day', Mary
wrote. Afterwards they had three more days in London and then returned
together to Devon.

Rosamond's *The Ballad and the Source* had enjoyed a huge success in the
United States and when sales passed the 600,000 mark she benefited by a
well-placed clause in her contract with the Hollywood film-producer
Walter Wanger. A windfall in the order of £40,000 enabled her to buy
the beautiful, rambling Georgian manor house at Little Wittenham, near
Abingdon in Berkshire.

> Did you notice at all as you entered the house,
>   Your dove-treed house,
> Traces of one who was there before you
> Imagining roseate company for you,
>   While the locked rooms lay in a drowse?*

* 'The House-Warming' (*Poems 1943–1947*, 1948).

The manuscript of this poem in King's College Library at Cambridge is dated 'Little Wittenham, May 5' and this is the best guide there is to when this place, built under the shadow of Paul Nash's Wittenham Clumps close to the Thames and 'a weir's deep humming', became Cecil's second home. Over the next four years, with interruptions, he would spend much of school term-time there, monopolizing the dining room for his work, with Rosamond fulfilling numerous social engagements at nearby Oxford, regretting his departures and that 'mischance or folly' which prevented his being more than a visitor.

> But here may you find, for all his fretting
>   And gaunt regretting,
> Between the dove-tops and the weir's
> Undying fall, how broken years
>   Can sing to a new setting.

The carefully-placed and well-varied trees, the spacious and flower-surrounded lawns, the mellow red-brick house and its bow windows, all give a great impression of ease and harmony: where Brimclose and its surroundings look like a natural growth, this Manor House and its grounds appear classical, ordered, rational, grand. Not all Cecil's responses were rational, but he fitted into the prevailing elegance. 'I always thought of her house as a dream fulfilment of my ideal Thames Valley manor, with its purity of design, its warmly mellowed brickwork, and ancient history embedded in every field around', remembered John Lehmann in 1960.

Cecil was back at Brimclose for Mary's forty-fourth birthday on 12 May and gave her a Wedgwood cameo brooch. Two days later she followed him to London to attend the Society of Authors poetry recital at the Wigmore Hall. She found herself sitting in the same row as Rosamond, but they did not make contact. It was a notable occasion, attended by Queen Elizabeth and her two young daughters, and starting with a prologue written and delivered by the Poet Laureate, John Masefield. Among others who read from their own work were Walter de la Mare, T.S. Eliot, Edith Sitwell, Louis MacNeice and Dylan Thomas (who at one stage in the proceedings was seen to flick his cigarette ash in the Queen's lap). Cecil, in good form, read Robert Browning's 'Confessions' and Thomas Hardy's 'At Castle Boterel' in the first half; and his own 'The Lighted House' (a love poem for Rosamond) and 'Birthday Poem for Thomas Hardy' in the second.

Later that month Cecil wrote to John Hayward, for many years friend and companion to T.S. Eliot, saying he had been asked by *The Times* to write Eliot's obituary. 'I have told them I do not feel able to tackle it without the help of a close friend of his, and they agree I should ask you to collaborate in this melancholy task. Will you? – I'd be immensely grateful and pleased if you could, for I do want to do T.S.E. proud.'

Another task Cecil unwisely accepted in this year of uncertain prospects was editing the comprehensive ninth volume of the *Oxford Junior Encyclopaedia* devoted to 'Recreations'. This would involve persuading over a hundred contributors to provide more than five times that number of short articles on every leisure activity from accordian playing and acrobatics to whist and yodelling. John Arlott, then a BBC poetry producer as well as a cricket pundit, was his guest at Brimclose for the weekend of 1 June and gave what help he could.

I came home from school as usual for a few hours on Sunday and was more than awe-stricken to discover that I was in the same house as a man who had once been twelfth man for Hampshire. Arlott was sufficiently impressed by our earnestness to invite Cecil and his sons to join him in his commentary box at Taunton for the Somerset *v* India match in early August.

T.S. Eliot had once advised Cecil that he should ration his appearances at school speech days. He found this a difficult rule to keep during his last twenty-five years, when he was constantly in demand, as he rather relished the platform role, knowing from bored experience that he could improve on the performance of ninety-five per cent of those who pontificate at such occasions. One of his first assignments of the kind was at Tennyson's old school, King Edward VI Grammar School in Louth, where the headmaster was Hedley Warr, a Cheltenham colleague. Cecil gave what he called 'a sales talk about poetry', an art which could help the sensitive young to 'unravel the tangle of your own feelings'. He ended by describing in detail the genesis of his one poem that grew directly from his experience of the London blitz, 'In the Shelter', which germinated some five years after the event.

One night in London, during the blitzes, I popped into an air-raid shelter. The Luftwaffe was getting a bit too close for my liking. It wasn't at all a deep shelter. There were a lot of grown-up people there, and we were all quite a bit frightened and pretending we weren't – making jokes and so on. One old man, I remember, was sitting on a bunk and shaking, shaking, shaking, shaking like an aspen leaf. Every bomb that fell seemed to start another rivet in me, and a bit more fear leaked in. Then a small girl entered the shelter. She must have been about seven or eight years old: a pretty little girl carrying a doll half as big as herself. Her grandmother – some old woman anyway – came in behind her. The little girl sat down on a broken-backed chair in the middle of the shelter, still nursing the doll, her long black hair falling over it. A stick of bombs fell close. The shelter seemed to rock and settle back again. I was watching the little girl. She bent closer over the doll as the bombs shrieked down; she was murmuring to it, comforting it. She seemed extraordinarily alone there, in the midst of the crowded shelter. Alone, but not lonely. The shelter was whitewashed glaring white, lit by naked electric bulbs. But this small girl seemed to me to be shining too, glowing, like a storm-lantern or a night-light. She looked absolutely self-possessed, self-contained she and her doll. I simply couldn't take my eyes off her. And after a bit, the raid ended. And

I realised that ever since this girl, this little night-light had come in and I'd begun to watch her, I'd forgotten to be frightened, I really had hardly heard the bombs and the barrage. There was she, absorbed in her doll; and there was I, intent on her, on the almost unearthly beauty of her face and her pose as she comforted her doll. . . .

> Dear sheltering child, if again misgivings grieve me
> That love is only a respite, an opal bloom
> Upon our snow-set fields, come back to revive me
> Cradling your spark through blizzard, drift and tomb.

At the beginning of that June at least two of the MacSpaunday poets were greatly exercised over the publication by Faber of *Talking Bronco*, the latest volume of verse by Roy Campbell, the South African poet who had fought for Franco in Spain and was now working at the BBC. The book is mainly devoted to 'satires' presenting that 'joint MacSpaunday . . . a cerberus-hyena commercially collectivised', as a cowardly, greedy and hypocritical monster. Left-wing poets made fiercely belligerent noises in time of peace, encouraging both war and utopian dreams; then at the outbreak of war they left others to fight, took safe positions at the rear and made money. Campbell ruined his case by overstating it; and yet Cecil did have exposed nerves in this area and they were touched. One poem called 'The Volunteer's Reply to the Poet' uses Cecil's *Word Over All* title 'Will it be so again?' as its sub-title. 'But hush! for the Poet-Civilian/Is weeping, between the cigars/Mellifluous, sweeter than Cadbury's/The M.O.I. Nightingale (Hush!)/Is lining his funk-hole with Bradburies', is a fair sample of the poetic and intellectual quality. Stephen Spender, who is personally attacked in another 'satire', was first to rise to the bait. Cecil wrote to him from Brimclose on 7 June.

Many thanks for your letter, and for the one you sent to Campbell, which seems to me just the thing he needs: I shall be interested to hear what he replies, if anything. I have not read his book of poems, but must try to get hold of it. What is Louis' reaction? As he is a colleague of Campbell at the BBC, much seems to depend on his viewpoint, since my own first impulse is that we should raise such a stink that C. should be chucked out of the BBC as a Fascist and an irresponsible calumniator and therefore a person not fitted to direct any civilised form of cultural expression. I agree with you in a dislike of taking such a business into the Courts: a libel action in such a case as this always suggests pique and vindictiveness on the part of those who bring it: it is essential that what we attack and expose in his book should be his vilification, through us, of the Spanish Republicans and all who helped them. And I think you, Louis and I, though we would not pretend to be unhurt by the personal attacks, can honestly say that it was this vilification which we feel most deeply about. I certainly agree that a letter should be sent to the Press: perhaps, when you are back, we might compose one with Louis. But I do not think we should necessarily stop there. What we must aim at is a public apology from Campbell, and I think only the most forceful methods are at all likely to wring an apology from him.

By the way, in 1941 Roy Campbell came into my office at the MOI, with Dylan Thomas, both fairly drunk. Campbell was shaking like a leaf. He kept on saying, 'I know you must hate me. I know now that I was wrong, I admit I was wrong'. I gathered he meant about his line during the Spanish War. So now he has turned his coat twice. I shall remind him of this when I see him, as I look forward to doing soon. He then asked me if I could get him into the Marines and tried to borrow some money, which I did not lend him. Maybe he thought that, if he said he'd been wrong about Spain, I would fall on his neck and offer him my wallet. I'm told that he offers a version of this incident in another poem in this new book, and it has evidently rankled with him for a long time. However, my secretary was present, and she may be able to remember just what did happen.

T. S. Eliot, at his most vague and unworldly, had accepted *Talking Bronco* for Faber without realizing that the 'satires' were directed more or less libellously, and with no camouflage, at four poets for whom he professed considerable admiration. When told what he had published he was shocked. Fortunately for him and Campbell none of the poets felt inclined to pursue the matter very far and when Cecil wrote to Stephen Spender again, from Little Wittenham on 26 June, he was taking a lighter view of the matter. 'Campbell is so childish and incorrigible that he ought to be made to stand in the corner with a dunce's cap on', wrote the schoolmasterly Cecil. 'Edith [Sitwell], from whom Rosamond received an indignant letter today, is girding herself up terrifically for the fray; if we are not careful, we shall find ourselves caught up in one of those Sitwell Charges of the Light Brigade: I must try to gag her somehow!'

Meanwhile Cecil and John Hayward were continuing to take trouble over the Eliot obituary, for which they were to share five guineas from *The Times*. 'You will see I have abbreviated some of your admirable material to make room for a longish critical paragraph, and patched some of my utility writing into your beautiful garment, I will not say shroud', Cecil wrote to Hayward on 21 June. 'I hope you feel that my reference to his private tragedy is passable; I am sure some reference is necessary and mine gives away nothing distastefully personal to the ordinary reader.'

The obituary, two-thirds of a column long, was filed in *The Times* morgue in August. The reticence with which Cecil dealt with the mental illness of Eliot's first wife was very characteristic. 'At the same time, a long drawn out private tragedy which darkened his middle years left deep impressions on his verse: the rawness, the shuddering distaste, the sense of contagion, the dry despair which emerge from certain passages of *Ash Wednesday*, for instance, and *The Family Reunion*, are traces of it. But for this emotional wound, so long unheeded, his poetry might well have been more genial, less ascetic: but equally it might well have been less intense.'

In mid-June Cecil wrote to John Lehmann from Musbury saying, 'I have just had a letter out of the blue from Chatto and Windus, offering me the job of literary adviser. I shall tell them that I have an arrangement with another publisher, and the nature of this arrangement. Their offer puts me on the spot a bit: on the one hand I would rather work for you; on the other hand, you naturally cannot be certain yet that, when our present arrangement for a year terminates next spring, you will be in a position to take me on permanently as reader and literary adviser.' He suggested that he should go temporarily to Chatto leaving Lehmann with the option of taking him back. 'I am terribly keen on getting this sort of job permanently so that I can have a basic livelihood (and such a pleasant one) and pick and choose more in respect of my own writing', Cecil revealed.

Lehmann decided to release him and it was agreed that he should start his new work as senior reader at Chatto and Windus, after a long summer holiday at Musbury, on 30 September. Cecil's recruitment for Chatto was mainly the work of one of its directors, Ian Parsons, who had reviewed his poetry for the *Spectator* in the early 1930s and was then commended by Cecil as being the first critic who has 'gone into my poems deeply and come out at the other end'. The firm had been without a principal reader since Oliver Warner went to the Admiralty in 1941 and, rather living on its pre-war past, was in need of revival. When Parsons asked J. R. (Joe) Ackerley for a recommendation, that MacSpaunday associate and respected literary editor of the *Listener* unhesitatingly proposed Cecil. The Chatto senior partner, Harold Raymond, accepted the idea and thus Cecil joined the firm he was to read for until a few weeks before his death more than twenty-five years later.

At first, that October, Cecil treated Tuesdays and Wednesdays as his Chatto office days; later he attended in alternate weeks. The tall, ramified premises are in William IV Street at the bottom of St Martin's Lane, and the claustrophobic view of walls and roofs from Cecil's small back office included part of the distinctive globe at the pinnacle of the adjacent Coliseum Theatre, at that period reverberating year after year with the American musical comedy *Annie Get Your Gun*. He learned his new trade as he went along, needing all his MOI and book-reviewing experience for recognizing good work quickly, and then editing wisely.

'Reading for a leading publisher is hard, exacting and unselfish work, illuminated by the occasional "discovery" and subsequent rejoicing,' said Cecil's predecessor Oliver Warner. 'At one stage some 800 manuscripts passed through my office every year and the rate cannot have been very different during Cecil's time. A few of those works needed close attention, and the art is to spot which they are. This is the result of experience, a rapid look, and an extra sense which a Reader acquires, with time, if he becomes skilled. Every Reader has his virtues and shortcomings. Cecil had both acumen and exceptional patience. He used to find the work restful in the physical sense, but arduous in its demand on the concentration needed for appraisal and editing. His long period of working for authors far less gifted than he was should be thankfully remembered when the sum of his achievement is considered.'

Ian Parsons admired Cecil's ability to manage a large volume of work; his 'first-rate skill' as a blurb writer; his well-constructed reports on books, anything up to a thousand words long; and his sensitive skills as an editor.

He was just a shade self-satisfied here and there, but was absolutely sweet-natured and humble-minded about corrections and suggestions to authors. He was good at taking trouble with authors and wrote such charming letters when a book was turned down that the recipient often felt more consoled than offended. He was quick to recognize talent and, remembering his youth, he erred on the side of being kind to young poets. He also had some flair for knowing what would sell, though he nearly drove us mad through his unwillingness to make decisions: having made his report he would ask, 'Do you think we should publish or not?'

Later he was made a director and was very glad about this. But he was never the complete publisher, more an outstanding publisher's reader. He was never interested in sales figures, he was really uninterested in whether books made money or not and never opened his mouth at board meetings when profits and loss were under discussion. He kept his life in compartments. This meant that he never took a book home and never found books for us; we were disappointed in our hopes that he might bring some of his writing friends to us. But he loved discipline and was a stickler for observing the official duties of a director: he hated parties, but he willingly came to the firm's annual outing to the theatre or into the country.

For a salary starting at £1,500 a year Cecil was a bit of a bargain.

Cecil became especially fond of the younger partners: Ian Parsons, Norah Smallwood, and Peter Cochrane, who was to be Cecil's executor.

His new job in publishing did not however give Cecil a new surge of life as a poet. When he wrote to Rupert Hart-Davis from Little Wittenham on 29 November he revealed that he had scrapped 'all or nearly all' of a long poem of six hundred words, 'the best part of a year's work wasted, but it simply was not good enough, except for the "Married Dialogue" which I do think is good'.

> But it's useless to argue the why and wherefore.
>   When a crop is so thin,
> There's nothing to do but to set the teeth
>   And plough it in.*

Cecil spent most of January 1947, at Brimclose and on the eighteenth he wrote from there to John Lehmann saying, 'I am still engaged in brooding over the bits which survive from the long poem I was writing, and which

* 'A Failure' (*Poems 1943–1947*, 1948).

I tore up last autumn, trying to decide which if any of these bits are worth working over again.' He added: 'Look after Rosamond in Paris, won't you, and don't let the Frogs take any liberties with her.'

On 1 February, when he left Musbury for two months at Little Wittenham with Rosamond, Mary wrote in her diary, 'I'm sick of this half life.' By this date the great snow blizzards of the famous 1947 winter had started. 'How lovely it looked when first it fell ... and how soon we were sick of it and never wanted to see the stuff again', wrote Cecil in the *Brimclose News* that I edited at that time. And in retrospect how cruel it seems to Mary that he should have written about Rosamond's place in our family paper!

Beginning to fall into a depression Cecil was somewhat consoled by the February publication of *The Graveyard by the Sea*, a lovely limited edition of five hundred printed in Verona with Paul Valéry's French text facing Cecil's translation. In April his characteristically practical sixteen-page reader's guide, *Enjoying Poetry*, was published for the National Book League by the Cambridge University Press. On 31 March *The Poetic Image*, the six Clark Lectures given by Cecil the previous year, came out from Jonathan Cape. This is dedicated 'In dutiful memory F.C.D–L–K.B.D–L', to his father and mother; and the foreword contains a generous but decently veiled tribute to 'the one who, from first to last, with gentle encouragement and delicate criticism helped me over the exacting course I had set myself when I chose *The Poetic Image* as my subject' – Rosamond.

Beside the cheerfully combative *A Hope for Poetry* (1934), designed as propaganda for MacSpaunday, *The Poetic Image* is thoughtful and undogmatic in its broad sweep through English poetry from Chaucer to Auden. The references to Cecil's discomfort at turning from artist to critic, a role about which he was always highly critical, are belied by the apparent ease with which he changes back and forth between the two functions. 'Again and again one recognizes the practical tone that one hears in Dryden's and Wordsworth's prefaces and in Coleridge's *Biographia Literaria* – the voice of the workman speaking with the peculiar knowledge that comes from having handled the materials and wrestled with the problems of the actual job', wrote Clifford Dyment.[4]

In late June this was followed by Nicholas Blake's *Minute for Murder*, his first post-war detective novel. 'The public will be relieved to know that the Government Department in which the action of this book takes place never did, or could, exist. I hereby assure my late colleagues, to whom this book is dedicated, that, whereas every disagreeable, incompetent, flagitious or homicidal type in it is a figment of my imagination, all the charming, efficient and noble characters are drawn from life', wrote Blake. Whatever the public's opinion, the Ministry of Morale in this book is a caricature of the Ministry of Information as seen by Cecil. Nigel Strangeways sits in Cecil's editorial chair and has lived at his club since Georgia, his wife, 'was killed in the blitz of April, 1941' – the time when Cecil began his relationship with Rosamond. According to Blake her death had left Nigel 'mentally crippled', as he had relied on 'her keen intuitive power' in his cases. (I can remember Cecil announcing at some Brimclose meal that he had 'got bored' with Georgia and so had killed her off.)

In April Cecil was feeling more weary than ever before, withdrawing where he could, arranging for a ghost to take over the chore of receiving and editing the articles for his volume of the *Oxford Junior Encyclopaedia*, refusing invitations. 'I'm so sorry I shall not be able to get to your party tomorrow – please give Christopher [Isherwood] my affectionate respects, if you have a moment', he wrote to John Lehmann on the fourteenth. 'Is that sum of money, which was offered to me last year to clear out of the country, still available? Rosamond and I hope to go to France in June, and perhaps to Czechoslovakia later, so it would come in useful.'

In fact it was at the end of 1945 that the Society of Authors' Travelling Scholarship Fund Committee, including Edith Sitwell, Stephen Spender and Harold Nicolson, as well as Lehmann, had divided some £300 between the prose writers William Sansom and V.S. Pritchett, and Cecil. It was maybe considered amusing to try to tempt Cecil abroad, as he was well known for his unwillingness to travel. Now, under Rosamond's wing, he thought that a change of scene might lift his depression.

He passed his forty-third birthday with the help of Nick Roughead, who came to stay for the weekend, and he tried digging in the garden to clear his head. He was also, unwisely, making one of his frequent attempts to give up smoking. 'My advice to anyone who contemplates giving up smoking is, DON'T. Depression, irritability, a foul taste in the mouth, pricking soles of the feet, inability to concentrate on work or to enjoy normal pleasures – these are some of the results of breaking a habit which is, after all, quite a harmless one', Cecil wrote in the *Brimclose News* of 30 April. After giving his rules for those who wanted to stop smoking he concluded that 'the quickest and most infallible method is to drink a pint of any good, reliable poison: which you will want to do anyway, after you have laid off tobacco for a day or two'.

The reference to poison was a wry joke. Cecil was deeply depressed when he left for his two Chatto days on 30 April and the next two months were going to be agony for him and those who loved him. He made the first of several visits to his sympathetic doctor at Axminster on 5 May, but he did not explain the root of his trouble and he was merely told that he needed a long holiday.

In better days he had looked up to the hill above Brimclose and written of 'Buzzards Over Castle Hill', recording that there always seemed to be three such birds 'wheeling/On the glass sky their skaters curves', speculating that they might be 'earth-souls doomed in their gyres to unwind/Some tragic love-tangle wherein they had mortally pined'. Cecil's own triangular

love-tangle had now become so difficult for him that he tried to stop looking up to the hill and cried,

> I will not lift mine eyes unto the hills
> For there white lambs nuzzle and creep like maggots.
> I will not breathe the lilies of the valley
> For through their scent a chambered corpse exhales.
> If a petal floats to earth, I am oppressed.
> The grassblades twist, twist deep in my breast.*

He saw himself 'Pent in a vicious circle of dilemmas' and had reached
the point where, as this poem says, 'Each onward step required the sweat
of nightmare,/Each human act a superhuman strength. . . .' It must have
been worrying for the unfortunate Terence Delaney, who had agreed to
be ghost editor of Cecil's *Oxford Junior Encyclopaedia* volume and came to
Brimclose to receive instructions during the weekend of 24 May. Delaney
escaped on Whit Monday the twenty-sixth, and later that day the dam
burst. Cecil talked, saying that his divided love had become intolerable to
him and that he could not take the strain much longer. Afterwards Mary
recorded that she was 'very tired and upset – cried for an hour, off and on,
I wish the situation could be cleared up'.

He went to London next day, and when he returned on the late train
of Thursday the twenty-ninth he and Rosamond had decided that the
present arrangements were too much of a strain on them, and that he must
leave Brimclose permanently and without pause for further agonizing.
Next day he went to the doctor again, complaining of chronic indigestion,
and was relieved to be told that no X-ray was needed. On Saturday he
did a little work on his boat at Lyme Regis and watched me playing in
a cricket match at Allhallows. On Sunday I was given my usual few hours
of release from school, between matins and evensong, and somehow
managed not to hear, see or feel anything out of place. Yet that day Mary
wrote in her diary, 'Cecil in state bordering on insanity, can't make up
his mind between Rosamond and me'; and later, 'Ghastly evening with
Cecil, life becoming intolerable, he can't see why he shouldn't leave me'.
By the early hours of Monday 2 June he had at last managed to say that
he would be going to Little Wittenham that day and would never be coming back. Mary's extraordinary stoicism disappeared, she broke down completely and begged him to stay.

They left in the Hillman at 7.30 am to catch the first train from Axminster
to Waterloo: he grey and grimly silent, she at the end of her resources,
saying nothing, crying uncontrollably. They had driven about half the
three miles to the station when Cecil suddenly stopped the car and, now
furiously angry, turned back. He accused Mary that by making it impossible for him to leave she had robbed him of 'the love of my life'.

* 'The Neurotic' (*Poems 1943–1947*, 1948).

In all its centuries Brimclose cannot have contained so much unhappiness as it contained that day, with Cecil brooding alone in his study and Mary equally alone and tortured in her kitchen. At some point Cecil telephoned Rosamond, his voice shaking with self-pity, to say that he would not be coming to her after all. He concluded that this must be the end of their relationship, and in a way was insisting on this loss so that he could feel the more sorry for himself. He, who had in psychological terms married his mother and had thought himself now ready to leave home, felt profoundly angry with himself that he had been unable to take this natural, healthy, inevitable step. Mary believed that marriage was a sacrament, that the vows they made at Sherborne Abbey more than eighteen years before were for always. It was unthinkable that Cecil should leave her; there was a sense in which he could not leave her. Such was her resilience and gritty optimism that she actually wrote in her diary that evening, 'Perhaps the garden will become a garden now and not an escape.'

It was not a pleasant week. 'Bad day with Cecil – had a varicose vein cut in hospital – this life at present is HELL', Mary wrote on Tuesday the third. 'Ghastly day again', she recorded on the fourth. 'Dismal evening', was her entry for the fifth. Laurie Lee had been asked for: he was a link with Rosamond and the one person whom Cecil believed able to lift him out of his depression. Laurie treated Cecil's malaise as an emergency, cancelled his previous arrangements and arrived at Axminster on the sixth with a bad toothache. Next day Cecil was already better, mowing the Brimclose lawn while his friend went to Seaton for treatment of an abscess. On Sunday it was Mary who fetched me from school: Cecil did not appear even for meals and I was told that he must stay in his study with Laurie, who was suffering from depression and needed Cecil's comforting presence. I was much impressed by Cecil's compassion and care, and went back to Allhallows that evening still none the wiser.

Next day Mary wrote that 'Cecil and Laurie seem happy together. Why can't he talk to me, I'm not always so dumb. He and Laurie have decided to go on holiday together, I wish *we* were going.' On Tuesday the tenth the two friends left on the early train to London, and Cecil resumed his Chatto work. Mary went to her friend Barbara Cameron for comfort and announced, 'Cecil hates me to cry, I shall never do it again.' When Cecil returned to her on the twelfth, and they had a long and inconclusive talk about their predicament, she remained dry-eyed and in control.

> Take any joy – the thread leads always on
> To here and now: snow, silence, vertigo;
> His frozen face, a woman who bewails not
> Only because she fears one echoing word
> May bring the avalanche about her ears.*

* 'The Woman Alone' (*Poems 1943–1947*, 1948).

Her control remained when she realized that Cecil was renewing his loving relationship with Billie Currall. Cecil and Billie's son William was a pretty boy of seven now, athletic and with a gentle manner and large, reproachful eyes. Often he walked up the lane past Brimclose after his bus from school had dropped him in the village. On one evening at the start of that terrible May a storm broke around him as he trudged upwards and Mary gave him shelter until the rain had passed, glad that he still remained ignorant of the link between them. That month Cecil gave Billie a ring belonging to his mother, a ring she has always worn since.

On 23 June Cecil was cheered by a letter from George Barnes, head of the BBC Third Programme, saying that he had 'often heard from mutual friends of your singing of Tom Moore's melodies and I am wondering whether you have ever broadcast any of them. If not, would you care to spend an hour one day or one evening singing them over a closed circuit in Broadcasting House? Your "turn", as described to me, seems well suited to the Third and I should so enjoy to have an opportunity of hearing how it comes through the mike. We might then, with your help, construct a programme around the melodies.' Cecil replied on the twenty-seventh that 'Yes, I have sung Moore twice on the air, but only a couple of songs each time: I'd certainly like to do a longer prog of them, if it could be arranged, I'm just off to Copenhagen for a few weeks: perhaps we might have a go over closed circuit when I return.'

On 30 June he left for his holiday in Denmark with Laurie Lee, the first time he had been outside the British Isles apart from his weekend in Paris in 1938. They stayed at the Hotel Cosmopallie in Copenhagen, Laurie recalling that he 'planned the holiday to be purely enjoyable, as Cecil had lately been so withdrawn and depressed. In fact, it worked and was a success – lots of food, friends and sunshine on the beach.'

Cecil was back at Brimclose on 17 July, bearing what Mary called 'small Danish presents'. Cecil was much better in spirit, and most enthusiastic about the plenitude of Danish food and the culinary habit of garnishing almost everything with a fried egg. His indigestion returned three days after he was restored to Mary's excellent home cooking.

On 21 July Rex Warner arrived at Brimclose to make his contribution towards Cecil's recovery. 'Cecil and Rex out most of day', wrote Mary on the twenty-second. It would be an exaggeration to say that Rex went to Musbury as an emissary from Rosamond, but he was close to her and no doubt able to reassure Cecil that if he should make another approach to her she would not be unsympathetic. Cecil and Rex left together on the early train of the twenty-third, and a week later Mary's heart sank when she received a letter saying that there would now be a return to the old compromise. Cecil would be spending most of the school holidays at Musbury and most of the terms at Little Wittenham, and he and Rosamond had once more agreed that they should abandon thoughts of full-time marriage until all their children were 'launched'. How unconsciously fitting that the *Daily Herald* should choose this moment to use the side-heading 'DOUBLE LIFE' over a gossip column item about Cecil's dual role as a poet and detective novelist.

August and September brought no change in our lives at Brimclose. There was a lot of cricket; Cecil tried me out as a tennis player on the courts at Seaton and allowed me to win three games in every set; he and Nick frequently went sailing at Lyme Regis while I went engine spotting at Seaton Junction; Roughie and John Garrett visited.

In the week of 8 September Cecil and Mary were in London together, showing Westminster Abbey and Greenwich Observatory and the American musical *Oklahoma* and other landmarks to Nick. They also went to the Academy Cinema to see the French film *Nous les Gosses*, shown in Britain as *Us Kids*, and the starting point for Cecil's second adventure novel for boys, *The Otterbury Incident* (1948).

On 19 September he took Nicholas to Sherborne for his first day at Harper House, thirty years almost to the day since his own father had delivered him there with those mysterious circumlocutions afterwards discovered to have been a sex talk. In my experience Cecil did not attempt to interfere in this part of our education: Mary gave me a book to read, with clear diagrams and no biological evasions, a year or two after a forward fellow pupil at school had given us the same facts in a vividly illustrated dormitory lecture.

I have a dim memory that somewhere about this time in 1947, fetching me from school one Sunday, on the last leg of the drive up through the village to Brimclose, Cecil tried to tell me about Rosamond. I did not know what the word 'mistress' meant, unless a female school-teacher, and I sensed enough about Cecil's tone of voice to realize that it would be best to remain in ignorance. The conversation fizzled away before we reached home, I having proved just as useless a consellor as was Cecil when invited to advise his father about remarrying.

Rumours that Cecil had been ill were circulating and at the end of October George Barnes, still hoping for his Tom Moore programme, asked Rosamond about them. She replied on 2 November, 'Cecil is now very well. He has been here all the month of October, but unfortunately left about an hour before your letter came. He had a near breakdown a few months ago – but he has wonderful powers of recuperation and is completely restored.'

That Christmas, surprisingly perhaps, the Day-Lewis family was still intact. Cecil read to us from *Oliver Twist* and helped to decorate the Christmas tree. On Christmas Day he joined the rest of us at morning service in St Michael's, Musbury, where Nick was now in the choir, and Mary considered he sang the hymns 'very loud'. On the twenty-seventh Cecil and Mary exchanged wedding anniversary presents as usual, a book for her and green bottles for him. He left for London early on 31 December for the reading by Robert Harris and Cecil Trouncer of his 'New Year's Eve' ode and meditation commissioned by the Third Programme.

> Between cast-iron past and plastic future;
> But equally, haunters of this unnatural pause,
> Remorse for what is to be,
> Doubt of all that has passed.

On 4 January 1948 Cecil took part in the BBC Home Service programme *Time for Verse*, produced by Patric Dickinson. His co-reader that evening was Jill Balcon, an actress who had reached her twenty-third birthday the day before. She was highly susceptible to poetry and poets and had read his work and hero-worshipped, if not loved, Cecil since 1938, when she was thirteen and he had visited her school, Roedean, to adjudicate the annual verse speaking competition. The following year she was in the Roedean choral team, declaiming Milton's 'Blessed Pair of Sirens' at the English Festival of Spoken Poetry in Oxford, and Cecil was on the adjudicating panel. She noted how, on this day at the BBC, Cecil appeared 'like a ghost, ravaged and tortured'. He behaved 'gravely and courteously but he was not communicative and we talked only about the programme and its production', she remembered. They were to meet again.

On 13 May Mary wrote, 'It is nearly a year since Cecil decided not to go, he has gone most of the way.' Two days before this diary entry he had left with Rosamond for the journey which would be enshrined as *An Italian Visit*. 'It started when I had a fan letter from Bernard Berenson about *The Ballad and the Source*', remembered Rosamond. 'We were already half-planning a visit to Italy and when he invited me to stay, asked Cecil and me together, we decided to complete our plans.'

Cecil's verse sequence gives a more or less accurate account of their journey. They flew from London to Rome, he uneasily conscious of the dangers of flight in those piston-engined days, specially when he looked down for the first time on that awe-inspiring air view of 'the atrocious Alps'.

> Their ambush –
> A primeval huddle, then a bristling and heaving of
> Brutal boulder-shapes, an uprush of Calibans –
> Unmasks its white-fanged malice to maul us.
> The cabin grows colder. Keep height, my angel!
> Where we are, all but terra firma is safe.*

They looked about the 'glorious junk-heap' of Rome, jaunting over the seven hills in a jarring carrozza, eating wild strawberries and sipping cool Frascati, impressed by St Peter's and glad to leave behind the ancient 'glum

---

* 'Flight to Italy' (*An Italian Visit*, 1953).

mementoes' of the Palatine and the Forum, comfortably at home with the
burial mounds of Keats and Shelley. They took a bus to Florence by the
Cassian Way, stopping in Siena long enough to admire 'the swan-necked
Mangia tower', the scallop-shaped square, the 'flight upon flight' of images
on the west front of the cathedral. Arrived in Florence they took a taxi
into 'the mint and myrrh of Tuscan hills' through Fiesole to Settignano
and the home of the sage of the Villa I Tatti.

Berenson, a frail little Polish-American Jew with a small head and a neat
white beard, had researched Italian Renaissance painting, attributed it,
shared his knowledge and made much money in the process. If he had not
managed the last of these accomplishments his achievement of the first three
would doubtless have brought him less attention. As it was he presided
over an international court for artists, intellectual pundits and beautiful
women. He was more adored by his female than his male guests and in
his cool way he, whose appreciation of beauty did not altogether coincide
with that of Michelangelo, reciprocated this bias. Men who were used to
being at or near the centre of attention were not attracted to this arrangement whereby, in John Lehmann's words, Berenson was treated as 'a
mixture of the Oracle of Delphi and God the Father'.

Cecil did not like B.B., though he fell in love with the Tuscan surroundings at first sight, but their host made impression enough to provide an
exterior for Dr Piers Loudron, a murder victim of Nicholas Blake's *The
Worm of Death* (1961).

Dr Piers came forward and took both her hands, gazing at her [Clare Messinger,
the sculptor and mistress of Nigel Strangeways] for a moment, his old eyes blue
as lapis lazuli.

'My dear, this is a very great pleasure to me. The genius I have long recognized;
but I had not known that such beauty went with it. . . .'

Rosamond was doubtless greeted in some such manner before Berenson
turned reluctantly to Cecil in that autumn of 1947. Before the end of the
visit Cecil was persuaded to sing some Tom Moore ballads and to read
his 'O Dreams, O Destinations', the sonnet sequence which Rosamond
came to think represented his 'negative philosophy': and whatever he may
have thought of their host he was greatly moved by seeing his love displayed in this beautiful place.

All woman she was. Brutalizing, humanizing,
Pure flame, lewd earth was she, imperative as air
And weak as water, yes all women to me.
To the rest, one of many, though they felt how she was rare
In sympathy and tasted in her warm words a sweetness
Of life that has ripened on the sunny side of the tree.

> To herself a darker story, as she called her past to witness –
> A heart much bruised, how often, how stormily surmising
> Some chasmal flaw divided it from whole felicity.*

During the days they went down to the still 'pot-holed boulevards' of Florence to admire the works of Michelangelo, da Vinci and Fra Angelico, Cellini, Botticelli, Brunelleschi, Giotto, Donatello and Masaccio; Cecil looking to them to illuminate his selfhood.

> And if I miss that radiance where it flies,
> Something is gained in the mere exercise
> Of strenuous submission, the attempt
> To lose and find oneself through others' eyes.†

Cecil returned to the English south-west for the weekend of 28 May. When he departed for London Mary wrote, 'The keel is more even than this time last year, but the boat is still becalmed.' In August she and Rosamond wrote to each other for the first time, a friendly and inconclusive exchange. Mary had by then been disturbed by Cecil's *Poems 1943–1947*, four of which advertised the numb state of the marriage; and did so, to some extent, by putting himself with feeling, perception and sympathy, into her mind.

The volume was published by Jonathan Cape at the end of October with a dedication to Laurie Lee. The forty poems include the two translations from Valéry and Cecil's verse tributes to Emily Brontë, Thomas Hardy, Walter de la Mare and Edmund Blunden. Over the years the critical response to this book has been less favourable than that given to *Word Over All* (1943), and Ian Parsons chose to exclude half its contents when preparing his 1977 selection of Cecil's poems. It has been felt that Thomas Hardy ʳvas allowed to approach too close. Against this Clifford Dyment has pointed out that 'in the tradition Day-Lewis shares with Hardy he has found a home in which he can be *natural*, do without affectation or pretence, feel under no compulsion to follow the smart and fashionable but be free to create his personal atmosphere of seriousness and charm'.[5] Whatever else Cecil does he certainly lays out his insides for inspection in this clearly revealing book.

Published a month earlier was Cecil's *The Otterbury Incident*, illustrated with all his characteristic feeling for atmosphere and space by Edward Ardizzone. It was dedicated to Jonathan Fenby (son of Charles and June) and Richard Osborne (son of Tony and Eileen), Cecil's two godsons. The name Otterbury was derived from Ottery St Mary in Devon, but the town to which the French story, of schoolboy war games leading to crime detection, was transposed was roughly modelled on Sherborne. The 'Incident' of the

---

* 'Elegy Before Death' (*An Italian Visit*, 1953).

† 'Florence: Works of Art' (*An Italian Visit*, 1953).

title was a derelict site where one of Hitler's stray bombs exploded during the war. The book, intended by Putnams for boys between eleven and fourteen or so, has proved a lasting success, and having been bought by schools for over thirty years has sold around 250,000 copies to make it very much the author's best seller.

In the early months of the new year, Cecil was working on *An Italian Visit* and more than once reported that he was 'miserable with indigestion'. On 1 March 1949 he turned down an invitation to compose a BBC feature on Matthew Arnold, pleading, 'I'm pretty well out of circulation this year because I am writing a long poem'. Four days later he was somewhat discouraged to discover that John Lehmann was not keen on 'Dialogue at the Airport', the opening section in which aspects of Cecil named Tom, Dick and Harry discuss the Italian experience before them. He replied on 5 March from Little Wittenham: 'I'm sorry you did not greatly care for the poem, but hope you may like it better when you see it in position with the rest of the work. Anyway, it is nice to have someone seriously enough interested in one's poetry to reject some of it – if you see what I mean.'

On 14 March Ronald Lewin of the BBC talks department, reported in an internal memorandum that he had 'a long talk with Cecil Day-Lewis about Virgil'. They had discussed the possibility of translating parts of the *Aeneid* for radio use and Cecil had suggested doing the first six books. 'He would need nine months to translate because he insists on verse and can only average some 20 lines per day. He cannot begin until the end of the year as he is at present working on a long poem of his own, the subject of which should surely interest the Third Programme in view of the Goethe bi-centenary series, for its theme is his reaction to his first visit to Italy, which he made last year.' Harman Grisewood, who had succeeded George Barnes as Third Programme Controller, was also interested and set about organizing a meeting with Cecil and the classical scholar W.F. Jackson Knight.

Knos, now nearly seventy-five but still as interested and gently teasing as ever, made her first and only post-war visit to Brimclose that April. She arrived on the twenty-sixth, the day before Cecil's forty-fifth birthday, and he and Mary gave her no cause to worry about the stability of their marriage. They were able to thank Knos for the many parcels of meat which she had sent from Ireland to supplement our ration, without letting it be known that the stuff was almost invariably bad by the time it reached its destination.

She stayed until early May and three days after her departure Cecil left for London: first to install me in an Ebury Street bed and breakfast house, from whence I was supposed to be attending a course in shorthand and typing; and then to join Rosamond at Little Wittenham. On the seventeenth Mary was writing at Brimclose, 'I miss Cecil, but when he is here his heart isn't.' Two days later he and Rosamond left for the South of France, where they were to stay with Somerset Maugham.

At this time the Villa Mauresque at Saint-Jean-Cap-Ferrat was a court rather like that of Bernard Berenson's I Tatti, except that Maugham preferred to surround himself as far as possible with the young and beautiful of his own sex. This 'Master' had become, to borrow from Anthony Curtis's 1974 BBC radio portrait, 'the great awe-inspiring, Oriental-looking host of the Graham Sutherland canvas'. The entrance hall offered a seemingly infinite vista of black and white marble and the drawing room looked to be large enough to house several railway trains. Martinis were mixed at 12.30 and 'Willie' would appear from his writing just before lunch at one. The ritual was repeated at six o'clock, with more martinis and a dinner for which everybody was expected to change.

In 1947 the writer had set up his Somerset Maugham Award, administered by the Society of Authors and offering £400 to enable deserving writers to travel abroad. Cecil had been one of the first judges, with C.V. Wedgwood and V.S. Pritchett. Beyond this slight connection the two men had little in common: Maugham had small feeling for poetry and he was not one of Cecil's hero prose-writers. As at I Tatti, rather more attention was devoted to Rosamond, a fellow prose-writer who could to some extent match Maugham's penchant for sharp-tongued gossip. Cecil was not much of a gossip and had a fairly limited fund of anecdotes, and despite Rosamond he still felt some lingering social inferiority.

He enjoyed the sun and the swimming and the occasional drive to Monte Carlo and elsewhere, but he could never feel that he belonged amidst such extravagance. Maybe there were also shadows of doubt in his mind about himself and Rosamond now, though they certainly were not revealed to her and she saw him going through the motions with as much loving care as ever. He was beginning to approach 'Elegy Before Death', the centrepiece of *An Italian Visit* which would be a summation of, and memorial to, their great love. 'I never thought at the time that it was more than a beautiful, romantic farewell to an idyll', remembered Rosamond. 'Though with hindsight it does seem strange, as if he was already denying us a future together.'

If thoughts about being overwhelmed by Rosamond really had formulated themselves, Cecil proved as underwhelmed as usual when he returned to Brimclose for Whit on 2 June. 'Cecil isn't really back', Mary told her diary. At the end of the month she added: 'Cecil out when I'm in, we haven't done one thing together, I'm only a bloody housekeeper.'

That July both she and Rosamond, had they both been granted telepathic vision, would have suffered equal distress. At the English Festival of Spoken Verse, held at the Institut Français in Queensberry Place, Cecil again met Jill Balcon. L.A.G. Strong, once more taking a hand in Cecil's destiny, had invited her to give a demonstration recital, reading from Emily Dickinson, Robert Frost and Thomas Hardy. Cecil sat next to her at the Festival dinner in the Rembrandt Hotel and afterwards heard the recital. This time he did notice her long-eyed, black and white gypsy beauty, and her addiction to him and his works. He felt the first pangs of love.

Next month, when he was 'keeping warm' my room in Ebury Street, Victoria, while I was on holiday in Devon, he invited Jill to dinner at the Maison Basque restaurant in Dover Street. After, they took a long walk together down the Mall and through Tufton Street, Westminster, which was Jill's childhood home. Before the walk was done he took her arm, a gesture which from Cecil meant more then she knew at the time. They parted good friends.

That summer saw publication of Nicholas Blake's *Head of a Traveller*, dedicated to Rosamond's children, Hugo and Sally. With its Housman-derived title it is set at Plash Meadow in the 'messy Oxfordshire village' of Ferry Lacey, otherwise the Manor House at Little Wittenham. Living in the house are the Seatons: including a poet failing, as Cecil did, to realize his ambition of writing 'something in the nature of *The Dynasts*' about the 1914–18 war; and an ebullient Sally-like teenage daughter. The story is a variation on Beauty and the Beast and was very close to Cecil's heart. The muse of the poet had been rendered into a trance by Rosamond's surroundings and is awoken by the arrival of the poet's bestial brother, the traveller of the title. The poet's wife wishes to keep him and his muse where they are, and so murders the brother. There is a horrific scene in which a sculptured head falls out of a tree. It splits on impact to reveal the previously missing and now decomposing head of the traveller.

Cecil was not with Rosamond when I saw him off from Victoria station on 8 September for a PEN conference at Venice. The official proceedings of this conference no doubt had as much and as little value as all writers' occasions of the kind. More notable things happened outside on the Piazza San Marco. Natasha Spender snapped the 1930s triumvirate of Auden, Spender and Day-Lewis sitting together at a café table, taking the only known picture including all three: pale Auden laying down some outrageous new law, well-browned Spender sheepishly admitting that he had recently broken that law, bow-tied and gaunt Day-Lewis an appreciative umpire in the middle.

Spender seems to have been something of a butt. At one point Wystan and Cecil were left alone, 'soaking up grappa beside the Grand Canal'. They discussed the news that Stephen was writing an autobiography, *World Within World* (1951). Wystan wanted to know why Cecil had not stopped this project: 'You know perfectly well, Cecil, that *no* poet should *ever* write an autobiography.' A proposal that they should go and burn the manuscript was abandoned. Later Spender was supposed to have been shocked when in the moonlight, on the square where Claudio Monteverdi once walked, Cecil joined forces with the Irish writer Kate O'Brien in the singing of several of Tom Moore's melodies and a not specially Venetian setting of 'Credo in unum Deum'.

I was still in London that autumn, awaiting call-up to the Royal Air Force, having a weekly lunch with Cecil, and on 1 November I went to Broadcasting House to hear him record part of *An Italian Visit*. A week later he invited me to the *Sunday Times* Book Exhibition at Grosvenor House, for an Apollo Society recital he gave with Peggy Ashcroft and the pianist Angus Morrison. After the performance I was introduced for the first time to Rosamond; and to Jill Balcon, who was then out of work and selling on the André Deutsch book-stand. There was a puzzling contrast between the warm responses of Cecil and Jill together, and the matter-of-fact calm which appeared to mark the relationship of Cecil and Rosamond.

It was Rosamond who asked me to come and see her a week later. On 16 November, the day I received my calling-up papers, I called at the Charlotte Street pied-à-terre which both she and Cecil used when they were in London. She gave me dinner at a small restaurant beside the flat and seemed to me all pastel shades and sweet warmth and kindness. I was absurdly gauche for an eighteen-year-old and, as I had been a main cause or pretext for Cecil's inability to marry her, she might well have felt resentful of my existence: yet her objective was clearly to make friends, and this she did. 'I thought you were a duck! – and so communicative, specially after a glass of wine. Cecil told me you'd be very shy, but you were not', she remembered.

No doubt she wanted a clearer idea of what she was dealing with now that Cecil was becoming almost as withdrawn in her presence as in that of Mary. She believed this new black ice was partly caused by my departure from home, the dreaded moment of 'O Dreams, O Destinations' which in turn made him conscious of his advancing years. 'He had fallen into a long depression which was connected with your going into the RAF', she recalled twenty-five years later. 'He dreaded, or said he dreaded, not finding you at Musbury; it made his home life more and more unreal and gloomy.'

He was at Musbury in November when he heard Jill Balcon playing Ottima in a Third Programme radio adaptation of Browning's *Pippa Passes*, at the same time as she heard a recording of him reading Walter de la Mare's 'To a Candle' at the Cheltenham Festival of Literature he had attended with Mary in October. Their fan letters crossed and out of them sprang a suggestion that they should arrange a dinner with Sir Jacob Epstein, then working on a head of Jill.

One day in December Cecil announced to Rosamond that he could not spend an evening with her as he had been invited by the actress Jill Balcon to have dinner with her and the sculptor Epstein. Rosamond asked if she was invited; Cecil assured her it was not the kind of occasion she would enjoy, and she fell to teasing him about his susceptibility to his 'schoolgirl' admirers. Epstein chose the Caprice for dinner; Cecil was not at his most scintillating, but the mutual admiration continued over the table. Rosamond, on her way back to London by train after a visit to her son Hugo at Cambridge, had a presentiment of doom. She decided that if Cecil was back at their flat when she returned there his presence would be a sign that all was well between them still, if not, something had gone wrong. In the event Cecil was forty-five minutes later than she was, and came in 'looking sheepish'. She did not treat the matter calmly. Ironically, Cecil and Jill were never alone that evening; he had left the Caprice before her and the Epsteins.

December was also worrying for Mary. She and Cecil coincided at Euston Station on the seventh to see me off to the RAF recruits' reception camp at Padgate. 'Why did we have to meet, and part. Why did I have to choose one who could not last. How I hate this mask of indifference, this cloak of service. How I need just now warmth and tenderness and companionship', Mary wrote afterwards.

At Christmas I was given leave and the Day-Lewis family went through the usual motions. On the seventeenth Cecil and Mary gave a sherry party, the guests including St John and Nora Ervine, who had lived at Seaton through this decade. On the twenty-second Cecil went for a pub crawl with Billie and John Currall. As a Christmas present for Jill he sent *The Way to Poetry*, an anthology by E. Ellerington Herron for which Cecil had written a foreword. He and Mary kept their twenty-first wedding anniversary on 27 December, and three days later Cecil left to see in the new decade with Rosamond. 'There is nothing in anything I do to compensate for this gap, this unfilled heart. I am so tired and bewildered and unhappy', wrote Mary to herself.

4
~1950–1964~
Easier Walking

He might
Have noticed how, mile after mile, this road
Made easier walking – noticed a lack
Of grit and gradient; there was a clue.
Ah yes, if only he had listened to his feet!
But, as I told you, he walked in a dream.★

Here Cecil wonders if the right road for the man may be the wrong road for the poet. His route through the 1940s had been tortuous and strewn with obstacles. There were vistas of beauty and joy and plains of guilt-laden gloom; roses and thorns. Where the ground had been volcanic it was uncomfortable for the man but provided the poet with all the working material he needed. In 1950 he would tear himself free from this route and take a new road promising peace and contentment, easier walking. Was this bad for the poet? One school of thought holds that his verse lost force after the 1940s. Another finds that he improved with age, that he benefited from the pause of the early 1950s and made his most valuable contribution with the four volumes he published in his last fifteen years. The opinion that he wrote too much, expressed by himself as well as his critics, covers those years as well as earlier periods. In time the man learnt that for him all roads must, sooner or later, arrive at grit and gradient.

This reflected the background to his progress. The condition of Britain in 1950 did not fulfil the Communist dreams of the 1930s, but there had been five years of evolutionary social democracy faintly uncomfortable for those who had anything to lose. Far from struggling on towards the magnetic mountain the people decided for easier walking. In late 1951 the Conservatives were returned to power and remained there for thirteen years, maintaining the welfare state and the status quo, shedding the burden of the Empire, learning that they no longer had the power to impose their will on other nations.

Cecil's 1950 began with an addition to his previous divisions. He saw the New Year in with Rosamond and her family and he returned to Musbury 'seemingly depressed', according to Mary, on 2 January. On 12

★ 'The Wrong Road' (*Pegasus*, 1957).

January he and Jill again had dinner together at the Maison Basque in Dover Street. This time she led him on a longer walk through London diversity.

It was a cool night but they became less cool. Eventually they admitted their feelings, kissed passionately and found they were outside George Eliot's house in Cheyne Walk, Chelsea. They carved their initials outside and walked on together to Jill's flat at 4d Clarendon Street, in Pimlico. Cecil declared them to be 'one in the sight of George Eliot' and their love affair began. She said that even if the affair only lasted that night she would feel abundantly blessed. He said, 'I have had a lot of happiness, a lot of pain, a little ecstasy, but I have never known such peace.' Next morning he gave her a copy of *Poems 1943–1947*, inscribed 'Friday the 13th'. He was approaching forty-six, and she was just twenty-five.

Cecil returned to Brimclose on the sixteenth and spent a week there, nursing a cold, helping Mary to shop, taking Nick to the cinema, considering his future in silence. He was back in London on the twenty-third and telephoned Jill, saying 'I want to spend the rest of my life with you.' That evening he went back to the tiny flat in Clarendon Street, with its one small bed and its single table that had to be used both for eating and translating the *Aeneid*. They started planning the future.

Jill Balcon is of Eastern European Jewish stock on both sides; her father's family were refugees from Riga, Latvia and her mother's from Poland. In 1950 she was invariably described by newspapers as 'actress daughter of film chief Sir Michael Balcon'. At that time, just before television was developed to replace the cinema as the chief medium of mass entertainment, the head of Ealing Studios was in the British context a very important man indeed. He had received a knighthood two years before. His recent run of Ealing comedies – *Passport to Pimlico*, *Whisky Galore*, *Kind Hearts and Coronets*, and that year *The Lavender Hill Mob* – was considered at the time to represent the most distinguished work emerging from the home industry. Sir Michael Balcon was born at Birmingham in 1896, and began his film career some twenty years later as a Midlands distributor. He produced his first picture, *Woman to Woman*, in 1922. Two years later he married Aileen Leatherman, who had become the love of his life when she was still a schoolgirl visiting England from her family home in South Africa.

Jill was their first-born, brought up in and around London. Film-making was sufficiently lucrative for her to be sent to school at Roedean. She found this tolerable until, in the first year of the war, it was evacuated from Brighton and re-established in the Lake District at what had been the Station Hotel, Keswick. 'Being, like her father, given to the dramatization of minor events, she wrote to us complaining that on arrival at Keswick she had had to carry her luggage from the station', wrote Sir Michael in his autobiography.[1] 'It was only when we visited her some months later we realized that the school was practically on the station platform.' After her final escape from Keswick she took up a place, aged sixteen, at Elsie Fogerty's Central School of Speech Training and Dramatic Art. Her course began at the Royal Albert Hall in London, but the school was evacuated to University College, Exeter, just in time for the raids of April 1942, which obliterated the centre of the Devon county town. She completed her training in London before starting, in 1943, on a year with ENSA: officially the Entertainments National Service Association, affectionately known as Every Night Something Awful, which had been providing drama and variety for troops and factory workers since 1940. Jill moved on to the BBC in 1944, still a teenager, and spent the rest of the war making her voice familiar as a continuity announcer. Since then she had been building a reputation as an actress and verse-reader and was getting parts, just below star billing, in the theatre and cinema as well as radio.

She had been reading poetry since she was five – 'It was part of my organic life' – and she already knew more or less everything Cecil had written. She also listened a lot and had deduced from his radio voice a nature of 'attentive kindness'.

For Cecil nothing was ever simple. He was much aware of being an 'old lag', full of years, a good starter of love affairs but one who found it hard to sustain marriages. At this moment his moral sense did not for once run entirely counter to his perennial need of new beginnings. There would be no escape from his accumulation of guilt, but he had experienced enough of 'this blind numb grinding severance/Of floe from floe', which had long been the way of marriage at Brimclose, to believe that such compassionate inaction, turning to 'sterile, impotent pity', was ultimately more hurtful than the unhappiness and bitterness, the wounds and tears he would leave in his trail after cutting himself free. He believed that the same argument could be applied to his relationship with Rosamond. Moreover he was in love and his self-doubt demanded that he should prove his commitment, to himself and Jill and the world, by undertaking marriage and accepting its responsibilities. Jill would give him the new beginning, the 'renewal' and the refuge he felt that he needed both as a poet and a man.

They knew that that there would be money worries and the strongest possible disapproval from her parents. Yet she was earning, and in so far as she had an uneasy relationship with her father Cecil could cast himself in the role of rescuer. He also considered that Jill's interest in poetry, and her sensitive ability as a reader, would help towards lasting companionship; and because he was older and more experienced, and to some extent a poetic idol for Jill, he was likely to be the dominant companion in a way not possible with Rosamond.

Jill and Mary were opposites in almost everything apart from their love for Cecil, and to an extent they lacked each other's strengths and weaknesses. In some ways it was paradoxical that he should turn to Jill for peace:

such an impulsive, vivid nature could never be peaceful for long, it seemed to observers, however successful Cecil might be in providing soothing emotional security. Yet Mary's peaceful stoicism contributed to Cecil's boredom at Brimclose. Jill would be more complementary to him, more demanding on his nervous energy, and would help him to generate more, unless and until they were both enveloped by the law of diminishing returns.

As for Rosamond, Cecil began to convince himself that it was his instinct for self-preservation, his need to protect his ego against another just as strong, which had made him turn his car round when going to his new life with her in 1947. He dreaded the scenes that would be involved, but this time he would show himself that he did have the strength to make a 'clean break' with the past.

In the next week one of Rosamond's presents to her Sally on her sixteenth birthday was an Apollo Society recital at their Little Wittenham home. Cecil read and sang, Peggy Ashcroft was his co-reader and Angus Morrison was the pianist: the same artists in fact who had performed the previous November at the *Sunday Times* book exhibition, to an audience that included both Rosamond and Jill. Cecil wrote to Rosamond saying he was looking forward to this, that he would be singing just for her, and assuring her of his love. The recital was given according to plan and was enjoyed by the guests assembled at the Manor House, but Rosamond noted that off the platform Cecil was 'in a terrible state, white and twitching and sweating and holding my hand'. He was 'very gay but in a nervous, exaggerated sort of way'. He stayed the night and went back to London next day.

'A day or two later I received a great thick letter from him. As soon as I felt the envelope I could tell that this was different from his usual thin letters', remembers Rosamond. 'He told me that he had been in a state of despair, of black melancholy, that he had fallen in love with Jill, had gone to bed with her and would be staying with her to renew himself. I threw the letter in the fire and thought to myself it just can't be true. I had such complete faith and trust in him and his love that I could not believe that he would act as he did. I sent Sally back to school and asked him to come and see me. . . .' They met on 28 January. Rosamund, still incredulous, said she felt Jill must be a passing fancy and asked him not to see her for three months, so that they could discover if they really did care for one another. He agreed.

Cecil went home to Brimclose in the afternoon of Tuesday 31 January but said nothing about the new turn in his life until the following Friday evening, the day after Mary had been alerted through a letter from Rosamond. On Saturday he wrote to Jill.

Yesterday I talked to my wife about you and me. It was not, as it turned out, a surprise to her as R. had written to her about it the day before (my intuition was not so very far out) saying that I must be stopped from this 'act of madness'. Mary thinks (as others will) that it can only be the sort of infatuation for a girl that a middle aged man often falls victim to. I told her as kindly but plainly as I could, that it is nothing of the sort, and said I wanted her to divorce me. She is dead against this at present, but I think if I am kind and patient with her, she may come round. I said that whether she divorced me or not, I intended to go and live with you. In a way, this was bluff on my part: not that I wouldn't live with you on any terms as far as *I* am concerned, but I cannot help realising that, without marriage, it would be leading you into a blind alley – it would make it so difficult for you to have children, and *in the end* you might well bitterly resent my having done it. Anyway, we can jump that fence when we come to it – and it won't stop me flying to you with the speed of light on April 28 or whatever the date is. I am putting all this as coldly and detachedly as I can, my darling love, because I can't bear to release any emotion – except what I feel for you. Last night was a terrible ordeal for me, you can imagine, and terrible for M. – the trouble is that she loves me still (heaven knows why), while I have great affection and respect for her, and nothing more. But she has never done me any harm, which makes it so much more difficult to do this to her. One thing I'm sure of – bloody as these three months will be, they can prove to me, better even than being with you, how firm and real and overpowering my love for you is.

Mary wrote of this interview in her diary: 'Jill Balcon comes into the picture. Everything has the feeling of nightmare, I broke down.' She recovered her composure and achieved the sort of numbed dignity with which she survived the next few months, while despair quietly grew within her. After Cecil left for London on 6 February she wrote, 'I have no idea what I ought to do, I want to sink into oblivion.' She knew that he would not be seeing Jill, but that gave small comfort. 'He kept getting her letters and going off to the lavatory to read them', she told me. Four days later, just before Cecil returned to Brimclose 'tired but more cheerful', Rosamond rang Mary as an ally and suggested a meeting in London later in the month. 'I almost dread this numbness passing', wrote Mary as she and Cecil prepared to assume the face of normality for my long weekend leave from the RAF, and a visit to Nick at Sherborne. She was in London on the twenty-fourth consulting Rupert Hart-Davis, the close friend of Cecil she found most sympathetic; and having lunch and tea, and a long and revealing talk with Rosamond at the Mayfair Hotel.

Of the two betrayed victims Mary was naturally the more disabused. She considered that Cecil became bored with women when he no longer found them sexually exciting, and the trouble was as simple as that. Rosamond, new to knowledge of Cecil's infidelity and newly shattered, still thought that 'there must be a fit of temporary madness' which had led him astray at this moment. She suggested that he should be persuaded to see a psychiatrist, and with some scepticism Mary agreed.

The psychiatrist idea was relayed to Cecil from Rosamond by a mutual friend. He wrote to Jill saying he had agreed to go and see 'a Wimpole Street quack', partly for the pleasure of talking to somebody about his love for her and partly because the man might produce a report which would help Rosamond to 'become more detached'. He went to the consultation on 6 March, explained himself and emerged confirmed in his belief that he was still in full possession of his senses. At the end of that week Rosamond again rang Mary at Brimclose, and next day Cecil returned home saying that he would not be making a second visit to the psychiatrist. Mary confessed herself 'still in a state of complete bewilderment'.

For Cecil the three months abstention was passing quite quickly, thanks to the pleasures of correspondence. Once he lunched at Antoine's with Jill's friend since her BBC announcing days, Elizabeth Jane Howard. She was a golden haired beauty, less than two years older than Jill; her first marriage to the bird conservationist Peter Scott had broken down, and she had just published her first novel, *The Beautiful Visit*. In the middle of the decade Jane and Cecil would draw closer, but at this time she was a mere emissary sent by Jill to make possible what she called 'a kind of second-hand communication'.

Neither Rosamond nor Mary could now see any purpose in the separation and Cecil was given permission to return to his new love after collecting what belongings he had left at Little Wittenham. He went back to the Manor House on the evening of 20 March and there followed a terrible few hours which gave him and Rosamond the maximum of distress. Her initial disbelief had turned to bitter fury: he was trying for a 'scorched earth' policy, burning his attachment to her out of his heart.

'What was almost the worst thing to bear, for both Mary and me, was what appeared to be his complete change of personality towards us both after he had struck us down', Rosamond recalled. 'He wore a triumphant smirk, and seemed convinced that he was completely justified. We both felt that we were nothing but obstacles in the way of his desires and determination. No kindness, no courtesy, sympathy or (apparently) conscience. I daresay this was temporary but it was very appalling. My reproaches became simply subjects of resentment. It suited him, of course, to feel resentful towards me: it made it easier for him to feel how much better off he'd be with Jill.'

For his part Cecil was trying to cultivate whatever he could find in himself of the determined desperado, the ruthless eraser, and at one point he even referred to his capacity to destroy himself, though it may be that the 'smirk' which Rosamond observed was as much a sign of nervousness as triumph.

Waiting for him at her flat in Clarendon Street that night Jill was in a state of acute anxiety, not because she doubted Cecil's love for her, but as the early hours ticked away she wondered what had happened to him. She paced the small room wondering if Cecil had been physically injured or worse, knowing that at best he must have missed the last Didcot to Paddington train. He eventually arrived at three o'clock in the morning, 'looking as though he had been tortured', asking for money to pay off the hired car he had had to take after a five-mile walk from Little Wittenham.

Next day Mary was in London. She went straight to the psychiatrist, who 'merely confirmed my own views'. Afterwards she had lunch with Cecil who was 'very tired after a gruelling meeting with Rosamond'. Mary decided to withdraw from any kind of joint campaign to try and persuade Cecil not to marry Jill, and to see if she could arrive at her own compromise. 'Rosamond and I got on perfectly well I think. I found her sympathetic, but I just wondered which of us was going to have Cecil if we did get him back', drily commented Mary.

Cecil's private affairs were not quite all-consuming at this time. On 26 January he wrote with mild impatience to Harman Grisewood of the BBC Third Programme, asking if any decision had yet been made about which passages of the *Aeneid* he was to translate. 'I must start on this soon or begin on something else. I am all lined up and ready to start when you give the word,' he said. He added: 'I have an idea (immodest and possibly delusive) that I could give a good talk in the *Personal Pleasures* series.' Grisewood replied, 'The only help I can give at this stage is to say that I feel we can put on the air a translation of all the 12 books pretty well as they are. The size of your task, therefore can be regarded as a translation for radio of the whole of Virgil's poem.'

The work was given added impetus by the government proposal to stage a Festival of Britain in 1951 to impress overseas visitors of the nation's postwar capacity and, more importantly, to improve morale and pride at home. It was 'in the Corporation's interest to be able to offer the work during the Festival year even if it had to start after the Festival period had strictly concluded', wrote Grisewood in February. He offered Cecil £1,000 to do the translation, if possible within two years, and did not haggle when the translator suggested that £100 per book, £1,200 in all, would be a fairer fee. By March he had made a start on the 9,896 lines and Basil Taylor had been appointed to produce the huge project.

On 25 March the classical scholar who had helped to originate the project, W. F. Jackson Knight, came to stay at Brimclose and go through the translation of Book One – 'correcting, suggesting, encouraging', as Cecil put it in his grateful foreword to the published version. 'Cecil read first book of the *Aeneid* for an hour, very exciting', wrote Mary the following day. The same day Cecil wrote to Jill, 'I have been having a gruelling but most enjoyable time, picking over my translation with Jackson Knight: he is not far short of a genius, I suspect; and he lets nothing pass, not even the finest shade of meaning, till we have argued it out: but he is willing to be convinced. So, after 24 hours hammer and tongs – we have reached Line 250. He seems pretty pleased with the translation as a whole, though. A tubby, twinkling little man, with a voice like a castrated seagull.'

In 1939 the Treasury agreed to double a Pilgrim Trust grant of £25,000 towards encouragement of the arts. Thus was born the Council for the Encouragement of Music and the Arts, which in 1945 became the Arts Council of Great Britain. These organizations gave what little money they had to the 'performing arts', musical and theatrical, and the visual arts, painting and sculpture. Literature was not helped until 1949, when Cecil found himself on Sir George Rostrevor Hamilton's Arts Council committee, with Richard Church, Christopher Hassall and L.A.G. Strong, asked to suggest how poetry might be included in the Festival of Britain. This led to a huge poetry competition open to all comers from the British Commonwealth, and a vote by the Council to institute a permanent poetry panel. It had its first meeting at the beginning of 1950 under the chairmanship of Joseph Compton – with Church, Day-Lewis, Hassall and Hamilton attending – and began its work of distributing a little over £500 for the encouragement, mainly, of public readings. Out of this small beginning grew the much more powerful, and more generously funded, Literature Panel of the present. Cecil, who would move permanently to London before the end of the year, had announced himself as a writer available for public duty.

To the innocent eye, mine for instance, that April Easter at Brimclose was quite a happy time. Nicholas came home from Sherborne, I on leave from the RAF; Cecil, grinning with huge pleasure when we were all assembled in the living room, said that he was to receive a CBE (Commander of the British Empire, or 'Commander of Broken English' as he would put it when replying to letters of congratulation) in the King's birthday honours list; and Mary managed to smile with apparent contentment. Alone in his study Cecil wrote to Jill of 'this happiness business':

Well, of course it must be transient. The great thing is not to be intimidated by the knowledge that it is so – or having caught the winged joy as it flies, not to clamp it down under a microscope, nor tear off its wings by trying to keep it when the time has come for it to fly off again. Which things since they are thus, you are subject to a fine of at least 1s every time you dwell on your 'inadequacy' to preserve my happiness.... There is no reason why we shouldn't go on, either, making new kinds of happiness possible for each other, long, long after this first paradise of being together and utterly absorbed in each other has gently disengaged itself from us and gone. When in the future, you find me from time to time gloomy, depressed, morose, etc etc, for God's sake don't leap to the conclusion that its through any inadequacy of your own, *or* that you are inadequate because you cannot make me at once snap out of it. These bad moods of mine are nearly always self generated; and generally mean either that I've got indigestion or that I am about to have a poem!

On 20 April Mary received a letter from the heartbroken Rosamond telling of an incipient nervous and physical breakdown. It was not a happy portent as she and Nicholas took the London train from Axminster. They stayed at the Charing Cross Hotel and were joined for dinner by Cecil. Next day the three of them left for the Lake District, the place of so many King family holidays in younger days. They were attending the ceremonies for the centenary of William Wordsworth's death. 'Thrilled and saddened to see the hills again', wrote Mary; while Cecil complained with more fervour than before that he felt threatened by mountains rearing so close to him. The piquancy and poignancy of the weekend was increased by the presence of Cecil's old Sherborne friend and rival, Mary's beloved brother Alec King, now himself a Wordsworth scholar and in England with his wife Catherine and family on their first post-war sabbatical year from university English in Western Australia.

Cecil wrote to Jill from the Hotel Rothay, meeting her dislike of the Lake District resulting from her war-time evacuation there.

I am seizing a moment in between the frenzied orgies of the Wordsworth devotees to write to you.... Thank heavens it's only four days till we're together again. Well, the mountains are, you will be glad to hear, as revolting as ever: their lower slopes are dotted with sodden sheep and lumbering lady hikers in sensible skirts with humps on their backs and great big red bulging calves. (I speak of the hikers not the sheep.) ... The obsequies have been pretty dim so far – a pack of academic mediocrities paying their unasked for tributes to old W.W. – relieved by good lectures from Beveridge and Basil Willey, however. Also, I had a jolly chat with Herbert Read, who is going about in dark glasses lest the devotees should recognise him and tear him to pieces for having said in print that W.W.'s affair with Annette deeply influenced his poetry. Tomorrow morning we are to be harangued by the Archbishop of York and in the evening I do my turn. It has, I need not say, been raining all day.

The actual centenary fell on Sunday the twenty-third. The Day-Lewises and the Kings walked to Dove Cottage and saw a wreath laid on Wordsworth's grave. Helen Darbyshire gave what Mary described as 'a nice, colourless address' and in Grasmere Church, Cecil 'read the Intimations Ode most movingly'. He reported to Jill that 'The Wordsworth reading was not too bad, though I hate reading poetry in a church, it is so difficult not to start booming. The three readers were placed in a sort of loose box – one of those old family pews – near the choir: the temptation to begin my renditions by popping my head over the wall of the loose box and giving a loud whinny was almost over-powering.'

After this there were three days rowing on the lake and walks, Cecil courteous and mostly absent in mind. On 27 April, his forty-sixth birthday, they all returned to London. Cecil opened his presents from Mary and Nick and went off to spend the rest of the day and night with Jill.

In the same week Cecil published an article in *The Author*, the journal of the Society of Authors, about his working methods. He advised aspiring writers of verse or prose to appoint fixed hours of work every day. 'The habit and rhythm thus established make it easier to take up the work where it has been dropped the previous day and to "tune in". For me "waiting for inspiration" means only not beginning a poem until the unconscious has done its work on it, until I feel compelled to write the poem. Once I know roughly what the incipient poem is trying to say, what direction it is moving in, I can work my regular hours at it (normally 10 am to 1 am, and 5 pm to 6.30 pm).'

The restless Cecil ironically went on to write that 'a familiar room is better than a strange one'. He continued: '... the start of the poem is the trickiest period, since it requires the greatest concentration: I could go on writing a poem almost anywhere, once it had got momentum and direction, but I could only begin it in a familiar environment. Similarly with people: once the poem is underway, three people whom I know well, talking in the same room, would not distract me; one silent stranger would.'

On the motive for writing a poem Cecil suggested that it was 'a rediscovery', a 'rearrangement of once familiar data'. Unconscious processes were 'set in motion by some violent, novel and quite possibly irrelevant experience – a new personal relationship, a new country, a change of house or habit'. He said that 'a deep, violent personal experience is apt to produce about two years of steady verse-writing: then for a year at least I write nothing in verse. I am waiting for a new seam of discovery.' The final section dealt with method. He wrote that a long poem or sequence was planned ahead. 'I write as fast as I can, perhaps 20 lines a day, at the start, revising little: mistakes here do not matter so greatly.' With a short, concentrated poem, the reverse was true. 'One false word can ruin the whole thing: I write very slowly, three to five lines a day, especially at the start: a moment's lapse of attention, and the poem may have taken the wrong direction, into one of the innumerable blind alleys awaiting it.'

On 4 May, to a sigh of relief from Cecil, his 'Recreations' volume of the *Oxford Junior Encyclopaedia* was published at thirty shillings. It is a handsome, generously illustrated volume; Cecil retained his billing as volume editor and his ghost Terence Delaney is listed among the contributors. I was another contributor, receiving a 13s fee for a very short article on railway spotters' clubs.

Next day Cecil was able to send his translation of Book One of the *Aeneid* from his Chatto office to the BBC. He said it was 'in a more or less finished state'; he had also done Book Two, 'but I have not been over it with Jackson Knight yet'. Before the end of the month he heard from Harman Grisewood: 'I am delighted with Book One.... I feel greatly encouraged by the translation and am strengthened in my belief in the enterprise.'

Early in May Cecil and Jill had a snatched holiday in Sussex and Kent, staying for a while with their friends Patric and Sheila Dickinson in Rye.

Both Cecil and Mary's brother Alec were at Brimclose on 12 May for her forty-eighth birthday. It was a gloomy day for her; she got up early, not disturbing Cecil asleep in the far corner of their bedroom, and sat in the garden alone sipping tea. The three of them drove to Dorchester for a Hardy pilgrimage, and came home in time to hear recordings of Cecil reading from Yeats on the Third Programme. The knowledge that Cecil would be leaving permanently in September nagged all day.

It still nagged through the first weekend in June when Sherborne School celebrated the four-hundredth anniversary of its foundation with a visit from the King and Queen. Cecil spent 'two gruelling days' there, saw Nick in the chorus of 'Benedictines, cavaliers and scholars' of V.C. Clinton-Baddeley's chronicle play and provided a substantial 'Commemoration Ode' of sixty-two lines. His letter to Jill from this celebration indicated how strongly he was longing to get away. 'I long consumedly to get back to you', he wrote. 'Don't think I like crowds of people any better than you do – they bring out all my specious charm and insincerity, and the hollow hangover of emptiness that one gets afterwards!'

As in the 1940s, Cecil was leading a divided life – now between Brimclose and Jill's flat in Clarendon Street. He was at Musbury on 8 June when his CBE was announced. 'Telephone buzzing all day: I felt like weeping and did so: this makes everything more of a nightmare', recorded Mary. Newspaper callers ranged from the local *Pulman's Weekly News* – which described Cecil as an East Devon resident who helped to form the Musbury Home Guard, 'is fond of sailing and has played cricket and rugby football' – to the Pendennis gossip column of the *Observer*.

'The one poet whose name appeared in the Honours List, C. Day-Lewis, is a very public-spirited person, sitting on innumerable committees. At the moment he is on a committee with Rose Macauley and V.S. Pritchett which is choosing books for the Festival of Britain', revealed Pendennis. 'He has had one disappointment in connection with the Festival. He was a member of the panel set up to adjudicate poetry, but resigned from it in order to be free to submit his own entry, a poem in seven parts on a journey to Italy. Then he found that by broadcasting the poem on the Third Programme he had forfeited the right to enter it for the Festival award. He is at present engaged on a new translation of the *Aeneid*. Some believe that the CBE will not be his last official honour: they believe that he may one day be offered the exalted post of Poet Laureate.'

In mid-June Mary heard that Rosamond was 'about but looking ill' and on the twenty-third received a firm letter from Cecil which 'holds out no hope'. Mary nevertheless continued to hope, to believe that as her marriage could not end Cecil must return to it one day. She and Nicholas loyally attended at Buckingham Palace early in July to see him receive his CBE from King George VI. Next day they were all back at Brimclose and on the seventh W.F. Jackson Knight arrived for a weekend of work on the *Aeneid*.

Mary's continued devotion and suggestions of compromise proved abortive. 'Distressing letter from Cecil', she recorded on July 22. 'How can he do this to me? My ideas are not even acknowledged. I am very, very miserable about him.' In the next week Mary received a letter from Jill's mother saying that she and Sir Michael were desperately keen that a marriage between Jill and Cecil should be avoided, and urging Mary to support them. Mary felt unable to respond very warmly. Meanwhile Cecil was writing to Jill:

I am so happy. I am not intimidated by my past failures, I only wish I could be a less flawed person for you, but you couldn't have a more loving one.... To know that I can talk to you about anything and everything, to feel so vulnerable to your moods, – to be glad to be vulnerable above all – you don't know how marvellous it is for me ... you make me feel so alive, in a way I've never felt alive before.... Slogging away at the *Aeneid:* the race and the boxing match are extremely funny – athel, bugger it I will spell it right, athletes have evidently behaved all through the ages with the same mixture of exhibitionism, hysteria and unscrupulousness.

My brother Nicholas and I remained ignorant of the approaching break and, in early August, life at Brimclose seemed to us as amiable and well-ordered as it had always been. He was back from school at Sherborne, I from my current RAF station near Hereford. There was sailing and bathing at Lyme Regis, a Somerset cricket match at Taunton as well as the annual cricket encounter on our tiny Brimclose pitch between the Day-Lewises and the Hedges and Osbornes living over the valley at Colyton. When Cecil left for London neither he nor Mary had dropped the smallest hint of his permanent departure the following month.

On 20 August Mary wrote to me that 'Nick went off to camp at Rye on Thursday with a large knapsack, mackintosh and bike. He was to meet Cecil in London. I'm afraid that the weather is against happy camping, but he hasn't written to me yet.' Even then she did not give me the main reason why camping would not be happy, and the rest of the letter is concerned with a day at Lyme Regis, a birthday party of Jinnie Osborne's and the annual show of the Musbury Village Produce Association.

Nicholas, then sixteen, had been put in the picture that Thursday.

Cecil asked me to have lunch with him on my way through London. On the way back from the restaurant to Chatto's we stopped and watched one of those Houdini types extricating himself from chains, outside the National Portrait Gallery at the bottom of Charing Cross Road. We stood for what seemed hours, Cecil apparently in a complete brown study, but later, I realized steeling himself to the task of telling me about the impending divorce. Uncharacteristically, he was hurling silver to Houdini's assistant, every time the latter asked the bystanders if there was 'one good Irishman' among them.

The announcement, finally made once we had reached his office, was a tremendous embarrassment all round – very painful to him obviously, and leaving me utterly unbelieving. In fact, for months I had the feeling the whole thing was a dreadful mistake. At the time he told me he had been very cowardly and had simply written you a letter.... After the camping expedition I returned through London, parked my bicycle at the Cecil and Jill flat, had a *very* warm welcome from her, and stayed at a nearby hotel in Ebury Street I think it was. When I got back to Devon, Mother said, 'I believe he's told you already – he said he was going to wait until he finally leaves here.' And that was all that was said.

In fact Cecil's letter to me, on Chatto and Windus notepaper, was not written until Monday 21 August.

Dearest Sean, This is a difficult letter to write to you, but I must do my best. I think you are old enough now to understand what a serious problem it is for me. For about ten years now, Mummy and I have been growing apart. I want to impress on you that – so far as anyone can be blamed for this – the fault was entirely mine. She has always been good and forgiving. I fell in love with Rosamond Lehmann, who was my mistress for a number of years – I dare say you had suspected this. But, since I was unable to marry her, we parted. I always refused to consider breaking up my home till you and Nico were of a reasonable age. Well, now I am living with Jill Balcon, and am quite sure the time has come to leave Mummy. I have asked her to give me a divorce, because I want to marry Jill : we are not sure yet whether she will be able to; but in any case there will be a separation. This is a very hard thing for Mummy, I know: but I do badly need someone I can love, and who shares my interests. And, though I don't approve of people divorcing lightly, I think it is dishonest and in the end disastrous to go on living with somebody when your heart and mind are with somebody else. Mummy would go on living at Brimclose for a year or two at least, so Nico and you will have it to go back to for holidays. And of course I shall love to have you in London with me, whenever, you feel like coming, and I shall always be at hand to give you any sort of help, practical or otherwise, which you may need. Don't mention any of this to *anyone*, yet, I shall be telling Nico before you see him next; and I'll be coming home for two weekends in September when you are there. I'm afraid this will have given you a shock. And you may think I am doing wrong. But I believe, in the long run, it will prove to be the best thing I could have done under the circumstances. Anyway, write to me when you can, and don't be afraid to say whatever you want to say about this, when you have got used to the idea. With best love, Dadda.

In shock I did tell my news to the nearest fellow Aircraftman Second Class. He did not telephone the *Daily Express* but told me I was 'old enough to know these things happen and not take it badly'. I managed a more or less coherent reply to Cecil and his second letter to me was despatched on 28 August.

Dearest Sean, I was very glad to get your letter, and that you wrote as you did, saying clearly and honestly just what you thought. I will answer your questions in the same way. First, Mummy knew about Rosamond after the first two years of my association with her, but agreed to let it continue – for my sake – on condition that I spent half my time at home. She knew about Jill, also, because I told her as soon as I fell in love with Jill. This was last January. And I told Mummy then that I felt I must leave her – could not stand any longer the mental agony of trying to divide myself between two people: apart from which, I knew it was not fair either to M. or to J. to do so. When you were last at home, therefore, Mummy did know – and had known for some months – what I intended to do. I only held back my last letter to you because I was not sure of the number of your Hut: my decision was not taken quickly – I do particularly want you to realise this. It was the result of many years of trying to live a divided life, of slowly being made to realise how wrong and difficult this was, and of being *absolutely* certain in my own mind that Jill was the right person for me (and I for her); also, it was easier to make such a decision now than it would have been a few years ago, when you and Nico were that much younger. Now, as to Mummy. She does not 'agree wholeheartedly' with my decision. She feels that she and I should have persevered longer in trying to keep our relationship going. This – I'm being very frank with you – is because she still loves me, whereas I have not loved her for a long time, though I admire her goodness very much and have a real affection for her. My own feeling is that there is no longer any real, living relationship left between us: our only common interest (as far as I was concerned) was in you and Nico, and in keeping a home together for you. Mummy, then, does not agree *whole-heartedly* with my decision, but she does agree that it seems the best thing to do now: she is very unhappy about it just now, but she will not be 'driven to despair' by divorce proceedings. She will be provided for financially by me, of course: she has you and Nico still: and I am hoping that she will be able to 'begin again' – in the sense that, when the worst is over for her, her life may become easier through being relieved of the problems I created for her by my association with other women. A clean break generally is preferable to a ragged wound – or an amputation to a limb dangling by a thread. No, Sean old boy – *no* pinch of salt about my being glad to see you in London: I want you to be with me *whenever you can*, though Mummy of course must have first priority. What you said about having had a happy child-hood touched me more than I can say – for I never felt I was a grade-A father, though I wanted to be. I hope this answers some of your questions. Please go on asking them if there are other things it would be a help for you to know. Best love, Dadda.

So began Cecil's last days as a planted, but never quite rooted, Devonian. It was almost exactly twelve years since he and Mary settled in at Brimclose, refugees from the political involvement of Cheltenham; a decade since he had stood with a farmer on this 'hill flank overlooking the Axe Valley' watching for German invaders, and the world began to think that he had found his home as a poet of the Hardy tradition. His last twenty-two years were to be spent, like so much of his childhood, as a Londoner.

At the end of August I returned to Brimclose for a fortnight of leave, and next day Diana Jordan, Mary's devoted friend since they met in Sher-borne twenty-two years before, arrived to take up position as a buffer. Cecil stayed from Friday 1 September until Monday the fourth, punctuat-ing the silence of that bleak weekend with the explosions of a bad cold.

The final weekend began on Thursday the seventh. The next morning he wrote to Jill:

I feel no reservations in my love for you.... It has tapped some sort of reserve tank of love in me, which I never knew I had. Before, though I have loved very deeply and passionately I have always kept a part of myself back; been afraid of being encroached on by a stronger (or more loving) personality, but with you, my beloved, I am too much at peace to feel I need ever say 'thus far but no further'. I wouldn't care if you did swallow me up; and because I don't care I know there is no danger of it.... I am feeling better today – really – cross my heart, though the cold is still clinging tenaciously: I hope to be snuffling, hawking, spitting and moping no more with it when I return to you on Monday.... Roughie is turning up in time for dinner tonight, which will be a relief: these last things do take their toll of one.

Nick Roughead was a man who normally contrived to avoid all emotional problems, but bravely faced up to this one, his normal cheer somewhat muted. 'Lumbago, tears and cold', wrote Mary the same day. 'Dull, heavy, damp, everything seems covered with fungus, I wish I could be drunk all day. The boys, Cecil and Roughie, went out twice', she wrote next day. There were no quarrels and no wailing, just a touch of low-key bitterness when Cecil pointed to the few items of furniture that he wanted sent after him: Mary numbly protested and he complained, 'I must be able to sit down.'

Sunday the tenth was fine and sunny. I retain one image from the mellow afternoon of that last day. Cecil had been making a farewell tour of the garden. It was never an easy garden to work because of its heavy clay soil, but Mary, who had a gift for making things grow, ensured that it never lacked colour. Now Cecil walked beside her devotedly tended herbaceous border, his face a grey mask of pensiveness. He once wrote that through the 1940s 'I was never long free from the sense of guilt, oppressive with disaster like the atmosphere before a storm that will not break....' It was this tightly bottled thunder which now showed on this face.

> Before you condemn this eminent freak
> As an outrage upon mankind,
> Reflect: something there is in him
> That must for ever seek
>
> To share the condition it glorifies,
> To shed the skin that keeps it apart,
> To bury its grace in a human bed –
> And it walks on knives, on knives.*

At 7.30 next morning, a car arrived from the village to take him and Nick Roughead to the London train at Axminster. There would be no

* 'Almost Human' (*Pegasus*, 1957).

turning back this time, the wheel was out of Cecil's hands. Some instinct made me get out of bed and help Mary see him off. He departed in silence and took no backward glance as the car was driven swiftly away down the lane. 'You *could* have at least let me do that alone', said Mary as she went back to her room, convinced that she was a failure in all things. 'Very, very tired and numb', she wrote in her diary.

'Self-exiled, I left what seems in retrospect a little paradise', wrote Cecil ten years later. 'But, as Proust so wonderfully showed, for certain tempera-ments the only Paradise is Paradise Lost....' In this rhetorical paragraph from his autobiography he looked beyond this departure in the half-light to his early years at Musbury when he enjoyed being a member of the vil-lage community. 'Did the place and the people really mean so much to me?' By 1950 it and they meant little to him.

At the end of the month Mary decided to give Cecil the divorce he wanted. Her reactions were always delayed and it was not until Christmas, fortunately spent at Bromsgrove in Worcestershire with her tenderly caring sister-in-law Ann and brother Charles, as well as a large gathering of other King relations, that her body protested at the strains of that terrible year now ending. She caught influenza and that turned to pneumonia. On the last day of 1950 she was in Bromsgrove Cottage Hospital 'somewhere between earth and heaven', and it was almost as if she had decided that as there was no further point in living, she would leave. She narrowly sur-vived the crisis, to keep Brimclose for twenty-two years more.

She lived alone and tried to compensate for her loss in close friendships with other women; she provided a home for her sons which, in the mind, I can never leave; as far as her temperament allowed she was an active member of the village community, president of the Women's Institute, a member of the Parish Council, a Liberal Party worker, a producer of mime plays, a churchgoer partly through belief in its social value. Some might say that, in Cecil's words, she went 'to seed in that soft, unexacting climate of the mind', and certainly her mind did not become more flexible or recep-tive with age. Sometimes her bitterness showed through her natural dignity and reserve. Yet in all those solitary years there was no withering of the roots or her love, her loyalty, her taste for what she had always enjoyed or her gritty maintenance of her own standards of consideration and beha-viour. After Cecil died her Musbury friend Barbara Cameron asked her if she would have had him back, had he wanted to return. 'He knew he could come, any time,' she replied. It was only after his death in 1972 that she was psychologically able to sell Brimclose. She moved back to her native Sherborne, made another wondrous garden at her tiny new house. It was there that she developed the cancer which killed her in early 1975.

She was not the only woman left sorrowing on that grey September day in 1950. Over the brow of the hill above Brimclose there was Billie Currall who also had a lonely sense of loss. She was always poor, and some-

times her son William suffered because of his origins. She had never used
him for moral blackmail and never would. At bad moments she considered
writing to Cecil for help but, she said, 'I did not do so because I was afraid
of being hurt.'

Far away at Little Wittenham there was the heartbroken Rosamond,
who found it harder to forgive the hurt done to her, and to her daughter
Sally. In *The Swan in the Evening* (1967) she gives her view of the way Sally
was 'shocked into sick, pale-cheeked, brooding dumbness by falseness in
word and deed, double dealing and other varieties of emotional treachery'.

She was obliged to witness a catastrophe of this nature at close quarters, and at
an impressionable age. A pattern of relationships she wholly trusted in collapsed
without warning: she saw the effects of this upon a person she had been accustomed to love happily. Unable to swallow what confronted her, she withdrew
for a time into herself and suffered deeply; equally for fear of contagion, I set
a distance temporarily between us. This perhaps was the most hateful aspect of
the full reckoning I was trying, and failing, to contend with.... *Almost a mercy
killing*.... A few years ago I came across this phrase. The poem in which it occurs
is, if I remember rightly, a philosophical justification of ruthless destructiveness
in certain relationships of love. I was particularly struck by the word 'almost'.

> Pitiless love will mean a death of love –
> An innocent act, almost a mercy-killing:
> But loveless pity makes a ghost of love,
> Petrifies with remorse each vein of feeling.
> Love can breed pity. Pity, when love's gone,
> Bleeds endlessly to no end – blood from stone.*

Rosamond, like Mary, had some of the life knocked out of her by this
break. She sold her Manor House and moved back to London, and found
it hard to maintain her earlier creative fertility and social energy. Her Sally
fared better, and worse. She lived for a time with her father and stepmother,
narrowly missed a First in English at Oxford, married the poet and critic
P.J. Kavanagh and in September 1957, sailed with him to Java where he
was to take up a teaching job with the British Council.

Just before they left she had a last brief meeting with Cecil. With Jill
he was buying cherries from a barrow in Davies Street, where she and
Kavanagh saw him. 'At first she wanted to walk past, but I sensed she was
hesitating, so it was easy to make her turn back and join him at the barrow',
remembered Kavanagh. 'I walked on, and after a few minutes she rejoined
me, looking glad. That's all really. We were both pleased, I think. A piece
of the past had been brought out into the open and looked at, and that's
usually a pretty good idea.' As Rosamond remembered this meeting, Sally
thought Cecil looked lined. 'She was shocked by what she saw as his
changed appearance and expression, the disappearance of his earlier beauty.'

*Love and Pity' (*Pegasus*, 1957).

In Java the following year Sally contracted poliomyelitis and died at the age of twenty-three. Cecil was one of the many who mourned her; in his later years no death so shocked him. Her brief life is enshrined in Kavanagh's beautiful autobiographical book *The Perfect Stranger* (1966); and her mother's *The Swan in the Evening*, which describes the mystical experiences, the spiritual communication with Sally, which have led her to the certain conviction that death is not the end of consciousness.

Turning his back as best he could on the ruins, the scorched earth he had left in his wake, Cecil arrived at 4d Clarendon Street on 11 September, to begin his new life, to recover his youth, with Jill. There was a burden of guilt to be carried, but he could now enjoy married happiness such as he had not known before. When I encountered them for the first time after they had set up house together the release of all inhibitions was palpable. Their continuous endearments and physical touchings, their constant close proximity to one another, suggested that they could hardly believe their luck and were clinging on in case it went away. My discomfort about this doubtless said as much about the quite opposite atmosphere at Brimclose as about the tiny hothouse in Pimlico. The clamour of demonstrativeness was not excluding: Jill extended her generous warmth to her newly acquired 'stepsons' and did her best to conquer our inbred, country-cousin diffidence. There was also a lot of laughter: Jill could make Cecil laugh, a gift he placed among her most endearing features, and she was the most overtly appreciative audience he ever had.

One reason for close proximity was the size of the Clarendon Street flat, which was not designed for two, not even two who felt they were one. Earlier that summer they had been witnesses at the marriage of Laurie Lee and Kathy, conducted at Kensington Register Office in Cheniston Gardens. Leaving the ceremony they looked in the window of the nearest house agent, and saw that 73a Bedford Gardens was offered. They eventually secured the lease of this reasonably capacious studio flat, off Kensington Church Street. They were able to move in with Cecil's 1,500 or so books on 19 September.

The large window overlooking the tree-lined street made the place very light. The furniture was mainly books, but there was room enough for an eating-table as well as Cecil's Pembroke working-table at which, conscious of his difficult financial position, he often sat for a seven-day working week. There was a small kitchen at the back where Jill quickly improved her cooking skills: Cecil appreciated her castle puddings, but was moved to say that her apprentice pancakes reminded him of Keats's death mask. Above there was a gallery where they slept. From the start they managed a lot of entertaining, though overnight guests had to be placed with friends in the neighbourhood.

Even during the move Cecil was at work on Book Six of the *Aeneid* and this task was approaching the half-way mark. On 1 October he and Jill resumed, appropriately at the Bristol Old Vic, the reading partnership which had begun with their *Time for Verse* appearance in January 1948, and was destined to last a quarter of a century.

Jill has given her appreciation of Cecil's reading voice and technique in her foreword to *A Lasting Joy* (1973), the anthology derived from their 1972 BBC Television series.

I would say that he was endowed with one of the most spell-binding voices I have ever heard: in turn gentle, contemplative, passionate, urbane, witty. The articulation was all purity and clarity.... As a poet and also a trained singer, he had an inborn lyricism, sense of rhythm and capacity for breath control, and therefore phrasing. He never lost the hint of Anglo-Irish pronunciation that was his inheritance. In talking to people about poetry he was never pompous or pedantic, never solemn when he was serious, never lost his infinite capacity for enthusiasm and joy.

There was little histrionic display, still less show-biz razzamatazz, about their public recitals. They would walk on to the platform carrying their marked books, the stage set with table and reading light, Jill smiling and Cecil blinking a little in the bright light. When Cecil read, Jill became a leader of the audience appreciation; when she read, he would assume the air of a schoolmaster modestly pleased with the progress of his pupil. They were both always very alert. She was not a pupil, of course: she was indeed the established professional of the two, meticulously rehearsed and yet fervent, and their performances were always nicely complementary. In Jill's memory they had 'total rapport' with the planning of their programmes, and during rehearsals often found themselves laughing, or crying, in the same places. 'Cecil always took a lot of trouble with any performance, but he had a mixture of caution and recklessness, he needed an element of danger and did not rehearse as much as me', she remembers.

After the visit to Bristol he wrote to me on 6 October of its success, and other things:

I don't think you need worry about Mummy doing anything 'desperate', not that I want to minimise the hardness of the time she must be going through. People do, sooner or later, get over these things; and it is not as if I'd been able to give her much in the way of love for a long time. I want you to feel assured, yourself, that at any rate she need not worry about money. She will have about £700 a year, free of income tax, to live on, which is a good deal for a single person: I myself, after paying tax and Nico's school fees, and giving her the greater part of this £700, will have little more than £1,000 per annum to support Jill and myself, and a possible family. M.'s only real financial difficulty will be in the keeping on of Frank [Parnell, the Brimclose gardener]: but I hope she'll be able to do this, and stay on at Brimclose. I do realise how 'fantastic – absurd' what has happened must seem to you: well, you know the saying, 'tout comprendre, c'est tout pardonner'.

The same day he wrote to Rupert Hart-Davis, hoping for an early meeting. 'I'm living here now with Jill, and hope to get a divorce soon. It has all been I hope you will believe, not so mad or bad as it must appear on the surface (and some way below the surface . . .).'

A week later he knew that the divorce was going ahead as planned. In accordance with the customary legal procedures a private detective arrived at their flat to discover him and Jill co-habiting. He collected his evidence and she continued preparing a celebratory dinner party for Nick Roughead.

That month they had nine Dorset days at the New Inn, Piddletrenthide, an unofficial honeymoon. They had a private sitting-room where Cecil could stick to his working hours, while Jill read Hardy by the fire. They also gave Nicholas a day out from school at Sherborne and visited the Crichel home of Edward Sackville-West, Raymond Mortimer and Desmond Shawe-Taylor.

They were back in London at the beginning of November, Cecil taking part on the eighth in a radio discussion about poetry with Paul Dehn, Patric Dickinson, Laurie Lee and Henry Reed. Next day at Brimclose the divorce petition arrived for Mary's signature; she found it 'devastating' and signed. On the tenth Cecil wrote to me that the news was no longer secret:

I thought I'd write at once to clear up the points you are in doubt about. First, you may now tell anyone you wish to about the divorce, as far as I am concerned. . . . I only wanted it kept secret before, until I knew for certain that M. was going to bring a petition for divorce. As the case is undefended, I do not have to appear in court; nor do you: M. does have to appear. It is she who is bringing the action against me – she is the 'innocent party' and will appear as such. She has filed her petition on the grounds of my adultery with Jill. . . . I know this is a miserable subject for you: but, if there is anything else on your mind about it, that I can explain or help over, do write and ask me – it is much better so than to keep doubts, difficulties, or criticisms or resentments bottled up inside oneself. . . .

I seem to have had nothing but committee meetings this week, planning for the 1951 festival, apart from the broadcast with Paul, Laurie and co, which went off better (or at least more fluently) than we expected, as a result of the BBC supplying us with three bottles of wine to drink during the rehearsal and recording of the programme. J.B. Priestley has asked me to collaborate with him on a play when I've finished the *Aeneid* (top secret), but as this seems to mean rewriting in verse a play he has already written in prose, I doubt if it's a good proposition. . . .

In the middle of December the Fifth and Sixth Books of the *Aeneid* were delivered to the BBC and the producer, Basil Taylor, who did not know Cecil well at this stage, began to agitate about the translator interfering with the production and casting. For his part Cecil had thought that he might be consulted over the production; but he had more respect for the judgment of professionals than seems to have been realized. At the end of the month J.C. Thornton, administrative officer for the talks department, wrote to Harman Grisewood explaining that Taylor did not want Cecil in the studio during rehearsals. 'The second point is that he fears Day-Lewis may want to take a hand in the casting. Taylor naturally wants to pick actors and actresses who are willing to work to him as a talks producer. . . .' Grisewood scribbled the words 'Taylor should be protected' at the bottom of the memorandum.

While writing, Cecil had inwardly 'heard' Jill doing the part of Dido, and he had urged her claim with what he considered to be professional objectivity, knowing that she was regarded within the BBC as one of the most accomplished of radio actresses; he thought Taylor would be glad of her services. When broadcasting began the following June, Catherine Lacey was Dido, and Jill had the longer part of Venus. Also in the cast were Alan Wheatley, Margaret Rawlings, Mary O'Farrell, Robert Harris and Alan McClelland.

In early 1951 few people not concerned with either the criticism of poetry or the university had heard of the position of Oxford Professor of Poetry. The chair had long been occupied by distinguished academic critics, and at this time Cecil's one-time tutor, the newly knighted Sir Maurice Bowra, was about to complete his five-year term. The university establishment considered that C.S. Lewis, the respected Magdalen English tutor and Christian apologist, would be a suitable replacement. Enid Starkie, a small but pugnacious Anglo-Irishwoman at Somerville College, considered otherwise, and now proceeded to make herself a name far beyond her own field of French literature, as the king-maker of the Oxford poetic throne.

The position is unique in that it is decided by an election in which the whole of Convocation, the 30,000 or so Masters of Arts of the university, are the electorate. It is the oldest Oxford chair, having been established by Sir Henry Birkhead in 1708 as a protest against the small number of lectures given by dons. In the early 1950s it paid a salary of £250 a year for which the Professor was expected to deliver three lectures a year, deliver the Creweian Oration in Latin at Encaenia in alternate years, and judge the entries for the Newdigate Prize and the Sacred Poem Prize.

Enid Starkie had first met Cecil, with Rosamond Lehmann, at a Bowra dinner party in the summer of 1944. Later that year she was invited by Rosamond to become a contributor to *Orion* and the acquaintance with Cecil was maintained. She now asked him if he would stand for the Oxford chair and, with little thought that he might sit on it, he agreed. Thus it was that the intense, unpredictable, fastidious Dr Starkie, dressed always in a beret and lurid red and blue jackets and slacks, could be seen in the early weeks of 1951, cycling fiercely about Oxford, collecting MA supporters for Cecil. She was a buccaneer with a considerable flair for publicity, and by the end of the month the election was arousing excited speculation even beyond the common rooms of the university.

Fortunately for Cecil there is a tradition that the candidates do not do any electioneering themselves. He could remain a glamorous mystery and was not required to live up to any of the fervent claims made by Dr Starkie about his greatness as a poet and his spell-binding perception as a lecturer. In the face of her campaign Edmund Blunden, who had earlier also been persuaded to stand, modestly retired from the context declaring it would be wrong of him to split the poetry party vote. Cecil wrote to him, 'I feel very distressed that I did not get my withdrawal in first – it's another case of Gresham's Law, I fear – if that is the law by which the higher is driven out by the lower ... I am awfully touched by your generosity.'

'Grim goings on at Oxford just now, contest for the chair of poetry and no holds barred between Slogger C. Screwtape Lewis and Man Mountain of Bedford Gardens', wrote Cecil to Nick Roughead on 2 February. 'Result will be known today week.' Voting had to be in person.

In the event Cecil had a narrow majority of twenty-one, polling 194 votes against 173 for Lewis. For the first time the dropping of the Day-Lewis hyphen may have had practical value, for Cecil was listed in the voting papers as C.D. Lewis. 'I attribute my narrow victory to a handful of aged voters who, though determined to support the eminent Magdalen candidate, through failing sight or powers of concentration confused C.S. with C.D. Lewis', he wrote afterwards.

This victory coincided with publication of *C. Day Lewis*, a Penguin selection of his verse from *Transitional Poem* to *Word Over All* made and introduced by Cecil himself. In his preface he wrote that looking back over his last twenty years of verse he was struck by its 'lack of development'; it looked to be 'a series of fresh beginnings, rather than a continuous line'. He thought his later work had more variety, 'a more sensuous appeal and a greater flexibility of line'. His interests had changed and his sympathies widened. 'At the same time, it is only fair to inform the reader that, in the view of some critics, my verse had deteriorated since the early "school of social consciousness" days into an anti-social or at any rate a-social pre-occupation with the past and with traditional forms.'

He writes that if he took the reader through a conducted tour of his verse he could

show where emotion, applied too raw, has eaten holes in the fabric of a poem, and where it has been more successfully depersonalized: where, through lack of patience, a poem has taken a wrong turning and ended up a blind alley; or the very place where some apparently adventitious thing – the need for a certain rhyme or cadence – gave me a line which altered in the right direction a poem's whole course. I could point out how, during my so-called 'political' period, most of my poems were in fact about love or death: how contrary to received opinion about modern verse, nearly all my poems 'rhyme and scan'; and how, contrary to the preconceived opinions of some, they are not less experimental in nature when they are more traditional in idiom: how an over-enthusiastic, often per-functory use of 'modern' imagery is gradually replaced by a more personal yet wider field of images: how certain characteristics keep cropping up throughout my work – hero-worship, fear, compassion, the divided mind, a prevailing sense of the transience of things: and how, whatever its apparent focus of the moment – politics, the birth of a child, love for a woman, youthful memories, the appre-hension or impact of war – however much its style is altered from time to time by the demands of some new experience or ruling passion, there runs through it all, an unbroken thread, the search for personal identity, the poet's relentless compulsion to know himself.

On 27 February Mary went to Southampton for the 'silly, dull, sordid, miserable' divorce hearing. This court had been chosen by her solicitor as a way of avoiding newspaper publicity, and though the *Sunday Times* carried the news on 4 March and the *Daily Telegraph* followed it up next morning, Mary was spared photographs and direct interviews. The decree absolute was obtained on 21 April and Cecil and Jill were able to complete plans for their own marriage ceremony six days later, on his forty-seventh birthday.

Jill's mother and brother attended the proceedings at Kensington Register Office, and the witness was her Clarendon Street home help, Mrs Pizzey. Afterwards there was a wedding lunch, paid for by the still dis-approving and consequently absent Sir Michael Balcon, in an upstairs room at the Ivy. There one of the guests, Elizabeth Jane Howard, remembered Jill 'glowing in rose pink, with the aquamarine earrings that Cecil had given her'. He was supported by his oldest friends, Rex Warner and Charles Fenby, and their wives, as well as Nick Roughead. Charles Tennyson, a grandson of the poet, made a speech and contrived to find a suitable passage to read from Cecil's *Noah and the Waters*. Tennyson also made available his cottage at Walberswick on the Suffolk coast for the short honeymoon.

They were back in London on 3 May so that Cecil could go to St Paul's Cathedral for the service of dedication marking the opening of the Festival of Britain, and attended by the King and Queen. Next morning Cecil was at the South Bank Exhibition with its Dome of Discovery, and sense of lightness, fun and optimism, for the visit there by the King and Queen. He could go to these ceremonies knowing that his main contribution to the Festival, his complete translation of Virgil's *Aenid*, was now finished and safely delivered to the BBC. For the rest he and Jill would be adding their quota of poetry recitals to the 500 and more official artistic events and twenty-two provincial festivals to be held throughout Britain over the next few months.

On 1 June, Cecil gave his inaugural lecture as Professor of Poetry at Oxford. It was called 'The Poet's Task' and began with the thought that 'it is a solemn and rather disquieting moment when a person finds himself upon his feet, about to profess a subject he has for most of his life-time practised'. He went on to deliver not the first, or last, of his eulogies to Bowra, before doubting if he could match the enthusiasm of his old tutor for the words of others. 'For throughout that long series of love affairs with Words which is the poet's working life, and wherein Thought must play the delicate dual role of chaperone and pander, he is as selfish and egotistic as any other lover: he is concerned with the love affairs of his colleagues only in so far as they may advance his own: he is out for what he can get out of them.'

The inaugural was warmly received and broadcast on the Third Programme, but Cecil was very aware of having added little to what he had said before in other words. That his subsequent lectures were also enthusiastically attended, sometimes 'packed to the rafters', was a tribute to his making much of little, as well as to the decorative presence of Jill at his side. It cannot be claimed that this Oxford performance as a whole was one of his successes. Some undergraduates complained that he was inacessible, and he was himself conscious that he said more in his much superior 1946 Clark Lectures at Cambridge.

'Three lectures a year for five years nearly killed me, I had nothing more to say. I only published about three, it wasn't at all a good performance', he said in a 1971 interview. The best, he thought, were one each devoted to Emily Dickinson and Edward Thomas, one on translating poetry, and a handful exploring various idioms of poetry: but he was temperamentally unsuited to such a long term of office. He saved his best new lectures, even in this period, for single appearances elsewhere: 'The Lyrical Poetry of Thomas Hardy' given to the British Academy in 1951; and 'The Grand Manner', given at Nottingham University the following year as the Byron Foundation Lecture.

In August Cecil and Jill travelled abroad together for the first time. They went at the invitation of Stephen and Natasha Spender, who had taken rooms for their friends at the Albergo Gardesana, a harbour inn at Torri del Benaco on Lake Garda. They had some financial anxiety about this Italian visit, selling a pair of silver coffee-pots, given them as a wedding present, to pay for the fares; and having to make a strictly limited ration of lire last for ten days. This helped to make for the idyll so lovingly recorded in Cecil's poem 'Time to Go'.

They returned to find Cecil being publicized. On 2 September he was the subject for the 'Portrait Gallery' of the *Sunday Times*, photographed pipe-smoking by Douglas Glass and identified as a writer of 'dazzling detective novels', Professor of Poetry at Oxford, poet of much variety, translator of Virgil, reader of verse, charming light tenor. 'How unfair that accomplishments enough to satisfy the pride of six men should be united in Mr Day-Lewis! It must, however, be grudgingly admitted that he is, or at any rate appears, no more vain of his voice than of his detective stories, his professorial chair or even his poetry.'

The other 'quality' Sunday newspaper, the *Observer*, followed this up with a Jane Bown picture and a more serious profile on 7 October. The peg was Cecil's *Aeneid*. 'The readings of the new translation, still in progress, are for some tens of thousands of listeners a rediscovery of the "father of Western civilization"; the critical talks which accompany them make a major contribution to the self-scrutiny of that civilization at one of its supremely critical junctures. Altogether, the present Virgil season offers a truly magnificent celebration of the Third Programme's fifth birthday.'

The anonymous writer saw Cecil as a man of 'worn and rather suffering good-looks' whose modesty was 'genuine as well as apparent'. His 1947 visit to Denmark had 'suddenly and radically cured him of insularity' and at forty-seven he was reacting to foreign countries 'with the passionate enthusiasm of novelty'. In his work there was less novelty, for 'he has magnificently matured since his gay buccaneering days of 15 years ago'. He had 'become a careful, thoughtful and eloquent poet; he has always been a gentle, sensitive and kind-hearted man.'

In September it was suggested by Dr Alex Comfort, just beginning to make his name as a sex freedom fighter, that Cecil might like to go to the Soviet Union in a delegation of the Authors' World Peace Appeal. On the eighteenth he replied, somewhat guardedly, from Bedford Gardens:

I am very much for the project in principle: whether I could go myself depends upon when and for how long the visit is planned, as I am terribly busy this autumn. Also, whether I am a good person to send I rather doubt, as I have no clearly defined political position, am not a good arguer, and doubtful whether my own 'current of thought' at present, such as it is, represents anything of general application among English writers of today. However, I think that the deputation should include as much variation of outlook as is reasonably possible, even at the risk of impressing the Russians as disunited, woolly or 'decadent'. I also think that, without making this a condition of going to Russia, we should suggest that a friendly match on our home ground would be a good thing all round – the Russian writers seem to have even more bizarre phantasies about what goes on in this country than we have about what goes on there. Anyway, I'll go if I can.

The AWPA had been started that year by the short-story writer A.E. Coppard, and Comfort was on its committee with Doris Lessing, Compton Mackenzie, Herbert Read, Naomi Mitchison, L.A.G. Strong and others as well as Cecil. Its objective was to make the public aware of the danger of nuclear war between the Soviet Union and the United States, then being encouraged by some to take advantage of its temporary arms superiority. It also tried to press for talks between governments which would reduce the tension of the cold war. In its attention to detail it even considered children's comics which treated 'the enemy' as something sub-human, and it took some legal action against the worst ones. At its peak the organization had several hundred members, including such apolitical figures as Dylan Thomas and Christopher Fry. It was sometimes labelled a 'Communist-front organization' but really it was more of a centre and left coalition. A fellow committee man, Robert Greacen, remembered Cecil as 'quiet and sensible, but I think that with his many other commitments he was unable to give us as much of his time as he would have liked'.

A minor war was being fought that autumn within the Old Vic Company. In Tyrone Guthrie's blood-soaked production of Christopher Marlowe's *Tamburlaine the Great* the name part was performed by Donald Wolfit, playing somewhat against Jill's Zenocrate. She later had the more comfortable role of Titania in Shakespeare's *A Midsummer Night's Dream*, but it was generally a fairly nerve-racking season and this no doubt helped her decision early the following year to opt out of the company's visit to Africa following its two months' tour of Britain. She decided that her stage career was not worth the periods of separation from Cecil that it must inevitably involve. She was still playing in *Tamburlaine* at Stratford-upon-Avon when Cecil wrote to her from Bournemouth, where he was visiting his stepmother, Mamie, at the end of October:

My stepmother seems remarkably cheerful and recovered [she had just had a cancer operation], is sitting up in her bedroom and has a nice Irish nurse. Unfortunately my Butler cousin is still here, an old bore of Test Match standards and I shall have to get to bed at 10 sharp simply to get away from her. Just been listening to *Aeneid* 7 which is very nearly as tedious as the Butler cousin. Oh, how horrible Bournemouth is – I should like to blow it all up and bury the squalid remains under quick lime.

The year ended with a 'satirical' criticism of Cecil by the poet John Heath-Stubbs in the literary quarterly *Nine*, the complaint being that he had snatched the Oxford chair from the abundantly qualified C.S. Lewis, partly through greed for money. When asked to subscribe to the journal Cecil replied on 23 December in friendly but firm terms to the editor, Peter Russell.

I have just received a subscription form for *Nine*. It is an odd thing, being asked to subscribe to a magazine in which the Professor of Poetry at Oxford is called 'a knave'. The statement is, I am advised, gloriously actionable; so I think my subscription should take the form of not bringing an action. I don't want to be unkind to poor Heath-Stubbs, but he should check his facts – the salary of the Prof. is not, alas, the huge one he mentioned, but £250. This letter is for your own information, not to be printed or commented upon in *Nine* – keep the space for more important matters.

This led, on 20 February 1952, to a second and longer letter in which Cecil spelled out his fastidious distaste for the publication of personal abuse.

You ask what I think about the question of satire. Well, first, I think that if we have learnt anything from Freud (and, for instance, Auden) it is to examine out motives very carefully: and, if we do so, it is extremely difficult to take up an attitude of moral indignation about other people's shortcomings. *Personal* satire seems to me not civilised any more (though I indulge in it in private, all right): Pope and Swift were civilised; Walter Winchell is not. And this difference goes beyond their respective literary merits. I think if we are going to write satire now, it should be directed against types, against 'trends of thought' and ways of life; or against the dishonesty and nastiness we find in ourselves; not against individuals. Personal satire, such as [Roy] Campbell's, seems to me nowadays nearly always a parade or a bolstering-up of the writer's own ego, not a genuine detestation of what the satiree stands for: this need not prevent it being good poetry, though I think Campbell's best poems – like 'Choosing a Mast' or 'Zebras' – come out of self-forgetfulness, not self-inflation.

You say that one should 'accept public criticism without resentment'. One should, no doubt; but, since we are none of us superhuman, we do resent it. I have had my share of it – scurrilous abuse from Grigson, for example; and on the other hand a most severe criticism by Edwin Muir of one of my early books, which I resented equally at the time, but soon saw the justice of, and got great benefit from. Grigson, I dare say, felt he was being 'sincere and honest' – people do, who believe they have a mission to clean up the literary or some other scene: but the *tone* of malice always betrays itself. Such people have not examined their motives thoroughly, or not acted upon the result of doing so, and therefore sincerity and honesty are not words I would apply to them. There is a difference between stringent literary criticism and calling a man a knave. I was hurt by this (who would not be?). I have done many things of which I am bitterly ashamed – perhaps even Heath-Stubbs has: and because I have, I should never use that word in public (and have not used it in private, for that matter) about anyone else....

I'm very glad you are enjoying Hardy. Now there was someone whose sweetness and goodness of character breathes up at you out of his poems. O si sic omnes, including myself!

That January Cecil was carefully rehearsing for *Blame Not the Bard*, an hour-long Third Programme radio feature in which he was to play and sing the part of Tom Moore, the centenary of whose death would fall in February. This was really the summit of his singing career, as well as his combined début and swan song as a radio actor, and he considered the BBC somewhat mean in only offering a fee of twenty guineas exclusive of expenses. 'This is considerably more than we are accustomed to pay to other people for a similar engagement', claimed the BBC bureaucracy when Cecil wrote to complain.

He was on the air again on 8 February, taking part as a reader in a 'Mourning and Consolation' compilation, broadcast on all channels as a response to the sudden death of King George VI two days earlier. This time the fee was ten guineas. Such small sums would not solve Cecil's financial problems. On 12 February he received an invitation from Rayner Heppenstall to write something for the Third's *Imaginary Conversations* series. He replied next day saying, 'I've got to write a detective novel double quick, to save us from the work house: after that I'll cast about in my mind and see if there is anything there which might do.'

In the middle of that month Jill left home on a British provincial tour with the Old Vic production of *A Midsummer Night's Dream*. Her absence gave Cecil the chance to renew his love affair with Italy. At the invitation of Brian Kennedy-Cooke, the Anglo-Irish head of the British Council in Rome, he agreed to undertake a lecture tour. It began in Turin on 10 March and included appearances at Milan, Bologna, Venice, Padua, Verona, Florence, Rome, Naples and Palermo, before ending in Rome on 30 March. Writing to Jill from London two days before his departure Cecil said he was 'seething with resentment and fury at going abroad tomorrow'. Once in Italy he responded contentedly to 'the usual stimulus', though he had his difficulties: 'The lecture did not go so well at Milan as at Turin – that is to say, a smaller proportion of the audience was able to follow it closely, for linguistic reasons. It is really more exhausting than I'd anticipated, trying to put the thing over to a foreign audience, particularly when, in the Italian manner, some of them stroll in long after I'd started while others stroll out long before I'd finished as if one was conducting a service at a Roman Catholic cathedral', he wrote from Bologna. By the time he reached Florence on the twenty-second he was beginning to take a jaundiced view. 'Italy is absolutely wasted on me without you to share it, and I'm depressed by the utter futility of lecturing to these cow-eyed women and earnest, worried-looking men who can't understand half I say', he complained to Jill. 'Bugger British culture and Italo-British relations. Viva the hearth and the bed!'

In Rome he met Praz, Ungoletto, Moravia 'and such like Italian writers', and he was impressed by Pompeii as 'without any question the most remarkable place I've ever seen', but such things did not match the pleasure of his London reunion with Jill at the beginning of April. Almost at once they went to Piddletrenthide for a week of Dorset holiday. Then working as a reporter on the local edition of the *Bridport News*, I met them at Lyme Regis. Cecil drove us in his extravagant and decadent-looking second-hand Ford V8, the latest in his long line of cars, across the border into Devon, past the gates of my old school at Rousdon, down into the Axe Valley and through Musbury to Axminster. Not much was said and we did not stop or see anybody who might have recognized us. It was the last glimpse Cecil would catch of his 'lost paradise', though for the moment he was in a paradise regained.

> Now is a chink between two deaths, two eternities.
> Seed here, root here, perennially cling!
> Love me today and I shall live today always!

> Blossom, my goldenmost, at-long-last spring,
> My long, last spring!*

In June Cecil and Jill were given the loan of Laurens van der Post's Half-Crown Cottage and attended the Aldeburgh Festival for the first time. William Plomer was that year working on the libretto for Britten's *Gloriana*, and a regular Festival lecturer was Sir Kenneth Clark. A friend made that year was the Cambridge Professor Emeritus, Elsie Butler, a scholar of German and another of those life-enhancing Anglo-Irish-women to whom he was so easily drawn.

Other new friends made at this time were Franta Belsky, a sculptor working close by the Day-Lewis home who managed a serene, life-like head of Cecil, and his cartoonist wife Margaret; and the artist Ronald Searle, creator of St Trinian's, and his wife Kaye Webb. In the *News Chronicle* of 3 July the Searle-Webb team featured Cecil in their 'People Worth Meeting' series. Below a headline proclaiming 'POETIC DON WHO WRITES WHO-DUNNITS' there was a respectful pen-and-ink drawing by Searle, giving the subject just a little too much height of brow; and a view by Webb of 'a disarmingly young and romantic don, with lively hair, furrowed brow and an aloof rather noble expression, as if he actually *thought* in Latin'. She judged him to look 'exceedingly English; the part of him which belongs to Ireland emerges only in his talent for reassurance, his readiness to laugh and, of course, his poetry'. Since youth casual acquaintances had reported him 'hard to know, almost forbidding. Only his intimates discovered that this was a mask created painfully through boyhood to conceal his own un-certainty.' The following year Cecil provided an admiring preface and 'short dirge' for Ronald Searle's book *Souls in Torment*.

For the most part Cecil kept his old friends, several of whom Jill had known before they met. This meant that to an extent they moved in the same social circuit which he enjoyed with Rosamond in the 1940s. Any resentment was largely hidden, but there were moments when Jill's nerve of guilt was touched. She did not, for instance, altogether enjoy the 24 August weekend spent at Woodstock with Rex Warner and his wife Barbara – who remained entirely loyal to Rosamond.

For Cecil this visit had a greater significance. He met the poet George Seferis, since the previous year a counsellor at the Greek Embassy in London and later to be the Greek Ambassador to Britain and a Nobel prizewinner. Four years older than Cecil, George Seferiades, to give him his real name, was a man who had seen much of the world, as a student in Paris, and as a diplomat who had worked in Africa, the Middle East and Turkey as well as Europe. Being equally accomplished as a man of action and as a poet, he quickly fitted into Cecil's hero category, and was further elevated there when he declined to serve or live with the repressive military regime

* 'On a Dorset Upland' (*Pegasus*, 1957).

which took over Greece in the 1960s. The fact that Rex Warner was his English translator also inclined Cecil to join the most devoted admirers of Seferis's verse. When he died in 1971, the same year as Sir Maurice Bowra, he was coupled with Cecil's Oxford tutor in a single memorial poem, 'Hellene: Philhellene'.

That August ended for Cecil and Jill at Stratford-upon-Avon, where they gave an Apollo Society recital with the young pianist Noel Mewton-Wood. They were back in London for the publication on 4 September by the Hogarth Press of his translation of the *Aeneid*, dedicated to W.F. Jackson Knight. In a foreword he writes of his task, and the impossibility of finding a modern English equivalent to Virgil's language, his melodic variety and complexity of rhythm. He had decided that 'a translation which is not somehow based upon the language of its own time will never begin to come near the poetic quality of its original', and that the translator would be 'a little more "like his author" if he writes in verse'.

Harman Grisewood of the Third Programme wrote next day thanking Cecil for sending him a copy of the book, which reminded him of broadcasts that 'remain one of the major achievements of the BBC'. In the United States the translation has sold nearly 400,000 copies, the best seller of all Cecil's books. With paperback reprints and academic use it has done almost as well in Britain. The reviews were mainly respectful, though some critics detected that the translator had not been so engaged by his work this time as he was with the *Georgics*.

The day after publication he and Jill again left for Italy, invited by Brian Kennedy-Cooke, the British Council boss in Rome. From Rome they went by bus to Siena and Florence, following the route taken by Cecil and Rosamond during the 1948 journey that became *An Italian Visit*. In Cecil's mind there was an element of exorcism about this journey. After looking at pictures and sculpture in Florence, with particular attention to the works used in the parody section of Cecil's verse sequence, they went on to Torri del Benaco. There they found Stephen and Natasha Spender entertaining the American poets Robert Lowell and Allen Tate. With so many poets about there was small chance of writing poetry. The atmosphere was nevertheless sufficiently lulling for Cecil to accept at least one engagement which he later rather regretted. On 20 September he wrote from Torri undertaking to give four talks constituting 'An Examination of Modern Poetry' for the BBC Home Service the following January. According to the producer Gilbert Phelps, Cecil was at first 'reluctant to undertake this series and there was much groaning of spirit. Then he began to get interested.'

He and Jill were back in London on 27 September and nine days later they went to a dinner given by the Incorporated Society of Musicians for the eightieth birthday of the composer Ralph Vaughan Williams, due the following Sunday. Cecil was proud of being an honorary member of this

Society and on this evening attended in white tie and tails with the CBE about his neck.

At the same time Cecil agreed to replace Steuart Wilson, in hospital with gall-bladder trouble, as the speaker in a performance of Vaughan Williams's *An Oxford Elegy*, to be given as part of the birthday concert at Dorking on 11 October. As this work for speaker, wordless chorus and orchestra sets parts of Matthew Arnold's 'The Scholar Gypsy' and 'Thyrsis' it was appropriate that the Oxford Professor of Poetry should be heard, but Wilson had taken the speaking part in the first public performance at Oxford that June and was angry at missing the repeat. 'I wish I wasn't missing the party – I could wring my gall-bladder's neck and give it to Cecil Day-Lewis to eat', he wrote in a birthday letter to Vaughan Williams. Ironically, when the work was recorded at Cambridge in 1970, Cecil had to drop out through being in hospital for a bladder operation, and the actor John Westbrook was substituted.

Cecil had now begun a stage play, *The Exiles*. 'I've been bulldozed into giving four talks on modern poetry (ugh!) for the Home Service in January, and then I must get back to a play I've been trying to write', he wrote to the BBC producer Rayner Heppenstall. He completed the play, but it was never produced. It had a cold war setting and was tuned to its period, but Cecil never gave himself enough time to work at the playwright's art. He was sufficiently discouraged, by the unwillingness of any management to take up the script, not to repeat the attempt. After his death Hallam Tennyson, assistant head of BBC Radio drama, looked at the play and found it 'very skilfully constructed' with 'some effective scenes'; but the main plot devices and the love scenes did not work well, the ending was unsatisfying and the writing was 'very uneven'.

Before the end of 1952 Cecil and Jill had decided to start a family, and their first-born was conceived that Christmastide. They both looked to the New Year with great happiness.

Cecil's *An Italian Visit* was eventually published by Jonathan Cape on 26 January 1953, about three years after it had been ready for the press. The problem was that Rosamond had withheld consent to the publication of the sixth of its seven sections, 'Elegy Before Death: At Settignano', and Cecil wanted to publish the complete work. Only in 1952 were short notes exchanged, in which Rosamond agreed to publication and said she would like to retain the dedication, 'To R.N.L.'. This was by no means Cecil's last love poem, but it was maybe the last in which he surrendered himself completely; after this there was usually a tinge of irony. He and Jill gave a small dinner party at the Bedford Gardens flat to celebrate publication. The guests were the poet Henry Reed, to whom the volume as a whole is dedicated, and Elizabeth Jane Howard.

The verse book was followed that year by the tenth Nicholas Blake novel, *The Dreadful Hollow*. This begins with an eminent financier, soon pushed over the edge of a quarry, asking Nigel Strangeways to investigate a plague of anonymous letters which has infected his native Dorset village, Prior's Umborne, otherwise more or less Piddletrenthide. Cecil had lately visited the Black Museum at Scotland Yard, where he been fascinated by a pair of binoculars which let loose two needles from its eyepiece when the user started to twist the focus dial. Such an instrument is sent to one of the Chantmerle sisters, a couple whose looks and characteristics enabled the writer to throw odd shafts of light on his continuing thoughts of Rosamond. There is an autobiographically revealing passage in which Nigel/Cecil reflects on the 'opportunist' attitude of women to the truth: 'One's always being tempted to soften or sweeten or pare down or exaggerate the facts for them, so as to satisfy their vanity or avoid wounding their quivering sensibilities or bolster up their perpetually-crumbling egos', he says.

A third book which came out at this time from Peter Nevill was L.A.G. Strong's *Personal Remarks*. In discussing Cecil's performance over the years he declared that 'to me, his work says more than that of any poet since Yeats. What he has accomplished is remarkable, and, to judge from his latest work, he promises even better things to come.' The 'cardinal fact' about him was that 'he uses his whole life in his poetry', as poets of the ancient times had done.

In early February Cecil and Jill embarked on the first of their Arts Council sponsored reading tours of the English South-West, after which she took on a North of England tour with Christopher Hassall. She performed as a good professional does, but her pregnancy was making her feel continuously sick. While she was away Cecil worked on his 'Pegasus' – the poem which some believe to be his masterpiece – his reflection on the Greek legend in which the golden bridle won by Bellerophon is poetic inspiration. 'If "Pegasus" goes on going as well as it has started I think you and I might open the Festival Hall recital with it, reading alternate stanzas', he wrote to Jill.

On the twenty-eighth they flew to Ireland for the first of their many joint visits to Cecil's native land. They stayed at the Shelbourne Hotel in Dublin, and called at Knos's Monkstown flat to visit her and Cecil's 'droll recluse' uncle, the Rev Willie Squires. They also visited an old friend of Cecil's, Robert Collis – doctor of medicine, healer at Belsen, fearless horse-rider, traveller, writer and Irish rugby international – at Bo Island under the Wicklow mountains.

In January Cecil had given his four talks on modern poetry for the BBC Home Service. Now it was hoped to send the talks to the United States. Cecil wrote to Dylan Thomas, eight months before the latter's death: 'I used two poems of yours in the series of talks, and the *particular* points I made with them could not be made by substituting somebody else's poems. Will you therefore in this case, consider removing the ban placed on using your work in a Transcription programme for the USA? I hope you will. If not, we shall probably go no further with the project as I think your "On the Death of a Child . . ." [presumably "A Refusal to Mourn the Death, by Fire, of a Child in London"] and Edith's [Sitwell] "Still Falls the Rain", were the best poems that came out of the war, and I can't substitute anything by anyone else, and make that claim for it.'

The Bedford Gardens flat was comfortable for two but impossible for a family, and on 28 July Cecil and Jill moved into a small but elegant house round the corner at 96 Campden Hill Road. There had been the usual problems about borrowing money, but the change was safely made two months before Jill's child was due.

About this time Cecil became involved with another film produced by Basil Wright, and directed by Adrian de Potier. 'The narration for *The Drawings of Leonardo da Vinci* was written by Michael Ayrton', Wright remembered. 'We had Laurence Olivier to speak the narration and we were going to have Dylan Thomas to be the voice of Leonardo speaking passages from his notebooks. Then Dylan got into one of his disappearing moods and so we gave the whole thing up and sat beating our heads against the wall. Then I suddenly said, "Well, how stupid, Cecil, he has got a beautiful voice which he knows he can produce perfectly." So we got on to Cecil and we recorded at Beaconsfield. I drove him down there and he did it beautifully. It was a very successful film, one of the most successful art films ever made.'

Jill was well enough to go to stay with Patric and Sheila Dickinson at Rye on the Sussex coast at the beginning of September. Labour pains started on the fifteenth, almost a fortnight early, and she was admitted to Queen Charlotte's Maternity Hospital in Goldhawk Road, Hammersmith.

Lydia Tamasin was born at 7.45 that evening, 17 September, and now Cecil had the daughter he had always wanted. 'Lydia was chosen because it is a sound classical name: as for Tamasin it is a name suggested by the character of Thomasin in Hardy's *The Return of the Native* and Ivy Compton-Burnett's Tamasin', he told one gossip columnist. When mother and baby returned from hospital the kindly and expert Nanny Minny Bowler, who was to relieve the child-rearing burdens of the Day-Lewis household for the next nine years, was already installed at No 96. Tamasin was christened before the end of the month at the church of St Martin-in-the-Fields, Trafalgar Square, by the Rev Austen Williams. He was a godparent together with Lillian Browse (the art historian and a long-standing friend of Jill's), Nick Roughead and Elizabeth Jane Howard. As Jane has written, the vicar was the only one of the party 'really up to standard from the holy point of view',[2] but the ceremony was nevertheless 'a serious affair' and testified to the lasting admiration felt by Cecil and Jill for this particular clergyman. If such things were allowed to the divorced they would have liked Williams to have married them.

The growth of BBC Television had now begun and at the end of September Cecil was invited by the producer Paul Johnstone to take part in an impromptu 'Russian Sleigh' or 'Balloon Debate' in which he, with his friend Noel Annan of King's College, Cambridge, and the historian Arthur Bryant, would be prosecuting counsel trying to determine whether Alfred the Great, Mrs Beeton or Bernard Shaw should be thrown out first to save the craft and the other two. G.M. Young, Nancy Spain and Maurice Colbourne were to be the defending counsel. Cecil had no confidence whatsoever in his abilities at the kind of spontaneous chat that was seemingly required by television producers. 'Many thanks for the invitation', he replied on 2 October. 'I'm afraid I must decline, as bitter and humiliating experience has taught me how bad I am at improvising in public.' Instead he went off to recite at the Cheltenham Festival of Literature and the Oxford University Poetry Society, something he knew he could do well.

At Christmas I was at 96 Campden Hill Road for a dinner party at which Sir Kenneth and Lady Clark were guests. I found the proceedings daunting and explained this in a letter to Cecil. His reply was written on the notepaper of the Students' Memorial Union at Queen's University in Kingston, Ontario.

I was very interested – and sympathetic – in what you said. It seems to be a law of life that people can talk more freely to friends, or other relations, than to their parents. I was certainly very much the same as you at 22: had no confidence with my father, and found myself tongue-tied in his house with people who came there. I daresay I'm as shy at opening up on serious subjects, with you, as you are with me: but I don't think one should feel bad about this, as long as one continues to feel affection for one's father or son, as the case may be. At a certain stage, one's growing-up and maturing *must* be done outside the home – and the parents can do little more than to provide practical help, and not get in the light. I'm sorry you've tended to pick nights when we have had people like the Clarks to dinner: such folk are rather overwhelming at first. But you shouldn't worry too much about not being able to play your part in the conversation: it's a good thing for a writer, especially when young, to take in rather than give out – one stores up material, often unconsciously, in the process. But, as a matter of fact, – for what that is worth – you give the appearance of being interested and reasonably at ease with these rather formidable seeming folk, much more than I did at 22. I suppose I seem to live in 'a whirl of social activity'; I wish I had less of it: but we don't really go to or have so many parties as you might think, and I keep my working days pretty intact: also, I have many years of solitude – as a boy and young man – to drawn upon like capital. ... I'm having a splendid time here, but extremely exhausting – shall have given about 15 lectures, informal addresses, or readings, before I go.

Cecil had flown to Canada in January 1954. Extracts from his letters to Jill tell of his experiences in Kingston:

I have a bedroom, bathroom and quite charming sitting room all to myself at the Students' Union. On entering the suite I was dismayed to find a notice saying that no alcoholic beverages may be consumed. However, I then went over to have a drink with the Vice Chancellor [Dr W.A. Mackenzie] and his wife, and on their learning that I was mad about rye and dry, which I sampled on the aeroplane, they gave me a bottle of rye from their own store for solitary consumption in my suite! This is only one example of the immense friendliness, thoughtfulness and generosity I've met everywhere here. The V.C. turns out to be one of the three greatest economists in the world and not at all stuffy, extremely good company. . . .

A stiff day yesterday: private talk with students, then an address to the classical society, then one to the medicals: the latter were a particularly pleasant, good-looking and intelligent lot of young men – the elite of the university. This afternoon I'm talking to the philosophers: on Friday to the English Club, then going to the university revue: on Saturday I'm giving another broadcast (190 dollars): on Sunday a recital of poetry and being drawn by the local painter. What a prog! I've been asked out to meals nearly every day in people's houses, and have had to refuse quite a few invitations. Kingston is evidently the Boston of Canada, without Boston's complacence or starchiness. Conversation is amusing, wide-ranging, with a nice edge to it, but not feline in the Ox-Camb manner. I have had a quite undeserved number of verbal bouquets about my activities, which have made me feel that apart from the dough the visit has been well worth while. . . .

Cecil returned to London for a February of many public engagments. The most notable occurred at the Royal Festival Hall on Sunday 14 February, a memorial recital for Dylan Thomas, who had died in the United States the previous November. Over 3,000 people attended and a profit of £633 was made for his widow and children. Cecil was joined on the platform by Stephen Spender, Louis MacNeice and Vernon Watkins, and he gave a first reading of his 'In Memory of Dylan Thomas', later included in *Pegasus* (1957).

> Now we lament one
> Who danced on a plume of words,
> Sang with a fountain's panache,
> Dazzled like slate roofs in sun
> After rain, was flighty as birds
> And alone as a mountain ash.

That month I noted in a diary that 'Cecil has been lecturing at Swansea and Oxford, he is tired and has rheumatism in one leg, he is getting any number of reading and speaking engagements'. In the first week of March he was invited to serve on the Council of the Royal Society of Literature, proposed by Lord Birkenhead and seconded by Christopher Hassall. He replied saying he was honoured by the proposal. 'Frankly, I do not see how I could attend eight meetings a year: my work at Chatto's to mention only one thing, involves being there on alternate Mondays, and I have a lot of other affairs. However, if the Council felt it could put up with rather irregular attendance on my part, I would gladly accept.' In the event he was as punctilious over the RSL as over his other public activities and began work for the Society on a lecture about Edward Thomas: one of the 'extremely short list of poets we had little hope of ever equalling' made by Cecil with W.H. Auden at Appletreewick in 1927. The research began a lifelong friendship with Helen Thomas, the poet's widow.

The Nicholas Blake novel *The Whisper in the Gloom*, published that spring, is dedicated to Franta and Margaret Belsky and has a title extracted from lines of Lionel Johnson. The time setting, as for Cecil's unperformed play *The Exiles*, is the height of the cold war between Stalin's Soviet Union and the West.

The place setting is largely that square of Central London, bounded by Park Lane and Kensington Church Street, which Cecil had got to know as a boy and had settled into again as a resident of Bedford Gardens and Campden Hill Road. The story begins in Kensington Gardens with the liquidation beside the Round Pond of a Welshman presumed to know too much about the spy ring to which he was scarcely attached. Nigel Strangeways, walking in the park, becomes involved by accident, and so does a group of innocent but resourceful young boys who do much to help, and hinder, his investigation.

As the story opens Nigel is having his portrait head shaped in clay by the highly regarded sculptor Clare Massinger; rather as Cecil had his head rendered soon before the time of writing by the dedicatee of the book, Franta Belsky, whose Bedford Gardens studio provides the background to their scenes. Clare is twenty-six, an 'unwordly artist' who had known Nigel for four years without realizing he was a detective. She would remain his girl for the rest of his career, a kind of Cecil ideal who was independent, unpossessive, relaxed, beautiful, talented, resourceful, intelligent, creative, who did not require marriage or children or his constant presence, but was always available to give succour and comfort when needed.

Before the end Blake takes the story to the John Constable country around Dedham and Flatford, and has the boy heroes Bert and Foxy kidnapped and imprisoned at Stourford Hall; a house 'like a Sleeping Beauty's palace, unreal, lapped in a cataleptic trance' recalling the Manor House at Little Wittenham in *Head of a Traveller* (1949).

Cecil was much taken with Constable and his River Stour countryside in East Anglia at this time. He returned to it with 'Dedham Vale, Easter 1954', a *Pegasus* poem dedicated 'for E.J.H.', Elizabeth Jane Howard. The dedication marks the blossoming of that 'loving friendship' of which she wrote soon after Cecil's death.[3]

A month or two later, she remembered, 'we were having dinner together', she in low spirits because her latest novel was not flowing as she would like; her private life was 'in its usual chronic chaos' and she did not enjoy living alone. Next day Cecil, who had lately become a director of Chatto and Windus, invited Jane to join the firm as a part-time reader. When she protested that she had no experience of the work he replied, 'I think you will soon get the hang of it.'[4]

'This kind of unobtrusive and imaginative kindness was one of Cecil's major characteristics,' she said. 'The way in which he did this kind of thing often meant that the people he did it for had little or no idea of the trouble and effort involved.'

At first they shared an office, Cecil being excited by Jane's company and at the same time endeavouring to give her an editorial training as rigorous as that which he had received from Max Parrish at the Ministry of Information thirteen years before. In her memory much of the time was spent eating; the less appetizing the book to be edited, the more they used food for relief. Cecil maintained the 'quite unself-conscious and insatiable pleasure in chocolates, buns and cakes' he had first developed as an antidote to his frugal public school diet at Sherborne. She also remembered that 'we worked hard as well'. Later their working hours coincided rather less: they took alternate weeks at the office and at home writing, but they arranged other meetings.

Jane accompanied Cecil, Jill and Tamasin to the New Inn, Piddletrenthide, in early July. There was some sun, Tamasin's first picnic and a verse reading for the Dorset Drama League at Stinsford House. Jane was able to make progress with *The Long View* (1956). Nursing the ten-month-old Tamasin, Jill observed the loving friendship of Cecil and Jane, rather as Mary, nursing me at an even younger age in 1931, watched the friendship of Cecil and Alison Morris.

On 29 July Cecil and Jill were at the Royal Albert Hall for the first public performance of Sir Arthur Bliss's *A Song of Welcome*, given as part of a Henry Wood Promenade Concert. Cecil had provided the words for this slight but spirited piece for soprano and bass soloists, chorus and orchestra, marking the 'joyous occasion' of the return of the Queen and the Duke of Edinburgh from a Commonwealth tour. The words were written to order, designed to be sung, influenced by the composer's formal design which was largely modelled on that of Purcell's songs of royal welcome. It exhibits the kind of rhetoric normal in the 1950s atmosphere of royalty worship, when Cecil would have made such a vigorous Laureate. There were no sneers from the music critics. Neville Cardus in the *Manchester Guardian* said, 'Bliss has set the poem of Day-Lewis with serious musicianship warmed by imagination; and it is a fine poem. . . . The audience called Sir

Arthur Bliss vociferously to the platform, C. Day-Lewis should have been with him.'

Bliss, who had been appointed Master of the Queen's Musick in succession to Sir Arnold Bax the previous year, recognized in Cecil a poet who loved music and had the technical resources and understanding needed to provide singable words. He hoped that one day they could collaborate on an opera and meanwhile, in early September, he invited Cecil to write a sonnet for the pianist Noel Mewton-Wood, who had just taken his own life. The Bliss setting of the sonnet was given at the Mewton-Wood Memorial Concert at the Wigmore Hall the following January, a programme that also included the first performance of Britten's canticle *Still Falls the Rain* using Edith Sitwell's poem. For this occasion Cecil did not need rhetoric; he and Jill knew Mewton-Wood as a friend and neighbour, and as a gifted fellow artist in Apollo recitals. Cecil's words came from the heart.

There were two more publications in the last three months of the year. The minor one, intended to capture the Christmas market, was *Christmas Eve*: a single poem published with Edward Ardizzone illustrations as a pamphlet in the Ariel series by Faber. This was followed on 2 December by a major enterprise, the joint Cape and Hogarth publication of the *Collected Poems of C. Day Lewis*. This handsome volume contained all the verse he was willing to own from *Transitional Poem* (1929) to *An Italian Visit* (1953). He allowed no example of his juvenilia as it appeared in *Beechen Vigil* (1925) and *Country Comets* (1928). He was also hard on his political verse of the early 1930s. In his preface he wrote 'in principle, I think a *Collected Poems* should offer everything one has written. In practice, I have excluded most of the last 14 pages of *A Time to Dance*, and all but two choruses of *Noah and the Waters*. Cuts might well have been made, too, in the first three books, particularly *The Magnetic Mountain*: but, since they were written as sequences, I decided to let them stand.'

'Reading over my verse written during the last 25 years, I have felt both surprise and regret: regret, that so much energy should so often have run to waste; surprise, to hear a buried self speaking, now and then, with such urgency', he wrote. He was not one of those who could rewrite and improve earlier work, for 'the selves who wrote those poems are strangers to me'. The only link between his buried selves was their 'constant themes', constituting his 'personal tradition'. All he could ever do was to 'write another poem, feeling my way along the same themes with the self I am now'.

The critics were generally respectful rather than enthuasistic, and G.S. Fraser in the *New Statesman* gave a glimpse of the kind of reviewing that would, at best, now follow Cecil whatever he did. His volume was buried below the *Collected Poems of Stephen Spender* and the inevitable comparisons followed. 'As a verse craftsman, he has a more consistent and various dexterity than Mr Spender . . . but perhaps a less unified poetic personality and, because of the many skilfully absorbed influences, a less individual tone of voice.'

The Times found that Cecil had 'settled into an accessible and eloquent upholder of accustomed poetic virtues' and was a poet who 'will go on pleasing when more spectacular performers have ceased to dazzle'. Richard Church in the *Sunday Times* wrote of Cecil's early 'struggles to reconcile his political conscience (that of a young and sensitive nature) with his personal demon (a mercilessly egoistic one that insisted on testing all experience against his own needs and longings)'. He considered that the reconciliation had now been achieved and Cecil had in recent years produced some 'masterly' work 'likely to be of permanent endurance.... Mr Day-Lewis has had to stretch himself to the full, as a poet, to contain the variety and inner conflicts which have made his career in the art so stormy and so agonizing.'

When he was visiting Dorset or thereabouts Cecil loyally called on his stepmother, Mamie, in the Branksome district of Bournemouth. He had never loved her, but his pity for her had turned to a kind of admiration. Her eighteen years of lonely widowhood had done nothing to widen her interests or bring her any closer to him in taste or outlook. She went to an Anglo-Catholic church on Sundays, but otherwise stayed at home guarding her 'things': that grim collection of heavy Victorian furniture, seedy oil paintings and ugly ornaments displayed under glass domes or in cabinets, which restricted movement at her home, 'Edwinstowe', as it had previously done at Edwinstowe Vicarage. Her sole companion was her Irish cook.

Since her cancer operation in 1951 her health had slowly deteriorated. Cecil wrote in his autobiography of her 'rooted obstinacy', which had enabled her to survive the hectoring, bullying moods of his father. This quality had 'in the years of her widowhood and last illnesses, transmuted itself before my eyes into a patience and courage wholly admirable'. Mamie died at her home on 13 January 1955, aged eighty-three.

In the days of his idealistic, romantic youth Cecil had sometimes preached to his 'stepdragon' about the wrong of unearned, inherited wealth. She had received this message. She left Cecil and each of his acknowledged children £1,000 each. The rest of her fortune of over £40,000 she bequeathed to homes for dogs.

Mamie's death was followed after only three days by that of Cecil's favourite uncle, the Rev Willie Squires, aged eighty-six. He had had nearly eleven years of retirement in the Monkstown flat, overlooking the sea outside Dublin, which he shared with his faithful sister Knos. She looked after him to the end, he lapsing into increasing silence so that some days he never spoke to her from morning until night. Cecil did not remember his silences, only the inexhaustibly kind Uncle Willie who had entered so easily into his childhood mind, in those long summers at Monart before the First

World War. Knos, now eighty, was free to live her own life for the first time since early in 1909, when she had come to London to look after Cecil, and his father, after the death of his mother.

Cecil could make no claim to Knos's kind of selflessness, but among poets he was unusual in the amount of help he was prepared to give almost any apprentice of the craft who approached him. At the Chatto office Elizabeth Jane Howard noted how 'he always tried to be kind enough not to dash' the young poets.

His kindness can be exaggerated: his initial letter was invariably helpful but he could become as impatient as the next man if a correspondence threatened prolixity. This can be seen by following through the case of a young Newcastle-upon-Tyne journalist, Bryan Reed, who sadly died before his poetic talent had been properly focused and developed. Cecil began on 25 February, writing in longhand.

The Stars. Pleasant: unaffected: striking no attitudes: lacks decisive phrases or a key image. I think you're playing about on the surface of memories, not plunging boldly into the depth of possible meaning below. For *my* taste (there are plenty of others) the poem needs more concentration. This is partly due to the form you use. I'd always ask, what is there in the subject or development which *demands* a relaxed, free-versey form, and recompenses one for losing the concentrative aid of strict metre, rhyme etc. If you'd not said that you didn't want advice, only comment (but isn't any useful comment bound to be advice?) I'd suggest your writing this poem again as a sonnet, and seeing what happens....

Reed took the advice or comment about 'The Stars' and rewrote it as a sonnet, sending it to Cecil for any further observations. Cecil wrote again on 3 March in a somewhat less expansive vein: 'Yes, surely it's much more alive and interesting as a sonnet. Sorry I haven't time to comment on the other two, but I'm desperately trying to clear up a lot of work here before going on a recital tour for a fortnight in Yorkshire: but I like the first 12 lines of "From the Window" very much, and the "Coastline" appeals to me almost throughout.'

The Yorkshire tour, a series of recitals given by Cecil and Jill, began at Sheffield and took in Wakefield, Scarborough, Leeds, Harrogate, Aysgarth, York and West Hartlepool. Reed travelled to meet them towards the end of the tour, and was impressed by Cecil's courtesy and interest. Early the next year he asked if Chatto and Windus might be interested in his first slim volume of verse, *The Wind and the Sea*. The answer this time was typed from dictation on 26 January: 'Yes, send along your poems. We do sometimes publish first volumes of verse: but it is only fair to tell you that, under present conditions, we cannot take on much poetry, and that we have accepted all the volumes of verse we can afford to publish for some little time ahead.'

The final letter was dictated on 26 February 1956.

I have now read the collection of poems you were kind enough to send us. I am afraid we are not able to make you an offer for them. In my opinion, although there are some exciting lines and interesting passages in the collection, very few of the poems are thoroughly integrated: I also felt that you are too often visibly striving for an effect, and this makes your work rather confused and hectic in manner. I am returning the typescript herewith.

On 25 May a selection from the poems of Robert Frost was published in the Penguin Poets series, with an introduction by Cecil. In this he claimed an English stake in Frost's poetry, 'though it is American to the core', as the writer had lived in Britain before the First World War and belonged to 'a common tradition'. Like Hardy, 'Frost found his style young and has not needed to alter it. ... Not long ago Mr Robert Graves declared that, of 20th century poets, the best influences for young writers were Thomas Hardy and Robert Frost. It is a view I am much in sympathy with.'

To celebrate this publication Frost himself dined at 96 Campden Hill Road, and Elizabeth Jane Howard was invited to make a fourth. 'I could see easily why Cecil and Frost got on so well', she has written. 'They both had a quiet, dry, but devastating sense of humour, they understood and admired each other's work, and in the same curious way both their faces had kindred beauty.... Both had the same unfailing courtesy and enjoyment of the simplest things. It was one of the best evenings.'[5]

That month Cecil and Jill went to Rome, again as the guest of Brian Kennedy-Cooke. It was during this holiday, sitting and drinking in the Piazza dell'Esedra, that Cecil tumbled on the idea for an opera libretto to be presented to Sir Arthur Bliss. In the centre of the square is a fountain; at the turn of the century Rutelli was commissioned to adorn it with sculptured groups, and the two curvaceous naiads wrestling with marine monsters are said to be modelled from two sisters, well-known musical comedy stars of their day. The sisters in their old age used to walk to the fountain every day because it reminded them of their lively youth, and once a year Rutelli travelled from his native Sicily to give them dinner. The fountain and the sisters were to be the starting-point of the opera. Cecil worked at it through the rest of May and June and submitted a first draft of the libretto to Bliss at the beginning of July. The composer asked for changes and these Cecil willingly carried out. On 19 July Bliss wrote to say 'the opening is too like La Bohème don't you think? I shall willy-nilly ride into Puccini, and I don't want farce.' Bliss quietly let the project slide away. No copy of Cecil's libretto could be found among the papers of either the composer or the poet on their deaths.

Neither in his London youth nor in provincial manhood had opera been part of Cecil's way of life; it had seemed to him an artifical, strident, even decadent, way of bringing together the worst of several worlds. His conversion happened gradually in the late 1940s when he discovered Italy and began shedding the austerity which had been part of his youthful idealism. Even then he did not manifest the indiscriminate zeal of the convert. He came to join the adulation of the time for the soprano Maria Callas and later, to some extent, for Joan Sutherland, but really he always wanted the work to be by Verdi: just as he eventually wanted any play he saw to be by Shakespeare or Chekhov. At the end of 1955 he did review Sir William Walton's new opera *Troilus and Cressida*, as produced at Covent Garden, for the Third Programme's *Comment*, but that was about the limit of his involvement with music theatre.

That July, Cecil presented the prizes at the Berkhamsted School for Girls in Hertfordshire. The future Mrs Alison Claybourne was one of those honoured and she remembered the occasion well: 'He spoke with a pleasing diffidence, unusual in Commemoration Day celebrities, and with the right Irish "t" sound, which my father noticed with approval.' It may be significant that Cecil's use of a soft Irish 't' was noted at this stage. Until now his Irish background had been a fallow part of his personality, touched upon in his novel *Child of Misfortune* (1939) and a few of his detective stories, but not directly in his verse since *Country Comets* (1928). His memories, his 'whispering roots', were maybe stirred by the deaths of Mamie and Uncle Willie in early 1955. He now began to develop his Irishness and the element of apartness which it gave in an English context, even while his verse became ever more firmly rooted in the English tradition. During the second half of the decade he once again recognized in himself the symptoms of a 'long-rootless man'; and it was a help to build up a background of stability in his Irish connection.

There was no sudden change. He had never disowned his Anglo-Irishness and had sometimes publicized it; he had always found himself drawn to others of the same background from the novelist Elizabeth Bowen to the arts administrator Brian Kennedy-Cooke; during the troubles of 1916 to 1922 he had been ' "on the side of" those whom our English neighbours called rebels and murderers', though he saw this as 'perversity, or at best a romantic patriotism like my inveterate partisanship of the Irish international rugby teams'. There was a gradual change, as he increasingly cultivated what his friend Ian Parsons has called his 'self-willed romanticism' about Ireland, spoke more in public of 'we Irish', more obviously gave his English public school, or Oxford, accent something of a gentle Irish lilt and intonation.

During this summer his enthusiasm moved on from his opera libretto to a murder case from the early years of the century, which he was adapting as Nicholas Blake's *A Tangled Web*. This was the first time that Blake operated outside the Crime Club imprint of Collins, and used a real event for his plot outline.

I got the idea from the memoirs of Sir Patrick Hastings [he explained to the readers of *Books and Bookmen* the following March]. The case he describes there under the title of 'The Case of the Hooded Man' was the first in which he led for the defence. The young man in the dock was charged with the murder of a policeman at Eastbourne: a young man of gentle birth and remarkable agility, what we would call a 'cat burglar'. He had a mistress, a girl whose singular beauty created a sensation in court. Another man, William Power, plotted against them and betrayed them to the police in a detestable manner, with a malice worthy of Iago. The girl visited her lover in his condemned cell, with their new-born baby. It is a story of tragedy and pathos: I became obsessed by it, as deeply obsessed as I am by the theme of a potential poem.

The book was published at the end of January 1956, and dedicated to A.D. Peters, appearing later in the United States as *Death and Daisy Bland*.

On 16 January, Cecil made his delayed debut before the television cameras, being paid twelve guineas to appear with J.B. Priestley in a *Books and Authors* discussion. 'The programme is an informal one,' promised its producer David Attenborough. 'Mr J.B. Priestley will be wearing an ordinary lounge suit, and it assists the cameras if speakers can avoid wearing a pure white shirt. We meet at 7 pm for refreshments, talk and rehearsal, and transmission is at 9.45 pm for 15 minutes.' Jill went along to watch the proceedings.

Cecil looked well enough on television and was reasonably fluent, but he was always a quiet debater who found it impossible to be outrageous in public, and difficult to express the kind of unqualified and uncomplicated opinions which are necessary in the quick-fire timetable insisted upon by television controllers. He did not have a natural gift for popular address, as did Priestley.

Nine days after this, supported as usual by Jill, he made his last appearance as the Oxford Professor of Poetry. Already the glint of battle had returned to Enid Starkie's eyes and she was again gadflying about the university on her bicycle, ensuring that W.H. Auden should be elected as Cecil's successor at the election on 9 February.

Though Cecil and Rosamond were permanently estranged he and her brother, John Lehmann, saw no reason why they should not continue to work together. When commissioned to produce *The Chatto Book of Modern Poetry*, Cecil invited Lehmann to be his co-editor. 'I would rather collaborate with you than anybody, but will quite understand if you prefer not to do so', he wrote. Lehmann agreed to collaborate and enjoyed his frequent visits to the Chatto office and 96 Campden Hill Road in 1955. The book was published on 28 June 1956, as an 'attempt to show the range and variety of the last 40 years' of poetry. Poets under the age of thirty were not included, because the editors felt they could 'not judge their work fairly'. The five poems by Cecil were 'Emily Brontë' and 'Marriage of Two' from *Poems 1943–1947*, 'Departure in the Dark' and 'The Album' from *Word Over All*, and 'Sonnet' from *A Time to Dance*. To some extent, no doubt, this represented Lehmann's choice.

By early September Cecil was able to write to Lehmann, 'Our anthology is nearly up to the 6,000 mark, and still selling 20 a day on average – which isn't bad at all. I have just heard that your mother has died. Please accept my deep sympathy.'

By August, when Jill embarked on her second pregnancy, Cecil had assembled enough new verse to make a new book. That the gap between books of verse should have been the longest of his career is not so surprising after a look at, for instance, his activities during October, the month of the abortive Anglo-French invasion of Egypt. He provided an introduction for a new edition of Charles Dickens's *The Mystery of Edwin Drood*; he went to Newnham College, Cambridge, to deliver the Henry Sidgwick Memorial Lecture on 'The Poet's Way of Knowledge', discussing the relationship of poetry and science; with Jill and Julian Bream he gave an Apollo recital at Abingdon in competition with a rehearsal of the local bell-ringers; for the Third Programme he reviewed a New Watergate Club Theatre production of Arthur Miller's *A View from the Bridge*; he worked with other editors assembling a PEN anthology; he attended in alternate weeks at his Chatto office; and he worked on his Nicholas Blake detective novel *End of Chapter*, set in 'a very different kind of publishing firm'.

This autumn was also marked with a visit from Knos. With the help of Cecil's silently given financial aid she had, at eighty-two, managed her first flight. I remember her on this visit, more frail than she was when last in England, but as excited as a child by her first experience of travel above the clouds. She teased and she smiled and her selfless love for Cecil shone as brightly as ever.

In 1934, four years after his appointment as Laureate to George V, John Masefield had been instrumental in establishing the King's Gold Medal for poetry. The first had gone that year to the young Laurence Whistler, and the second was accepted in 1936 by W.H. Auden. In 1952, with the arrival of Elizabeth II on the throne, it became an annual award and at the end of 1956 Cecil had agreed to join the small committee of advisers which considered the prize. His first letter on the subject was written from 96 Campden Hill Road on 13 January 1957. 'I think there are two young poets well worth considering for the Queen's Medal – Thom Gunn and Philip Larkin', he wrote. 'The latter shows perhaps more technical accomplishment, a greater ease in the medium: but he was born in 1922, so he may just come outside the age-limit. [There was no age-limit.] Thom Gunn, who was born in 1929, is a more uneven poet, to my mind, but at his best – which he quite often is – shows greater promise than Larkin, more passion, a deeper poetic sensibility.'

The work of the committee was conducted entirely by post. In the last letter of the series, written on 19 June, he said that his first preference was for Thom Gunn. 'But if there were a preponderating vote for Siegfried

Sassoon among the committee, I should be very glad to see him get the award.' It did go to Sassoon.

Cecil's second son Nicholas had followed the charted course from Sherborne to Wadham College, Oxford, but had extended the family tradition to the extent of being a successful RAF officer and aircrew navigator during his National Service, and of reading engineering at university. He had now become engaged to a chemistry undergraduate and was proposing to travel with her to live and work in South Africa. 'We went down to Oxford on Saturday to inspect Josephine Pike, and were very favourably impressed', Cecil wrote to me on 18 February, the day after Nick's twenty-third birthday. 'I fear the parents must be rather the Stockbroker-Tudor type: this enormous wedding and pretentious reception they plan fills me with some foreboding – much though I look forward to seeing you forced into Moss Bros tail-coat and top-hat for the occasion.'

In March, with Jill now in the last stages of pregnancy, Cecil flew away on his first visit to the United States. He was undertaking a month-long 'whistle-stop' tour of lectures, readings and seminars, involving immense distances and many airports from New York to Colorado, from Ohio to South Carolina. The timing was not deliberate. It had arisen from a nine-month delay in obtaining a visa, which suddenly ended when Hugh Gaitskell, the leader of the Labour Party whom Cecil had got to know through the Balcon family, and R.A. Butler, deputy leader of the Conservative Party and a friend through his presidency of the Royal Society of Literature, had agreed to be his joint sponsors. The Butskellite Solution, then considered a main factor in the consensus dominating British politics, enabled Cecil to set out on an itinerary so hastily constructed that it was all geographical zig-zags.

The difficulty over admission was caused by the question asked on all American visa application forms, 'Are you or have you ever been a member of the Communist Party?' In his autobiography Cecil described his encounter at the American Embassy in London. The 'nice American lady' at the counter asked why and how he had left the party in 1938, and he explained that he had just drifted away to Devon village life. 'But didn't they try to get you back?' she asked. 'No, they did not. I wasn't important enough. I suppose', he replied. The counsellor found this hard to believe and asked, 'Well, of course you published some sort of renunciation after you had left the Party?' Again Cecil had to disappoint her.

'I tried to explain', he wrote, 'that at the time when I left the Party I was not hostile to Communism and that, even if I had been, public renunciations or denunciations were extremely distasteful to me, and seemed quite unnecessary anyway. I had become sick of myself as a public figure and wished only to retire into a private life and write poetry: leaving the Party in a blaze of publicity ignited by my own hand would, under these circumstances, have been both folly and falsehood.' Such honesty left American officialdom still puzzled.

The tour began in New York City, where he stayed at the Yale Club, and was entertained by his Harper and Row publishers and celebrities ranging from e.e. cummings to Burl Ives. 'I fancy this place is my spiritual home – the New Yorkers being so eager to give, and I so willing to receive', he wrote to Jill. Extracts from his other letters to her, written between 3 March and the end of the month, tell something of his further progress...

From Chicago, March 7. I found New Haven and Yale particularly agreeable. On arrival I was given a comfortable guest suite – then walked round by Gordon Haight to see something of the town. The lecture went with a bang – a very large and appreciative audience. After it I had dinner with Haight, Purdy (the Thomas Hardy bibliographer), Norman Pearson who did the anthology with Wystan etc. Then I was taken to the Elizabethan Club, and shown a first folio of *Hamlet*, and one of the only three extant copies of the first edition of Shakespeare's sonnets, amongst other treasures. Then I was taken to hear Artur Rubinstein playing and after the concert had supper and a long chat with him – he's a charming, incredibly vivacious man.... I have an extremely comfortable suite in the Arts Club here, with a view of the lake and several madly attractive male negroes attending to my immodest needs and beaming from ear to ear. Chicago is far too big, and there's a permanent sweetish taint in the air – blood, hides etc from the stockyards and slaughter houses I assume.... The horrors of itinerant lecturing have been wildly exaggerated. If one doesn't get into a flap about missing connections, or getting into the wrong aeroplane, it is possible to relax for long periods. Over here the human being tends to be less efficient and reliable than the machine, but Anglo-Irish phlegm can see one through the occasional moments of American helplessness and sub-hysteria. It is, of course, a great help to positively enjoy flying, and to have a rather sordid knack for showing off to strangers.

From New York, March 10. You will be relieved to hear that I haven't used any of my box of drugs, no sinus, catarrh, oozing boils, hang-overs. With iron self-control I confine myself to a maximum of two martinis and two to three highballs per evening. The changes of climate are drastic – cold winds off the lake at Chicago, snow and sun in Ohio, and violent rainstorms which threw the aircraft about as we approached New York this afternoon. Well, one week of the four has gone quicker for you than for me.

From Charleston, March 15. I arrived here two hours late last night. I was met by my host who is a teacher of the Citadel, the Sandhurst and Woolwich of the South, and driven here through banks of azaleas in full bloom. It was like an English midsummer night. Temperature 70, balmy, tree frogs reeling away. I was woken up at 7 am by a tropical rainstorm and violent lightning and thunder. This soon cleared up and I was taken for a long drive by a 60 to 70-year-old Southern lady who must have been a knock-out belle in her day, and writes novels and rides horses still. 'Ah've been throw-wun from mower ho-worses than ah cain't remem-bah', she said. And 'Ah lahk ray-erd roses in a bay-erd'. ....

Tomorrow I return to Washington, then the long flight to Denver via Chicago. Edith Sitwell's all right, she's turning up at Washington on Sunday. It is so hot I've been going everywhere in my shirt sleeves.

Nicholas Blake's *End of Chapter* was published on Cecil's return to London, dedicated to the two Chatto partners to whom he was closest, Norah Smallwood and Ian Parsons, 'with great affection from their unsleeping partner in a very different kind of firm'. It is different no doubt, but the fictional publishing firm of Wenham and Geraldine apparently occupy the A.D. Peters premises only five minutes walk away from Chatto and Windus. With a façade of dark-crimson brick, dazzling white paintwork and the exquisite moulding and fanlight of the doorway, the house 'created an impression of solidity and grace, charm and decorum, altogether appropriate to the imprint'. In these premises a libel problem turns into a murder case, for a Nigel Strangeways more than ever a show case for Cecil's attitudes. Now living in a Campden Hill flat, he muses that 'as middle age advances and one's youthful illusions recede, almost the only way to get the sensation of starting again, of being reborn, is to move house....' He is even afflicted, as Cecil was, by cigarette addiction resulting in 'paroxysms of coughing which set his sinus aching'. On the staff of Wenham and Geraldine is a poet responsible for 'an acrid masterpiece tracing a man's love for a woman through all its stages from passionate faith to savage disillusionment'. Nigel suggests that after being subject to this experience the poet 'determined never to be vulnerable again; he retired into himself, scorching the earth behind him – and the poetic seed got burnt up in the process'. Cecil talked of scorched earth when detaching himself from Rosamond Lehmann, but he never lost his vulnerability; in fact, to the consternation of his wives, he preserved it with determination.

Jill's second child, Daniel Michael Blake Day-Lewis, was born in the front room at 96 Campden Hill Road on 29 April, two days after his father's fifty-third birthday. He was fairly formed and he thrived. The name Daniel was chosen because it mixed Jewish Old Testament associations with those of Daniel O'Connell, the barrister who fought for Catholic emancipation in Ireland during the early nineteenth century. Michael was adopted from his grandfather, Sir Michael Balcon, and Blake is one of Cecil's family names carried by his mother.

> Welcome to earth, my child!
> Joybells of blossom swing,
> Lambs and lovers have their fling,
> The streets run wild
> With April airs and rumours of the sun.
> We time-worn folk renew
> Ourselves at your enchanted spring,

> As though mankind's begun
> Again in you.
> This is your birthday and our thanksgiving.*

In 'The Golden Bridle', the last of his 1964–5 Harvard lectures published as *The Lyric Impulse* (1965), Cecil describes the writing of this poem, to illustrate his belief in the use of strict poetic form.

When my youngest son was born, seven years ago, filled with euphoria I dashed off a poem about this event, a poem in four-line rhyming stanzas. I had not gone far when the poem stalled. I raised the hood and examined the engine: it had seized up – yes, obviously; but what should I do next? I decided to start again, with – so to speak – a new engine. Perhaps I could distance myself from my still raw emotions by employing a more complex stanza form. So, for the four-line stanza I substituted one of ten lines, rhyming a b b a c d b c d b. There were still several misadventures on the way; but the poem 'The Newborn' got to its destination.

Daniel was also christened at St Martin-in-the-Fields by the Rev Austen Williams, who only insisted that one of the godparents should be a practising member of the Church of England. Peter Cochrane, Cecil's Chatto colleague and future executor, accepted the responsibility of making the responses. The other godparents were Ian Parsons, Ursula Vaughan Williams, and Julia Gaitskell, a daughter of the Labour Party leader.

On 1 June Cecil was at Haworth in Yorkshire addressing the annual meeting of the Brontë Society on 'The Poetry of Emily Brontë'. The theme of this lecture was Emily's ruling passion of freedom, something which Cecil shared with similar ambiguity. 'What her poetry gives us, finally, is not an image of freedom but an image of man's inveterate, vain yearning for it; not the unbounded Empyrean, but the beating wings,' said Cecil with feeling. 'And she had the poet's right instinct for rooting her work in the most vulnerable, most wounded part of herself – in the deep cleft between the two opposed sides of her nature.'

On his return from the north he and Jill entertained Robert Frost. During his stay Cecil took the New England poet, then eighty-two, to see some sheepdog trials in Hyde Park, and they took the same delight in 'the miraculous game'. In writing a poem about this event, dedicated 'for Robert Frost', Cecil attempted to match the 'classical, realist, conversational' idiom of the American he so much admired. On the eleventh the two poets went to Broadcasting House to record an unscripted conversation about poetry for the Third Programme.

The other event of that month, from Cecil's point of view, was the publication by Jonathan Cape on the eighth of his *Pegasus and Other Poems*. This book, dedicated to Jill, is divided into three parts. The first consists of the title poem and three others based on Greek legends, the second of thirteen

---

* 'The Newborn' (*The Gate*, 1962).

poems is to some extent outward-looking to the state of humanity and art, and the third part of twelve poems is a record of personal experience. The collection gathered together anything, apart from the *An Italian Visit* sequence, that Cecil thought worth preserving of his work since *Poems 1943–1947*. Some of the poems included were indeed quite venerable: for instance 'Father to Sons', in which Cecil looks back to his Cheltenham period and wonders how his first two sons will remember his 'guardian stance', first appeared in the *Listener* in April 1949. This unprecedented time-span made for more breadth of style than showed in his 1940s books, or to put it another way, as the reviewers inevitably did, his voice was a variable one.

The nine-part sonnet sequence 'Moods of Love' in *Pegasus* was the first love poem to be sparked by extra-marital involvement since the very different 'Elegy Before Death' of *An Italian Visit*. By comparison with the old days Cecil is very knowing, almost impersonal, as he accepts his sexual instincts and greets again 'the old Illusionist' and love begins the tightening of 'knots no one saw tied'.

> Admire the 'fluence of this conjuring
> As once again he runs the gamut through
> Of tricks you can neither fathom nor resist,
> Though well you know the old Illusionist
> Employs for his whole repertoire only two
> Simple properties – a rod, a ring.

In 1950 Cecil had spoken of himself as 'an old lag', a recidivist who had grown into the habit of falling in love, before escaping or being released after his term in its thrall, and he doubted his ability to keep out of further trouble. Later he reacknowledged this as a symptom of the vulnerability that he felt bound to cultivate as a poet. In *The Lyric Impulse* (1965), the published version of his Harvard lectures ending that year, he declared, 'To write a good lyric of love today, the poet must have surrendered to the feeling of love and been possessed by it.' In the *Pegasus* poem 'Almost Human' he asked those who would condemn him to reflect that there was something in him 'That must for ever seek/To share the condition it glorifies'. So here when love himself 'comes back insidious and subdued/ As an old jailbird begging one more chance', the poet unresistingly allows this chance and once more is locked into 'the merciful illusion' when 'Two are reborn as one': When the 'gross hurricane' has passed he is rewarded with

> A world more lucid for lust's afterglow,
> Where, fondly separate, blind passion fused
> To a reflective glass, each holds in trust
> The other's peace, and finds his real self so.

Yet in the 'paradox and mode' of sexual love what is 'least enduring is the most enthralling'. For afterwards 'love breeds habit' and 'habit brings estranging'. Moreover, to sit about idolizing the past of 'love's high noon' unhealthily divorces body and mind yet leaves them both sadly twined in 'soft regret'. There is no rest, the explorations and repetitions must continue.

Ten years later Cecil would write to a friend, 'Thank God I'm too old now to face or stand the strain of two-way loving: it *always* ends in tears: which is not to say that it isn't worth it. I don't approve the moral desperado inside me (I've had seven mistresses – statistic, not boast), and try to prevent him getting out, with only moderate success so far.' Of the seven either two or three figured during his second marriage.

He was not a womanizer or a notable sexual athlete or artist – it may even be that he was as much pursued as pursuing – but he certainly was susceptible to the bright and beautiful young women writers who brought their books to him at his Chatto office. The mood of 'Moods of Love' is a bit melancholy; but Cecil also had great enjoyment of love, part of the panache, *élan* and zest for life which he had in good measure and which he responded to so wholeheartedly in others. As a lover he was at once tender, uninhibited and enthusiastic. In his fifties he had a not unusual need to prove his virility to himself, but, though he now believed that guilt could be 'a kind of self-indulgence, or at least a futile surrogate for the moral action one cannot, dare not take', he still carried his share of guilt-feeling into his love affairs.

There were other paradoxical forces at work. The main objective of Cecil's life was to be a good poet. In theory it would have helped him greatly in this if he had lived with the solitude, and the comparative lack of financial responsibility, of a single man, but after his solitary childhood this was psychologically beyond him.

He was always much concerned in his verse with limitations, boundaries, frames, the rather sexual image of the smallest aperture providing the greatest force. This concern was reflected in his life. Without really having tried freedom he decided that, as he put it in his *Pegasus* poem of the early 1950s 'A Riddle', he was a bird who 'sings best in a cage'. Like Emily Brontë, he did not want freedom so much as the yearning for it, the sensation of 'beating wings'. So it was that in 1950 he had moved on from a loose marriage which, with his children leaving home, would have given him the solitude he needed, to a close marriage where he was rarely left alone for long. His late 1950s poem 'An Upland Field' confirms that in his second marriage he found the serenity he craved, and pays a tribute to 'she, who gives me peace/Wherein my shortening days redouble.'

Yet contented poetry is something of a contradiction and Cecil's happiness in the first half of the decade made for a comparative lack of poetic productivity. Though the man was comfortable, the poet came to recognize that there was 'a lack of grit and gradient' on his road, just as he knew from long experience that he needed 'some deep violent experience' working 'like an earthquake' to provide his raw material. Included in this realization was his belief that his creative impulse needed him to be 'in love', a state which for him was synonymous with 'new beginnings'.

The case for his love affairs was therefore a strong one, even though they added to the clutter of his life and further reduced his ration of solitude. He did not fall in love in a mechanical way; it mattered who his partner was, and he was specially drawn to clever novelists writing in the feminine vein, where Rosamond Lehmann was pre-eminent. There was also an element of professional cold-bloodedness which Cecil himself acknowledged in a 1965 letter to novelist A. S. Byatt. Some poems, he told her, were 'a sort of consummation, as when two bodies (not in the legal sense but in the sense of for the first time working perfectly together) reach a point which can never be excelled, only echoed. And then again it is also true that poets do tend to fall in love with a woman (sometimes consciously even) in order to beget a poem upon her; and when that's done, gradually withdraw.'

If a mistress withdrew first, as one did for Jill's sake, Cecil could be as bitter as he was in his late 1950s poems 'An Episode' and 'A Loss'. In the first of these he wrote of her, 'Who had been his love and any comer's whore' and whose 'betrayal must deserve/What his own agony felt like'. He had 'walled her up alive' but the 'blank wall grew eyes ... neither forgiving nor beseeching'.

> His bloody fingers tore at the wall,
> Demolishing what could never salve nor seal
> Its crime, but found in the nook where he had placed her
> No twisted limbs, no trace at all.
> His heart lay there – a mess of stone and plaster.*

In the 1960s he enjoyed a loving friendship with the Indian novelist Atha Hosain. He was 'a good kind friend to me from the time I first met him as my editor at Chattos', she remembered years later. He helped to support her through the painful last illness and death of her brother. 'He also gave help and advice to my daughter and translated couplets from the poems of two of our greatest Urdu poets for a film she had made – though the language and its images were alien to him'. Cecil talked of 'the moral desperado' within him but he was also enlivened by contact with a race and culture previously unkown to him. He was sympathetic towards her experience as an expatriate in limbo and encouraged her to write a novel on her feelings of alienation.

The poem she inspired was published in Britain as 'Seven Steps in Love', included in the 1965 collection *The Room*. In the United States it came out

* 'An Episode' (*The Gate*, 1962).

as a longer sequence of eleven sections, rather than seven, called 'A Course in Love', and was included in the 1964 collection *Requiem for the Living*. The longer version has the lovers sitting at a restaurant table, she 'the dark unknown/Which makes him an explorer'. She is 'gentle as snow on branch' and 'never would she contend/For more than he could give'. When he is away from her, thoughts of her keep recurring, so that 'Making a round/ Of firelit friends, he can/Take nothing in/But her who is not there'. The final section has him ringing a bell and her opening the door, with a mien 'acquiescing/In what had come – had come for them both too late. . . .'

> She greets him, eyes downcast as if to acknowledge
> The shadow of parting that always followed close
> At his heel; looks up, and now an impossible hearth-fire
> Between them glows.

She also appears in Nicholas Blake's 1963 detective novel, *The Deadly Joker*, under the name of Vera Paston and living in a Dorset village because married to an undeserving business man who has bought the big house. She has a kind of withdrawn, elusive grace, an extraordinarily beautiful face, causing both the elderly narrator and his journalist son to fall in love with her, before she becomes the murder victim.

Clearly such affairs were hurtful to Jill. Cecil did his best to avoid emotional confrontation and yet also apparently needed the explosions which, as he recognized, would inevitably follow from his courses in love.

> It mounted up behind his cowardice
> And self-regard. Fearing she would expose
> His leper tissue of half-truths and lies
> When, hurt, she probed at him, he tried to gloze
> That fear as patience with her sick mistrust
> Of him . . .
> A spate of her reproaches, The dam broke.
> In deluging anger his self-hatred spoke.*

The last such explosion occurred in the summer of 1965 when Cecil and Jill were on holiday in the West of Ireland with Tamasin and Daniel. Jill went at Cecil's request to fetch a packet of cigarettes from his coat pocket in their hotel bedroom and a *billet doux* fluttered to the ground. Cecil had passed beyond the stage of sexual involvement and was trying to satisfy his needs with literary-erotic friendships, *amitiés amoureuses*, but this was no great comfort to Jill. Jill went off alone from the family for part of two or three days. Tamasin and Daniel were anxious and mystified; Cecil would only tell them, 'Your mother has had an awful letter.'

In younger days Cecil had, as he wrote in his autobiography, been 'able to feel at one with people in their sadness and bewilderment', and this was

* 'The Dam' (*The Room*, 1965).

evident in such poems as his 'Married Dialogue' with Mary in the 1940s. To some extent, he now felt Jill's pain as well as his own. Once more he was severely shaken and this time he recognized that his system could no longer cope with such earthquakes. Two years later he wrote, 'I very nearly destroyed my marriage by having a letter discovered which I'd only received three days before. I shall never again risk the slightest chance of another such blow-up.'

Nicholas was to marry Josephine Pike in August, and as both Cecil and Mary would be attending they decided they had better have an exploratory lunch first. They had not set eyes on each other since that early Monday morning in September 1950, when Cecil left Brimclose for the last time. They smiled and shook hands and had a quiet and courteous lunch together. For the next fifteen years such lunches became a regular event, every time Mary was in London. They were always amiable and affectionate times, but conversation was inclined to run out: she realizing he was not passionately interested in her present concerns; he ruminating on how far she was removed from the world that now interested him. In 1959, when he and Norah Smallwood of Chatto's were looking through his old photograph albums to illustrate his autobiography, they came upon a picture of Mary as she looked when he was courting her. 'She was very good-looking,' said Norah. 'She was a golden woman, a golden woman,' replied Cecil.

Nick's full-dress wedding ceremony was conducted at St Martin-in-the-Fields by the Rev Austen Williams and there was an expensive reception afterwards at the Dorchester Hotel, at which Cecil was accompanied by a discreetly unshowing Jill. As soon as this ordeal was over, he and Jill set out on their first journey to Greece. They travelled to Venice by train and boat and then joined one of Swan's Hellenic cruise liners for a suffocating ten days in a lower-deck cabin.

Like Nigel Strangeways and his Clare in Nicholas Blake's *The Widow's Cruise* (1959), Cecil and Jill avoided some of the lectures which are supposed to be one of the attractions of these tours, though they already knew Professor 'Bill' (W.R.) Stanford, a classics don from Trinity College, Dublin, and met others on board whom they also found amusing rather than solemnly scholarly. They sailed down the Adriatic, into the Ionian Sea, through the Corinth Canal and so to Athens, the Aegean and the islands of the Dodecanese. Five years later it would be Delos that Cecil would most fruitfully revisit. This time he looked at the sights in a desultory sort of way, began constructing romantic generalizations about the loud and lovable simplicity of the Greek character, and decided he felt more at one with mellow Italy than harshly lit Greece.

Back in England in September they joined the 'Save the Third Programme' campaign, designed to preserve the existing scope of the service now threatened with economy cuts. T.S. Eliot and Ralph Vaughan

Williams led a deputation to Broadcasting House; and Cecil and Jill took part with others in a 'Third Programme Entertainment' at the Royal Court Theatre; but Sir Ian Jacob, the BBC Director-General, no friend of what he called 'long-haired listening', considered those running the campaign were more interested in the work provided by the Third than in hearing its output.

Ralph Vaughan Williams was at the Royal Festival Hall on 9 October for his eighty-fifth birthday concert given by the Royal Philharmonic Society. Acting on an idea of Ernest (T.E.) Bean, the manager of the Festival Hall, Jill read a birthday ode written for the occasion by Cecil.

Back in June the poet Jon Silkin had been staying at 96 Campden Hill Road, and one Sunday morning encouraged Cecil and Jill to drive to Greenwich and look at a Georgian house on Crooms Hill advertised for sale. They found that the journalist Nicholas Tomalin had made an offer ahead of them. But in October, Jill heard that another Crooms Hill house was being put on the market. Cecil, working at home that day, at once climbed into his car and drove to inspect the somewhat decrepit No 6. He made his offer before discovering whether or not he would be able to raise a mortgage and bought what was destined to be his last home, for £5,990.

At the end of 1957 Cecil changed two homes. As well as moving to Greenwich he left the Savile Club, after his fourteen years of membership, on his election to that bastion of church and state, the Athenaeum. He was proposed by Dr E.V. Rieu and seconded by Richard Church, both to become fellow vice-presidents of the Royal Society of Literature. Bishops and vice-chancellors were still more evident in the Athenaeum Club than writers and Cecil was never much at home with the resounding silence of so many distinguished men in massive leather armchairs. However he agreed to join because the premises were only a short walk from his Chatto office, and because he rather enjoyed the idea of becoming an Establishment figure.

Old Greenwich, built between a steep escarpment and a broad curve of the Thames, is an oasis in the drab south-east quarter of London. It includes a superbly coherent array of seventeenth- and eighteenth-century buildings: there is the Royal Naval College and the Queen's House, and a park climbing away to the Old Royal Observatory and Flamsteed House, and the brass strip which in 1884 became internationally accepted as the dividing line between the eastern and western hemispheres.

Crooms Hill forms a western border for this extraordinary panorama of English history, most of its Georgian houses looking straight out to the park. No 6, to which Cecil and Jill moved on the last day of 1957, is at the bottom of the hill, facing what was then a derelict music hall, converted in the 1960s to the present Greenwich Theatre. The house has a capacious basement and four storeys above that, and the masts of the nineteenth-century tea and wool clipper the *Cutty Sark*, which had been installed in a dry dock in 1954, can be observed from the top windows. Built on at the side is a doctor's surgery, of which Cecil had become the landlord.

On that first cold day when they had neither fuel nor power to make them comfortable, Cecil and Jill had already decided how the dark elegance of the house would be arranged. His study, wood-panelled and soon to be book-lined as well, was to be the front room at street level, looking out on the Crooms Hill traffic. Behind on this floor were the similarly panelled dining-room, and the kitchen. Above on the second floor would be their drawing-room – the first room to be made beautiful – their bed-room and bathroom. The third floor was for Tamasin, Daniel and Nanny Bowler, and the fourth was for lodgers and guests. By the time the children arrived from the care of their Balcon grandparents, life at No 6 was more or less possible.

There were disadvantages. The London to Greenwich was the first rail-way of the metropolis, but it was not specially well favoured by the South-ern Region of British Railways in 1958. Underground lines do not pene-trate to that part of London, and the bus journey to the West End, either by road or river, requires time.

Cecil's compensation was that he became fascinated by his immediate surroundings. When at home, his routine meant work in the morning and, usually, a solitary walk in the afternoon, before returning to his desk after tea. He loved the river path downstream from the *Cutty Sark*, passing Wren's buildings of the Royal Navy College and the bow-fronted Tra-falgar Tavern – used by Dickens and the artist Tissot – and continuing beside the seventeenth-century Trinity Hospital almshouses, the stark power station built to support the era of electric trams and the romantic and still less salubrious wedges of nineteenth-century commercial development beyond. Sometimes he would vary this by walking up the hill to capture the long view across south London to St Paul's Cathedral and beyond, or through the under-river subway to the forlorn Isle of Dogs, so that he could look back to Greenwich as it was seen by Canaletto. Above all he loved watching the throbbing river traffic, passing in and out of London Docks, quickly becoming an expert about shipping as a boy who has caught the railway or aircraft bug.

In his poem 'Ideal Home', written at this time, Cecil again equates mov-ing house with moving from one loved one to the next, as a means of achieving the illusion of rebirth. He concludes that 'the footloose traveller' who indulges in this drug 'will soon be back where you started':

> On the same ground,
> With a replica of the old romantic phantom
> That will confound
> Your need for roots with a craving to be unrooted.*

* 'Ideal Home' (*The Gate*, 1962).

This did not make the illusion any less exciting at the time, and I can still hear the echoes of Cecil's early enthusiasm for his new home and water-front, an enthusiasm which reverberates through Nicholas Blake's *The Worm of Death*, published two years later.

In England through 1957 and into 1958, Mary's brother Alec King was on sabbatical leave from the University of Western Australia with his family. Despite the divorce, Cecil and Alec, the rivals of the treble singing contest at Sherborne forty years before, still had much affection for each other. They met several times during those fourteen months. 'There was something alike and of equal power or depth in their minds', deduced Alec's son Francis, who in 1970 edited a memorial volume of his father's essays, lectures and verse, to which Cecil contributed a poem.

This harmony had spread into the next generation, for I had fallen in love with Alec's seventeen-year-old daughter Elizabeth and proposed that we should spend the rest of our lives together. This idea was not greeted with rapture by our King relations, and Liz herself, at that time, remained more or less heart-whole. Cecil's fatherly perception was evident in a letter he wrote to me on 10 January. 'The Alec Kings came down for tea last Sunday – all but Liz. Speaking of whom, why don't you marry her? You're not worried about the first-cousin thing, are you? – there's nothing against the marriage of first cousins, provided the stock on both sides is sound. Forgive me poking my nose in like this, but I do like Liz so much', he said.

I replied thanking him for saying what I wanted to hear about my cousin and explaining that although I would have loved to take his advice I had been rejected. Cecil sympathized over the 'unbearable parting' when the Alec Kings began their voyage back to Australia in mid-January and was struck by my ability to accept rejection with resignation. In Nicholas Blake's *The Deadly Joker* (1963), where the young journalist Sam is a kind of idealized version of me, the narrator who is Sam's father muses that 'his generation is less romantic than mine, more easily capable of cutting its losses – or so it seems to me'.

The one publication in the first half of 1958 was Nicholas Blake's *A Pen-knife in My Heart*, dedicated to his friends of Bedales School, Barbara and Geoffrey Crump. It is more of a thriller than a whodunnit, and as there is no mystery for Nigel Strangeways to unravel he and Clare are, as in *A Tangled Web*, left out of the proceedings. The story begins in the summer of 1955 and its starting point is a variation on Cecil's own experience at that time. Edwin Stowe is a dramatist named after the village of Cecil's Nottinghamshire youth, engaged on a clandestine meeting with his mistress Laura at an unregarded East Anglian seaside town, while his wife Miriam seethes at home. 'Do I look like a desperado?' he asks at one point. 'You do sometimes. A sort of contained excitement, like a pot simmering with the lid on. I noticed it last night', responds Laura.

The ruthless Charles Hammer perceives the situation and gradually draws Edwin into a contract by which Charles will murder Miriam and, in exchange, Edwin will murder the uncle who stands between Charles and his ambition of inheriting a factory and a fortune. The book concludes with the conscience-stricken Edwin sailing the small boat containing him and Charles into the path of a large steamer. It is Charles who describes how before the war he sailed from Wandsworth to South Shields in a gas collier, the voyage Cecil undertook to research his film script for Basil Wright's *The Colliers*. Elsewhere the writer clearly identifies more with Edwin who, for instance, suffers from Cecil's claustrophobia at cocktail parties and his tendency to nervous indigestion.

Thanks to an introduction by Sir Kenneth Clark, the Day-Lewises' circle of friends now included the distinguished engraver and stone-carver Reynolds Stone and his family, who lived at Litton Cheney, a village lying between the sea and the main Dorchester to Bridport road. Staying that July at the nearby Ilchester Arms in Abbotsbury, Cecil enjoyed this happily occupied family 'seasoned/In dear pursuits and country gentleness', and their beautiful surroundings. It was a feeling reflected in a poem sparked off by the young daughter of the house, Phillida, called 'This Young Girl' and included in *The Gate* (1962). It was fitting that at this time Cecil should be working on his introductions for new editions of Hardy's *Tess of the d'Urbervilles* and *Under the Greenwood Tree*, to be published in the Collins Classics series at the end of that October.

In mid-August Cecil and Jill managed a short holiday in Ireland. In Dublin they found Knos in reasonably good health; but were shocked to read in an evening newspaper on 17 August the news of L.A.G. Strong's death, at the age of sixty-two. He and Cecil had not been particularly close in recent years, and Cecil, who like most people was irritated by his own faults found in others, privately complained that Leonard was too obliging about non-writing invitations and so had failed to make the most of his talent. This increased Cecil's sadness at the death of the man who had shown him such beneficence for over thirty years. Returned to England Cecil gave one appreciation in the BBC Radio programme *World of Books* on 12 September, and another at the memorial service on 3 October.

In the latter address Cecil said that Strong's 'imaginative work, in prose and verse, was visibly shaped by that quarrel within', which his friend W.B. Yeats had pointed to as the raw material of poetry.... 'His piety – a natural feeling of reverence for his Victorian roots in Ireland and Devon – went with a considerable irreverence for the puritanic, the stupidly conventional, the self-righteous, wherever he found them.... I myself – and I am only one of many – will never forget the encouragement Leonard gave me as a young writer.'

Nicholas Blake's *The Widow's Cruise* came out early in 1959, dedicated to Peter and Louise Cochrane, a fruit of the Hellenic journey undertaken by Cecil and Jill in the summer of 1957. Nigel Strangeways and Clare Massinger are both on board and Clare the artist is allowed some of Cecil's characteristics. 'Well, I'm going to concentrate on the lions,' she announces when they are on Delos. Nigel 'knew from her tone that she wanted to be by herself for a while' and he trails off to the Roman quarter and Apollo's cave on Mount Kynthos. Clare muses on the lions and feels 'refreshed, reinvigorated, and wonderfully sleepy'.

Cecil was now writing his autobiography. 'You know perfectly well, Cecil, that *no* poet should *ever* write an autobiography,' W.H. Auden had explained to him sipping grappa beside the Grand Canal in Venice in September of 1949. 'A poet should keep his experience for his poetry, and let sleeping images lie till they awake of their own accord when a poem begins to dawn. Besides, his proper concern is with the object to be created – an object which, however much of himself goes into it, must end up as a not-self; whereas, for the autobiographer, his personality is not the scaffolding but the foundation and fabric of what he tries to build.'

Cecil accepted this but now had decided that

in autobiography we can ask different questions, or ask them more directly, and in a sense answer them more truthfully, than in poetry – more truthfully, because less has to be left out. Till a few weeks before I started it, I had never imagined that I should want to write this sort of book. Yet the idea must have been forming imperceptibly, just as poems and many of the major decisions of my life have ripened within me to emerge, whether fruitful or disastrous in their issue, with the compulsive force of waters that have stealthily massed behind a dam, and often with the unexpectedness of an ultimatum delivered by insurgents who have achieved a revolution before one has even suspected a conspiracy.

Although the book dealt mainly with his young life he added a short postscript describing his existence at Greenwich as he saw it on 28 April 1959.

Yesterday was my 55th birthday. J. gave me a telescope. Now, sitting by the Thames, I can bring closer to me the great cargo-liners rounding the Isle of Dogs, the tugs and their strings of lighters, the wharves, warehouses, power stations, the skyline restless with cranes, the blue-diamond lights of welding and the indigo smoke from tall chimneys – all the river life which, here at Greenwich, overlooked by the palace and the park, enlivens their elegance with a workaday reality. I am happy, living in this place where old and new can be focused together into a historic present. Heavy traffic between the Blackwall tunnel and the Rochester road may shake down one day my early-Georgian house; or the bomb will fall. But, fortunate beyond words in my wife and children – yesterday was also the eighth anniversary of my second marriage – I shall play my luck while it lasts. A least I am learning to live with myself, to view in some kind of focus and in some degree to reconcile the contradictory elements that make up the man of whom this book is a portrait.

The days whisk by very fast now, placid and ordered though my life has become.... One sits more easily to life as one grows older. The self-torture of youth far behind now, still distant the pains and physical ignominy of old age. Since I am no longer sodden with guilt for things done and left undone, I can accept other people for what they are, not needing to turn them into mirrors, props, blue-prints or Aunt Sallies.... The sense of things passing is with me all the time, but it seems less poignant now that my own time is shortening so fast and there is still so much to do. I must put my sense of transience to work, not luxuriate in it.

Again this year Cecil wrote many letters to the Poet Laureate, John Masefield, about the Queen's Gold Medal for Poetry. 'I would like to put forward the following candidates, all under 35 I believe: Elizabeth Jennings, Thom Gunn, Philip Larkin, Ted Hughes', he wrote on 26 January. 'Gunn and Larkin have been considered before. I am much impressed by Miss Jennings' two books – *A Way of Looking* and *A Sense of the World* – hers is the kind of poetry that grows on one. Ted Hughes' *The Hawk in the Rain* has some good things, but he has only produced this one volume so far.' A second letter, two days later, agrees that Messrs Gunn, Larkin and Hughes should be 'shelved' for a while. 'I should, though, very much like Miss Jennings' work to be re-submitted, and in particular her last year's book to be considered, for I am finding her more and more a poet of rare distinction.'

A third letter, sent on 18 February, expressed 'surprise' that John Betjeman was on the list for consideration. He was still concerned with this point on 21 June:

My own inclination would be to have a ballot of the committee, each member voting for two of three names on your list, in order of preference. Were you to decide on this, I would myself vote for Charles Causley first and Mrs Cornford second.

I am still a little puzzled by the presence of Mr Betjeman on the list. Much as I like him and his work, I cannot see how so successful a poet could be considered for an award which, I had understood, if it went to an older poet, went to one whose work had not achieved the success we felt it deserved. If the Queen's Medal can be given to an older poet, irrespective of the prestige or popular success his work has gained, then should not Robert Graves (for example) be eligible for the Medal. I am sorry to go harping on this point, but I do not seem clear in my own mind about the terms of the award in reference to older poets.

Masefield's view, scribbled at the foot of Cecil's letter, was that it was 'difficult to know how well-known a poet really is, but we have to consider every name put forward by a member of the committee'. In his final letter, four days later, Cecil wrote that although he would have preferred Charles Causley for the award, 'I should quite happily vote for Mrs Cornford, if that would make the decision easier.' After that Frances Cornford was declared the winner.

For Cecil and Jill the 1960s began with another recital tour in the English South-West, this one organized by Cyril Wood and the South Western Arts Association. They set out on 7 February and for the first time they penetrated west of Exeter. They went just over the Cornish border at Launceston, the home of the poet Charles Causley, who was to be their host.

'I first spoke to Cecil at a beano run by the Royal Society of Literature in 1958, it was attended by the Queen Mother and held at the Skinners' Hall in the City of London', Causley remembered.

After the reading one or two other people were rather sharply moving in the direction of the Queen Mother, but it didn't occur to me to move to anybody but a man I thought and still think the greatest lyric poet of the century, and this is including Yeats and Hardy. I went up and waited patiently for some time while Cecil was talking to some friends. I somehow managed to pull myself together and I simply thanked him for everything that his poetry had meant to me. I remember being enormously struck by his kindness, he was a very kind man and very gentle, he was also diffident and withdrawn I think. He knew me by name, but I was at the age when I was quite certain that nobody knew who I was.

Causley, a school-teacher, was of the generation which had grown up to the MacSpaunday tunes. As a Launceston schoolboy he had found that it was these poets 'who spoke to me most clearly about the inevitability of war, whereas most of the newspapers and the BBC were pretending that nothing was going to happen, that everything would be all right'. Through his war service on the lower deck of the Royal Navy and in his early teaching years in his native town he had felt Cecil giving him 'a great deal of encouragement and support, because he went on working'.

At Launceston on this 11 February Causley entertained Cecil and Jill to lunch at the White Hart Hotel. 'We were on our best behaviour at first, and he was still calling me "Mr". I didn't exactly call him "Sir", but it was a damned near thing. He induced in me, very properly, this feeling of awe. He was as close as I had got to a Keats or a Shelley. He had the aura of a poet, he wasn't like a bank manager or a barman....'

There is no doubt that the admiration was mutual. Cecil saw Causley as a pure poet with an individual voice, accessible and strong in rhyme and rhythm. Above all he saw him as that most fortunate of beings, a rooted man, a writer like Hardy who was part of his own West Country landscape and took poetic strength from his place.

The recital that evening, according to Causley, was 'austere'. 'I think most of the people in the audience had never been to a poetry reading, but they were given an uncompromising programme. Cecil and Jill read a selection of very good poems very well, and did not make any allowances for anything. The good people of Launceston were impressed.' Causley thought Cecil best at his own poems. 'I was always conscious of him reading other people's poems, his voice wasn't kind of anonymous enough. Actors are able to melt away their own personalities, but with him it was not like pouring water into a jug so that it takes the shape of the jug.'

That spring Cecil and Jill at last found a Dorset retreat as welcoming as the New Inn, Piddletrenthide, had been in the early 1950s, and barely two miles away, up a steep and twisting lane at the even smaller village of Plush. The Brace of Pheasants had been converted from two thatched cottages and was reminiscent of Cecil's Devon home of Brimclose. They had a first weekend there starting on 6 May, an advance celebration of the publication on the twelfth of Cecil's autobiography, *The Buried Day*.

This publication, with its allusion to Meredith and the *double entendre* in the title, brought Cecil the first large fanfare of publicity since 1951. He was interviewed on television and radio; he was invited to present his choice of records in Roy Plomley's *Desert Island Discs* radio feature; and he received considerably more space than was ever allowed for his verse.

Inside a beautifully melancholy dust-jacket, designed by Reynolds Stone, the book severely echoes the Nigel Strangeways view that it was acceptable that autobiographers should be frank about themselves but not about others still living. 'The most crucial and agonising decisions I have been faced with have arisen from personal relationships', by which he mainly meant emotional and physical relationships with women. 'Of these I shall say little or nothing, where the others concerned are alive. To justify or condemn oneself in public is a squalid piece of egotism when it will hurt the living', he wrote. This means that the book, in which 'less has to be left out' than with verse, is in fact more reticent than his verse – which details all his agonies in full and repeatedly. He wrote that verse 'must end up as not-self', distanced and universalized; but Mary, for instance, was certainly more hurt by *Word Over All* and *Poems 1943–1947* than she was by the graceful tact of *The Buried Day*. Cecil was indeed so fastidious that the generous selection of photographs does not include one of Mary or of any of the other women he came to love.

Of the 244 pages the first 180 are spent getting the young Cecil as far as his Oxford graduation, and the book more or less ends in 1940. Appropriately it is dedicated 'To A.O.S.', otherwise Agnes Olive Squires, his second mother Knos. Despite its romantic gloss it is intensely honest, revealing and evocative. It is not officiously accurate about dates or chronology and has sometimes therefore led literary critics into error. Reviewers praised its poetic grace and modesty but disliked its reticence. Even such a friendly critic as the poet Philip Larkin, writing in the *Spectator*, saw it as 'a dull and somewhat arch book, much nearer, as writing, to Richard Church than W.H. Auden, and unlikely to send anyone in search of Mr Day-Lewis's books'. The *Times Literary Supplement*, on the other hand, found it 'not only a fascinating document, a record full of names, memories, attitudes spanning the past 40 years of troubled life in British social and political history, it is also a quiet reticent work of art in its own right'.

On 1 July at the Dorchester Hotel there was a Foyles Luncheon in honour of Cecil and *The Buried Day*, organized by the London bookshop of the same name. Not yet having been soothed by the more generous and understanding approach of most American reviewers, Cecil replied in his speech to those English critics who tended to write more about the author than his book. This was not a pleasant experience, particularly when it was said that he had lived an uneventful life. 'Well, it has been eventful enough for me', he declared. For a man who had lived so much in his own mind, it had indeed been eventful enough. In *The Buried Day* some of the events are made more tolerable, as he himself allows in his postscript, by the selection and subtle distortion of his 'personal mythology'; others are deliberately kept buried, with only their edges showing through the surface.

As always Cecil was encouraged by the letters of his friends. His pleasure is evident in a letter he wrote on 25 May to William Plomer, then living at Rustington in Sussex: 'Your letter gave me more pleasure than anything anyone else has said about the book (this is not an exaggeration). You pick out the things I hoped someone would, but nobody else has – e.g. that you hear my voice in it at times.... One of the innumerable advantages of growing old is to discover the people one is *permanently* fond of – amongst whom, in my case, I put very high and firm the Sage of Rustington.'

Through May 1960 I lived at 6 Crooms Hill. I was due to be married to Anna Mott in June, and I had just started work at the *Daily Telegraph*. It seemed then a household for the most part as 'placid and ordered' as it was said to be in *The Buried Day*. Each morning Cecil or Jill drove Tamasin, now six, to her studies at the infants' department of Blackheath High School, and each afternoon they collected her again. Otherwise she and Daniel stayed mainly on the second floor with Nanny Bowler. They appeared, beautifully arranged in their night-clothes, at bed-time, when Cecil would place them one on each knee and read to them from one of Mary Norton's series of 'Borrowers' books; they also appeared for family lunch on Saturdays and Sundays.

For the most part Cecil was enabled to work uninterrupted in his study, disturbed only by the rumbling Crooms Hill traffic outside and Jill's long and enthusiastic telephone conversations in the reverberating dining-room next to him. When she was out he liked waiting on me, getting my breakfast and coffee. Sometimes Jill and I both joined him on his riverside walk. Once or twice we played badminton together on his lawn, and as it was a new game for both of us he made up the rules as we went along, and contrived by these means to keep ahead. For this brief period we returned to our

Brimclose relationship, quiet and relaxed and respectful. On 11 June, wearing a bow tie and a smart grey suit, he dutifully attended with Mary at Hampstead Register Office and the ensuing lunch at the Venezia Restaurant in Soho. Then Anna and I departed on an Irish honeymoon, and always afterwards my meetings with Cecil were events, marked in my diary beforehand, never an everyday part of life.

Having completed a Nicholas Blake play, *Wanted – Bearded Man*, intended for television but never produced, Cecil was now beginning to assemble his *A Book of English Lyrics*, eventually published by Chatto and Windus the following May. A wide net was needed as the volume was to contain any 'true lyric' he could find produced in the British Isles between 1500 and 1900.

Probably the most popular talking-point in London during the second half of 1960 was the unsuccessful prosecution of Penguin Books under the new Obscene Publications Act for allegedly publishing 'an obscene book', D.H. Lawrence's *Lady Chatterley's Lover*. Cecil was the twenty-seventh of the thirty-five 'expert witnesses', or members of the literary establishment, called for the defence. He was called to the stand in Court No 1 at the Old Bailey on the fourth day, 24 October, when he was examined by his friend Jeremy Hutchinson, then married to the actress Peggy Ashcroft, briefed for the defence as one of the juniors to Gerald Gardiner QC. The jury were visibly stirred when Cecil admitted to being Nicholas Blake, but were entirely unmoved by the recitation of his other literary and academic qualifications. He considered *Lady Chatterley's Lover* not one of Lawrence's greatest novels, but still in a higher class than the average proficient novel or best-seller.

'Does the fact that the heroine of a book or novel is an adultress mean that the author is extolling adultery?' Hutchinson asked him. 'No, most certainly not. Lady Chatterley is certainly an adultress; she has committed adultery. I would not call her an immoral woman. She does certain things which one can call acts of weakness; but, as a whole, taking her character as a whole, I think there is more good in her than bad....'

'Do you find that the book recommends wickedness and vice?' – 'No, I find it very much the reverse. I find it is recommending a right and full relationship between a man and a woman.'

He was then cross-examined at some length by the senior Treasury Counsel, Mr Mervyn Griffith-Jones, on the line that Lady Chatterley and the gamekeeper could not have had a 'full relationship' because it consisted only of sex. 'Apart from meeting him in the park, I think, when she is out with her husband, can you point to any other occasion when these two people meet, other than when they have copulation?' – 'No. After their first meetings they do in fact copulate on each occasion. They are lovers and it seems to be perfectly natural they should.'

'Perfectly natural?' – 'Yes.'

'Perfectly natural that Lady Chatterley should run off to the hut in the forest on every occasion to copulate with her husband's gamekeeper? Not "perfectly natural", sir!' – 'Yes; it is in her nature.'

'It is in her nature because she is an oversexed and adulterous woman; that is why it is in her nature, is it not?' – 'No, I entirely disagree.'

'Why?' – 'I think it is in her nature because she is an averagely sexed woman, I would say. We have no particular evidence about her one way or the other, but she is a lonely woman who is not getting the affection and love that she needs and her nature sends her to the man who can give it to her.'

Among the four talks on BBC Radio which Cecil gave in the first half of 1961 was one on George Meredith called 'The Gracious Guard'. This was a favourite anecdote, sometimes varied in the telling; part of his 'personal mythology' no doubt. He had been lecturing on Meredith in Derby. Next morning he was sitting in a second-class compartment of a London-bound train when the guard appeared and asked if he would not rather travel in a first-class compartment. Cecil replied that he would rather, but did not have a first-class ticket. 'Never mind that,' said the guard, 'follow me.' Cecil was mystified but obediently followed to a first-class coach, where his escort ceremoniously brushed a seat for him and said, 'It's an honour to have you on my train, Mr Day-Lewis.' It emerged that the guard had not only been at the lecture but had a great-aunt who was Meredith's housekeeper.

A Thomas Hardy talk, 'A Half-open Door', was equally personal. It began with a familiar Cecil thought, this time clearly universalized: 'I suppose every man feels in himself from time to time those two opposing pulls: a need for roots and an impulse to tear them up.' He went on to say that if he had not been a poet he would like to have been a sailor or a farmer: though it might have been more accurate to say that he had to be a poet because his mind was so firmly divided between the mobility of the sailor and the roots of the farmer. He recalled with nostalgia the time he lived at Musbury, managing to be a bit of a sailor with his Lyme Regis dinghy, and a bit of a farmer, helping to reap the harvest of the Curralls of Bulmoor. (He did not in this talk say anything about sowing wild oats.) He believed it was now too late for him to put down roots, but 'if I could ever retire it would be to Dorset ... it is something to have found a countryside that welcomes me home, even as a visitor'.

He and Jill saw more than usual of Dorset that year, staying with the Reynolds Stone family at Litton Cheney in April, and taking an August–September summer holiday based at the Ilchester Arms in Abbotsbury. In June they made their first trip to Germany, reading for the British Council at the University of Frankfurt-am-Main. In connection with the definitive edition of Wilfred Owen's poems, which Cecil was preparing for Chatto and Windus, they experienced the luxury of Sir Osbert Sitwell's house at

Renishaw in Derbyshire: a double room each, nectarines on the breakfast trays, the beautiful manners of their host, who was surmounting the disabilities of Parkinson's disease. With the Irish poet Patrick Kavanagh, and William Plomer, Cecil was one of the judges for the 1961 Guinness Poetry Awards. This meant two expenses-paid trips to Dublin and the chance to visit Knos, at eighty-seven becoming more frail at her old people's home in the suburb of Rathmines.

Nicholas Blake's *The Worm of Death*, his Greenwich novel, came out in October. Nigel Strangeways and Clare are now cohabiting in sin higher up Crooms Hill. 'I love this place,' she had said on finding Crooms Hill for the first time, 'I can work here.' So they had rented two floors of a Queen Anne house overlooking the park, turned their double drawing room into a studio and acquired a comic charlady to set the story moving in the manner of an Agatha Christie play.

At the outset Blake admits to having taken three other liberties: altering the weather of February 1960; building a house where no house is – on a certain quay in East Greenwich; and installing Dr Piers Loudron, his daughter and two of his sons, in his house at Greenwich. The desirability of 6 Crooms Hill is soon underlined. 'My goodness, what a lovely room!' exclaims Clare as she is led into the first-floor drawing-room. 'And what exquisite proportions! It's almost a perfect cube, isn't it?'

Cecil's own fondness for the place is made clear through the responses of Nigel. 'Is there anything so exciting in the world as to see a ship steaming past the end of a street?' he asks himself during a visit to the Isle of Dogs. Both the ship movements and the landscape are lovingly observed. The book is dedicated to John Garrett, now retired from teaching and mortally ill after a stroke.

Cecil had not been directly involved with the Arts Council of Great Britain since the early 1950s, but he was approached during the autumn of 1961 by the Secretary-General, Sir William Emrys Williams, and asked if he would take over as chairman of the Poetry Panel, with an automatic seat on the Arts Council itself. Little realizing the work and aggravation he would be involved in, he agreed. On 2 October he received a formal invitation stating that the Chancellor of the Exchequer (Mr Selwyn Lloyd) wished him to serve on the Council for three years from 1 January. The Council would meet six times a year, on the fourth Wednesday of January, March, May, July, September and November, under the chairmanship of Lord Cottesloe.

It was left to Eric Walter White, the officer in charge of poetry, to let Cecil know precisely what he had let himself in for. They went to lunch at L'Epicure restaurant in Soho and, according to White's somewhat inventive hindsight, the conversation began with Cecil underestimating the work of the poetry panel.

'I understand the Panel meets about three or four times a year?' 'It depends on the business in hand, but we usually find we can get by with an average of about five meetings a year.'

'I don't suppose it'll be necessary for me to attend all the Council meetings as well?' 'I think attendance is absolutely essential. The Panel is only advisory, the Council is the sole executive body and all the important decisions are taken at that level.'

'Good heavens, that is another six meetings!' 'In practice it is eleven, one every month except August. Also there are two or three extremely important meetings of the Finance and General Purposes Committee, at which I shall expect you to fight tooth and nail to defend the interests of the poetry budget. There are several meetings of the Poetry Finance Committee, which makes grant recommendations, and also of the Manuscripts Committee, both of which you will chair. You are also likely to be involved with extra sub-committees, working parties, and informal meetings with people like the Chairman, the Secretary-General or myself.'

'God, if I'd realized all this when Bill Williams spoke to me I shouldn't have accepted the job. Do I get anything in return?' 'You get free tickets to all the events we support, and plenty of hard knocks in the press, specially the *Times Literary Supplement.*'

Cecil joined the Council in company with Lady Hesketh, Peggy Ashcroft and John Witt. The Poetry Panel he inherited included Thomas Blackburn, Charles Causley, Rumer Godden, Philip Larkin, George MacBeth, Kathleen Nott, William Plomer, James Reeves, Alan Ross, Janet Adam Smith, Helen Spalding, Anthony Thwaite and Constantine Trypanis. It was a lot of talent to spend a mere £2,815 13s 1d, which was the extent of the poetry budget in the 1961–2 financial year.

In May 1962 Jonathan Cape published Cecil's thirteenth volume of verse, *The Gate and Other Poems*, dedicated to Peggy Ashcroft and her husband Jeremy Hutchinson QC. The twenty-eight poems do not lack variety. There are 'The Disabused' and 'Not Proven', the latter an imagined version of what Madeliene Smith might have said on her deathbed seventy-one years after her trial for murder, both dramatic monologues broadcast by the BBC Third Programme in May 1960; there is 'The Unexploded Bomb', salvaged from the prologue Cecil wrote for the Campaign for Nuclear Disarmament's Midnight Star Matinée at the Royal Festival Hall in September 1959; there is 'The Christmas Rose', performed in a setting by Alan Ridout at St Paul's Cathedral in December 1961; and there is the longer 'Requiem for the Living', at that time still waiting for a composer.

The title poem is a reflection on a painting by the wife of his friend and publishing partner Ian Parsons, and is dedicated 'for Trekkie'. The book is indeed unusually full of dedications, speaking for Cecil's slightly despairing wish to write for friends rather than critics. The somewhat bleak 'View from an Upper Window' is for Kenneth and Jane Clark, the enthralling 'Sheepdog Trials in Hyde Park' is for Robert Frost, the stirring 'Not Proven' is for George Rylands. Added to which there is 'The Newborn', marked 'D.M.B.: April 29th, 1957'; 'Getting Warm – Getting Cold', a wish for the preservation of her childlike wonder 'for Tamasin'; and 'Walking Away', the poem saying that parental love is 'proved in the letting go' and inscribed 'for Sean'.

There was no poem dedicated to William Plomer, but the 'sage of Rustington' again wrote a kindly letter about the book, and Cecil responded to it with all the fervour of a poet who had suffered from more cool reviews: 'I'm so glad you picked out the poems you did – not everyone's pick, but "Walking Away" and "This Young Girl" especially are ones I had the feeling of having got through to something in – if you'll overlook this curious grammar. I borrowed the "chunnering" from "The chunnering worm doth chide" in *The Wife of Usher's Well*. I don't precisely know how one chunners but am fairly sure that D–L does a good deal of it.'

Cecil continued to find himself in a minority on the committee selecting winners of the Queen's Gold Medal for Poetry. Despite his rearguard action on behalf of Roy Fuller it had gone to John Betjeman in 1960. The following year there was such disagreement in the committee that no award was given. Cecil wrote to John Masefield on 21 May urging the claims of George Barker, Ted Hughes or R.S. Thomas above Christopher Fry, though it was Fry who gained the medal for 1962.

Having failed in this business Cecil set out with Jill the following month on their second visit to the Greek islands. They, and Ursula Vaughan Williams – who had been widowed since 1958 – were included in a caique-load of seventeen friends assembled by Cecil's Chatto partner Peter Calvo-coressi. This private taxi was something of a cockleshell, especially when being tossed about in a gale, but these three weeks in the Aegean proved less oppressive than the ten days partly spent below decks on a cruise liner. This time Jill paid the £90 fares from a legacy given by her maternal grandmother.

On Delos, Cecil contrived to detach himself from the others, as Clare Massinger had done in *The Widow's Cruise*, so that he could commune with the lions. It was then that he received out of the still air one of his most striking *données*, those poetic phrases or lines which came into his head from beyond 'the field of experience I am involved in or meditating at the time'. His record of this is to be found in 'The Golden Bridle', the last of his Harvard lectures in 1965.

For some time I had wanted to write an elegy for a certain woman I had never met personally, but had heard about from her widower – a brave and fascinating woman who had died of a hideous disease (cancer). But I could not find a way into the subject. Then on the island of Delos, communing with those beautiful, weather-beaten stone lions (who, if I may say so, are now old friends of mine)

I heard – almost as if the lions had spoken it out of the island's holy hush, 'Not the silence after music, but the silence of no more music'. To me, those words had an extraordinary momentousness. I connected them at once with the dead woman; and the elegy began to get written. . . .

> And silence – not the silence after music,
> But the silence of no more music. A breeze twitches
> The grass like a whisper of snakes; and swallows there are,
> Cicadas, frogs in the cistern. But elusive
> Their chorusing – thin threads of utterance, vanishing stitches
> Upon the gape of silence, whose deep core
> Is the stone lions' soundless roar.*

The woman was Fiona Peters, the wife of a North London pathologist Dr Michael Peters. The Elegy finds her 'At her charmed height of summer –/Prospects, children rosy', when the cancer attacks; and it tells how 'Three times flesh was lopped,/As trees to make a firebreak'; how in her 'Three years of dying . . . She wrote poems and flung them/To the approaching silence'; she 'Soft only to the cares/Of loved ones – all concern/For lives that would soon lack hers'.

She and her husband had become admirers of Cecil's work in the late 1940s and after her death Dr Peters brought her verse to him for his opinion. The verse was not good enough for publication, but Cecil was so moved by the story of her courage that he determined to write the poem that was just beyond her.

> Whither or why we voyaged.
> Who knows? . . . A worse storm blew. I was afraid.
> The ship broke up. I swam till I
> Could swim no more. My love and memories are laid
> In the unrevealing deep . . . But tell them
> They need not pity me. Tell them I was glad
> Not to have missed the voyage.

He and Jill returned from Greece on 7 July and he at once arranged to give a BBC Radio talk about his journey. He wrote to the producer Jocelyn Ferguson about how the talk might be billed: ' "The silence of Delos is concentrated in the stone lions which roar up at the mountain where Apollo was born. Mr Day-Lewis talks about the different kinds of silence we can hear, and about a cruise of the Aegean in a caique." I hope to goodness this is what I shall be talking about – one never quite knows till one opens the mouth.'

The talk was recorded, for September transmission, on 28 July. Jocelyn Ferguson declared that it had 'delighted us all', but added that a fellow producer (George MacBeth) had complained of Cecil facing the lions in the wrong direction. Cecil replied that 'George MacBeth is totally

* 'Elegy for a Woman Unknown' (*The Room*, 1965).

disorientated (in this respect): the lions do NOT have their backs to the
mountain: to be pedantic, they do not exactly face it, but roar up at the
terrain a little to the left of the mountain.'

During the financial year of 1962–3 his Poetry Panel had £3,285 to spend.
Some £1,000 of this went to the Poetry Book Society, and £500 to the
Apollo Society, but there were much smaller amounts for literary magazines such as *Ambit*, *The Review*, *Stand* and *Unicorn*. The smallest grant,
as always, was £9 11s 6d for the Cley Women's Institute for its annual
Little Festival of Poetry held at Cley-next-the-Sea in Norfolk. More provocative were the prizes for individual poets, which created plenty of jealousy amongst those not rewarded and which seemed to create a category
of officially approved writers that would be used by Cecil's enemies as a
stick with which to beat him.

On 28 November he was photographed for *The Times* at the Arts
Council drawing room, 4 St James's Square, with the two poets who had
just received the 1962 awards from him, Robert Graves and Edward Lucie-
Smith. Graves is clearly doing the talking while the other two assume
expressions of polite amusement. The picture perhaps illustrates a conversation which Cecil later had with P.J. Kavanagh. The younger poet asked
him, 'Is Graves a bore?' 'No,' replied Cecil after considering his reply, 'he
bores, but he's not a bore.' A valuable distinction.

For Christmas 1962 the Day-Lewis family went to the Reynolds Stones
at Litton Cheney in Dorset. Most unusually for those mild parts it began
snowing on 28 December, and continued snowing. There had been no
winter like it since 1947. Cecil had plenty of time to contemplate the snow-
bound world, a chance that led to the plot of Nicholas Blake's 1964 detective novel, *The Sad Variety*.

In the cold January of 1963 General de Gaulle closed the door on Harold
Macmillan's attempt to join the European Economic Community. At
home there was an increasing economic malaise and growing unemployment figures, and the heavily publicized scandal which brought
about the resignation of War Minister John Profumo was beginning to surface. Nevertheless the Conservatives had been in power for twelve years
and, with Macmillan still able to claim that the majority of the population
had 'never had it so good', this arrangement looked as permanent as ever.
Cecil did not object to this very stridently, but he was now a member of
the Labour Party and he was as saddened and demoralized as every other
liberal social democrat when its revered but exhausted leader, his friend
Hugh Gaitskell, was taken ill and died. He went to the memorial service
at Westminster Abbey on the thirty-first, and sat in Poets' Corner, contemplating the unfairness of life.

Cecil's translation of the *Eclogues* of Virgil was published by Jonathan
Cape on 25 February, and dedicated to his friend of Oxford days Wilfred

Cowley, otherwise 'the Baron'. In his foreword Cecil becomes mildly de-
fensive – 'We find here little of the realism of the *Georgics*, but there is
sharp observation, humour and unforced emotion' – so reflecting his doubts
about the work. In view of these he was quite pleased with the reviews,
as he explained in a letter to Elaine Hamilton, a university teacher in New
Zealand who had written to express admiration for his poetry.

The *Eclogues* had very good notices over here, which surprised me a bit as they
are not poems that I find altogether inspiring as a translator. I go to Harvard
in October of next year: for some extraordinary reason they have invited me
to be the Charles Eliot Norton Professor: I hastily accepted it before they could
have time to write again and say they really meant C.S. Lewis. ... Maurice
Bowra's matter is rather better than his manner as a lecturer, I would say: he
fires off erudition at you like blasts from a Bren gun. He can certainly be a bit
overawing in private: as his pupil in the Twenties, I used to compare him with
strychnine – a tonic in small doses, but if one took too much one bent into a
hoop and expired. ... I was very sad about Frost's death; but he had achieved
the ripeness which is all: lately, he and Seferis (who has been translated excellently
by Rex Warner) have been the only poets I wanted to read.

The Nicholas Blake novel for 1963, *The Deadly Joker*, came out from
the Collins Crime Club on 10 June. It is dedicated 'for J. and J.', otherwise
Joan and Jo Elven, the then proprietors of the Brace of Pheasants public
house at Plush. The story is set in a Dorset village called Netherplash Can-
torum, Plush by another name. Nigel Strangeways, maybe still nursing
the shoulder wound he suffered at the end of *The Worm of Death*, is not
included. He is replaced by John Waterson MA, a recently retired Inspector
of Schools, married to Jenny, twenty-five years his junior, who has 'given
me back my youth – or the illusion of youth'. By his first marriage he
has a romantic and sardonic twenty-two-year-old son who is a jounalist
working on a paper in Bristol. This journalist, Sam, has some of the traits
Cecil ascribed to me. In his autobiography, for instance, Cecil told how
the first time his son was set beside the sea at Lyme Regis he 'had given
it one look of profound distaste, then sat down on the beach with his back
to it and read a newspaper'. Here the infant Sam 'had given the sea one
look of loathing and turned his back on it and read a paper'. Waterson
himself has some of Cecil's characteristics, including his susceptibility to
the beautiful Indian lady of the manor. The story begins with a nocturnal
cuckoo, the bird that helped to keep Cecil and Jill awake on their first visit
to the Brace of Pheasants in 1960.

The summer of 1963 brought some bad moments. On 4 August Cecil
and Jill drove to Stratford-upon-Avon to give a recital and, as they came
off the platform, were telephoned by neighbours to say that they had been
comprehensively burgled. 'Our house was ransacked from top to bottom
and every scrap of jewelry and portable valuables was taken', Jill wrote
to a friend. 'This included even Cecil's CBE, a silver cigarette box he was

given by the boys of Larchfield, all the boxes with his verses for me and
Christmas messages, all poor Tamasin's things and her savings. Now the
children have got mumps and are missing all this rare sunshine, I could
weep for them.' Nothing of this haul was ever recovered.

Tamasin and Daniel did recover enough to travel northwards for a family
holiday in the West of Scotland, the first Cecil had ventured upon since
he was courting Mary some forty years earlier. They stayed with Deirdre
Bland, a sister of Rupert Hart-Davis, and her law-don husband Tony, and
their daughter, at the Ferry House, Ardpatrick, off West Loch Tarbert in
Argyllshire, and it was not a success. The place had grandeur enough but,
as Jill remembered it, this was a 'dismal holiday with very bad weather'.
Tamasin remembered it as a 'nightmarish' holiday full of quarrelling, and
one of the occasions when Cecil went more or less berserk with rage. Pulling the Bland dinghy into their private jetty one day he managed to slip
and fall into the water between boat and jetty. He went into the house
to get dry clothes, only slightly cross that his former sense of balance seemed
to be deserting him. When he tried the manœuvre a second time and fell
into the loch a second time he exploded.

It was characteristic of him that he should come home having largely
forgotten the unpleasantness of the holiday, but excitedly bearing a new-
minted anecdote that would have a permanent place in his anthology of
representative truth. ' "No songless people has ever been discovered", says
the Oxford Companion to Music; and it goes on to tell us that only men
and birds sing, not animals', he began the second of his 1964 Charles Eliot
Norton lectures at Harvard. 'This is not quite true: I myself sang last year
to a seal on the west coast of Scotland, and it replied to me, with a strangu-
lated but unmistakably melodious kind of mooing. I am satisfied that the
animal (or is it a fish?) was at least making a passionate attempt to sing,
to break out from inarticulateness.'

Waiting for him at Greenwich when he returned from Scotland at the
beginning of September was a letter with an Austrian stamp, from W.H.
Auden. 'I've always been meaning to write to you about your Selected Poems
[presumably the Penguin selection, given a second impression in 1957], to
tell you how delighted I was to find your later poetry so much finer than
your earlier. The critics, of course, think our lot stopped writing 25 years
ago. How silly they are going to look presently.'

One of 'our lot' would be writing no more. Louis MacNeice died on
3 September. Cecil was never particularly close to this fellow Sherborne-
schooled Irishman, for MacNeice was more sceptical and less in love with
life. Cecil's admiration was nevertheless generous and he gave two radio
tributes for the BBC, and attended the memorial service at All Souls, Lang-
ham Place, in October.

In September Cecil also spoke on the Home Service World of Books programme about Wilfred Owen, and his definitive edition of The Collected

Poems of Wilfred Owen was published by Chatto and Windus on the twelfth. The book was really an expansion of the previous editions by Siegfried Sassoon in 1920 and Edmund Blunden in 1931. It includes a selection of juvenilia, some other previously unpublished poems and an *apparatus criticus* giving Owen's own variants to the texts of earlier editions. The book was well-timed to coincide with the renewal of interest in the First World War that coincided with the fiftieth anniversary of its outbreak, and the widening of Owen's audience brought about by Benjamin Britten's *War Requiem* from its first performance at Coventry in 1962. In its first six months the 21s book sold 7,500 copies in Britain, and 1,000 more in the United States.

As an escape after a trying summer Cecil and Jill managed a short holiday in Ireland at the end of September. A high point of this was a pilgrimage to his birthplace, Ballintubbert House in Co Laois, the first time he had been there since his parents moved to England in his second year. He was encouraged to make the day trip from the Shelbourne Hotel in Dublin because of a short conversation in a lift at Broadcasting House in London earlier that year. He and Jill were in the lift together when the actor Sebastian Shaw stepped in to join them. 'I'm very glad to meet you,' said Shaw. 'I own the house where you were born.'

I was in Dublin that weekend, covering the theatre festival for my paper, and I joined Cecil and Jill for the journey on Sunday 29 September. We went first to Rathdowney on the Co Laois border with Tipperary and Kilkenny, for lunch with Cecil's cousin Trevor Goldsmith Squires and his family, before driving on to Ballintubbert.

'Another poem, still under construction, is to tell of his return to his birthplace at Ballintubbert . . .' I wrote for the November–December 1966 issue of *Ireland of the Welcomes*:

He had known the elegance and shabby charm of this house only by a single photograph. It had always been hung in dark places of his father's English homes, lest it should provide too blinding a reminder of the wife who died so young, and this added to the mystery. . . .

The house was unoccupied, apart from an elderly custodian. On the front lawn, where the original photographer must have stood, the grass was kept in check by unconcerned donkeys. The Anglo-Irish air of living beyond one's means was still in the air. No ghosts were seen but they had clearly been at work. In one room was a copy of Cecil's autobiography, *The Buried Day*, and in another was his first detective novel, *A Question of Proof*.

At last the question of 'what my mother could see, looking out one April morning, her agony done' (asked in 'The House Where I was Born', *Pegasus*, 1957), was answered. From the front windows there is a view of the ground rising gently towards the border of Co Kildare. It looks as uncluttered as it must have looked 60 years before, few trees and the new Ireland represented only by electricity pylons unobtrusively climbing the background. Wandering about the empty rooms no memories could be awakened, but Cecil grew pensive with the weight of the past. 'You should never come back', he said. . . .

Earlier that summer Cecil had done his work as commentator on a short film about Thomas Hardy made by David Jones for the BBC Television arts programme *Monitor*. He had said some of his piece at the Upper Bockhampton cottage, near Dorchester, where Hardy was born in 1840. By chance, the poet Henry Reed, the source of so many of the jokes on which Cecil dined out, was at the same time making a Hardy programme for Southern Television. Between them they built this coincidence up into a hilarious anecdote which had the lane jammed with outside broadcast units, a sea of crossed wires and cross technicians, and the two poets shouting infuriated insults to each other, Cecil pontificating indoors and Reed holding forth in the garden. Whatever the difficulties, the BBC film was completed and broadcast at the end of November.

Having been a member of the Royal Society of Literature's Council for ten years, and a Vice-President since 1959, Cecil now carried some weight. He had played a leading part in the institution in 1961 of the new honour, the Companion of Literature (C Lit), to be limited to ten writers at any one time and much less easily awarded than the Fellowships (FRSL) to which Cecil had been elected in 1944. On 29 February 1964, Cecil wrote to the Society saying, 'My votes go to, (i) Elizabeth Bowen, (ii) W.H. Auden (I believe he is now an American citizen; but British-born and all his best earlier work written before he took up US citizenship). If he is considered ineligible, I'd vote for Sean O'Casey. ... If I could be present, I'd make an impassioned appeal for Elizabeth Bowen as *outstandingly* the most distinguished living novelist, now E.M. Forster has ceased writing.'

Discussion went on until July. During these months it was reported to the Council that Graham Greene had refused the honour 'on the grounds that he did not feel at home in a literary establishment', T.S. Eliot because of a disagreement with the Society in 1961, Robert Graves because he had refused a CBE. J.B. Priestley was not asked because everybody was sure he would refuse, and W.H. Auden and Sean O'Casey because they were not sufficiently English. The wording of the scrolls, written by Cecil, decreed, 'In honour of his great gifts as a writer and in gratitude for his most excellent contribution to English letters, we, the President and Council of the Royal Society of Literature do hereby confer upon ... the dignity of Companion of Literature.' It was eventually agreed that the two new Companions should be Elizabeth Bowen and Cecil himself, though the presentations would be delayed because of his forthcoming visit to the United States.

On Sunday 26 April, the day before his sixtieth birthday, Cecil wrote what had become an annual letter to his New Zealand correspondent, Elaine Hamilton.

Am in a state of nerves just now, as I have to give a sermon about Shakespeare at Westminster Abbey this afternoon: the Dean calls it an 'oration' but I prefer the good old C of E word. Glad you liked the Owen edition: it was a fearful job and proved to me (not that I needed proof) that I am no scholar.... Graves' Clark Lectures [1954–5] were awful – he's so perverse, but then he's a very good poet, don't you think. I liked Edwin Muir's very much – so pure and sensible and not a trace of lit. crit. jargon. I'm re-writing my Norton ones just now: propose to enliven the proceedings by singing some examples of words-and-music.

The evensong service at the Abbey was devised to mark the quatercentenary of Shakespeare's birth. In his sermon Cecil stressed the range of the bard's creative imagination, a poet who had measured up to Walt Whitman's rhetorical 'I am large, I contain multitudes'. This favourite Whitman quotation is used at the start of part two of Cecil's *Transitional Poem* (1929), with the two previous lines, 'Do I contradict myself?/Very well then, I contradict myself'. In the congregation that day was the former Margaret Marshall (now married to Gordon McDonell), the 'sorrow's familar' of the poem, the disinterested friend who had helped Cecil to order his mind in Oxford days.

Cecil's only 1964 publication, apart from the American edition of *The Gate*, was *The Sad Variety* by Nicholas Blake. With a title taken from Dryden this is dedicated 'to all the Stones' and uses the setting of Dorset under snow as Cecil saw it from the Old Rectory at Litton Cheney at the turn of the year 1962–3. Nigel Strangeways is back at work dealing with a sinister manifestation of the cold war rather like that he encountered in *The Whisper in the Gloom* (1954). The conspirators kidnap the young daughter of a nuclear scientist, very much modelled on Cecil's Tamasin as she was at eight. She is taken to an isolated farm-house, based on the Eggardon holiday home of Sir Desmond Lee, the headmaster of Winchester College, near Litton Cheney. Nigel takes the leading part in the final rescue. He has the advantage of Cecil's Citroen car, with the device for elevating its body from the ground, which enables it to traverse snow-covered fields when conventional police cars are bogged down in snow-blocked lanes.

From the financial point of view 1964 was Cecil's most successful year. With his £7,500 Harvard fee and American fringe benefits to rely on he felt secure enough that August to take his family on the first of their holidays in the West of Ireland, a pleasure they repeated each year until the end of his life. In Dublin, Cecil was distressed to find how Knos had deteriorated from frailty into complete helplessness over the past year.

> ... Now, sunk in one small room of a Rathmines
> Old people's home, helpless, beyond speech
> Or movement, yearly deeper she declines
> To imbecility – my last link with childhood.*

The holiday began at Ballyconneely in Co Galway. While they were staying there, Tamasin rode in the Connemara Pony Show at Clifden and they all sailed from Cleggan to the island of Inishbofin in the Galway

* 'My Mother's Sister' (*The Room*, 1965).

hooker of the poet Richard Murphy. From there the family moved to the Old Head Hotel near Louisburgh, Co Mayo, below Croagh Patrick and overlooking Clew Bay. Nearby lived Charles Harman, an English judge, and his wife Sally, old acquaintances of Cecil and Jill's. Their Tully House was used in Nicholas Blake's final book, dedicated to them, *The Private Wound* (1968).

The family returned to London at the beginning of September, so that Cecil could tidy his affairs before setting out for Harvard. Jill was not keen on the prospect of being left behind: Cecil, as always, sent some of his mind away like advance luggage as the day of departure drew nearer. He arrived at Lowell House in the University of Harvard on September 29 and wrote to Jill at once:

I've been very much depressed all this week, realising how much I shall miss you – *not* only as bed-mate and house-keeper, whatever you may say: I knew all along I should, but I didn't say so (yes, I know I should have) because I didn't want to get morbid about it, and it seemed such a long way into the future, and in short I was afraid. Remember all the lovely things we've had together, and think of all the lovely things we shall have....

He 'chummed-up' with three 'very agreeable faculty members', apart from the Master of Lowell, Zeph Stewart and his wife Diana. The three were an assistant professor of English, Al Gelpi, 'who cannot decide whether his emotional immaturity should debar him from marrying his girl'; a lecturer on American painting, John Wilmerding, 'who is an expert on marine painting and has visited our Maritime Museum at Greenwich'; and an Irish Professor of Celtic Studies, John Kelleher, 'who told me that when Kevin O'Higgins, the great Free Statesman, was assassinated on his way to Mass, a Cork man said to him (the Prof.), "That was a wicked thing to do, sure why couldn't they wait an hour and shoot him when he was coming out of Mass."'

All these became close to Cecil during the next six months, specially Gelpi and his girl friend Barbara, who was teaching English at nearby Brandeis University. Gelpi had met Cecil on arrival at Boston Airport and they had progressed from there. 'My father had died of cancer and this somehow brought about a mutual recognition. We spent time together and Cecil started talking about his father', Gelpi remembers. 'I was confused about my relationship with Barbara as he had been before his first marriage. He wrote his parable "The Way In" which I could learn something from and was helpful to me personally.'

On a more trivial level he and his girl, and Wilmerding and Kelleher, all provided material for the penultimate Nicholas Blake novel, *The Morning After Death* (1966). It was Gelpi, for instance, who drove Cecil, nursing a hangover, on his Emily Dickinson pilgrimage to the house and grave at Amherst, a substantial scene in the book. It was Kelleher who gave Cecil the romantic notion that his Day forebears, who actually came from the South-East of England, might be the Ó Deághaidhs of Co Clare.

A letter to Jill written on 18 October told her that he had read some of his poems after a Ford Foundation dinner. 'The poems are going well, I've written no less than five since the beginning of the month, one of which is the best I've done for a very long time: some undergraduates here who run a hand press are going to print it as a broad sheet. . .'.

The poem was 'On Not Saying Everything', published the following year in *The Room*. It begins with the Coleridge-like image of a 'tree outside my window here', changed for the best lyrical reasons from an elm to a linden tree. The second stanza adds that a poem like a tree must have its form and limitations. This leads on to consideration of human relationships, and the wise development of a love affair into a more lasting settlement that respects the individuality of both parties.

> Each to his own identity
> Grown back, shall prove our love's expression
> Purer for this limitation.
> Love's essence, like a poem's, shall spring
> From the not saying everything.

He dwelt more on this in his final Harvard lecture, 'The Golden Bridle' – the bridle given to Bellerophon for his attempts to tame Pegasus. He asked his audience, what about 'the restraining function' of the bridle? He saw it 'from this aspect, as a symbol of poetic form. Paul Valéry wrote somewhere: "Why do I use strict form? To prevent the poem saying everything." This is an extremely profound remark. A poetic form (which conveniently rhymes with "norm") provides the poet with a system of checks and balances external to the memories, thoughts, images, which an incipient poem catches, and which – if not controlled – may run away with it.'

The first lecture, 'The Lyric Impulse', was given on 21 October. 'It does seem to have gone off extremely well – a huge crowd, applause some time after I left the platform, and this morning a number of faculty and undergraduates have stepped out of their way to tell me how much they have liked it', he wrote to Jill. Cecil was nervous, particularly before the first two lectures, and stuck very much to his text. He wore a microphone about his neck so that all should hear, but took this off whenever he had to sing. 'A professional performance', Al Gelpi considered. The second lecture was on 28 October, and after it he wrote again to Jill:

Lifelines are for emergencies: but if you are not now in that sense a lifeline you are very much my terra firma, the place where I live and move and have my being, even when I'm 5,000 miles away. . . . The lecture went well again last night – though, in spite of giving up smoking for that day, my singing voice was a bit gritty and not what it should have been: however, the audience burst into applause after the first stanza of 'Oh light was my head as the seed of a thistle'. . . .

I. A. Richards was charming about it afterwards, and Profs Bush and Bote (the Keats man): it never ceases to amaze me how English faculty members not only attend other people's lectures but go out of their way to express pleasure in them.... I work hard on verse every morning, on a variety of subjects – separation, illusion, and at present I'm doing one about Knos....

> So, still alive, she rots. A heart of granite
> Would melt at this unmeaning sequel. Lord,
> How can this be justified, how can it
> Be justified?*

Increasingly he was called upon to talk or read to groups and institutions in and around Cambridge and Boston. At a Jesuit College in Boston he was introduced to a priest who had kept everything that had been written about him or his work in American newspapers for thirty years. 'The SJ who drove me back said it was the best reading they'd ever had, clasped my hand in both of his, and said, "God bless you and keep you" – which nearly reduced me to tears', he wrote to Jill.

One weekend he went to Dartmouth, New Hampshire, as the guest of the poet Richard Eberhart – 'I was worked a bit too hard – a reading, a lecture, and relays of people I had to meet', he reported, and he was glad to get back to Lowell for Sunday lunch. Guests of the students that weekend were the poets Allen Ginsberg, a hero of the beatnik movement in the 1950s, and his friend Peter Orlovsky. Cecil was somewhat relieved to have missed their performance the previous day, and was somewhat perturbed when they entered the dining hall trailing a gaggle of students. Orlovsky stayed with the students, but Ginsberg engaged Cecil in animated conversation about poetic technique. 'What an intelligent person, what an intelligent person', Cecil was heard to say when the encounter ended.

Other poets were about from time to time: Cecil got on well with Robert Lowell in his calmer moods, and as always found Stephen Spender good company. Cecil took another two nights away to repeat his Westminster Abbey Shakespeare sermon at the National Cathedral in Washington; but he preferred to stay at Harvard, where he was 'more and more struck by the beautiful manners, ease and friendliness of the undergraduates' and 'the loudness and harshness of American voices'.

Before returning to London, for a Christmas break on 9 December, he spent a weekend with Rex Warner, who had tenure in the University of Connecticut at Storrs. He wrote to Jill from there on 3 December.

Rex has gone out to take a 2½ hour seminar on Thucydides, and I am sitting alone, except for his dog Corky, in his charming house, which is deep in a wood of birch and hickory with nothing in view but trees, squirrels and chipmunks. Yesterday I talked to Rex's class in the afternoon, and in the evening had a huge

* 'My Mother's Sister' (*The Room*, 1965).

and excellent audience for my poetry reading. Tonight R. and I go out to yet another dinner engagement. He is extremely popular here, and goes around bellowing with laughter, and flirting with the professors' wives. Everyone seems to have read *The Buried Day* and teases him about his young self as described in the book.

Cecil was back in Greenwich on 9 December, and Christmas Day 1964 went well and happily, both he and Jill being notably good givers, and receivers, of presents. It was in the early hours of Saturday the twenty-sixth that Cecil woke to find his pillow soaked in blood.

He thought it absurd to call in a doctor about a mere nose-bleed, and quite wrong to do so at a weekend. The slow haemorrhage continued, off and on, through that day and the next. By the twenty-eighth, when a doctor was called and he was rushed to the local Miller General Hospital, he had lost a lot more blood than he should have done. He received a transfusion and, with much difficulty, the flow was stopped. For some reason the doctors and nurses could not sedate him, though it was clear that movement would restart his bleeding, 'so they got hold of the largest nurse they could find to sit on my chest and keep me from moving', he explained later to a wide-eyed newspaper interviewer. 'Where science failed, the human touch succeeded. My life was saved by the heaviest nurse in Greenwich.'

His useful sense of humour could not disguise that his sixty years of good health were over. He might have been warned by his increasing tendency to impotence, but his medical advisers had not made the right deductions when he consulted them earlier that year. Now the impotence was seen to be part of a blood pressure problem. The 'physical ignominy of old age', which Cecil had regarded as 'still distant' when writing the postscript of *The Buried Day* in 1959, was now beginning to overtake him.

5
~ 1965–1972 ~
Time's Last Inches

And my thoughts revolve upon death's
Twisted attraction. As limbs move slower,
Time runs more quickly towards the undoer
Of all. I feel each day devour
My future. Still, to the lattermost breath
Let me rejoice in the world I was lent –
The rainbow bubbles, the dappled mount. *

It is the morning of 25 October 1972, and the church of St Martin-in-the-Fields, Trafalgar Square, is filling for Cecil's memorial service, which is also being broadcast live to a much wider congregation by BBC Radio 3. The Queen and the Prime Minister are represented. To the delight of press photographers, Sir John Betjeman, the new Poet Laureate, arrives with Jill on one arm and Tamasin on the other, gently declaring himself an unworthy successor. Among others in attendance are the Lords Annan, Birkenhead, Butler, Clark and Esher; Mr and Mrs Kingsley Amis, Dame Peggy Ashcroft, W.H. Auden, H.E. Bates, Lennox Berkeley, Cyril Connolly, Paul Dehn, Roy Fuller, Laurie Lee, George Rylands, Stephen Spender, Sir Charles and Hallam Tennyson, Rex Warner and Alec Waugh. Thanks to the imagination of Stephen Hearst, the controller of Radio 3, the service includes a performance of Fauré's *Requiem*, conducted through admiration of Cecil by Meredith Davies, and with Wendy Eathorne and Benjamin Luxon as the distinguished soloists. Through the imagination of Ursula Vaughan Williams the church is decorated with chrysanthemums: a reference to Cecil's much admired poem of the middle 1940s 'The Chrysanthemum Show', which looks back to his schoolboy time at Sherborne.

Every year at Sherborne, when the school marked its commemoration, Cecil heard the passage of scripture that begins, 'Let us now praise famous men'. With the Rev Austen Williams to speak the obsequies such praise was now being liberally applied in the church. Outside, people were reading in their newspapers of Dame Helen Gardner's *New Oxford Book of English Verse*, published that day. In making her anthology she had judged only one short poem, from Cecil's entire output of well over 400, worthy of inclusion: that one 'A Failure', the depressed work of *Poems 1943–1947*, which told of ploughing back a year's verse that he considered too poor

* 'Merry-go-round' (*The Whispering Roots*, 1970).

for publication. There would be further irony five years later when Ian Parsons published his wide selection of the verse he considered successful, *Poems of C. Day Lewis 1925–1972*, and left out 'A Failure'.

The critical response to this 1977 assessment was similarly contradictory and indicated that there was still little agreement about Cecil's value. The reviewers in provincial newspapers had a general tone of gratitude: many of the writers had apparently allowed themselves to be emotionally touched. Cecil might have commented that these reviewers had had the good fortune to avoid university education and so had not been blinded and blunted by the science of English Literature. The tone of the London reviewers ranged from guarded respect to qualified dismissal. Freely making use of the ammunition provided in Ian Parsons's introduction, the critics found all the usual weaknesses: Cecil wrote too much and was uneven; good poems often descended into bathos because of a faulty line; he was an imitative poet who let his influences show – 'an unhappy gift for mimicry', Julian Symons called it in the *Sunday Times* – and never found his voice. The longest and most serious review was provided by Samuel Hynes for the *Times Literary Supplement*. Professor Hynes concluded that although Cecil had 'the slightest individual gift' within the Auden Gang he had developed into 'a decent minor poet' who had 'worked steadily and honestly at his craft' and deserved his last resting-place beside Thomas Hardy for what he did to maintain the English lyric tradition, of which Hardy was the supreme modern exponent.

Cecil's small band of admirers had become accustomed to more hostile responses than these and were almost grateful for the cool of such as Professor Hynes. On the whole they did not much mind that Cecil had been influenced by other poets. It was more important that, as P.J. Kavanagh once put it, he had displayed 'the spiritual insides of a man's life' for the benefit of all; had, in the words of L.A.G. Strong, used 'his whole life in his poetry'. Those able to draw self-knowledge from this had no difficulty in hearing the voice behind it, on the page as well as on gramophone records; a voice of reflective retrospection which was no mere echo, but Cecil's very own.

Cecil himself had a divided mind on the question of his reputation, as on most things. He liked honours. He had hoped to live long enough to attain the status of Grand Old Man, perhaps to be rewarded with a place in the Order of Merit, or at least among the Companions of Honour; he rather presumed by virtue of his office as Poet Laureate and his public work over many years for the cause of English poetry, that he would be given a niche in the Poets' Corner of Westminster Abbey. Rightly or wrongly he early recognized the talent of W.H. Auden, his contemporary and friendly rival, as more significant than his own: yet, with the best will in the world, he never quite escaped from his youthful jealousy of Auden, and he would have been silently hurt if he had known that the 'Royal peculiar' and fashion-conscious Dean and Chapter of the Abbey had 'memorial-ized' Auden less than a year after his death in 1973, while telling the Day-Lewis supporters that posterity would have to judge whether he was worthy of a place.

His enjoyment of honours was partly a reflection of his enjoyment of life, partly a symptom of his ambition and competitiveness, partly a kind of family insurance policy. 'Are you glad to be Poet Laureate?' the tele-vision executive James Bredin asked him in 1968. 'Certainly; it is a feather in my cap, we Irish like feathers in our caps,' he replied. 'Why did you take the Laureateship?' asked the novelist A.S. Byatt, who knew him well enough to put the question as a challenge. 'For my children,' he replied gravely.

He knew better than anybody that such titles did not make him a better poet. After receiving advance word of the Laureateship, his first wife, Mary, wrote saying he must feel as he did when receiving the verse prize at Sher-borne. 'No,' he replied, 'in those days the news was merely confirmation that I was, or at least would be, a Great Poet: no such illusion possesses me today!' He was glad of L.A.G. Strong's remark that to him 'his work says more than that of any poet since Yeats'. He would like to have heard his friend Charles Causley describe him as 'the greatest lyric poet of the century'. He would have enjoyed reading, in Kenneth Hopkins's *The Poets Laureate*, that 'C. Day-Lewis was the most important poet to be born in the years 1900–1914. ... I believe Auden's overall achievement as a poet – impressive as it is – is too much of its time to be wholly accepted as time passes.'[1] Cecil would like it that such things were said, but he would not have believed them. 'I have a B+ brain with a B++ talent for writing verse,' he once said. He had come to the view that if he could get a thought from his own experience clear in his head he might, through verse, be able to help maybe half a dozen people, maybe fifty, by passing on such insights. He would like to have had a place in Poets' Corner for his widow and children, but in 1968 told an *Observer* interviewer, 'Such immortality as I ever want is for a few people to read my poems for a few years after I am dead.'

His persistent grumbling about literary critics betrayed his inability to leave them and their concerns behind. In interviews, lectures and his own prose writing he repeatedly listed the other poets who had influenced him, and so contributed as much as any critic to the myth that he never found his voice. He lacked the self-confidence simply to offer the evidence of his poem 'Final Instructions', which testifies to his all-important Renaissance belief that it was for the poet to provide craftsmanship and the gods to confer, or withold, the grace of art; add that he had read widely all his life and preserved his susceptibility to the work of others; and conclude that 'the way I arrived at this poem is my business, it is for you to judge whether it is useful to you'.

Cecil was very conscious of having 'written too much' and he would certainly be more highly regarded if he had discarded every poem with a faulty line. That he did publish his inferior work has been taken as evidence that he lacked a critical sense; it is said that he should more often have obeyed the impulse of 'A Failure'. It is also true that he saw publication as a means of disposing of a poem, moving it out of sight so that he had space to try again with something different. In a sense therefore the act of publishing a poem was a more critical reflex than the act of ploughing it in: the latter procedure might mean that more time had to be spent on cultivating failure. He was content to leave posterity to judge which handful of his poems, if any, were worth keeping available.

When I spoke to Stephen Spender about Cecil, at the time of the 'Young Writers of the Thirties' exhibition in 1976, he said he had a sense of the work being poetry before it reached the page. This may be another way of putting what Cecil's most severe critic, Geoffrey Grigson, found: that he was all masks and no reality. Others, who hold a higher opinion of Cecil's work, have agreed that he may have lived too much for poetry, instead of letting poetry emerge from living.

Like most views of him this is probably true and untrue. He was above all contradictory, paradoxical, divided, and he cultivated this, believing that it was from his divides that his poetry sprang. 'I knew that poetry was the point of my life, so all my momentum, all my force, such as it was, was put behind this activity, and anything else took a very secondary place indeed, and it always has done', he said to Elizabeth Jane Howard a few weeks before his death. Yet he also remained a man who wanted to belong, and his life had necessarily become a clutter of relationships and fringe activities which could not help but blur 'the point of my life' to an extent.

All this acknowledged, Cecil's last seven years did contain an unequivocal statement, arising, like the main tune of the last movement in Beethoven's Ninth Symphony, from the sea of contradictory and discarded themes. Both in his living and in his poetry he showed an extraordinary faith in life, its familiarity and its hope, which was heightened in inverse ratio to the lowering of his physical strength. In his 1944 children's book *Poetry for You* he wrote, 'When other men generally retire . . . the poet is still working as hard as ever to wring the last drop of poetry out of himself before he dies.' He might have been writing of himself. His will-power, as he kept his promise to himself to 'rejoice in the world I was lent' to his 'lattermost breath', demonstrated the kind of heroism which he quickly recognized in others but believed he lacked.

Cecil, still very weak after his haemorrhage, stayed in hospital for the first half of January 1965. Returned to his own bed at 6 Crooms Hill he was more grateful than he had ever been for the gift of life. 'I remember, with almost hallucinatory vividness still, how very simple is the mystical ingredient of happiness and how love is seen in the most commonplace objects', he wrote later in an American travel magazine. 'For a little while I shared the world of the child. This was not the euphoria I used to feel after a night of the London blitzes, when I was agreeably surprised to find myself still alive – as I say, I had no idea at this time that death came so close to me in hospital. It was something much more positive – a sense of being stripped of habits, of knowing my own limitations (I was still very weak), accepting them, and thus being reunited with the beautiful frailty of the world around me. . . .'

> Gently at last the angels settled back now
> Into mere ornaments, the unearthly sheen
> And spill of diamond into familiar raindrops,
> It was enough. He'd seen what he had seen.*

Now mortally ill, Sir Winston Churchill lingered on, but all knew that the end could not be delayed much longer and far beyond British shores newspaper obituaries were brought up to date, television film and radio tapes were compiled, messages and telegrams prepared and prayers offered. With such outpourings of words how could the poet compete? Despite everything Cecil tried and was sufficiently recovered to record his long poem 'Who Goes Home?', fifteen six-line stanzas, for the BBC Third Programme on 18 January, six days before Churchill's death.

His efforts were not universally appreciated. After hearing the tape the Third Programme controller, P.H. Newby, wrote to the producer, Terence Tiller, that 'if we had commissioned Day-Lewis to write a poem for the Third on this occasion I suspect he might have handled it differently. Do you think the point might be made, tactfully, that the last two stanzas in particular are a bit embarrassing. The occasion of the broadcast will no doubt ensure that we have an unusually receptive audience for language of this kind but I think, don't you, that Day-Lewis might reconsider some of it.' In the event Cecil had neither time nor energy nor inclination to do such reconsideration, and he included the whole poem as written in his 1965 volume of verse, The Room.

Newby was not alone in his disapproval. Later that year I had tea with W.H. Auden at an Edinburgh hotel, he reading at the Festival and I attending as a journalist, and he picked out 'Who Goes Home?' as an example of the kind of occasional writing Cecil should stop doing 'when he obviously doesn't believe in what he is saying'. Maybe this was one of the occasions where he believed in what he was saying only so long as he was saying it. Ironically, in his 1968 Hull University lecture 'A Need for Poetry?', Cecil approvingly quoted Auden as saying, 'A dishonest poem is one which expresses, no matter how well, feelings or beliefs which its author never felt or entertained.'

* 'A Privileged Moment' (The Whispering Roots, 1970).

Cecil was given medical clearance to fly back to Massachusetts on 2 February, armed with pills to meet every eventuality. He was not quite so productive with his verse as he had been in his previous term, but productive enough. At the end of the year he was able to tell an interviewer from the London *Guardian*, 'I wrote, I think, eight poems in eight weeks [at Harvard] which is an all-time record for me.' Clearly the solitude which Lowell House could offer was useful to him. More important than the quantity of the output was the quality: at least two of the Harvard poems, 'On Not Saying Everything' and 'My Mother's Sister', are among the best that he ever wrote.

At the end of February he wrote to Jill of going to the first of three of Al Gelpi's lectures on Emily Dickinson, in company with Barbara Charlesworth and John Wilmerding. 'A rattling good one again: apart from excellent matter and extraordinary fluency (he hardly ever *appears* to look at his notes) Al brings down the house from time to time with wildly funny digressions and impromptu asides delivered in a throwaway manner.' Afterwards, 'Al came over and told me he and Barbara got engaged last weekend (I was the first, family apart, to hear of this): he was suffering from reaction, doubts etc, so I told him pretty well everybody did, like delayed shock after an accident, took him out to dinner, and got him cheerful again.'

Cecil had done something to help along this engagement. Even the voluptuous girl who recorded his lectures for the Harvard radio station did not engage his attention so much as Barbara. Sukie, the heroine of Nicholas Blake's *The Morning After Death*, is partly her. Cecil more than once 'bearded' Al about her, believing that as he found them both so attractive they must be right for each other, and that all they lacked was the confidence to accept the inevitable. He wrote them 'A Marriage Song', included in *The Whispering Roots* (1970), for their midsummer wedding. He and they liked to think they conceived their first child, Christopher Francis Cecil, when they visited 6 Crooms Hill during their honeymoon that August.

Another new poem that term was one 'For Rex Warner on his Sixtieth Birthday', an anniversary that fell on 9 March, published later that year in *The Room*. On his birthday Warner wrote from the University of Connecticut that he 'was inexpressibly moved and delighted by your birthday poem for me ... certainly this makes up for all the birthday presents you've neglected to give me.... I liked the phrase "though bulkier", much better than "fatter", "more cumbrous" or other equally true descriptions.... But was it beyond you to have adapted metrically that fine phrase from the *Stroud News*: "Perhaps the most dangerous man in the West of England"?'

The death of T.S. Eliot that January was preoccupying Cecil, specially as Charles Eliot Norton, the teacher, was the man who had confirmed the young Tom Eliot in his devotion to Dante, and T.S.E. had given the 1932–3

Norton lectures partly as a means of escaping from his increasingly de-
mented first wife. After his last Norton lecture in early March, Cecil wrote
to Jill saying, 'I had a standing ovation at the end, having sung two stanzas
of "Where Have all the Flowers Gone?", and in short it was, you may
say, satisfactory.' He had agreed to provide a poem for an American
memorial volume about Eliot, and told Jill that this would involve visiting
East Coker, the Somerset village of the second of the *Four Quartets*, in May
or June. His 'At East Coker' was included in *The Whispering Roots* in 1970.

From Cambridge, Massachusetts, he flew in early April about as far as
it is possible to fly within the United States, to San Diego, California. Here
he was the guest of Professor Andrew Wright, and his wife Gina, at La
Jolla University.

I read at a settlement run by my Greek, Mr Fraggis. It is in a slum area, but
the people who came to my reading were not visibly slummies but a class of
disturbed persons who indulge in group therapy with Mr Fraggis and make just
about the best audience for poetry I've had. . . . Yesterday I flew to Los Angeles
for the Whittier College lecture, over which I draw a veil – by far the most awful
audience I have ever had. On my way back from fucking Whittier I heard the
latest news of Britain's austerity budget, well, we had it coming to us. . . . I missed
Julian Bream's recital in the evening. However he was brought along to a small
cocktail party Andy and Gina were giving and we fell on each other's necks.

On Good Friday, 16 April, he was reunited with Jill where they parted
the previous September, at Dublin Airport. After a weekend at the Russell
Hotel he was back in London on the 19 April, enjoyed his sixty-first birthday at Greenwich on the twenty-seventh and sat down at his Chatto desk
again on 3 May.

Three days later he was in Exeter receiving the first of his honorary university degrees. Looking worried about maintaining his preposterous ceremonial hat on his head, he was made Doctor of Letters by the Chancellor,
the Dowager Duchess of Devonshire. Mary and I were among the guests
at the subsequent refectory luncheon and heard him refer in a veiled way
to his ten years in East Devon. He explained that his main reasons for loving
the South-West now were Thomas Hardy and its geographical position
'half-way to Ireland'.

This was not the last honour of the summer. On 6 July Cecil attended,
with his Anglo-Irish friend Elizabeth Bowen, at the Royal Society of
Literature, where they received their scrolls as Companions of Literature
from the President, Lord Butler. 'It is a great honour to hold one of these
things,' Cecil replied. 'I made up a speech in my head, assuming I would
be given a scroll. I shall still make this speech because when you are given
a scroll you think of yourself as one of those orators immortalized in sta-
tuary, and when you think of orators you think of Cicero – at least I do.
When you think of Cicero you think of that famous Ciceronian opening
gambit: "I do not say that *all* the best English literature has been written

by the Anglo-Irish...." It gives me especial pleasure to be receiving this honour you have given me, together with a very old friend, a compatriot, a woman who has shed such lustre upon English letters....'

In 1964 Harold Wilson's first Labour Government had been formed and, though it was not successful in all ways, it was giving a heartening lift to the state's financial and moral support for the arts. The Arts Council no longer had to go to the Treasury to ask for money: Jennie Lee, the first Minister for the Arts within the Department of Education and Science, did the arguing, and as she was the widow of the revered Nye Bevan, and carried her own political clout, she was heard. In 1965 she was able to install her own man, the lately ennobled Lord Goodman, in the Arts Council chair, a man with the appearance of a Caliban, and the equipment of a Prospero particularly in the area of public relations. There was a feeling of optimism in the air.

At the beginning of 1965 Cecil accepted a second three-year term as an Arts Council member. On his return from the United States he discovered that Eric White, an administrator who had long wanted to broaden the Council's field from poetry to literature as a whole, had in the autumn of 1964 attended a useful meeting to this end between the Poetry Panel and the Publishers' Association. Cecil now found himself first chairman-elect of the Literature Panel, which met for the first time the following January and had £66,000 to spend in its first full financial year, compared with less than £5,000 given to the former Poetry Panel. The amount was still small in the context of the £5,700,000 spent by the Council as a whole, with opera and ballet taking by far the largest share, but it still demanded much thought about the most effective way of obtaining value for money. Of the nine new members who joined the Panel three were put forward by Cecil himself: Iris Murdoch, Ian Parsons, and V.S. Pritchett.

Among those to whom Cecil felt close on the Council was Hugh Willatt, later Sir Hugh Willatt and the Secretary-General. 'At Council meetings Cecil was largely silent', Willatt remembered.

Unless Goodman deliberately brought him into some discussion he really never said anything except when literature matters came up. This even applied at the meetings of the 'inner cabinet' held at Goodman's flat in Portland Place. Towards the end of his second term he looked sad and depressed at Council meetings, definitely bored with things outside his field. He did his own job thoroughly and clearly. He and Eric White really created the literature policy at that time, and Cecil gave a very lucid presentation of the current proposals for a public lending right. He was also very discreet, very good at keeping things to himself.

With his own Panel Cecil was, in Eric White's view, 'very patient and extremely fair, though he could be goaded by the more recalcitrant members. He made his own views clear, a man doing something he knew about and to which he was committed.'

Cecil was keen to extend the system of awarding prizes to individual poets for work done, to the conferring of bursaries designed to 'buy time' for writers to do new work. The principle was agreed by the Poetry Panel in 1964; the first bursary of £750 went to Martin Bell, and this was apparently accepted by the outside world without demur. It was not until the end of 1966, when the *Times Literary Supplement* was alerted by the Arts Council's 1965–6 annual report, that the storm broke and Cecil was for the first time involved in acrimonious public debate.

Cecil's Charles Eliot Norton lectures were published by Chatto and Windus in September, offset from the Harvard University Press edition, as *The Lyric Impulse*. 'The amount which most practitioners of poetry can say about their art is strictly limited', Cecil wrote in a foreword. 'They will draw a few sweeping – often too sweeping – lines, then leave the scholar and the critic to fill in the picture. I am no exception to this rule.'

The British critical response to this tracing of the 'singing line' in English poetry from the sixteenth century to the present held that the limitations were rather too obvious. 'The Americans seemed to like the lectures: over here the critics mostly jumped up and down on them, which was only to be expected as I'd pointed out in the lectures that critics are not God', Cecil wrote to Elaine Hamilton.

There was more jumping up and down two months later on publication by Jonathan Cape of *The Room and Other Poems*. According to the *Times Literary Supplement* this penultimate volume of verse consisted mostly of 'placebos and plastic blooms'. It is dedicated to Elizabeth Bowen and contains thirty works: the first fifteen described as 'fables and confessions' and the rest as 'others'. The second section begins with the Churchill poem, 'Who Goes Home?', and thus proceeds to 'Pietà' reflecting on the assassination of President Kennedy in 1963. The *TLS* reviewer picked out these two poems as 'positively embarrassing'. Cecil's Harvard time is remembered with 'Madrigal for Lowell House'; he slaps at cautious poets with 'Apollonian Figure' and at presumptuous literary critics with 'A Relativist'; and the book ends with 'The Voyage' translated from Baudelaire.

The more stern business of explaining himself to himself is contained in the first half. The title poem, marked 'for George Seferis', stemmed from the *donnée* 'To taste myself', received when 'I was sitting inoffensively in my study one day'. Cecil told of this in his last Harvard lecture, 'The Golden Bridle'. The poem, 'beneath the fable of a prince who must retire now and then from public affairs into a secret room of the palace … expressed my own need for solitude, to withdraw from the demands and irrelevancies to which even a poet is subjected when he becomes, in however small a way, a public figure'. Later, in 'St Anthony's Shirt', he declares that whatever his need to be alone, 'I was most/Purely myself when I became another'. 'This is not an arid paradox but a discrimination between love and self-love', he explained in a letter to A.S. Byatt. 'You will learn to live with your fear of being non-existent – I have. It's our old friend Negative Capability.'

Negative Capability or not, Cecil had survived another year and was managing even his disabilities with style. Reciting with Jill at Halifax in Yorkshire that October he became very worked up at the climax of his dramatic monologue 'The Disabused'. His false teeth shot out, he caught them, replaced them and carried on as though this was a natural part of the action. He was very proud of that catch, much more proud of it than of his reading, and he boasted about it afterwards, pointing out that he had made it left-handed.

When Derek Parker visited 6 Crooms Hill that autumn, to interview Cecil for the *Guardian*, he found him in his study. On the walls of the room were 'a powerful pencil portrait of Thomas Hardy, and one of the original drafts of Wilfred Owen's "Strange Meeting" scored through and scribbled over'. Cecil has working on his detective novel *The Morning After Death* and attending to 'the subtle rhythms and turns of phrase which distinguish Harvard English from Oxford English'.

Parker's article holds that Cecil's style had become less lyrical. 'What we call the poets of the Fifties have influenced me, I think, in the sense that they've rather encouraged me to get drier myself ... they tend to be awfully dull, but anyway they're not sort of mad dionysiac poets, and mad dionysiac poetry (the 1940s fashion) has never suited me much', Cecil is quoted as saying.

Cecil took the first months of 1966 quietly. On 7 April he and Jill went to Dublin for Easter, for the fiftieth anniversary of the Rising which led to the end of British rule in most of Ireland. He watched the commemoration ceremonies with the affectionate goodwill of a romantic exile. The visit to Knos was harrowing; in her ninety-third year, she had lapsed so far into a vegetable condition that it was hard to know if she even recognized Cecil.

In May, Cecil agreed to publish an explanation of the Arts Council's Literature Panel, and its policy, in *Socialist Commentary*, the monthly of the Labour Right for which I was then arts editor. The article caused no stir until printed in the Arts Council's annual report at the end of the year, when the *Times Literary Supplement* was sarcastic about Cecil's choice of journal. The Panel, he wrote, was 'concerned very much with the individual writer' and had to advise the Council how to use its money for the benefit of literature, 'and then *go out and find* the writers most deserving of financial help'. Much play was made later with this phrase, which Cecil emphasized with italics. Who, for instance, was going out to look for deserving epic poets in the Orkneys, particularly as they would not be entitled to help unless 'sponsored by a reputable member of the literary profession'?

Cecil's ideal was the establishment of 'a hard core of whole-time professional writers – men and women who can give their full energy, thought and skill to the practice of their art at the highest creative level of which each is capable. . . . Failing this professional elite, we can at least buy a writer a period of time in which to study and practise his art. . . .' He did not think 'the young writer, however talented, should have things made too easy for him'. He was more concerned about middle-aged writers who had done good but inadequately rewarded work for twenty or thirty years, and were running out of incentive. 'Ideally, it is this writer I should like to catch at the critical moment, to show him he is not forgotten, and restore his confidence.'

He announced that his Panel and the Publishers' Association were trying to evolve schemes to help individual firms produce non-commercial work, and to subsidize certain authors. Proposals would eventually be put forward for a public lending right scheme, under which authors would be paid for the use of their books in public libraries; and consideration would be given to ideas for extending the copyright period to benefit living writers, and for relieving the income-tax burden. 'I do not notice that British writers' substantial dollar earnings in the United States receive any export rebate. . . .'

The usual August holiday in the West of Ireland included a Yeats pilgrimage. Cecil and Jill drove to Drumcliff, Co Sligo, to see the poet's grave beneath bare Benbulben, and then called at Lissadell House where the Countess Markievicz, one of the leaders of the 1916 Rising, spent her early years. Out of this sprang Cecil's poem 'Remembering Con Markievicz'. Another poem arose from a visit to the thirteenth-century Ballintubber Abbey at Lough Cara in Co Mayo. Cecil was 'moved by the beauty of the place and its history of heroism; even more deeply moved by the sense it gave me of what I can only call illumination'. He told Father Thomas Egan, his guide, 'rather light-heartedly, that all he needed now for the restoration was a poem. Before I knew where I was, he had pinned me down to writing one. . . .'

That autumn of 1966 saw the publication of Nicholas Blake's *The Morning After Death*, dedicated 'to my friends at Harvard with apologies for resisting the temptation to put them into the book'. The title is the second line of Emily Dickinson's poem 'The Bustle in a House. . . .' Nigel Strangeways, having left Clare sculpting at Greenwich, has come to Cabot University, near Boston, 'for pure escape and to take a peek at your Herrick manuscript', but inevitably becomes involved in a murder investigation. He apparently senses that this will be his last case. 'The private investigator is *out* – in fact as well as in fiction. Crimes of violence can only be dealt with now by teams of professionals', he announces at one point. He is also conscious of his advancing years: the students 'look so young', he muses. 'Can I ever have been as young as that?'

The graduate student Sukie Tate, working on her Emily Dickinson thesis, gazes at him 'spellbound, like a child listening to a fairy tale, her fists clenched and the pretty breasts rising and falling rapidly under her sweater'. Throughout his long career Nigel has grimly resisted the attempts of his clients to seduce him and remained faithful to Georgina his wife and Clare his mistress, but Sukie and the impulse demanding a last fling proves too strong for him. At the last Nigel is saved from death by his hip flask, which takes a stiletto blow meant for him, and he is finally glimpsed standing at one end of the Cabot bridge watching the murderer hurl himself off the parapet into the Charles River far below. It is thirty-one years since the investigator alighted from a first-class railway compartment somewhere in England, to begin his first case in *A Question of Proof*.

The *Times Literary Supplement*'s onslaught on Cecil and his Arts Council Literature Panel began on 20 October with the first of three leading articles called 'The Panel Game'. 'Deciding who "our good writers" really are is a problem that has taxed finer minds than are assembled on Mr Day-Lewis's Panel', suggested the article. Looking into Cecil's mouth the writer discovered that his tongue was 'gilded with beneficent optimism'; looking at Cecil's words the writer professed to be 'depressed' both by his 'scoutmasterly' language in making his case and his 'easy assumption of some kind of absolute wisdom, not just in matters of literary discrimination, but also in life itself'. The article, like those which followed it, was clearer in its denunciations than its suggestions for remedies. In the end the writer appeared to draw back from his logical conclusion, that *no* public financial help should be given to any individual writer because of the impossibility of selecting the right beneficiaries, and he merely demanded more information.

'We're not replying to that sour article in the *TLS*', Cecil wrote to me a few days later. 'In fact, I haven't even read it. I *may* have a private word with the Editor, but from what Eric White told me about the article the author has over-reached himself badly and fallen into his own malice, so let him drown there.'

Such insouciance, reflected in the complete absence of any official response to the first article, was no doubt infuriating to those suspicious of Arts Council methods. In the *Times Literary Supplement* correspondence column on 3 November the publisher Tom Maschler of Jonathan Cape sternly asked that there should be a public reply, not the private one that would be characteristic of the Council. The novelist Anthony Burgess also wrote disapproving of Arts Council awards on the ground that the Panel members would have their own ideas about the worth of work, and would not necessarily take the lead from 'critics on both sides of the Atlantic. ... A State award for writers implies too many kinds of unseemliness – unseemly snooping, unseemly obligation (is not the needy writer's sponsor supposed to look over his shoulder and report progress?), unseemly assumption of a special adjudicatory gift, unseemly discrimination....'

After this Cecil, with Julian Mitchell as his junior, was persuaded to appear in Rediffusion's *This Week, the Arts* on Independent Television, to defend his ideas. In a superficial discussion they were faced by Burgess, more muted than he was in print, and the publisher John Calder, who attempted to prosecute the Arts Council both for spending its literature budget in the wrong way and for being too secretive.

On 10 November the *Times Literary Supplement* responded with the second of its 'Panel Game' leaders, claiming that the paper had received 'a large number of letters from writers, publishers and readers', and notification that the Arts Council itself would not be offering a reply to the first leader. 'This was decided at last week's meeting of the Literature Panel, a meeting attended by no fewer than ten of the Panel's 21 members.' The article went on to the question of Cecil's television appearance. He had given 'a spirited performance', though Anthony Burgess had shown him to be not as well briefed as he should have been.

As to our leading article, Mr Day-Lewis dismissed it as a 'low-level attack', 'an article which is factually null and critically disreputable' and of a level 'not much higher than a Hollywood gossip column'. Readers of our article will already have their views about its 'level' and 'repute' (they will bear in mind, of course, that this is a quality dear and unmysterious to Panel members) and although they will surely admire the virility of Mr Day-Lewis's rhetoric they will hardly be taken in by it. A letter in these columns *substantiating* his contempt for what we said would clearly have involved Mr Day-Lewis in rather more subtle arguments than he was required to marshal on television. Whatever his personal umbrage – and we made no criticism that was not relevant to his chairmanship of the Literature Panel – he is associated with a public body whose activities have been seriously questioned by a responsible journal. Such criticism cannot be brushed aside with fine patrician scorn, as if it were just another unfavourable review of a book of poems.

The drift of the last sentence may or may not be significant. The paper had, as Cecil said to the *Guardian*, 'jumped up and down on my last books of poetry'. Four years later it was to savage his entire poetic output. His 'fine patrician scorn', if that is really what showed, was no more than a bandage for his wounds.

The lay press now went about the business of stirring the squabble. On 14 November the Charles Greville column of the *Daily Mail* revealed that, whatever his disapproval of the system, Anthony Burgess had sponsored an application for a bursary by a Guyanese writer, Wilson Harris, and been turned down. Next day Terry Coleman of the *Guardian* disclosed that the *TLS* editor, Arthur Crook, had been given the opportunity to confront Cecil on television and had declined.

On 17 November the entire leader page of the *TLS* was devoted to letters on the subject. The first, from five English Literature dons at Oxford, including the poet John Fuller, said that the decision of the Literature Panel not to respond to criticism gave the impression 'either that it considers itself above criticism ... or that its procedures are indeed indefensible'.

Ursula Vaughan Williams defended the Panel. 'The vituperative personal attack on Mr Day-Lewis is one I should deplore to see made to anyone who has generously given time and energy to work for public good if he were a stranger to me; it is more painful because he is a friend of long standing. ... That you, Sir, are responsbile for these graceless and spiteful attacks has made me cancel my order for the *Times Literary Supplement*, a paper I had never thought to see behaving like the gutter press.'

Other published letters, more or less supporting the paper, were written by, among others, Geoffrey Grigson, Kathleen Nott, John Calder, Martin Seymour-Smith and David Holbrook. It was questioned whether the Apollo Society, with which Cecil had 'close ties', should get the largest subsidy for poetry-reading; it was remarked that Cecil was one of those paid for some of his contributions to the National Manuscript Collection of Contemporary Poetry.

Three days later Anthony Burgess returned to the fray in the *Sunday Telegraph* and referred to Cecil's 'scout-masterly euphoria' before repeating his view that individual writers should stand on their own feet, helped only as a tribe through a public lending right and support for widows and widowers through the Royal Literary Fund.

On 24 November the *TLS* was able to publish a short letter from the Arts Council Secretary-General, Nigel Abercrombie, in which he promised that all the ideas put forward by the paper and its correspondents would be examined or re-examined. The editorial footnote beneath was as long as the letter, and it brought forth another letter from Abercrombie on 1 December. Next day the whole matter was again thrust before a wider public with an Arts Council press conference announcing grants of £14,000 divided between fifteen prose writers. Leader-writers once more sharpened their pens, and the *TLS* proclaimed that it was 'the essence of our case' that too much of the literature budget was being allocated to individual writers, while remaining vague about how more generalized assistance would be worked.

Cecil, who so intensely disliked public controversy, meanwhile did his best to withdraw. It was left to Eric White to defend the policy in a Third Programme discussion with Karl Miller, literary editor of the *New Statesman*; and to Nigel Abercrombie to reply to the third *TLS* 'Panel Game' leader that appeared on 8 December.

The row gradually faded away, and the Literature Panel continued firmly along the path it had chosen for itself. The last word went to Elizabeth Thomas, literary editor of *Tribune*. She conceded that Cecil's original *Socialist Commentary* article had 'an aura of pomposity about it', but preferred the judgment of the twenty-one members of the Literature Panel to that of the *TLS* editorial writer 'who gives the impression of a vinegary and peevish maiden aunt'. He or she had produced a line 'of scorn and superiority backed by muddled alternatives which changed from editorial to editorial ...' The only pity was that some of the utterances of Arts Council officials had been 'silly and condescending', and that Cecil had 'given the impression, quite wrongly I am sure, of a lack of any concern about the rumpus over awards...'

Cecil had initially attempted to give the impression of a man who believed in what he was doing and would not be diverted from this, but in truth he lacked the stamina for a sustained political battle. He was more wounded by criticism than he would tell, and it was doubtless a main cause of the boredom and sadness which Hugh Willatt noticed on his face during his last year on the Council. In early December he was glad of such escapes as he could manage: one to Ireland where he gave a reading in Belfast; one to Switzerland, where he conducted a discreet interview with the detective-story writer Georges Simenon for the *Daily Telegraph* colour supplement.

On Christmas Eve, fifty-eight years and one day since the death of the mother she replaced, Knos died in Dublin. She was ninety-three, and her last years were a terrible burden to her and all who loved her. Her death was, as they say, a merciful release. It also broke Cecil's last link with childhood and thus caused a great, sad stir within him. It ensured that at the end of 1966 his mind was far away from the Arts Council of Great Britain and all its works. Knos had lived the most saintly life of self-sacrifice and disinterested love that he had known, he would have liked to be able to believe that she might now receive some reward.

In January 1967 Cecil went to dinner with the Library Association, in an attempt to win co-operation for a public lending right; and worked with the Master of the Queen's Musick, Sir Arthur Bliss, on a piece for the opening of the Queen Elizabeth Hall and Purcell Room next to the Royal Festival Hall on the South Bank of the Thames. Their 'River Music 1967' for voices alone was duly performed by Bliss and the Ambrosian Singers at the inaugural concert attended by the Queen on 1 March. 'Dr Cecil Day-Lewis', as he was called in the official papers, was afterwards presented to the Queen with Benjamin Britten, Peter Pears, Malcolm Williamson and other musicians. The next evening the Apollo Society, which, as Cecil knew too well, had suffered for sixteen years from the extraordinary shape of the Festival Hall's so-called Recital Room, inaugurated the more satisfactory Purcell Room.

On 1 April the British Museum opened an exhibition of its poetry manuscripts. In his preface to the catalogue, *Poetry in the Making*, Cecil pointed out that the idea of such a collection had been conceived by his Arts Council

Poetry Panel four years before. 'We thought it wrong that so much material by contemporary British poets should be housed in American universities, while there was no similar collection over here', he wrote. 'Which living poets will be remembered in 50 years' time? We decided to cast the net fairly wide, rather than risk what time might prove to be glaring omissions ... as the collection grows with the years and becomes more fully representative, it may be seen as a fitting memorial to the talents of our poets, the greater and the lesser alike.'

In March, Jill had contracted jaundice and in early May she and Cecil were in Dorset, staying with the Reynolds Stones, as part of her convalescence. From there Cecil wrote to Charles Causley congratulating him on winning the last Queen's Gold Medal of the Masefield era. 'I was absolutely delighted. Who better? Pity it's a little large to wear on a string round one's neck'. Two days later came the news of John Masefield's death at the age of eighty-eight, after a thirty-seven-year reign as Poet Laureate.

Almost at once there was public speculation, in newspapers, on television and radio, about his successor, and indeed the future of the post. 'The cultural consensus has broken down almost completely. For a great writer the Poet Laureateship is an inadequate honour. For a minor versifier it is an excessive one. So why not abolish it?' asked the *Observer*. In theory nobody can abolish the post except the monarch. 'The Laureate is a member of the Sovereign's household, and only the Sovereign is to decide how many parlourmaids, and how many gardeners, and how many laureates to employ', as Kenneth Hopkins put it in his *The Poets Laureate*.[2]

It was nearly twenty years since Cecil was first mentioned in a newspaper as probably the next Poet Laureate. Since then, his technical abilities had multiplied and he had become a public figure, but the arbiters of literary taste had put his star into a steady decline. Newspaper speculation now made him only one of the front-runners. His own public view, when he was interviewed on the subject, was that the post should go to the best British poet of the day, regardless of other considerations, which meant that Robert Graves should be appointed. Privately he knew that a willingness to accept the conventions of public life would weigh in the balance as much as poetic talent.

In practice the process of choosing a new Laureate has little to do with the monarch. The Patronage Secretary at 10 Downing Street arrives at a short list of three and, unless he is particularly interested in poetry or has time on his hands, the Prime Minister simply agrees with the first choice and passes this on as a recommendation to the sovereign. In 1967 the Patronage Secretary was Sir John Hewitt, a man of Cecil's generation who had a 'great admiration' for him. The papers about his consultations are subject to the thirty-year rule, which will keep them out of the Public Record Office until 1997. 'The core of it', Hewitt told me, 'is consultation at various levels until all the possible candidates have been considered, and

considered again and again. In the case of the PL the press always takes
an interest, and usually a helpful interest. The poetry societies, national and
local, have their say. So do the universities and the learned societies. And
so do very many individuals. All this volume of opinion and advice begins
to take shape after a time, and it is best not to rush it. . . .'

It was not rushed. It was not until the end of the year that Cecil was
asked if he would accept the honour.

Joseph Compton was a small, shrewd man, with the sadness and sparkle
of his Jewish ancestry, an amateur poet and anthologizer, director of education for the London borough of Ealing, first chairman of the Arts Council
Poetry Panel and the Poetry Book Society, for many years responsible for
the English Festival of Spoken Poetry and chairman of the National Book
League. He died in 1964 and under his will his residuary estate of about
£20,000 was given to the Arts Council for a Compton Poetry Fund 'to
further the Council's plans to bring poetry to a wider public and to help
poets'. After sitting on this for a year or two the Literature Panel had now
recommended the establishment of a new university post, the Compton
Lecturer in Poetry. British universities, apart from Oxford and Cambridge,
would take it in turns to benefit. Nigel Abercrombie and Eric White of
the Arts Council approached Hull University with an offer of the post for
its first three years. The Vice-Chancellor accepted and said he would like
to start 'at the top' with either Cecil or John Betjeman. The poet Philip
Larkin, the Hull librarian, was deputed to approach Cecil, and wrote to
him at the end of June. Cecil replied from Greenwich on 3 July.

Well now, what an extraordinary and pleasing suggestion! My first impulse was
to snatch at it for the simple pleasure of then watching the TLS go mad with
indignation at yet another example of the Arts Council's corruption, graft, nepot-
ism etc. But this would be unworthy. I do like the idea, and I am particularly
gratified because it comes from you. I cannot take on the job until I retire from
the Arts Council at the end of this year; and a year's tenure of it is all I can manage
– and indeed all you want. I shall still have to be at Chatto's alternate weeks,
but I can see, at present, no obstacle to my being at Hull for at least some part
of each of my non-Chatto weeks during the three terms. I have never done this
resident-poet thing anywhere else, and I am a little alarmed lest I should be found
to have started off the Compton Lectureship with more of a whimper than a
bang. I would very much like to have a talk with you about it. . . .

In August the Day-Lewises went to Co Mayo for a holiday that included
a pilgrimage to Yeats's Thoor Ballylee and what it left of Lady Gregory's
Coole Park, a day on Achill Island and another day at the Louisburgh races,
held at the coastal hamlet of Carrownisky. John Joe the butcher had
expressed a willingness to mount the thirteen-year-old Tamasin whenever
she desired, and on this occasion he provided her with an uncontrolled horse
known to dislike crowds. Jill took fright and said her daughter should not

take part on such an animal. Cecil was also alarmed but had some sort of fellow feeling about Tamasin's need to take risks. 'Ride, and be careful', he ruled. She rode fearlessly that day, a tiny figure in a red windcheater.

Four years later, in a train passing through Wales after his last visit to Ireland, Cecil saw a girl in a red jersey riding a horse, and was reminded of Carrownisky. He remembered the Irish farmers Tamasin was matched against, and the way she had reassured him as well as her mare by slowly taking the horse round the sand circuit to 'accustom her to a lawless crowd...':

> Our nerves too can taste of our children's pure
> Confidence and grow calm. My daughter rides back
> To me down that railside field – elemental, secure
> As an image that time may bury but not unmake.*

Returned to London, Cecil wrote to Elaine Hamilton:

We had a super month in Ireland – Dan caught his first trout, Tamasin came in second in a very tough horse race (the other competitors all being villainous horse-dealers and farmers), and I plunged intrepidly into the Atlantic every day.... I've written a number more of the Irish poems, but only published two ('Ballintubbert House, Co Laois' and 'The Old Fisherman, Co Mayo') in *The Dublin Magazine*. ... I'm taking on for a year a sort of poet-in-residence job at Hull University, chiefly because Philip Larkin persuaded me to, which will involve spending about two nights there every other week. On about November 22 I fly to Honolulu to address 5,000 American teachers of English at the banquet at the end of their annual conference, I shall be there about three days. ... John Betjeman came to dinner just before we went to Ireland, and we had a jolly chat about the horrors of the Laureateship.

One of the young poets whom Cecil took under his Chatto wing at this time was John Horder. He recognized a fellow spirit: a young man whose mother died when he was thirteen and who had had a difficult love-hate relationship with his father; who had experienced mental disturbance and psychoanalysis and had written verse 'trying to discover the truth about himself' and his prevailing sense of disembodiment. Cecil had already accepted his second book, *A Sense of Being*, and helped to get him two small Arts Council grants, when Horder took part that October in a book-burning demonstration in St James's Square. This time it was Eric White who went on television, to speak for the Literature Panel in BBC-2's *Late Night Line-Up*. On 17 October, after the programme, Cecil wrote to Horder from Greenwich.

Just as well I could not take part in *Late Night Line-Up*: I should have been a great deal ruder than Eric White was. I did see the programme. The 'protest' was an outburst of childish bloody-mindedness which I would never have associated *you* with. Leaving aside the Nazi-thug aspect of book burning, how could

* 'Remembering Carrownisky' (*Poems of C. Day Lewis, 1925–1972*, 1977).

any rational person suppose that the way to protest to the Arts Council is to burn the books of good poets? I do not know what victims there were other than the *Times* mentioned – Ted Hughes, Seamus Heaney, Anne Sexton and Peter Levi. But are these four supposed to be bad poets? or 'establishment' poets? – Heaney, who has had only one book published? Sexton, who has, I believe, had only one published over here? Are they supposed to have organised a campaign against the avant-garde? – Ted is the only member of the Literature Panel which, you implied, gangs up against the young poet. This is demonstrably untrue: we have always, on the old Poetry Panel as on the new Literature one, been at pains to make sure that its members are not a clique – that they should represent a large number of points of view about poetry. The views of the avant-garde *are* represented and will continue to be; but they would not be fairly represented by the sort of juvenile irresponsibles who staged that ludicrous and spiteful 'protest'. I strongly resent your implication that the Arts Council does not 'care' about poetry. Like many others, I have spent a great deal of time which I can ill afford, on the Council, its Panels and elsewhere, in caring for poetry and trying to help poets – old or young, avant-garde, derrière-garde, or any other garde – so long as I believed the individual poet was a good or promising one and could profit by the kind of help we can give. The fact that I accepted a book of yours for Chatto's should be evidence of that. To play down the grants the Arts Council gave you, because they were small ones, was not sensible: we have a limited amount of money available for literature, and it has to be spread amongst many activities in verse and prose. It is just too easy to suggest that any poet over forty, or whose work you do not yourself like, is an 'establishment' poet and therefore should be written off: too easy – and a flagrant example of cliquishness, for it implies that you and your friends are the only people who know what is good for poetry. Come off it, John, or come along here one day and we will argue further.

After Horder had written an explanation of his despairing state of mind, Cecil replied with sympathy. 'If you've ever come across a poem of mine, "The Neurotic", you'll know that I've not been a stranger to the state of mind you're in. There's been quite enough despair in my life too, so I know what you're talking about. I'd like to have a proper talk with you about your poems. . . .'

On 23 November Cecil took the long flight to the Pacific island of Honolulu, as far from the British Isles as he ever reached. He returned after four days, bearing fresh flowers on ice for Jill. That month Cecil also attended his last meeting at the Arts Council. 'It would have been unseemly, after the marathon meeting the other day, to take up more time in replying to the very kind things you said about me', he wrote afterwards to Lord Goodman. Another tribute came from one of his young Panel members, Giles Gordon (later to win one of the C. Day-Lewis Fellowships instituted by the Greater London Arts Association), in the course of a *Socialist Commentary* article questioning Arts Council literature policy. Cecil's 'real concern for, and shrewd and unprejudiced judgement of, young and serious writers I for one shall remember always', wrote Gordon. 'Mr Day-Lewis is one of our most distinguished poets, and some people, not least the anonymous *Times Literary Supplement* leader writer who attacked him for his 1966 article in *Socialist Commentary*, might pause to ask themselves what Mr Day-Lewis can possibly gain from spending so much of his time helping to devise schemes to assist, on the whole, third-rate writers.'

On Thursday 14 December a portentous envelope was pressed through the letter box at 6 Crooms Hill. The Prime Minister, Harold Wilson, wanted to know if he had Cecil's 'consent' to his advising the Queen that Cecil should be the new Poet Laureate in Ordinary to Her Majesty. Jill handed him the envelope and went out to do a reading at the Royal Society of Literature. When she returned he had not moved from his chair. He had been transfixed by the invitation which he regarded with a kind of pleased incredulity. Thoughts about the distractions of the job, and the extra opprobrium which would now be heaped upon him by his critics were then far from his mind. Just before Christmas there was a second letter signifying the Queen's approval, and adding that the announcement would be made on 2 January. 'It meant a lot of family giggling over Christmas', he told a *Times* interviewer on New Year's Day. 'My children – Tamasin, she's 14, and Daniel, who is 10 – have been teasing me. For me it has been rather like sitting on a volcano. Not too comfortable but very exciting.'

The office of Poet Laureate was instituted in 1668 with the appointment by Charles II of John Dryden. Cecil was sixteenth in a line that included Southey, Wordsworth and Tennyson. The only previous Irish-born Laureate was Nahum Tate (1625–1715), son of Dr Faithful Teate (sic), who provided the libretto for Purcell's *Dido and Aeneas* and the words for the hymn 'While shepherds watched their flocks by night' and 'As pants the heart for cooling streams'. By 1968 the Laureate had no duties, apart from presiding over the committee which selects the winner of the Queen's Gold Medal for poetry: he was not obliged to write a single line of court or public verse if he preferred to remain silent. Whatever he did his salary would remain at £70 a year, plus £27 'in lieu of a butt of sack'. Cecil made it plain to anybody who would listen that he would have preferred the sack, but he had to be content with the money.

He was the first of the Laureates to be reasonably at home on radio and television. Of his two immediate predecessors, Robert Bridges was an aloof man and John Masefield a shy one. The former resisted attempts to make him a public figure and though the latter appeared at public functions he was little known beyond his own circle. Cecil had ambivalent feelings about public life and the temperament of a man who started every new undertaking, from a love affair to the chairmanship of a committee, with a fervent enthusiasm he found it impossible to sustain. On the other hand his belief in the cause of poetry, and widening public consciousness of poetry, never wavered. Kenneth Hopkins was doubtless right when he judged, in his *The*

Poets Laureate (1973), that if Cecil had lived for ten years longer than he did, or had received the appointment ten years earlier, 'he would have raised the Laureateship to a position in the public consciousness which it had not held since Tennyson, and such as before Tennyson it had hardly held at all'.

On 2 January and during the fortnight following, the mass media did as much as it is ever likely to do towards building such public consciousness. On that first morning Cecil dominated the front pages of the *Daily Mirror*, the *Guardian* and *The Times*, and to a lesser extent the *Daily Telegraph*. He told Rita Marshall of *The Times* of his 'exhilaration'. 'But honestly I know absolutely nothing about what the post means. . . . Being Poet Laureate is considered by some an accolade, by others the kiss of death, I can't say I'm anything but pleased. I don't think today one has court poetry as in the eighteenth century. If something is very moving, something like Aberfan, or perhaps the day when Prince Charles becomes Prince of Wales, there might be an opportunity or a desire to produce a poem on such a theme. Personally I shall just go on writing poetry, that's what a poet should do. . . .' This was only day one. During the next week the house was both besieged and invaded by newspaper men and women, television and radio interviewers, film crews, photographers and magazine writers. One contingent from a United States television network walked through the front door uninvited and installed itself in the first-floor sitting-room.

As he went along Cecil polished his answers. The first time he was asked, 'What fringe benefits do you expect to accrue from your office?' he had no answer. A reply that pleased him came to him in the middle of the night. When he found the American team in his sitting room he asked the interviewer to put the question to him again and replied, 'I don't know much about fringe benefits, I know I have the right to be buried in Westminster Abbey, but I expect you would call that a beyond the fringe benefit.' There was polite laughter, but it was clear that the Americans were as unfamiliar with the theatre revue *Beyond the Fringe* as Cecil was with the unpredictability of the Dean and Chapter of Westminster Abbey.

The first Laureate effusion, 'Then and Now', commissioned by the *Daily Mail* for the first three-figure fee Cecil had received for a single poem, was a front-page, six-stanza contribution to the 'I'm Backing Britain' campaign, a bizarre manifestation of middle-class patriotism then current. He complained to the *Evening Standard* that most of his fees were going on stamps. 'I've had over 600 letters and telegrams to answer', he said. One such telegram, from his bank manager, said 'The whole Midland is rejoicing with you.' But the London weeklies soon began sounding sour notes, and in his book *The Pendulum Years*, about Britain in the 1960s, Bernard Levin wrote that Cecil had celebrated his appointment 'almost immediately with verse of a nature, and on a subject, that made many regret their impulsive rejoicing at the death of his predecessor'.[3]

Publicity generates publicity and there were long reports in both the

Daily Telegraph and *The Times* when Cecil gave his inaugural lecture, 'A Need for Poetry?', as Compton Lecturer at Hull University on 17 January. 'You, students, do not perhaps realize how extraordinarily stimulating it is for an old poet to be in contact, from time to time, with younger people and strange ideas. A poet's work is solitary: he throws his poems, like messages in bottles, into the deep blue sea, and it is very gratifying to him if he finds that other communication can be made', he said, to the 500-strong audience in the Middleton Hall.

With experience he was now able to provide the vivid overstatements which lead to newspaper headlines. One task left for the poet, he declared, was 'to purify the language of the tribe; to ensure that our English language shall be kept clean, resourceful, adventurous, alive'. This was 'rendered appallingly difficult by the vulgarity or cynicism with which so many people, from politicians to pop-singers, from with-it clergymen to woolly-minded publicists, corrupt the language'.

Under the terms of his lectureship Cecil received £2,000, half from the Arts Council and half from Hull University. On arrival at the campus that January he let it be known that he would be available to callers at the library's poetry room when he was in residence; but on his inaugural visit was left entirely on his own. He was not in residence all that much, taking a breakfast train from Kings Cross to Hull on alternate Wednesdays during term-time, and returning to London late the following day. Writing on 24 January, Professor R.L. Brett, head of the English Department, promised that in future there would be organized groups of volunteers so that Cecil was not left without company in the poetry room. 'People were a little shy to come on their own', suggested Brett. The new arrangement worked well enough, with Cecil going through particular poems in the seminar manner, and looking at the manuscripts of aspiring student poets.

He was also in demand in London. 'When I lunched with the Queen recently I broke the ice by placing both feet on one of her corgis, which was lying in a disciplined way beneath the table', he wrote to Diana Jordan. 'I thought it was a footstool and had to say "Ma'am, I have just put my foot on one of your corgis." This led to a conversation about (a) dogs, (b) about Prince Charles and whether he has any private life in Cambridge, and (c) about Ireland and my own children.' As well as lunch at Buckingham Palace, Cecil also went to dinner at St James's Palace where Lord Cobbold, the Lord Chamberlain, told him of the Poet Laureate's slight duties. He received a letter from the United States telling him he had been elected a Knight of Mark Twain, whatever that was.

Cecil set about reorganizing the committee which would select the winners of the annual Queen's Gold Medal for Poetry. His main idea was to honour the best poets who had been overlooked during the Masefield era. Charles Causley, Graham Hough, Philip Larkin and William Plomer agreed to serve with him, and he promised that decisions would be made over a good lunch rather than by correspondence. Having sacked the old committee and recruited a new one he claimed, half-seriously, 'I have assembled people who think like me so that I will be able to get my own choice.'

Nicholas Blake's twentieth and last novel, *The Private Wound*, was published on 1 May with Nigel Strangeways and Cecil transmuted into Dominic Eyre, an English novelist of the Isherwood vintage. It is the most directly autobiographical of Blake's books and entirely driven by memories of his love affair with Billie Currall in 1939 and 1940, she being only slightly disguised as the raffish Harry Leeson. The story was serialized by the *Daily Express* and advertised with posters juxtaposing the back view of a naked woman and a full frontal view of the clothed Poet Laureate. One day that May, Mary (the Maire of the book) was tending her Brimclose garden when John Currall (the Flurry of the book) spied her from the lane. He had been reading the *Express* and was not pleased, despite the rather affectionate account of Flurry. 'He may think I don't know what his story is about, but I do, damn his eyes,' said Currall as he disappeared up the lane. Mary never saw him again. He died from cancer the following year, nursed with devotion and fortitude by his wife Billie.

So ended the career of Nicholas Blake. In early 1969 Cecil did begin a new novel, to be called 'Bang Bang, You're Dead', which would have reintroduced Nigel Strangeways and Clare. It was set on the border of England and Wales and involved a popular historian turned 'television personality', and the explosive activities of the Welsh Freedom Army. Cecil had his heart in at least one short passage, where the historian explains to Clare Massinger, who is modelling his bust, his attitude to reviews. 'As you know I never read them now. What's the point? Why suffer heartburn when you can keep away from the food that causes it?' Cecil got as far as the blowing-up of the historian and a tenth chapter, 'After the funeral'. His manuscript ends on page seventy-seven, where he decided that the story had run out of impetus.

In early May 1968 Cecil and Jill flew to Rome as the guests of Johannes Schwarzenberg, then Austrian Ambassador to the Vatican, and his sculptress wife Kathleen. After six days in the Italian capital, when they were reunited with George Seferis and his wife, they had some time at the Schwarzenberg villa near Florence. Cecil was back in London on the fourteenth for a performance by the National Theatre company of *As You Like It*, a performance marking the 150th anniversary of the Old Vic and for which he had produced an occasional poem. Two days later he was at St James's, Piccadily, at the joint memorial service for Sir Harold and Lady (Vita Sackville-West) Nicolson. He read Vita's poem 'To Harold Nicolson' to a large congregation described by the *Evening Standard* as 'a solid chunk of the Establishment – literary and otherwise'. Cecil was observed by the reporter to be wearing his 'American-style suit, all the buttons done up, and carrying his umbrella'. The pressure was maintained for the next three weeks. He was at Hull, lecturing on 'The Thirties in Retrospect', he took part in a BBC recording of Richard Murphy's *Battle of Aughrim*, and on Whit Sunday he preached at Great St Mary, Cambridge, on 'The Creative Spirit'.

Cecil had not been seriously ill for over three years, but he was now visibly older and less strong. On 9 June, a day on which he was entertaining the poet Kathleen Raine at Greenwich, he was stricken with glandular fever. The illness was not at first diagnosed because it is unusual in a sixty-four-year-old, and it meant that he had to cancel all his engagements until the autumn, leaving Jill to deputize where she could.

He now took a complete rest, accepting a vice-presidency at the London Library as he did so, and wrote to Elaine Hamilton on 27 July describing glandular fever as 'a game of Snakes and Ladders – one day you crawl up a ladder and the next you slide down a snake....' He went on:

Having done nothing for weeks but lie about in the garden in the sun (when there was any) I've no more news than would an inhabitant of Limbo. However, there's something to be said for being bed-ridden – or *chaise-longue*-ridden: one learns to adjust the mixture of patience and apathy – like hot and cold taps for a bath. Also it's agreeable to have an incontrovertible reason for cancelling engagements already made – e.g. to read my Hardy poem at a memorial do for him at Westminster Abbey, and lecture at the Hardy Festival in Dorchester (all arranged, I suspect, by Harold Macmillan to sell his T.H. books). . . . Would you like me to be an Hon Litt D of Trinity College, Dublin? The board is putting up my name to the Senate in October – but, not a word till I know it's in the bag. My ancestor, Goldsmith, was there; and my father; so I feel a piety towards the place.

In early August he was subject to another outburst of publicity with the publication by the Society for the Propagation of Christian Knowledge of *Modern Liturgical Texts*, Cecil's response to a commission from the Church of England Liturgical Commission to put the traditional canticles into modern English. He had been asked to provide words that could be sung easily by church congregations which lacked the assistance of competent choirs and organists, and the composer Alan Ridout provided musical settings. Those who cared about the canticles – the *Te Deum*, the *Venite*, the *Magnificat*, the *Nunc Dimittis* and the rest – minded the loss of the old rounded phrases. Modernization work of this kind is not the way to get a good press.

The West of Ireland weather that summer was more characteristic of the Mediterranean than the Atlantic and Cecil returned from his annual Co Mayo holiday much revived. In late October he returned to his work at Hull, this time giving a recital with Jill as well as his venerable lecture on 'Emily Brontë and Freedom'. Of his three further visits to the university the most difficult was the occasion on 20 November when he struggled through lectures on 'The Dramatic Monologue' and 'The Lyrical Poetry of Thomas Hardy" with a tooth abscess, before going on to open a new public library at Goole.

After his final visit at the beginning of December he was seen off from the station with plaudits and gratitude ringing about his ears. He was succeeded as Compton Lecturer by two younger poets – Richard Murphy, whom he helped to recruit, and Peter Porter – and he did not suffer when comparisons were made. He was never an off-the-cuff lecturer, he always needed a complete text under his eyes, and at Hull he had little to add to what he had said elsewhere. Yet within these limitations he had become a very experienced professional, able to transcend his physical weakness with a psychic energy that kept his audiences on the alert.

In 1970, Cecil would be repaid for his efforts by being made an honorary Doctor of Letters of Hull University. At the ceremony Philip Larkin remembered that Cecil 'talked to our students with as much informality as they would allow; he performed on several occasions the not inconsiderable feat of packing this hall to its doors; . . . he was generous with his time in every conceivable way. It was a year that will live long in our memories, and the happiest inception to this national lectureship that could possibly have been hoped for.'

In mid-October Cecil had entertained his Gold Medal Committee. Their deliberations started at L'Epicure restaurant in Soho and continued in the Chatto board-room, but the members had little real difficulty in arriving at Robert Graves as the best British poet who had not yet received the award. Cecil had persuaded the Queen that it would be appropriate to present the medal in person, rather than have it sent to the winner by post. Accordingly Friday 6 December was marked down as the date for the ceremony. Graves arrived to stay at 6 Crooms Hill the previous night and was helped to smarten himself up. On the way to Buckingham Palace he was taken by Cecil to Jermyn Street, where he equipped himself with a regimental tie for the occasion. The resulting audience was recorded by Richard Cawston's BBC Television cameras filming the documentary *The Royal Family*. In discussion before the visitors entered, the Queen agreed with the television men that she would be filmed presenting Graves with his medal, and Cecil with the badge and chain which, she was advised, were intended for the Poet Laureate.

After Graves had received the medal he disconcerted the Queen by telling her that she and he were relations, both descended through Edward IV from Mahomet. He advised her to mention this in her Christmas broadcast for the benefit of her Moslem subjects. At a loss for a suitable response to this advice she turned to Cecil, saying she had to present him with the insignia of his office as Poet Laureate. With due deference Cecil said that he had not realized there were any such insignia. Unimpressed by this the Queen pressed the imposing chain upon him. 'What a magnificent thing, when will you wear it, Cecil?' asked Graves. 'I shall wear it on my pyjamas,' replied Cecil. The Queen was amused. Clutching his prize, Cecil bade farewell to Graves and went to work at his Chatto office.

A little later Jill received an apologetic telephone call at Greenwich. 'Her Majesty has inadvertently presented Mr Day-Lewis with the Badge and Chain of the Chancellor of the Order of St Michael and St George. The Viscount De L'Isle is waiting at the Palace to receive it', said the Palace voice. Some minutes later an emissary arrived at Chatto and Windus, William IV Street, to recover the object. Most of the film of the audience had to go straight to the BBC archives where it must remain unviewed for fifty years.

Two days later Cecil and Jill flew to Dublin. A shadow passed over him on this visit, and he approached the honorary degree ceremony at Trinity College in a black depression. 'They are only giving me this because I'm the Poet Laureate, they know as well as I do that I'm no good as a poet,' he said to Jill just before the banquet. It should have been an unclouded few days: Doctor of Letters at Goldsmith's old university, a place at last in the Irish Academy of Letters, a performance of Richard Murphy's *The Battle of Aughrim* on stage at the new Abbey Theatre, an evening with the actor Cyril Cusack, an introduction to Michael Farrell's vast Irish novel *Thy Tears Might Cease*, much lionization and pictures in the papers. He would rather have known that he had written one poem that would last.

When interviewed by the *Observer* at the end of the year he was in a more philosophical state of mind. He said that he felt 'a kind of old man's irresponsibility', which meant 'an opting out of certain things mentally, a diminution in the urgency and importance of the general load of duties and responsibilities ... it isn't *just* a slowing down. It is that I have decided which things are worthwhile thinking about, feeling about.' He wondered if 'when I come to die – which isn't so very far distant – I shall be clutching at any old straw'. At the moment, 'I don't feel the need to be preserved in any form: I don't think my individuality is worth preserving....'

The year of 1969 began with the pattern which had so tired Cecil the previous year. Lecturing or reciting at the new Ulster University of Coleraine, in Co Derry, at Lewes and Exeter, was followed by a British Council visit to Paris at the end of February. He now admitted to an admiration for French culture; it was Fauré's *Requiem*, not Verdi's, that he wanted played at his funeral, and he enjoyed this stay amidst the elegant comfort of the Hotel Lambert, which had associations with his beloved Chopin. He and Jill were entertaining by Enid and Charles de Winton of the British Council. They had lunch with the British Ambassador (Sir Christopher Soames) and Cecil's two lectures were politely received.

The second British Council journey that year proved less enjoyable, though not for want of hospitality received. Starting on 16 March this was a week of lectures, lunches, receptions and interviews on Malta. Cecil and Jill were the house guests of Peter Allnutt, the Council representative on the Mediterranean island, and his wife. Whether or not protocol strictly demands such demonstrations Cecil was, as a member of the Royal Household, piped aboard the small boat on which he was shown about Valletta harbour. He and Jill gave a recital at the eighteenth-century Manoel Theatre for which they received a standing ovation.

Throughout the visit Cecil felt unwell; he flew back to London in great pain and was at once admitted to the Miller Hospital in Greenwich 'for observation'. The diagnosis placed the blame on stones in his gall-bladder, but his doctors decided that in view of his general condition it would be prudent to avoid surgery if possible.

He returned to a full programme in May, though still far from well with, as he put it, gall-stones 'rattling about in my guts' and his dentist removing two of his teeth and 'uttering threats against my remaining old stumps'. He was in great discomfort when he went to Westminster Abbey on the eighth for a ceremony to mark the arrival of Byron in Poet's Corner. 'Mr C. Day-Lewis, the Poet Laureate, bent stiffly to put down a laurel wreath punctuated by red roses', noted *The Times*.

During the evening of 11 June Cecil was sitting at home with Jill listening to a record of Berlioz's *Harold in Italy*. At first he thought his chest discomfort was mere indigestion, something he had learned to live with, but before the symphony was over he had to rush from the room and go where he could be alone with his pain. A coronary thrombosis was diagnosed and next day he was back in the Miller Hospital. A few days later, thanks to the fee received for the cinema version of his *The Beast Must Die*, Cecil achieved his ultimate ambition in car ownership, a new Mercedes Benz. All he could do was to look wistfully at the dark blue vehicle from his hospital window, whenever Jill came to see him.

Despite his disabilities Cecil managed a poem of four six-line stanzas for the investiture of Prince Charles as Prince of Wales on 1 July. 'I won't have anything to do with the bloody *Times*', he told me when we were discussing where the poem might be placed. John Masefield sent his Laureate poems to *The Times* with a stamped addressed envelope, but Cecil blamed this organ for the repeated attacks on him in the *Times Literary Supplement*. He gave the *Daily Telegraph* first refusal as a loyal gesture to me, and a refusal is what he received. I suggested the *Guardian*, which subsequently devoted a large part of its 1 July leader page to the Poet Laureate's offering, printed side by side with a Welsh translation from the Archdruid of Wales, E. Gwyndaf Evans. Whether or not the heir to the throne found time to glance at this, Cecil's effort was not admired by other newspapers, nor by *Guardian* letter-writers.

Cecil had had to cancel all engagements for three months, but was well enough to go to the West of Ireland as usual in August. After returning to London at the beginning of September, he took the rest of the year quietly. But as president of the Greenwich Society he wrote a belligerent letter to *The Times* attacking a Greater London Council plan to build a 'by-pass' through the most characterful part of the borough; and as Poet Laureate he joined his selection committee in choosing Stevie Smith for the 1969 Queen's Gold Medal for Poetry. 'Thank God beastly 1969 is over – the New Year at least cannot be any worse', he wrote to Elaine Hamilton before Christmas. 'My health is still a bit rocky, but I now expect to live until 5 March, when my new book of poems [*The Whispering Roots*] comes out. I've just seen Cape's dust jacket for it, Celtic crosses, a round tower of other days, and a vast expanse of morbid liquid bog, God help us all.'

Soon after the start of 1970 the fates seemed to take Cecil's assertion, that this year could not be worse than the last, as some kind of challenge. He was now stricken with trouble in his bladder and the first signs of incontinence. 'I want to be put down', he told Jill when the misery of his ignominy first dawned. He went to Guy's Hospital on 22 January and was informed that he must have an operation for the removal of bladder stones.

In January he was interviewed by the poet John Horder. The resulting article, in the 18 March edition of *Queen* magazine, could have been more accurate about Cecil's past but was revealing about his present. He hoped first that his Prince Charles poem gave the Queen some pleasure, 'although I don't think that reading poetry in general gives her a very great deal'. He moved on to his thoughts on death. 'It's very odd having returned from the grave for a second time', he said, before going on to refer to his 'All Souls' Night' about to be published in *The Whispering Roots*:

> Existences, consoling lies, or phantom
> Dolls of tradition, enter into me.
> Welcome, invisibles! We have this in common –
> Whatever you are, I presently shall be.

'It is the act of dying rather than death itself I find so simply appalling. For once you have died you are presumably not around any more to tell the story.... I can honestly say I only began really enjoying life at the age of fifty-five. Time has gone by so incredibly fast ever since. Now it's just like water running down the plug hole; after the vortex has formed it's so much faster during that fatal last inch. It really is very sad that it should be like that. But it is.'

Cecil's last book of verse, *The Whispering Roots*, was published by Jonathan Cape at the beginning of March 1970, dedicated 'for Sean and Anna'. He had not told us in advance about the dedication, and had never given me such a pleasant surprise as when he gravely handed me a copy of the book in his study at Greenwich, and then with a conspiratorial grin suggested I should look inside more carefully than usual. Part One includes nineteen evocations of places and people in Ireland, and Part Two consists of fifteen miscellaneous poems on a variety of themes of which death and transience are the most persistent.

P.J. Kavanagh in the *Guardian* used *The Whispering Roots*, and a new paperback edition of *Collected Poems 1954* to look at the 'general opinion' that 'of the MacSpaunday poets ... Day-Lewis has worn least well'. He found that Cecil's work taken as a whole 'gives off the clash and bang of a hectically fought internal battle ... a rip by rip account of one man's tearing'. The reviewer wanted to use his blue pencil in places, specially in those 'last conclusion drawing stanzas ...'

There is nothing conclusive about Mr Day-Lewis as a poet. But it is his struggle to make himself so, marring work which was doing fine until he pulled himself together, this fighting quality is what makes him so alive and, to me, so attractive. It is like having the spiritual insides of a man's life laid out for inspection; the revelation is seldom explicit, is in the manner of the poem rather than its matter, in the shifts, evasions, defeats; one poem rings false, then hard on its heels, one that is nearer the hurting nerve of indecisiveness.

Cecil was admitted to a private room at Nuffield House within Guy's Hospital on 13 March and next day was, in his own words, 'safely delivered of three thumping great stones which have been pestering my bladder'. Visited in hospital he never displayed either his anxieties or his pain. In this case he displayed his bladder-stones, saying that when he also had his gall-stones to play with he would make a necklace from them all and wear it on ceremonial occasions as the Poet Laureate's insignia.

On 2 May Cecil was back at Hull to receive his honorary degree as Doctor of Letters. Three days later he and Jill flew to an unusually wet Tuscany in pursuit of his convalescence. They were again the guests of Kathleen and Johannes Schwarzenberg at the Villa Ugolino near Florence. It was a productive visit. Cecil wrote his memorial poem to his Sherborne friend and rival, and one time brother-in-law, Alec King, who had died of cancer in early March. Two other poems germinated: one reflecting on Masaccio's 'Expulsion of Adam and Eve from the Earthly Paradise' in the Church of Santa Maria del Carmine, and printed in New York as part of a tribute on W.H. Auden's sixty-fifth birthday; the second a rare attempt at light verse following an accident which might have been taken as heavily symbolic.

Kathleen had used Cecil's visit to model his head in clay. She completed her work and left it in her studio ready for casting next day. That night there was a sudden storm in the Tuscan hills and the Schwarzenberg villa was struck by something like a whirlwind. The head was blown to the floor where the impact returned it to its previous existence as a shapeless splodge of clay. The undaunted sculptress began again from the beginning and produced a result better than the first one.

A demon, jealous of the fame
That crowns the hard creative game,
BLEW – and turned back to brutish clay
The breathing replica of Day.
But Day survived and K. contrived
To keep her head and bring Day's head
To life again another day.*

Cecil was feeling reasonably well when the family left for the West of Ireland in early August. Tamasin and Daniel looked forward to these holidays for many reasons, not the least of them being that here Cecil seemed to shed his cares and his years and become the young father they wanted.

In many ways Cecil was the same kind of father to his last two children as he had been to his first two. He was always ready with practical advice; he knew exactly how to mix realism with encouragement; he was an uncomplaining material provider. His way of keeping an area of calm about him meant that his occasional volcanic outbursts of temper were all the more frightening. He normally took teasing and family jokes in his stride, or simply switched off, but a joke against him could touch him on the raw: according to family legend he once brought his fist down on the Greenwich dining-room table with such force that he cracked the table clean across. To a large extent he contrived to stay uninvolved with family trivia, and his Greenwich study was quite as much out of bounds to Tamasin and Daniel during working hours as his Brimclose one was to his first two sons. He kept a distance from all his children and aimed at a relationship of mutual affection and respect rather than relaxed friendship.

There were differences. In his sixties Cecil naturally had less energy for games. He once played tennis with Tamasin when she was thirteen, but that was the last time. The wider demands made on him during the years of his second marriage meant that family expeditions had to be events planned well in advance: there could be no spontaneous, spur-of-the-moment visits to the cinema as there were from Brimclose.

During his first marriage disagreements were largely bottled up; there was an outward tranquillity about domestic life, though the air was sometimes heavy with smoke. In his second family there were furious shouting matches which mostly cleared the air more quickly and his relationship with the children was different. Cecil could look at the Sean and Nicholas of 1950 as immature, insecure, accepting and needing the boundaries and the directives imposed by their seniors. We were, in other words, rather as he had been in 1920. To him the Tamasin and Daniel of 1970 looked to be something more confident. For one thing they were teenagers, a transient but ideal state of being, whereas we suffered from a disease called adolescence. Cecil was accordingly 'troubled and excited' by his younger

* 'Another Day' (*Poems of C. Day Lewis 1925–1972*, 1977).

children and saw them as more honest and open, and rather threatening him with the nebulous satisfactions of the 'unstructured life'. The young 'seem to value a kind of general freedom which to me is difficult to assess because my generation had to have something to be freed from', he said to Hallam Tennyson in their 1972 conversation for Radio 3. 'Just freedom in the abstract, general freedom, means anarchy, which may be an ideal state of things but is not a possible state of things. So my children, to whom I'm devoted and who are totally different characters, have much better manners than we had. They follow their own bent in a more determined way than we did. But I don't think they know where they are going because they've got almost no directives.'

Daniel had become a weekly boarder at Sevenoaks School, an establishment which used some progressive teaching methods, but was much like Sherborne or any other traditional public school in its non-academic mores. He was miserable there; and when he ran away it was not to Greenwich but to Bedales, proclaimed by Tamasin to be a paradise of freedom and care, sweetness and enlightenment. Cecil was at his best in such crises. He did not become over-excited, but patiently and quietly attempted to discover what was wrong and what was needed to put things right. In this case it was discovered that Tamasin's scholarship allowance would be increased if Daniel also went to Bedales, and a place was found for him.

Tamasin was something special for Cecil – a daughter. This did not necessarily make things easier for her. She remembers that through her teenage years her relationship with her mother became more tense, and when Cecil was brought in to adjudicate on their differences he thought it right to support Jill, though he would sometimes gives Tamasin some sign of 'peculiar understanding'. He came to think of her, as he told a student interviewer, Mark Featherstone-Witty, in late 1971, as 'a sweet girl and a tremendous tough'.

'I think he really got bored with being a father quite early in our lives,' Tamasin said. 'I realized that I would never get close to him unless I won his respect, and that I had to win his respect through my work. He was very good when we went through my English work and explained things elegantly and simply. He very rarely praised, but he was complimentary about an essay I wrote on T.S. Eliot. It was only his last two years that I began to win his respect. And there were other difficulties, of course.'

She remembers a bad scene at Old Head in that summer of 1970. Not yet eighteen, she developed a relationship with a Dublin boy and took to disappearing at nights. Cecil became anxious about this and one day summoned her to the sitting-room and asked for an explanation. 'I don't want my daughter to be a whore or a tart,' he said. Tamasin, who already knew a little of Cecil's sexual history, considered he was insisting on a double standard and those words of his have always remained with her. For his part Cecil had the normal protective instincts of fathers for their daughters, and was selective on her behalf.

The family returned to London in September and on the twenty-fifth Cecil attended a memorial service for V.C. Clinton-Baddeley, the one-time Sherborne prefect for whom he had fagged and written his romantic poem of the early 1920s, 'Once in Arcady'. Basil Wright, one of Cecil's fags at Sherborne, was also at this service. 'It is sad that at this stage in our lives we only met at the funerals of our friends. We had not seen each other since we both went to Dorset for the funeral of Wilfrid Cowley, "the Baron" of Oxford days. Cecil didn't appear too bad then, but he didn't look at all well at Clinton's funeral. And that was the last time I ever saw him.'

On 7 November Cecil and Jill set out on what was to be the last of their many Dorset weekends together, staying with the Reynolds Stones. The journey itself was frightening, with Cecil insisting on driving his Mercedes but lacking his formerly secure skill in judging distances. At the Old Rectory, Litton Cheney, they were both chiefly concerned with trying to hide the current issue of the *Times Literary Supplement* from each other.

Eight months had passed since the publication of *The Whispering Roots* and the paperback edition of *Collected Poems 1954*, and all this time the *TLS* had ignored both books. On 6 November they were used, with Cecil's Exeter lecture 'On Translating Poetry', as 'a base of operations' for a full page retrospective review. The article was written under the rule of anonymity maintained by the *TLS* editor, Arthur Crook, though Cecil did not need to make many inquiries before discovering that the author of it was the man who had been his chief scourge since the 1930s, Geoffrey Grigson.

Seven years later, when writing for the *TLS* about Ian Parsons's selection of Cecil's poems, under the very different editorial regime of John Gross, Samuel Hynes began with an apology for the Grigson article, in which 'the reviewer had taken the occasion to launch a general assault against his subject, in terms that seemed to me crude and vicious. The poet, he said, was all masks and no reality; his poems were mere acts of the will; they were frigid, wordy, and vulgar, and somehow threatened the good health of literature. There were, apparently, no exceptions, not one good word to be said about even a single poem. It was not so much a review, I thought, as a literary mugging.' This was not an exaggerated account of what Grigson wrote.

At the time the review seemed to Cecil's friends to be cruel as well as unjustified; he no longer enjoyed the maybe exaggerated reputation he had been given in the 1930s. He was a sick man, perhaps a dying man, now full of doubts about the value of his work. In its next two issues the *TLS* printed only two of the protesting letters it received from Cecil's friends, one from Professor Andrew Wright of La Jolla University in California, the other from Hallam Tennyson asking how the reviewer could imagine 'that the careful selection of a few weak lines from the less important poems constituted an act of serious criticism?' His Greenwich neighbour John Grigg also wrote in Cecil's defence: Crook the editor replied that he would not publish the letter unless an allegation of malice by the *TLS* was withdrawn, but Grigg declined to modify what he had written.

Cecil had his defence mechanism against bad reviews, consisting of either not reading them or pretending that he did not read them. In this case it took him and Jill a while to discover that they had both read the article and were trying to protect one another from it. A characteristic Cecil smokescreen was that raised for his old friend of Cheltenham days Frank Halliday: 'I never see the *TLS*, nor do I get press cuttings: but one or two friends have told me that, on internal evidence, the writer of that piece must have been no less a person than my old *bête noire* and persecutor, Geoffrey Grigson! Poor old sod. I blame the editor chiefly. He has censored, or refused to print, several other letters. About time he censored his reviewers for a change.'

The article, following unusually hostile reviews of his two previous books of verse and of his work as chairman of the Arts Council Literature Panel, plus a succinct sneer on his appointment as Poet Laureate, convinced Cecil that the editor, Crook, must have some kind of grievance against him. Crook emphatically assured me that this was not so, and that there was never any kind of campaign against Cecil.

And what motivated Geoffrey Grigson, a man of letters held in much respect and affection, to spend so much space and energy attacking a poet who, by his own arguments, did not merit a fraction of such attention? In 1975 I went to see him in the comfortable Wiltshire farmhouse where he maintained such a formidable literary output, looking to solve the mystery. Far from being dyspeptic he appeared to be enjoying marriage to one of the best cooks in England, his wife Jane, and he showed no discernible sign of malice or defensiveness or even personal involvement.

The two men had met in a bodily sense only once, when Grigson was a BBC producer in the 1940s, working on a radio programme about Crabbe, and Cecil was his reader. 'He was a marvellous reader and the best dressed English poet, we got on amiably', Grigson recalled. 'I remember he was moved by an extract new to him – from one of Crabbe's later stories – about autumn and shooting and how the distant gun's report proclaimed to man that death was but his sport.'

He said that in the 1930s 'few poets, or few of the ones I knew, thought well of Day-Lewis's poems. I remember talking about them with that man of fierce integrity, Norman Cameron. We found them thin, and considered they were politically or sub-politically modish. We felt a contradiction between his politics and his practice – and some of his actions, such as becoming a selector for the Book Society, then very much a symbol of bourgeois self-satisfaction and indifference to the Real Thing. It seemed odd that someone of our age, who was politically further to the Left than most of us, should be poetically so far to the Right and the ordinary, and so acceptable to critics and poet-proclaimers we despised, such as Richard Church or T.E. Lawrence or G.M. Young....'

He felt that Cecil had in some way deviated from and betrayed modernism on behalf of 'the drab English centre'. He also believed, according to an interview given to Hugh Hebert of the *Guardian* in 1974, that 'praise for the undeserving is a robbery of the deserving' and that the use of the critical bill-hook in 'an effort to clear the way, to make room for better things' is 'I suppose the only justification for savagery and satire'. How did he now see his savagery against Cecil? 'Perhaps I did ride that hobby horse a little too hard.'

Judging by his letter to Elaine Hamilton on 27 November, Cecil had relegated the *TLS* to the back of his mind again by the end of that month:

I have been to Doncaster reading poetry, to Lancaster ditto; judging an *Observer* young people's poetry competition; and dealing with my car, which had a bad bash a fortnight ago, though nobody was hurt.... I have at last penetrated the Penetralia of the Establishment, having been elected to a club called The Club, which was founded by Dr Johnson and whose members seem to be all ex-Premiers, Lord Chamberlains, Foreign Secretaries, and that kind of riff-raff, and a few friends of mine, like K. Clark. No club rooms. Just an expensive restaurant dinner once a month. Puffed up by this I've resigned from the Athenaeum. You can get an idea of the rarefied, though smokey, air of The Club when I tell you that Mountbatten's name was howled down when somebody proposed him as a member. I'm so glad *The Whispering Roots* have found their way at last to your far-flung country. They and the *Collected Poems* have caused an obscene notice in the *TLS*, having been sent to G. Grigson, an old enemy, for review, and pulverised by him. We had a splendid month in Ireland, and I did quite a lot of bathing in the icy Atlantic and ate quantities of soda bread. Nothing much laid on for the future, except a visit to Rome to attend the Keats 150th year celebrations.

1971 began with a second severe bump to the ill-fated Mercedes, this one caused through the iced-up brakes of an oncoming car failing to work on a remote Sussex lane. Driver and passengers were shaken but unhurt.

One who met Cecil at his Chatto office that month was Robert Greacen, a fellow committee member of the Author's World Peace Appeal in the early 1950s.

I had written to Cecil in December, telling him that our mutual friend Clifford Dyment was seriously ill with cancer of the liver and in need of financial assistance. We had a chat and I was of course unaware of the nature and seriousness of his own illness. He talked gaily about his hospital experiences and joked about the dreadfulness of the 'instant potato' they always wanted him to eat there. He added that he was now only allowed expensive drinks like champagne. I thought he had many years in front of him. His sympathy for Clifford Dyment's plight was apparent and he got in touch straight away with Victor Bonham-Carter of the Royal Literary Fund.

Cecil and Jill left for the last of their Italian visits on 21 February. In Rome they were the guests of the British Ambassador, Sir Patrick Hancock, and Cecil led the Protestant cemetery ceremony marking the 150th anniversary of the death of Keats. He was supported by some 120 others – British, American and Italian. According to the Associated Press news agency 'the mood was mournful, as if Keats had died a year ago.... Mr Day-Lewis stepped up to the clover-strewn grave with a wreath of laurel leaves in his hand and said: "Keats came here to Rome in a last desperate attempt to throw off the disease that was killing him. He died in despair and felt he was a failure. Today, we see him in a very different light as one of the greatest Romantic poets. His name will be in the hearts of every man and woman who loves Romantic poetry."'

In late March Cecil was attacked by jaundice, and was admitted to Guy's Hospital on 5 April for an exploratory operation. The surgeons found an inoperable cancer on his pancreas. Jill was told the worst news she had ever received and was advised that Cecil should not be told the truth about his condition; he had 'a possible year' to live but should be able to go on living in hope. She agreed to this and Cecil was able to write to his friends that they had 'scythed off' his gall bladder. Jill shared the truth with one or two of her closest friends, and with me, and decided that she must keep it from Tamasin and Daniel for as long as possible.

Cecil was allowed home in the middle of the month and had his sixty-seventh birthday there on the 27 April. Two days later he had become badly dehydrated and was told by his Greenwich doctor that his pancreas had 'gone crazy', and that he must return to Guy's for further treatment. Diabetes was diagnosed and he was told that he would have to spend the rest of his life on a diet. His main dread at this point was that he would also have to spend the rest of his life injecting himself with insulin. 'I've just changed over from insulin injections to insulin pills, to see if the latter work as well as the former', he wrote to my wife Anna on 4 May. 'If they don't, I shall be condemned to a life of kicking against the pricks.'

For a moment during that last visit to hospital Cecil must have felt like the drowning man who is supposed to see his past life flashing before his eyes. He received a message that one Billie Currall had telephoned and left her number. Despite *The Private Wound* he had had no contact with her for well over twenty years, and he felt that she would not have called unless something had gone seriously wrong for her. He struggled to the public telephone and called her back, only to discover that he had been given a wrong number. He did not know that somebody in Musbury had told her that he was seriously ill.

Cecil was driven back to Greenwich on 9 May, convinced that there would be a gradual improvement in his condition. A letter from Billie Currall awaited him, enclosing a portrait drawing of him she had done. He replied on 16 May saying that the portrait was 'great fun – a mixture of Angus Wilson, Harold Wilson and myself'. He enclosed a reciprocal present: 'I send my last mystery – familiar happenings shifted to the West of Ireland. . . . I have been in hospital far too much the last five years – high blood pressure, a coronary, two operations, glandular fever. Hope the last bout, which has left me with diabetes, is the last for a bit. . . . I remember the bluebells so well.'

Over the rest of the year he wrote eight letters to Billie.

I remember so much about 'the happy, carefree days', but they weren't that *all* the time. . . . I had forgotten about the topaz ring – I'm glad I gave you something more romantic than the pram. I have lived such a rackety life since then – God knows how they came to make me Poet Laureate. Now at last I seem to be settling down into dull old age: not that I don't enjoy uneventfulness – it makes a change, anyway. . . . When you are in London you must have lunch with me. June or July. Pick me up at Chatto's. You're very welcome to stay the night at Greenwich – Jill, my wife, would like to meet you, but you may not be able to or want to. . . . I loved your last letter, not least the four proposals of marriage! – you must have worn a good deal better than I have. . . . John Garrett retired from Bristol Grammar School, went to live in Wimbledon, and died about a year ago – he was an amiable old queer, but had a stroke and didn't enjoy his last years. Yes, I remember now it was he who dried you on his shirt – unorthodox for a headmaster.

In June, Cecil was back in circulation. My wife Anna and I, and Cecil's grandchildren Keelin and Finian, made a river trip that month to Greenwich from our home in Hammersmith. Cecil was in surprisingly good form, making what fun he could from the powder he was obliged to put on his food, and the extraordinary collection of pills that was supposed to keep his many ailments in check. We all went out into Greenwich Park; Cecil pushed his grandchildren on the swings, still showing that elegant style in movement that had always been one of his hallmarks, and we returned home with a camera full of pictures.

On the third he was at the Royal Society of Literature to take the chair for Professor Andrew Wright, his host at the Californian university of La Jolla in 1965 and his defender in the columns of the *Times Literary Supplement* the previous year. On the twenty-fourth he and Jill were again at the RSL, this time giving a recital of Keats, mixed with some poems from Shelley, Hardy and Day-Lewis. Cecil's reading seemed to me to be a triumph over adversity, the slurrings of speech caused by his permanently parched mouth almost imperceptible. At the end the woman sitting next to me, who knew nothing of his illness or of my connection with him, complained that a young voice was needed for Keats's poetry.

On 28 June Cecil and Jill went to the dinner at 10 Downing Street

given by Edward Heath for the Italian Prime Minister, Signor Emilio
Colombo. Cecil was allowed to sit for the reception and could not enjoy
the excellent food and wine as he would once have done, but he liked being
part of the Establishment. On 4 July his Oxford tutor and friend of so many
years, Sir Maurice Bowra, died. Four days later Cecil went to Oxford for
the funeral. It was a hot day, with a temperature of 90 degrees, but he followed the coffin to the graveside. Afterwards he looked so ill that Colette
Clark, daughter of Sir Kenneth, suggested to Stuart Hampshire, new Wadham warden, that he should be given a lift to the station. Cecil was consequently conveyed to his train in the hearse, a vehicle about which he joked
bravely.

On 18 July Cecil and Jill gave what was destined to be the last of the
hundreds of public recitals which they had offered together over twenty-
one years. It was organized by Douglas Cleverdon at the Shakespeare Institute as part of his eighteenth Stratford-on-Avon Poetry Festival. It included a wide selection from Cecil's more recent work: 'The Disabused',
requiring much power from the reader; 'Elegy for a Woman Unknown',
'A Picture by Renoir', four of the Irish poems from *The Whispering Roots*,
and 'The Expulsion', still unpublished.

With his family, Cecil embarked on his final visit to his native land on
Saturday 7 August. They took the Mercedes and crossed the Irish Sea by
way of Holyhead and Dun Laoghaire. The Old Head Hotel was once more
safely reached. Cecil enjoyed the place as he always had done, though his
walks were much restricted and his swimming and diving days were over.
His worst moment was when he was sitting in the front of his stationary
and safely parked car, and it was run into by an ill-controlled horse
and cart. The beautiful but accident-prone Mercedes had to be taken into
Castlebar for a new windscreen and other repairs.

From Old Head, Cecil wrote to Billie Currall.

I hope my lunch invitation has not gone astray, and that I didn't annoy you by
my crazy suggestion that you might care to stay in Greenwich. At any rate do
come to London – I don't know how long I have to live and it would be nice
to see you before I am trundled off to the tomb.... We'll go to a nice, dark
restaurant near Chatto and Windus, where nobody will notice a 'fat old woman'
or a man who resembles a human skeleton.

The journey back to England began on 30 August, Jill driving through
Enniscorthy, Co Wexford, a farewell to the 'land of milk and honey' of
Cecil's blissful childhood summers, before catching the boat at Rosslare.

In London, Cecil continued to go to his office every other week, showing
the determination of a man who still hoped that if he behaved as though
nothing was wrong his ills might tire of the struggle against him and go
away. Writing to Charles Causley about the 1971 meeting of the Queen's
Gold Medal committee, he did not even mention his health.

On 26 October he dined with The Club and next evening Jill drove him in her new Renault to give a recital at Stoke Poges in Buckinghamshire, the scene of Thomas Gray's 'Elegy Written in a Country Church-Yard'. It was a bad night. The side effects of his medicines and diseases were making it more difficult for him to control either his temper or his bowels, though he still contrived to keep such problems from everybody but Jill.

On the thirty-first Stephen and Natasha Spender brought W.H. Auden to lunch at 6 Crooms Hill. Cecil noted that Wystan now had a very limited stock of jokes and conversational gambits, which he repeated over and over again, though the pedagogic finger was jabbed as vigorously as ever. Wystan guessed at a first glance that Cecil had cancer and that this would probably be the last time he would ever see his old friend and colleague. Three days later Cecil, feeling 'limp to the last degree', was interviewed at his Chatto office for a Durham University paper by Mark Featherstone-Witty. With pleased affection in his voice Cecil bracketed himself and Auden as 'old fogeys'.

On 4 November the Queen's Gold Medal committee met as planned at L'Epicure and afterwards in the Chatto boardroom. Cecil had some difficulty in gaining the prize for Stephen Spender, but after a rearguard action by Philip Larkin it was eventually decided to go ahead with the Spender recommendation, on the strength of his latest book *The Generous Days* 'and, to a considerable extent, in recognition of his past work'.

On the twentieth he and Jill drove to Sussex. They started with the Balcons at Upper Parrock, for after years of tension Cecil and Jill's father could talk very amicably together; and they went on to stay with Ian and Trekkie Parsons at Juggs Corner near Lewes, where William Plomer was another guest. Cecil felt very ill during the car journey back to Greenwich, and it became clear that this kind of expedition was not worth the suffering involved. Though he was well enough to dine again with The Club on the thirtieth.

Also that month he managed the promised lunch-time reunion with Billie Currall. 'Alas, the film project is *off* so I'm getting nothing at all from *The Private Wound*', he wrote to her afterwards. 'But I'd like to give you this paltry cheque (£25) to help with your holiday or your winter coat or whatever you like to put it to. It was nice seeing you, looking so well and cheerful and blooming – it quite bucked me up.'

The news that Cecil had cancer now spread, and some generous gestures resulted. The poet Paul Dehn, who himself died of cancer five years later, but who was then being well-rewarded as a cinema screenplay writer, sent a cheque for £200 as 'an act of homage'. With Jim Rose, then running the Westminster Press, Elizabeth Jane Howard organized a fund to which Cecil's friends contributed £1,200 to give him extra comforts during his last months. Kenneth Clark brought a first edition of Coleridge, pretending that he was having to dispose of his library at Saltwood Castle before moving into the lodge.

His children also did him well that December. Tamasin was offered a place at King's College, Cambridge, one of the first group of girl under-graduates to invade that institution. Daniel, already showing signs of having inherited the acting talent of his parents, was an excellent Florizel in the Bedales production of Shakespeare's *The Winter Tale*. Cecil, who had taken the same part in that Sherborne production forty-eight years before when he fell in love with his Perdita, watched with approval. On the night of the performance he was black and blue with bruises sustained when he had lost his footing and fallen down some stairs.

It was surprising that he did not have more such falls, for he had become a six-foot-tall bundle of skin and bones, and it was will-power that kept him going about his business as 1971 turned to 1972. I remember giving him lunch, for a change, at a restaurant in St Martin's Lane, near his office, just before Christmas. It was an expensive establishment but, as always at that season, uncomfortably full. Cecil's chair, wherever he moved it, had a fatal attraction for the distracted waiters and he was repeatedly bumped. He remained patient and uncomplaining, relishing his mineral water as though it was best claret. He was decidedly pleased at the news that his second son Nicholas had found the courage to break free from the unsatis-factory marriage that he had begun with such ceremony at the nearby St Martin-in-the-Field church fourteen years before. Cecil and I parted in the street outside. I looked back and saw him striding across the road wearing his dashing, wide-brimmed hat. It was not the gait of an old man, much less a sick one; it seemed impossible that he would soon be snatched away, and all his panache and presence with him.

On 14 January 1972, he was writing to Mollie Patterson, the secretary of the Royal Society of Literature, about the candidates then being pro-posed for the honour of Companion of Literature.

I've tried to ring you twice but you're evidently enjoying a well-earned holiday. I hope to attend on January 24, and will propose Angus [Wilson] – as a *quid pro quo* for supporting Leslie [Hartley], whom I don't really think up to it. David Cecil certainly. My health being so up and down, if I'm baulked at the last moment I'll ring you, so can you take this scrawl as assenting to all those parties.

In the event Cecil did get to the RSL Council meeting on the twenty-fourth, proposing Angus Wilson for a Companionship of Literature after Lord Birkenhead put up Lord David Cecil and Robert Speaight spoke for L.P. Hartley. Cecil was clearly very ill and had to be placed at a corner of the table next to the electric fire so that he could keep warm. That he attended at all was proof of his extreme devotion to the Society of which he had been a Fellow for nearly thirty years.

Cecil had recorded a twenty-five-minute broadcast of his own poetry transmitted by Radio 3 on New Year's Day. This heralded a three-month period during which he did as much broadcasting as at any time of his life.

By far his biggest undertaking was a series of six poetry programmes for BBC Television, transmitted after his death as *A Lasting Joy*. This had been instigated by Norman Swallow, a Greenwich friend and neighbour, then head of arts features. The majority channel had never been used for the uncompromising dissemination of poetry. 'We three had had many animated, but often inconclusive discussions as to *how* one could present poetry on television, and even if one could do so at all', Jill wrote in her foreword to the Allen and Unwin anthology made from the series. Cecil was nevertheless drawn to the idea of 'using the latest means of communication to put over the oldest of the arts' and eventually Swallow, knowing that Cecil was very ill but not knowing he was dying of cancer, had taken the 'enormous risk' of commissioning the series.

But it was obvious that Cecil was no longer well enough to be transported to the BBC Television Centre in West London. Swallow decided that the filming must somehow be managed at 6 Crooms Hill and it was explained to Cecil that there had been an artistic decision that his home atmosphere would provide a necessary intimacy not possible with a studio set. The first-floor sitting-room, so lovingly described in Nicholas Blake's *The Worm of Death* (1961), was chosen for the shooting. A second difficulty, that could not have been foreseen, was that recording coincided with a miners' strike, a fuel emergency and power cuts. The BBC had to provide a generator. Recording began on 16 January with Swallow himself as director. Cecil managed his introductions and his readings, but was so exhausted when the first programme was completed that morning that he had to go and lie down. The same afternoon he got up and recorded the final programme of the sequence, this time with Sir John Gielgud joining him and Jill as readers, finding some reserve of strength that was not really there. He clearly spoke from the heart in introducing Gielgud's reading of Dylan Thomas's 'Do not go gentle into that good night'.

The other four programmes were recorded at irregular intervals during the next month, Cecil and Jill doing all the reading, except on 10 February when the actor Marius Goring joined them in 'Satire and Hatred'. Cecil more and more frequently collapsed with exhaustion between filming sessions but his determination, and the technical skill and patience of the film crew ensured that the series was satisfactorily completed. As Jill put it, 'a painful situation' was transformed into 'an exciting new adventure'.

On 26 January he and Jill gave a dinner party at 6 Crooms Hill, for Paul Dehn and his friend the composer James Bernard, and for Lennox and Freda Berkeley. Cecil was given much pleasure by the music made that night, as he was two nights later at the Royal Festival Hall, where Sir Arthur Bliss had arranged that he should have the Royal Box, and the use of a lift to get there. Appropriately the second half of the London Symphony Orchestra programme consisted of Fauré's *Requiem*, the reassuring work played at his memorial service later in the year.

By 28 February he should by all the rules of nature have become permanently bed-ridden. He was so thin that nothing could keep him warm and his feet had become so painful that walking was a misery. Yet on that day he returned to his Chatto office and went on afterwards to the House of Lords for a dinner of the Byron Society. Presided over by Lord Boothby, this marked the 160th anniversary of Byron's maiden speech to the House: Cecil read extracts from the speech. Doris Langley Moore, one of those present that evening, afterwards wrote to the *Daily Telegraph* about Cecil's last public appearance.

The Poet Laureate, though even then very ill, read the famous oration – against the imposition of the death penalty on the Nottingham Luddites – and it was a magnificent performance. His fine and fiery voice will never be forgotten by anyone who was present. I for one had never fully appreciated the courage and just indignation which had inspired a poet of 24 until I heard his words read by a frail and mortally sick man of 67.

The physical effort was too much and by the time he got home he was in a state bordering complete collapse and had to rest in bed for a day or two. On 7 March he was one of twenty-three members of the British arts Establishment who signed a letter to *The Times* calling for the end of detention without trial in Northern Ireland; but there were to be no more attempts at public appearances.

His second son Nicholas came from South Africa to see him in March, something of a stranger from another world. 'On my last visit to England I think we had completely lost touch', Nick recalled. 'He listened to me politely, but I don't think I got through to him at all. And when I finally left, I said goodbye to him in his chair. He had visitors (Ian and Trekkie Parsons) and was already talking to them again, without a glance in my dirction, before I reached the door of his study.'

I had come to collect Nick and drive him to London Airport. I witnessed this scene and hoped very much he had not noticed Cecil's apparent indifference. It was doubtless part of Cecil's scheme for conserving his energy and avoiding distressing scenes, for not wasting what little time he had on futile regrets. His special friends, among whom Ian and Trekkie Parsons were numbered, had now become all-important to him. He would light up with their presence and, more or less, collapse exhausted on their departure.

Another visitor that month, working on an interview for *Vogue*, was Elizabeth Jane Howard, now Mrs Kingsley Amis. The published part of their conversation began with Cecil's realistic view of the Laureateship and proceeded by way of his poetic daemon to his Oxford time, his debonair turn-out, his residual optimism and his mature belief in an economic use of indignation. The interview ended with Cecil's reflection that in life it is unwise to have too many principles, because they are so expensive and energy-demanding. 'Yes and so with people. One *conserves* one's love for them; one knows who one loves, and just as one doesn't waste one's dwindling capacity for indignation, so one doesn't waste one's rather dwindling capacity for affection and for love: one keeps it for people one knows one has it for, and those are my very last words to you.'

This was a harrowing visit for Jane. She could feel the almost unbearable atmosphere of jagged tension which then permeated what had become a rather dark house. The strain on Jill would have been huge even if she had been a physically powerful trained nurse, without emotional involvement. As it was, she had to watch the person she loved more than all the world decline day by day; she had to maintain the pretence of a better future, and she had to cope with the physical business of dealing with a patient who could do less and less for himself. Jill had not slept a whole night through for months. At times they both became exasperated, as much as anything with their own lack of physical strength. When Tamasin or Daniel were about life for them was bleak in the extreme. I can remember leaving the house at this time with the feeling of having been caught in a vice, so powerfully did the troubled atmosphere press down on the visitor. Thanks to good fortune and her own generosity Jane was able to help.

Jill had landed a part in an Associated Television drama series, *The Strauss Family*, which meant a week of recording at Elstree studio in Hertfordshire. Jane and Kingsley Amis were living in a large eighteenth-century house at nearby Hadley Common and could provide both a ground-floor room, and the nurse presently looking after Jane's invalid mother. Cecil, who dreaded the idea of going into hospital while Jill was filming, happily agreed to the idea of a week's 'holiday' in the Amis establishment.

At Greenwich Cecil received a letter of whole-hearted conciliation from Rosamond Lehmann, who had heard of his illness and 'how courageously you are fighting to recover'. She was nearly sure that 'Sally and I and the appalling tragedy that overtook us' must 'sometimes be in your thoughts', and she wondered if he would like to see her. He somehow managed to avoid betraying any realization that a letter such as this must signal the approaching end, and replied that he would very much like to see her again when he was at less of a 'low ebb'. He added, 'Sally's death was terrible to me', and that he was glad to have had a final friendly conversation with her.

Other friends continued to call. There was a visit from William Plomer, who called on 4 April and three days later wrote to Rupert Hart-Davis: 'I saw poor Cecil on Tuesday, quite enfeebled, quite clear in the head, *modestly* courageous.'

On Thursday 6 April, a sunny day, Cecil was helped out of his Crooms Hill home and was driven by Jill, with Tamasin and Daniel, to Lemmons, the Amis home above High Barnet on the northern outskirts of London.

All his life the 'rootless man' in Cecil had loved changes of scene, had felt renewed by a change of house as by a change of love. Now the magic worked once more.

Cecil at once 'professed himself delighted with the whole set-up', as Jane has written.[4] His room had a bathroom and a sheltered courtyard attached, at the east end of the elegant house. Kingsley Amis and Cecil were not political allies but found they had more in common than they suspected, and became increasingly attached to one another. Each morning Kingsley would ask for Cecil's recorded music order. He would choose some 'grand' Handel or some 'soppy' Chopin, and he fell in with the preposterous and self-denying Amis dictum that the main achievement of J.S. Bach was in fathering C.P.E. Bach. He took enormous pleasure in the simplest things: a bunch of flowers, a toasted bun, a new thriller, ice cream, the bird-table outside his window, sweet-smelling soap. One day he was able to sit in the court-yard and look at the trees as they began to leaf and flower, and once he went for a ride round the extensive garden in the electric chair belonging to Jane's mother, responding with enthusiasm to both the vehicle and the place.

After a week Jane asked Cecil if he would like to stay until he felt 'really better'.[5] 'I would like to stay for months, and I am very anxious to give Jill a proper rest,' he replied. Jill gratefully agreed that they should stay for as many weeks as there were, and, on Cecil's orders, went out to buy him a notebook so that he could thank the household with a poem. After two days he reported, 'It is very difficult to work on a quarter of a cylinder.' Ten days later his last poem, 'At Lemmons', was completed.

> Round me all is amenity, a bloom of
> Magnolia uttering its requiems,
> A climate of acceptance. Very well
> I accept my weakness with my friends'
> Good natures sweetening every day my sick room.

At this time he was also signing copies of his new birthday hymn for Shakespeare; and writing the occasional postcard, one of them to the anthologist James Gibson, commending him on his work with *Let the Poet Choose* (Harrap, 1973), in which each of the forty-four contributing poets was allowed to choose two of his own poems. 'May I suggest as my two poems the last sonnet of "O Dreams, O Destinations" (*Word Over All*, 1943) and "On Not Saying Everything" (*The Room*, 1965)', Cecil had written to him. 'The sonnet because, though I wrote it 30 years ago, it still stands up and says something I feel to be truthful about the human condition: "On Not Saying Everything" because I believe so strongly in the doctrine of limitations it speaks for – that everything, a tree, a poem, a human relationship lives and thrives by the limits imposed on it.'

A steady stream of visitors made the journey to Hadley Common: Norah

Smallwood, his Chatto friend and colleague for so many years; writers such as Philip Larkin and V.S. Pritchett; Peggy Ashcroft, the great actress with whom he had performed in so many recitals; the lawyer Jeremy Hutchinson ('very funny without being too noisy') and the academic Noel Annan; and others with less resounding names though equally dear to Cecil. Each was warmly greeted and gave him a little new lease of life, before their departure and the resulting exhaustion.

Three birthdays were celebrated at his bedside that April: Kingsley Amis's fiftieth on the 16th, Daniel's fifteenth on the 29th, and, in between, his own sixty-eighth on the 27th – this last also being the twenty-first anniversary of his marriage to Jill. He took pleasure in all these, particularly his own. His bed was piled with presents and he opened each with apparent excitement, either gallantly feigned or simply true. He was dressed up for the occasion and as carefully shaved as ever, though one side of his face was still badly bruised from striking it against the side of the bath in one of his falls.

Kingsley Amis took to having an evening drink in the sick-room, though he had to be warned against making Cecil laugh too much. Cecil's 'air of always being delighted to see you, and his cheerfulness, which could take a wry and sardonic turn' still made it 'refreshing to be with him', Amis wrote afterwards.[6]

He gave us all, those in the household and the many friends who came to see him, an unforgettable object lesson on how to die. Nobody can say with certainty whether, or how far, he understood what was in store for him ... at no time did he mention his death. My own strong feeling is that he came to draw his own conclusions from his physical decline and increasingly severe – although happily intermittent – bouts of pain, but, out of kindness and abnegation of self, chose not to discuss the matter.

My feeling is roughly the same. Maybe he felt that to discuss the matter with Jill would be altogether too painful for them both, and if he could not discuss it with her it would be wrong to do so with anybody else.

Jill telephoned me on 18 May saying that Cecil was suddenly much weaker, and that Tessa the nurse had suggested it was time to start thinking about funeral arrangements. Two days later he received a visit from his agent and working partner A.D. Peters who, himself on the verge of eighty and with less than a year to live, arrived soaked in the middle of a thunderstorm. I went out to Lemmons on Sunday 21 May. I kept a diary of those oppressive last days.

'Jill meets me in the Renault at High Barnet station. She is outwardly in control, seems really courageous, expresses worry that I will be distressed by Cecil's appearance. She says he has not been able to shave himself for two days. On Thursday he enjoyed her reading from *The Mill on the Floss*, but on Friday did not take in much when Jane read from *Pride and Prejudice*.

He is off music now. He is more or less comatose when I enter the familiar room. Ursula Vaughan Williams is here helping as Tessa has a weekend off. I am asked to help in turning him and for some reason hold my breath as if to detach myself from those skeletal legs and hips which cannot be part of Cecil. After the turning he laces his fingers together and places them on his chest as if he has arranged himself to die like an effigy on a tomb.

'I am left alone in the room with him. He murmurs to himself, "This is all right for two or three days, but how long oh Lord, how long...." This might mean that he still hopes to get better, or that he wants to die quickly.... After lunch I ask about V.S. Pritchett's *Midnight Oil*, though I think this is only beside the bedside because Ursula Vaughan Williams is reading it to herself. He starts talking of Pritchett's "remarkable achievement, nothing else quite like it". He says he is keen to show me "the moon of my delight', a round balsa and paper lampshade hanging from the ceiling. "It is like a moon ...", he says, but is unable to continue with the thought. He tries again, "It is like ..." "A moon," I suggest. "It is certainly like a moon," he says with a smile, his lips quivering as if some joke were close. He reminds me at this point of his own portrait of his uncle, the Rev Willie Squires, and Knos. He drifts into sleep and then apologizes, "You come to see me and I go to sleep, it is most indecent."

'He constantly becomes uncomfortable because there is nothing between his bones and his bed, but once he is moved he says, "I'm in heaven." I am left alone with him to make my farewell. He says, "Thank you very much for giving me such a lovely afternoon, I have enjoyed it so much." I think this is the formula for departing visitors, his instinctive courtesy. I say, "See you soon," as always, but he does not repeat this as usual. I feel that we should have said profound things to one another.

'At the station Jill says she cannot bear the idea of cremation and favours the words of the Church of England burial service. We talk about possible burial places. She thinks Dorset and I suggest Stinsford and as I say it we both know that is right ...'

After I left, Jane had settled down to read to herself in Cecil's room. Suddenly he said, 'When are you going to begin?' She reads him a chapter of *Pride and Prejudice* and thought he had gone to sleep. 'Read me one more chapter,' he asked. When she had done this he said 'marvellous stuff' and drifted away again. Later Tamasin went to his room to say goodnight. Cecil looked at her and said 'goodbye'. Soon after this he went into a spasm of pain and Tessa, recalled from her weekend off, summoned the doctor who administered a strong injection. Jill, who had been telephoning for Daniel to catch the first train from Bedales next day, only just caught Cecil's last words. 'It's Jill,' said Jane. 'I know,' said Cecil.

Cecil never recovered consciousness but slept peacefully on through the night, Jill constantly at his side and letting others take it in turns to hold his hand. Tamasin called me at 7 on Monday morning and said I should come back to Lemmons at once. I was there by 8.30 and found Cecil's bed surrounded by women in dressing-gowns, a sort of Greek chorus of devotion. Jill was so tired she could scarcely stand, but she announced to Cecil, 'Sean is here.' By intention or coincidence he responded to this with a kind of conversational groan.

There was much anxiety about whether Daniel would arrive in time. He came at 10; he went into the sick-room with Jill, and they watched as Cecil peacefully expired. There was no movement of his eyelids now and all colour had gone. His face had a look of stretch as though, at the last, death the destroyer had to tug the life out of him. There was an immediate exodus from the small room as Dan and the women in their dressing-gowns dispersed to different parts of the house to mourn in their own way. Something compelled me to kiss Cecil's forehead in a priestly gesture before following the others.

Monday 22 May 1972. . . . President Nixon of the United States was in Moscow and spent 105 minutes with the Soviet leader, Mr Brezhnev. The forces of North Vietnam launched an offensive on three fronts as part of their drive southwards. Ceylon became the independent republic of Sri Lanka. In Derry there was fighting between official and Provisional members of the Irish Republican Army. In Dublin the Irish Prime Minister, Mr Jack Lynch, promised to 'crack down on terrorists'. Princess Anne had laryngitis on board the Royal yacht *Britannia* visiting the Channel Islands. In Rome a Hungarian-born Australian was accused of smashing Michelangelo's Pietà in St Peter's. There was an even first day between the MCC and the Australians at Lords. The actress Dame Margaret Rutherford died aged eighty.

Obituary tributes for Cecil by newspaper, television and radio were not lost among these other happenings. Stephen Spender was one of those who spoke on the radio, describing Cecil as 'a fine lyric poet, old-fashioned by today's standards' but to be mentioned in the same breath, on this evening anyway, as Edward Thomas and Wilfred Owen. Also that evening BBC2 transmitted 'Death and Immortality', the final programme of *A Lasting Joy*, the television series Cecil and Jill made in January and February, and which was to be shown complete by BBC1 in July and August. It was hard to connect the hundreds of public words written and spoken with the scene of mystery and grief and relief enacted at Lemmons that morning.

On Friday the twenty-sixth a party of thirteen of those who had been close to Cecil during his last days met at the barrier of No 13 platform at Waterloo. The train took us to Dorchester and the Dorset landscape to which, like the other places of his life, he had never been more than a visitor, but from which he always felt a kind of welcome home. The short funeral service was held in the little thirteenth-century church of Stinsford, Thomas Hardy's Mellstock. The Rev Austen Williams pronounced the ritual sentences, all were invited to join in saying Psalm 121, and Julian Bream seemed to bring Cecil's spirit closer with his playing of three movements from Bach's lute suites. Presently Cecil's coffin was gently lowered into place close beside Hardy's heart, and with it a wreath made from laurels in the Amis garden.

From the train windows, as it moved away from Dorchester to return us to London, we day-trippers gazed back across the Frome valley to Stinsford. Pangs at the thought of Cecil left behind beyond those damp fields were overtaken by gladness that he was at last at rest and rooted in a place where the tradition he served with such devotion will be cherished for as long as the language is understood. In his poetry he had left the world his life, and that is where his life belonged. A few months later a stone was placed to mark his grave, bearing the epitaph he had written for himself in 1944. It directs the pilgrim back to the poems where he still breathes.

> *Shall I be gone long?*
> For ever and a day.
> *To whom there belong?*
> Ask the stone to say,
> Ask my song.

Appendix I

Epithalamium for C. Day-Lewis by W.H. Auden

This morning any touch is possible,
Who loved last year to-day shall love afresh
And sunlight on your pillow and the wall
Confirms for you what dreaming rumoured; now,
Stand like the sparrowhawk we watched who stood
Still in the sky, stop while we speak to you
And hold the excited animal in leash
Being so close upon a certain good.

The light and shade fall unfamiliar here
On all of us who know that hundreds sit
Working on afternoons and no one there,
That hundreds daily die and clay receives
A favour never asked; whom now you summon
To eat and drink with you under those eaves
Where soon the night will come to celebrate
The accurate matching of a man and woman.

That period perhaps comes to your mind
Pride hurt itself on corners everywhere
And lust howled in a boot-hole underground,
You marched for months, and she still further off;
Or how to Sherborne came a pretty boy
And splendid seniors bought his photograph,
Taller to-day. Yes, she is here, she's here,
And you shall taste this summer absolute joy.

Now for a little you may love in quiet
You go to-morrow to a district where
Are no sudden noises but the chicken's riot
At breakfast or the collie's rattling chain
At night sometimes, and now and then a gun
Tells that some jay will suck no eggs again
In pheasant woods across the valley; there
In fine weather she shall conceive your son.

Be quick; later you will not wake because
Of shooting round the house; will see too long
How excellent hands have turned to commonness,
The powerful taken an inferior way.
The mind, ashamed so, shall declare a fast
Touching no water till the cool of the day
When shadows make the blackbird tire of song
And you will pass as men have always passed.

The corridors are still
Within the empty school
The shadow of the mill
Is cast along the pool.
The hatches are let down
And the night meets the day
The spirit comes to its own
The beast to its play.

This was written on the occasion of the marriage of Cecil Day-Lewis to Mary King at Sherborne on 27 December 1928. It is published here for the first time: Copyright © 1980 by the Estate of W.H. Auden.

Appendix II

Verse-letter to C. Day-Lewis
by W.H. Auden

Time flies, Cecil; hardly a week ago
I left your Scotland, and to Berlin now
Across a frozen Europe come; where I
Am cold and homesick, listen eagerly
For postmen, not being one of those that choose
To live in Paris or to marry Jews,
Nor pimpled schoolboy at an aunt's expense
Dispatched to gain a European sense:
I like our cooking, envy none his joys
With girls in Prague, in Caucasus with boys.

Though neither book nor letter satisfies
Yet I today, wishing to exercise
My hand in writing and to please a friend
Have worked some hours for pleasure and now send
These fruits, ill-sorted, immature, and few
Of reading Dryden and remembering you.

I spoke of books, and think how we have sat
Taking this poet from the shelf or that,
Read them aloud, discussed them one by one,
With praises of Middleton and then of Donne,
Of Housman, wondering which theory right
On what the excitement was which made him write,
Affairs with soldiers or attacks of 'flu,
Of Owen's iron pity, Lawrence who
Remains an invalid and worships Will,
From illness loving, and from loving ill.

We found these moderns best, though seemed to see
Conceit in Yeats, in Eliot gravity;
While Wolfe, the typists' poet, made us sick
Whose thoughts are dapper and whose lines are slick.

I spoke of friends and now there come to mind
Associations of a different kind.
I see the features and the voices hear
Of Margaret, doctor, Christopher severe,
Of Rex who looked at much and much saw through,
And many others whom you never knew
As Gabriel who through flattery remained
Discriminating, simple, self-contained,
Dick, loved no less although not known for long
Whose mind is muscular, whose body strong ...
I speak as if their names in writing could
Be fit expression for my gratitude
But say to them and each unmentioned friend
That love continues though a list must end.

I turn again to you, for we are one
In choice of calling and ambition,
To wonder if there's room for you and me
When ten tons of new prose and poetry
Is the day's normal output. Papers say
'Five masterpieces have appeared to-day'.
The mind is hungry; – promptly to its needs
Come – 'Baby's poems' – 'What a statesman reads'
'A boxer's faith' – 'The memoirs of a whore'.
Each book expensive and each page a bore
We laugh at them, but they were serious;
Their writing pleased them though it wearies us,
For we write better – every writer does.

Should poets marry? You have done, and I
Engaged, may hope to be so presently.
What do we offer wives? They can expect
But disappointments, penury, neglect
And kept for nothing, they will often feel,
But washing dishes and to hear the bell,
Pitied by relatives who only see
In poetry a game for after tea,
Charming in lovers, in a husband mad,
Whom all think lazy, and most think a cad.
At best we shall succeed. What does this mean?

We're mentioned in a highbrow magazine:
Schoolmistresses send photographs and quote
With praise bad poems which we never wrote.
Suppose we fail, we shall not be excused
For chances offered now which we refused.
The fools condemned us, but the fools were just.
Our wives will have had nothing, yet they must
Bear with our tempers when our memories are
Aching in every narcissistic scar.

I send you these lines, Cecil: forgive in me
Their imperfections, their solemnity.
I wrote them out, alone on a dull day,
Wishing to speak with you, and so would they.

This was written from Berlin 'instead of a bread and butter letter' after Wystan
Auden stayed with Cecil and Mary Day-Lewis at Helensburgh in Scotland from
22 February to 25 February 1929. It is published here for the first time: Copyright
© 1980 by the Estate of W.H. Auden.

Appendix III

Selected Discography

(C. Day-Lewis reading his own verse)

The Jupiter Anthology of 20th Century English Poetry, Part 2. Recorded 1958. In-
cludes C. Day-Lewis reading his 'Maple and Sumach' from *Overtures to Death*;
'A Hard Frost' and 'Birthday Poem for Thomas Hardy' from *Poems 1943–1947*.
Jupiter JUR OOA2.

Poets Reading, No. 1. Recorded 1959. Includes C. Day-Lewis reading his 'Sheepdog Trials in Hyde Park', 'View from an Upper Window' and 'The Gate',
all from *The Gate*. Jupiter jep OOC1.

The Georgics of Virgil. Recorded late 1950s. C. Day-Lewis reads substantial
extracts from his translation published in 1940. Argo RG 27.

C. Day-Lewis. Recorded early 1960s. 'My love is a tower', 'Desire is a witch',
'With me, my lover makes the clock' from *Transitional Poem*; 'Beauty's end
is in sight', 'Rest from loving and be living', 'Do not expect again a phoenix
hour' from *From Feathers to Iron*; 'But two there are', 'Let us be off!', 'Nearing
again the legendary isle' from *The Magnetic Mountain*; 'The Conflict' and 'In
Me Two Worlds' from *A Time to Dance*; 'Passage from Childhood' from
Overtures to Death; 'O Dreams, O Destinations' 3 and 9, 'The Innocent', 'Jig'
and 'Hornpipe' from *Word Over All*; 'A Failure', 'The Christmas Tree', 'The
Neurotic' from *Poems 1943–1947*; 'A Letter from Rome' from *An Italian Visit*;
'The Committee', 'Love and Pity', 'Moods of Love' 5 from *Pegasus*; 'Sheepdog
Trials in Hyde Park' and 'The Gate' from *The Gate*. Yale Series of Recorded
Poets, Carillon Records, New Haven, Connecticut. YP 319.

The Poet Speaks I. Recorded 1964. Includes C. Day-Lewis reading his 'The
Christmas Tree' from *Poems 1943–1947*, 'Flight to Italy' from *An Italian Visit*,
'The Fox' from *The Room*. Argo RG 451.

The Poetry of C. Day-Lewis. Recorded 1964–5. 'Now she is like the white tree-
rose', and 'Do not expect again a phoenix hour' from *From Feathers to Iron*;
'In Me Two Worlds' from *A Time to Dance*; 'Newsreel' from *Overtures to*

Death; 'Where are the war poets?', 'The Poet', 'Will it be so again?', 'O Dreams, O Destinations', 'Jig', 'Hornpipe' from *Word Over All*; 'Birthday Poem for Thomas Hardy' from *Poems 1943–1947*; 'Baucis and Philemon' from *Pegasus*; 'Walking Away' and 'View from an Upper Window' from *The Gate*; 'My Mother's Sister' from *The Room*. Spoken Arts, New York. SA 1068.

The Voice and Pen of C. Day-Lewis. Recorded 1968. 'Jig' and 'Hornpipe' from *Word Over All*; 'The House Where I was Born' from *Pegasus*; 'My Mother's Sister' and 'Fishguard to Rosslare' from *The Room*; 'Ballintubbert House, Co. Laois', 'Avoca, Co. Wicklow', 'Sailing from Cleggan', 'Golden Age, Monart, Co. Wexford', 'The Whispering Roots', 'Near Ballyconneely, Co. Galway', 'Land', 'At Old Head, Co. Mayo', 'Ass in Retirement', 'Harebells over Mannin Bay', 'Kilmainham Jail: Easter Sunday, 1966', 'Remembering Con Markievicz', 'An Ancestor', 'Goldsmith outside Trinity' from *The Whispering Roots*. Saga Psyche PSY 30004.

British Poets of Our Time, C. Day-Lewis. Posthumous compilation of 1973. 'My love is a tower' and 'With me my lover makes' from *Transitional Poems*; 'Now the full-throated daffodils' and 'Beauty's end is in sight' from *From Feathers to Iron*; 'You that love England' from *The Magnetic Mountain*; 'The Ecstatic' and 'Learning to Talk' from *A Time to Dance*; Extracts from *The Georgics* of Virgil translation; 'The Rebuke' and 'Departure in the Dark' from *Word Over All*; 'The Christmas Tree' and 'A Failure' from *Poems 1943–1947*; 'Pegasus' and 'Final Instructions' from *Pegasus*; 'An Episode' from *The Gate*; 'The Room', 'On Not Saying Everything', 'Elegy for a Woman Unknown' 3, 'The Fox', 'Derelict' from *The Room*. Argo PLP 1187.

Appendix IV

Alternative American Titles

Short is the Time (Oxford University Press, 1945) includes poems from *Overtures to Death* and *Word Over All*.

Requiem for the Living (Harper and Row, 1964) includes poems from *The Gate* and *The Room*.

Shell of Death (Harper and Row, 1936) is Nicholas Blake's *Thou Shell of Death*.

The Summer Camp Mystery (Harper and Row, 1940) and *Malice with Murder* (Pyramid, 1960) are Nicholas Blake's *Malice in Wonderland*.

The Corpse in the Snowman (Harper and Row, 1941) is Nicholas Blake's *The Abominable Snowman*.

Death and Daisy Bland (Dell, 1960) is Nicholas Blake's *A Tangled Web*.

References

Chapter 1

1 *Daily Telegraph*, 28.4.04.
2 Graham Greene, *Collected Essays*, Bodley Head 1969.
3 Robert Graves and Alan Hodge, *The Long Weekend*, Penguin 1940.
4 *Sunday Times*, 4.6.72.
5 *Scrutiny*, September 1932.
6 Geoffrey Handley-Taylor and Timothy d'Arch Smith, *C. Day-Lewis, The Poet Laureate, a Bibliography*, St James Press 1968.
7 Stephen Spender, *World Within World*, Hamish Hamilton 1951.
8 *Sunday Times*, 4.6.72.
9 Stephen Spender (ed), *W.H. Auden, a Tribute*, Weidenfeld and Nicolson 1974.
10 Samuel Hynes, *The Auden Generation*, Bodley Head 1976.

Chapter 2

1 W.H. Auden, 'The Public vs. the Late Mr William Butler Yeats', *Partisan Review 6*, New York, Spring 1939.
2 Samuel Hynes, *The Auden Generation*, Bodley Head 1976.
3 Frank Halliday, *Indifferent Honest*, Duckworth 1960.
4 Leonard Woolf, *Downhill all the Way*, Hogarth 1967.
5 Margaret Gardiner, 'Auden: a Memoire', *New Review*, July 1976.
6 *Guardian*, November 1974.
7 Howard Haycroft, *Murder for Pleasure*, Peter Davies 1942.
8 Stephen Spender (ed), *W.H. Auden, a Tribute*, Weidenfeld and Nicolson 1974.
9 Louis MacNeice, *The Strings are False*, Faber 1965.
10 John Lehmann, *The Whispering Gallery*, Longmans 1955.

Chapter 3

1 Winston Churchill, *Their Finest Hour*, Cassell 1949.
2 John Lehmann, *I Am My Brother*, Longmans 1960.
3 Stephen Spender, *World Within World*, Hamish Hamilton 1951.
4 Clifford Dyment, *C. Day-Lewis*, Longmans Green 1955.
5 Ibid.

Chapter 4

1 Michael Balcon, *Michael Balcon Presents*, Hutchinson 1969.
2 Elizabeth Jane Howard, *Sunday Times*, 30.7.72.
3 Ibid.
4 Ibid.
5 Ibid.

Chapter 5

1 Kenneth Hopkins, *The Poets Laureate*, E.P. Publishing 1973.
2 Ibid.
3 Bernard Levin, *The Pendulum Years*, Jonathan Cape 1970.
4 Elizabeth Jane Howard, *Sunday Times*, 30.7.72.
5 Ibid.
6 Kingsley Amis, *Observer*, 28.5.72.

Index

A LASTING JOY

C. Day-Lewis

Childhood, heroism, love, hatred, nature and death – perhaps the dominant themes in our poetic heritage – are the subjects of this anthology and to each C. Day Lewis lends a freshness and energy which brings both familiar poems and lesser known or out of the way ones suddenly to life.

C. Day Lewis's comments on them are as enjoyable as the poems themselves. He had an instinct for exactly what appeals in a poem, for the emotional spring which it touches off. By a brief aside or throw-away remark he often succeeds in setting a poem in its landscape or, by giving a fragment of history or a biographical detail, illuminates a poem. In C. Day Lewis's own words 'poetry is one of the most durable products of the human mind'. And it is this lasting joy which he seeks to convey.

'a superb, life-affirming anthology, well titled "A Lasting Joy". Besides familiar classics from Shakespeare to Yeats there is less familiar poetry which will yet delight by its relevance to the chosen themes: childhood, human heroism, satire and hatred, love and friendship, times and seasons, death and immortality' – *The Press and Journal*

'The delicacy and aptness of his choice, and the perception of his linking commentary make this a poignant reminder of him' – *The Sunday Times*

THE INKLINGS
Humphrey Carpenter

The scene is an Oxford pub: 'There goes C. S. Lewis – it must be Tuesday,' remarks a character in a detective story of the nineteen forties. This gives some indication of how much Lewis and his friends were part of the Oxford scenery in the years during and after the Second War. They drank beer on Tuesdays in the 'Bird and Baby', and on Thursday nights they met in Lewis's Magdalen College rooms to read aloud from the books they were writing; jokingly they called themselves 'The Inklings'. J. R. R. Tolkien was one of them, and in this company *The Lord of the Rings* first found an audience. So did C. S. Lewis's *The Screwtape Letters* and his science-fiction novels, while another prominent member of the Inklings was Charles Williams, poet and writer of supernatural thrillers.

Humphrey Carpenter's *The Inklings* won the Somerset Maugham Award in 1980 for the best biography.

The Inklings tells the story of the group, and bases its account on a mass of unpublished letters and diaries to which the author was given special access.

'A skilful and sensible biographer . . . excellent book.'
– *Philip Toynbee, The Observer*

'He is that rare phenomenon, a biographical artist, combining a capacity to give us a well-researched record of fact with the power vividly to recreate human beings.'
– *David Cecil, Books and Bookmen*

A Lasting Joy *C. Day-Lewis*	£1.95 ☐	
J. R. R. Tolkien: a Biography *Humphrey Carpenter*	£1.95 ☐	
The Inklings *Humphrey Carpenter*	£3.50 ☐	

All these books are available at your local bookshop or newsagent, or can be ordered direct by post. Just tick the titles you want and fill in the form below.

Name ....

Address ....

....

....

Write to Unwin Cash Sales, PO Box 11, Falmouth, Cornwall TR10 9EN.

Please enclose remittance to the value of the cover price plus:

UK: 45p for the first book plus 20p for the second book, thereafter 14p for each additional book ordered, to a maximum charge of £1.63.

BFPO and EIRE: 45p for the first book plus 20p for the second book and 14p for the next 7 books and thereafter 8p per book.

OVERSEAS: 75p for the first book plus 21p per copy for each additional book.

Unwin Paperbacks reserve the right to show new retail prices on covers, which may differ from those previously advertised in the text or elsewhere. Postage rates are also subject to revision.